Ukraine
Russia's War and the Future of the Global Order

edited by
Michael Cox

Published by
LSE Press
10 Portugal Street
London WC2A 2HD
press.lse.ac.uk

Text © The Authors, 2023
Book first published 2023
Previous versions of all chapters were first published in the Ukraine Special Issue of the PPR journal, LSE Public Policy Review (2023), Volume 3, Issue 1: *Russia's war in Ukraine and the future of the global order*.
https://ppr.lse.ac.uk/10/volume/3/issue/1

Cover design by Diana Jarvis. https://www.roamland-studio.co.uk/
Cover photo: Anna Pasichnyk/Shutterstock

Print and digital versions typeset by Siliconchips Services Ltd.

ISBN (Paperback): 978-1-911712-14-5
ISBN (PDF): 978-1-911712-15-2
ISBN (EPUB): 978-1-911712-16-9
ISBN (Mobi): 978-1-911712-17-6

DOI: https://doi.org/10.31389/lsepress.ukr

This work is licensed under the Creative Commons Attribution 4.0 International License (unless stated otherwise within the content of the work). To view a copy of this license, visit http://creativecommons.org/licenses/by/4.0/ or send a letter to Creative Commons, 444 Castro Street, Suite 900, Mountain View, California, 94041, USA. This license allows for copying any part of the work for personal and commercial use, providing author attribution is clearly stated.

This book has been peer-reviewed to ensure high academic standards. For full review policies, see https://press.lse.ac.uk/

Suggested citation:
Cox, M. (ed.) 2023. *Ukraine: Russia's War and the Future of the Global Order*. London: LSE Press.
DOI: https://doi.org/10.31389/lsepress.ukr License: CC-BY

To read the free, open access version of this book online, visit https://doi.org/10.31389/lsepress.ukr or scan this QR code with your mobile device.

This volume is dedicated to the memory of
Christopher Coker (1953–2023), who passed away
as this volume was going to press

LSE Public Policy Review Series

This series republishes in book form selected issues on interdisciplinary themes from the LSE Public Policy Review journal.

Series Editors
Professor Timothy Besley, Department of Economics, LSE
Dr Tania Burchardt, Department of Social Policy, LSE
Professor Nicola Lacey, LSE Law School, LSE
Professor Susana Mourato, Vice President and Pro-Vice Chancellor (Research), LSE
Professor Andrés Velasco, School of Public Policy, LSE

LSE PPR editorial team
Dr Irene Bucelli, School of Public Policy, LSE (managing editor)
Nicholas Reed Langen (content editor)

Titles
Wellbeing: Alternative Policy Perspectives (2022)
Populism: Origins and Alternative Policy Responses (2022)
Afghanistan: Long War, Forgotten Peace (2022)
Ukraine: Russia's War and the Future of the Global Order (2023)

Contents

List of Figures viii
Editor ix
Contributors xi

1. Introduction: The International System in the shadow of the Russian war in Ukraine 1
Michael Cox

2. The War in Ukraine and the Return of History 11
Christopher Coker

Part 1: Russia 31

3. Who Supports the War? And Who Protests? The Legacies of Tzarist Social Divide in Russia 33
Tomila Lankina

4. Rewriting History and 'Gathering the Russian Lands': Vladimir Putin and Ukrainian Nationhood 59
Björn Alexander Düben

5. The Securitised 'Others' of Russian Nationalism in Ukraine and Russia 91
Eleanor Knott

Part 2: Ukraine 115

6. The Making of Independent Ukraine 117
Serhy Yekelchyk

7. Russia's Networked Authoritarianism in Ukraine's Occupied Territories During the Full-Scale Invasion: Control and Resilience 145
Tetyana Lokot

8. Ukraine's Decentralisation Reforms and the Path to Reconstruction, Recovery and European Integration 163
Tamara Krawchenko

Part 3: Impact 185

9. Uprooting and Borders: The Digital Architecture of the Ukrainian Refugee Crisis 187
Myria Georgiou and Marek Troszyński

10. Weaponised Energy and Climate Change: Assessing Europe's Response to the Ukraine War 209
Robert Falkner

11. New Dynamics, New Opportunities: Trends in Organised Crime in Ukraine After Russia's Invasion 227
Global Initiative Against Transnational Organized Crime

Part 4: The West 255

12. War in Ukraine in a Polarised America 257
Peter Harris, Iren Marinova and Gabriella Gricius

13. Europe and Russia's Invasion of Ukraine: Where Does the EU Stand? 277
Nathalie Tocci

14. After Merkel: Germany from Peace to War 293
Kristina Spohr

Part 5: The Rest   333

15. Comrades? Xi, Putin and the Challenge to the West   335
Michael Cox

16. The Global South and Russia's Invasion of Ukraine   359
Chris Alden

Part 6: The Economics of War   379

17. Mr Putin and the Chronicle of a Normalisation Foretold   381
Jagjit S. Chadha

18. Reconstructing and Reforming Ukraine   403
Erik Berglöf and Vladyslav Rashkovan

Annex A: Ukraine's Timeline: From Independence to War   433

Annex B: The Geography of War   441

List of Figures

4.1 Graphic from 1926 Soviet population census report depicting percentage of ethnic Ukrainians	74
17.1 Lower natural rate of interest	392
17.2 Higher natural rate of interest	392
17.3 The monetary policy trade-off	395
17.4 The negative supply shock	396
17.5 The negative supply shock and steeper Phillips curve	397
17.6 The negative supply shock, steeper Phillips curve and shifting target	397
A.1 Assessed control of terrain in Ukraine and main Russian manoeuvre axes as of 8 August, 2023, 3pm ET	441

Editor

Michael Cox is a Founding Director of LSE IDEAS and Emeritus Professor in International Relations at LSE. He was appointed to a Chair in International Relations at the School in 2002. His more recent publications include a new edition of EH Carr's *The Twenty Years' Crisis* and a collection of his own essays entitled *The Post-Cold War World*, which was published in 2018. 2019 saw the publication of his new edition of JM Keynes's *The Economic Consequences of the Peace*, and in 2021 he edited and brought out EH Carr's 1945 long out of print classic, *Nationalism and After*. His most recent book, *Agonies of Empire: American Power from Clinton to Biden*, was published in 2022. He is currently completing a volume for Polity Books called *Comrades: Xi Jinping, Putin and the Challenge to Western Liberal Order*.

LSE Public Policy Review Series Editors

Irene Bucelli (managing editor) is a Research Officer at the LSE School of Public Policy and programme coordinator for the Beveridge 2.0: Redefining the Social Contract initiative. She is also a Research Officer at the Centre for Analysis of Social Exclusion (LSE) where her research focuses on multidimensional inequality, poverty and deprivation.

Nicholas Reed Langen (content editor) is a writer and commentator on legal and constitutional affairs. He was a Re:Constitution fellow from 2021 to 2022. His writing has featured in the *London Review of Books*, *Project Syndicate*, the *Church Times* and other publications.

Contributors

Chris Alden is Professor of International Relations at LSE and Director of LSE IDEAS. His research focuses on comparative foreign policy and on China and Africa in particular.

Erik Berglöf is Professor of Economic Practice at the London School of Economics and Political Science, and previously he was Chief Economist of the European Bank for Reconstruction and Development. He has published extensively on institutional transformation, transition economics and governance.

Jagjit S. Chadha is Director of the National Institute of Economic and Social Research. His main interests are in macroeconomics and the design of monetary, fiscal and financial policies.

Chistopher Coker (1953–2023) was Director of LSE IDEAS and Professor of International Relations at LSE. He twice served as member of the Council of the Royal United Services Institute, and was a former NATO Fellow.

Björn Alexander Düben is Assistant Professor at the School of International and Public Affairs, Jilin University. He holds a PhD in International Relations from LSE.

Robert Falkner is Professor of International Relations at the LSE. His research focuses on global environmental politics and global political economy.

Myria Georgiou is Professor in the Department of Media and Communications, LSE. Her research focuses on migration, communication practices and media representation in relation to citizenship and identity.

Global Initiative Against Transnational Organized Crime (GI-TOC) is an independent civil-society organization, headquartered in Geneva, Switzerland. The chapter in this volume was authored by the GI-TOC's Observatory of Illicit Markets and the Ukraine Conflict, established in March 2022.

Gabriella Gricius is a PhD candidate at Colorado State University's Political Science Department and a Research Fellow with the North American and Arctic Defence and Security Network (NAADSN). Her research interests broadly cover Arctic security, the role of experts in security decision-making processes, and the centrality of narratives in foreign policy.

Peter Harris is Associate Professor of Political Science at Colorado State University. His research focuses on US foreign policy, international security, and international relations theory.

Eleanor Knott is Assistant Professor at the Department of Methodology LSE. Her 2022 book *Kin Majorities: Identity and*

Citizenship in Crimea and Moldova explores the (geo)politics of identity and citizenship in Moldova and Crimea in the wake of Russian annexation.

Tamara Krawchenko is Assistant Professor in the School of Public Administration at the University of Victoria and member of the Institute for Integrated Energy Systems (UV) with expertise in comparative public policy and territorial development.

Tomila Lankina is Professor of Interrnational Relations at the LSE. Her latest book with CUP is entitled *The Estate Origins of Democracy in Russia: From Imperial Bourgeoisie to Post-Communist Middle Class.*

Tetyana Lokot is Associate Professor in Digital Media and Society at the School of Communications at Dublin City University. Her research focuses on digital media, networked authoritarianism, digital resistance and internet freedom.

Iren Marinova is a PhD candidate at Colorado State University. Her research centres on issues of international security, foreign policy, climate change politics, and international relations theory.

Vladyslav Rashkovan is a member of the IMF Executive Board, where he represents Ukraine and 15 other countries. Previously he was Deputy Governor of the Central Bank, responsible for the financial sector reforms and central bank transformation in Ukraine. He currently focuses on building reform and recovery architecture and creating mechanisms for financing the post-war reconstruction of Ukraine.

Kristina Spohr is Professor at the Department of International History, LSE. Her work has focused on post-1989 Germany and, more recently, on the world order and the Arctic.

Nathalie Tocci is Director of the Istituto Affari Internazionali, and Honorary Professor at the University of Tübingen. Her research interests include European integration and European foreign policy, the Middle East, Eastern Europe, transatlantic relations, multilateralism, conflict resolution, energy, climate and defence.

Marek Troszyński is the Head of the Digital Civilization Observatory at Collegium Civitas, Warsaw. His research focuses on analysing discourse concerning Ukraine and Ukrainians in the Polish media and investigating media coverage of the Russian-Ukrainian war.

Serhy Yekelchyk is Professor of Germanic and Slavic Studies at the University of Victoria. His research focuses on Modern Ukraine, including this nation's historical relations with Russia and Europe.

1. Introduction: The International System in the Shadow of the Russian War in Ukraine

Michael Cox

The war in Ukraine may hold many lessons, but one rarely mentioned is how difficult it has been for even the best informed experts to forecast how it was likely to unfold. Thus, most analysts never thought Putin would launch a full-scale invasion of Ukraine in the first place; yet, he did. Many then assumed Moscow would win in a matter of weeks. But it did not. We were then informed that the Russian economy would fold under the pressure of Western sanctions. And so far it has not. The war, we were then told, would prove unpopular amongst Russians. But both the elite and the wider Russian public appear to have rallied around the flag. Finally, quite a few pundits assumed the West would fail to react to Russian aggression in anything like a united fashion. But so far, the opposite appears to have happened, with Finland and Sweden having become members of NATO and Ukraine inching ever closer to membership of the Alliance [1].

The war has also brought into question what many military theoreticians once thought about the nature of war in the modern era. War, the new gurus of conflict told us, would bear little resemblance to the conflicts of old. Major manoeuvres of massed formations, tank battles and prolonged artillery exchanges would be replaced by cyberattacks, high-tech sabotage conducted from satellites up in space and the use of artificial intelligence (AI). Even territory and its defence or capture had become passe in an era of so-called new wars. Yet, as Christopher Coker shows in his essay, the conflict in Ukraine has been something of a wake-up call for those who might have hoped that the old style of war was a thing of the past. Comparisons with World War I can be overdone. Even so, the 'orgy' of destruction that has been visited upon Ukraine with its 'trench-scarred landscape' now littered with millions of mines suggests that modern war might not be so modern after all [2].

Meanwhile, as the war grinds on, the most we can do at this stage is provide an interim report on the conflict and its wider significance. One rather badly informed American politician with presidential ambitions told his followers in the spring of 2023 that because the war in Ukraine was only of local significance, it was not of 'vital' importance for the United States [3]. Nothing could be further from the truth. In fact, the longer the war has gone on, the greater the impact it has had and will continue to have on the international system as a whole. At the start of the war, it was fairly normal to talk of the conflict changing the security landscape in Europe [4]. But as the essays here demonstrate, as the war has unfolded, it has become increasingly clear that the war has begun to redefine the world as a whole [5].

The most obvious place to start in making sense of what has happened is with Russia itself, though even this might be viewed as controversial, given that a number of critics have laid most of the responsibility for the war on the United States and NATO for previously having failed to take account of Russian security needs [6]. Still, at the end of the day, it was the decisions made in the Kremlin by Putin that occasioned the conflict; so, understanding what his reasoning was in launching the war would hardly seem unreasonable.[1]

Three connected essays attempt to deal with this issue. The first, by Tomila Lankina, seeks to explain what may seem difficult to explain to outside observers: why the majority of Russians continue to support Putin and have proved vulnerable to his official propaganda. To understand this, we have to move beyond the upper layers of Russian society and look at the broader swathes of Russian society from the rural communities and small towns. As she points out, people in Russia have remained remarkably susceptible to his message, even as he 'wages' what Lankina terms his 'brutal and genocidal war against Ukraine'.

In the next essay, Björn Alexander Düben focuses on Putin's own strongly held belief that far from constituting a sovereign country with its own history and culture, Ukraine in effect does not exist (and never has) as a nation separate from Russia. Düben admits that Putin's 'calculus for launching the invasion combined a variety of different motives, including geopolitical concerns about systemic threats to Russia's national security and domestic considerations of shielding his own authoritarian regime against potential pro-democratic "spill-over" from across the border'. But as he goes on to argue, 'there is much to suggest that Putin's personal readings of Ukrainian and Russian history, combined with deeply held ethno-nationalist and irredentist beliefs, have been one of the core factors motivating his decision to unleash a full-scale military assault against Kyiv'.

Eleanor Knott further examines Putin's ideas, making the important point that while 'the stakes of Russia's war against and invasion of Ukraine are ethnic, imperial, and civilisational', they are also 'existential'. This suggests that the decision to invade and continue with the war is as much, if not more, about Russian identity as it is about power. Knott also goes on to argue that there will be no easy exit from this conflict, not only because Ukraine as a 'victim' must be allowed to set the terms on which the war ends, but also because the war has come to define Russia as a nation while legitimising the repressive character of Putin's rule at home.

The next section moves on to Ukraine itself with an opening essay by Serhy Yekelchyk, who deals with the period since the collapse of the USSR. He takes the narrative from Ukraine's independence in 1991 – that 'unfinished revolution' as he calls it – right through to the invasion in 2022, which in his view has completed the transformational process consolidating 'a modern Ukrainian identity as separate from Russia both politically and culturally'. A number of other observers have insisted that the war was avoidable. Yekelchyk, though, believes it was more or less inevitable. Indeed, having continued to assert itself politically after breaking from Russia (in stages), a final clash between aspiring Ukraine and the former imperial power was something close to a foregone conclusion.

In her contribution, Tamara Krawchenko then examines the significance of the year 2014 in the evolution of Ukraine. While 1991 was clearly a landmark moment, it is only with the Maidan 'revolution of dignity' 13 years later that the country began to embark on a set of reforms – which she feels Ukraine must continue with if the country wishes to become fully democratic within an 'integrated Europe'. However, as Tetyana Lokot points out, there is at least one obstacle standing in the way of democratic renewal: the Kremlin's interventions into the information spaces and telecommunications infrastructure in temporarily occupied Ukrainian territories. This not only increases Russia's control of the territory it has conquered, but it also reduces Ukraine's potential for resistance and resilience.

We then go on to look at some of the costs and consequences of the war, beginning with the refugee crisis. As Myria Georgiou and Marek Troszyński point out, millions of Ukrainian refugees have been forced to seek a temporary home in Europe – almost a fifth of the country's population. Though they have generally been given a warm welcome often denied to other refugees, their rights to protection remain 'precariously dependent' and will stay that way until the Western countries commit themselves fully to 'the recognition of the universal right to refugee protection'. And, if they do not do so, there is a risk that the very real welcome given to Ukrainian refugees might one day turn into 'suspicion'.

Robert Falkner looks at another costly and significant consequence of the war: the biggest energy shock to Europe since the 1970 oil crises. In his view, this has laid bare what he believes was the 'strategic blunder' of becoming overly dependent on 'Russian energy supplies'. Fortunately, it has not, as yet, led to European leaders reducing their commitment to the net zero goal or pulling back from their decarbonisation efforts.

In the last essay in this section, a number of authors jointly look at the impact the war may have had (or is already having) on organised crime. As we know from previous wars, such as the Balkan Wars of the 1990s, organised crime can often be a beneficiary of conflict. It is essential therefore, that trends in organised crime remain a priority area of focus for 'policymakers, researchers, civil society and other key stakeholders'.

But how has the West responded to the war, and how in turn has the war shaped Europe and the United States? Peter Harris, Iren Marinova and Gabriella Gricius first look at the US, pointing out that 'Biden's policies of support for Ukraine have engendered a rare instance of cross-party unity in Washington'. But how long, they ask, 'will US support for Ukraine endure' in an America where there are still ongoing discussions around what is really at stake in Ukraine – an America where there is at least a chance of a more sceptical Republican party returning to the White House in 2024?

Turning to Europe, Nathalie Tocci is in little doubt of the transformational impact the war has already had on the continent. There is, however, some 'bad news' for those who were hoping that Europe in the future would play a stronger role on the global stage. Strategic autonomy might remain an aspiration for some. But if the war in Ukraine has shown anything, it is the degree to which Europe still relies on the United States for its security. It is perhaps in Germany though, where things may have altered most. Many may doubt how far Germany has really changed. However, as Kristina Spohr suggests, the shift away from 'Merkelism' has been real. Even so, if Germany truly wants to lead in Europe, Chancellor Scholz must ensure that its *Zeitenwende* is implemented and endures for the longer term.

The two essays that follow shift attention away from the 'West' towards the 'Rest', including perhaps most importantly, China, whose political support for Russia in the war has been serious and significant according to Michael Cox. Chris Alden then looks at the Global South and its response to the conflict. The war in Ukraine has illuminated much about the modern world, especially about the gap that now exists between perceptions of the conflict in the 'North' and many of the developing countries. Countries like Brazil and South Africa may not openly approve of what Moscow has done in Ukraine. On the other hand, they have been remarkably reluctant to condemn Russia. But as Alden notes, even if many in the West have shown a marked impatience with those who refuse to see the war in the same ways they do, it is still important to explain what is 'behind the seeming indifference and even hostility in the Global South to the Western position on Russia'.

The last section addresses two big economic issues. One of immediate concern is the impact the war has already had on what was already a distressed world economy. As Jagjit Chadha points out, the 'invasion of Ukraine came at a precarious moment for a global economic order still trying to recover from the impact of the Covid pandemic'. Inevitably, the war has made the situation all the more precarious by leading to a 'sharp increase in energy and food costs'. These, he notes, not only threaten 'price stability but has also asked severe questions of the monetary and fiscal frameworks which coped so well with stabilising the global economy over the previous quarter of a century'.

But what about the economic challenges facing Ukraine itself, if (or when) the war finally comes to an end? Erik Berglöf and Vladyslav Rashkovan are under no illusion of the uphill task confronting a war-shattered country. But as they also remind us, even if all the 'difficult choices involved in reconstruction and reform, including the use of donor resources' may be shaped by outside actors, ultimately, the 'key decisions' must be made by

Ukrainians themselves. A war Ukraine did not seek, and for which its people have paid a high price, has been fought by Ukrainians. It follows that, when peace comes and the task of rebuilding a shattered nation begins, it must be 'owned by them' too.

However, this lies in the future. Meantime, the war shows little sign of concluding any time soon. China and a large number of countries in the Global South might talk about the urgent need for peace. Ukrainians, however, have made it clear that there cannot be peace at any price, especially if the price involves the loss of any of its territory. Nor does Putin seem likely to bring the war to an end. Victory may not be in his grasp, but he cannot afford to lose either. Furthermore, with the Russian army dug in behind well-protected fortifications from the south to the east of Ukraine, he has every incentive to fight on and even escalate the war. Destroying Ukraine's infrastructure and preventing the export of its grain to the rest of the world may look like desperate gestures from a leader with his back to the wall. And continuing the war further may well turn out to be futile. But that is not how it looks to Putin. Rather than accepting what appears obvious to some in the West (and perhaps even in Beijing) – that Russia cannot win – he has instead continued to make Ukraine (and thus its Western backers) pay the heaviest price possible for their continued resistance. A famous writer on strategy once opined that all wars end, and no doubt this war will end one day too. Still, nearly two years into a conflict that some believed would be over in a matter of weeks, we are no nearer to knowing when the conflict might end, on whose terms and with what long-term consequences for the world at large. The tragedy in Ukraine looks set to continue for some time to come.

Note

¹ There is now a burgeoning literature on why Putin launched the war against Ukraine. For a sample of the most recent studies, see citations [7–13].

References

1. Rachman G. Putin, Ukraine and the revival of the West. *Financial Times*. 2022 April 15 [cited 2023 August 10]. https://www.ft.com/content/7d9f69b9-2f04-451a-a0d5-e1242a2bcb99.

2. The Economist: Battlefield report: Warfare after Ukraine: Special report. 2023 July 8–14 [cited 2023 August 10]. https://www.economist.com/special-report/2023-07-08.

3. Quinn M, Navarro A. Ron DeSantis says U.S. support for Ukraine in war not a "vital" national interest. *CBS News*. 2023 March 14 [cited 2023 August 10]. https://www.cbsnews.com/news/ron-desantis-american-support-for-ukraine-war-russia-not-a-vital-national-interest/.

4. Morenatti E. Remembering the past – looking to the future: How the war in Ukraine is changing Europe. *The Conversation*. 2022 March 2 [cited 2023 August 10]. https://theconversation.com/remembering-the-past-looking-to-the-future-how-the-war-in-ukraine-is-changing-europe-178151.

5. Lehne S. After Russia's war against Ukraine: What kind of world order?. *Carnegie Europe*. 2023 February 28 [cited 2023 August 10]. https://carnegieeurope.eu/2023/02/28/after-russia-s-war-against-ukraine-what-kind-of-world-order-pub-89130.

6. Mearsheimer J. Why the Ukraine crisis is the West's fault: The liberal delusions that provoked Putin. *Foreign Affairs*. 2013; 93(5): 77–89. http://www.jstor.org/stable/24483306.

7. Matthews O. Overreach: The inside story of Putin's war against Ukraine. London: Mudlark; 2022.
8. Harding L. Invasion. London: Guardian Faber Publishing; 2022.
9. Plokhy S. The Russo-Ukrainian War. London: Allen Lane; 2023.
10. McGlynn J. Memory makers: The politics of the past in Putin's Russia. London: Bloomsbury Academic; 2023. DOI: https://doi.org/10.5040/9781350280793.
11. Ramani S. Putin's war on Ukraine. London: Hurst Publishers; 2023.
12. Etkind A. Russia against modernity. Cambridge, UK: Polity Press; 2023.
13. Miller C. The war came to us: Life and death in Ukraine. London: Bloomsbury; 2023.

2. The War in Ukraine and the Return of History

Christopher Coker

> Russia's invasion of Ukraine came as a surprise. The West believed for a long time that Great Power conflict was a thing of the past, that war itself was no longer a central feature of international relations. It was not a view shared by the rest of the world, and certainly not by Russia. The Ukraine war is in part a product of the misreading of history. It is also threatening to become for the Russians an existential struggle that they cannot afford to lose. What if the European peace we have come to celebrate is just a 30-year experiment sandwiched between much longer phases of conflict?

'You should move to a small town where the rule of law still exists. This is the land of the wolves now. And you are not a wolf.' (Del Toro in Sicario)

At the conclusion of his magisterial history of the world, Simon Sebag Montefiore writes that the war in Ukraine marks the end of an exceptional period in human history – 70 years of peace between the world's Great Powers divided into two phases: 45 years of the Cold War, and a quarter of a century of American unipotency. 'The Russian invasion is a return to normality. Normal disorder has been resumed' [1]. Unable to achieve swift regime change, Putin has settled for eliminating Ukraine as a functioning country. To the 16% of the population that has been internally displaced, thousands have disappeared (many of them children sent to Siberia); the four annexed republics have been ethnically cleansed, its cities taken apart by drone strikes. The wanton butchery and terror that has characterised Russian operations from the very beginning remind us what history was like in times when there were no mobile phones to record the atrocities.

In this essay, I am going to argue that we had simply forgotten the role that war has played in history and is threatening to play once again. Instead, we told ourselves comforting stories of a globalised world where ethnic identity and national chauvinism have lost out to the logic of the market. The Europeans have long claimed to have discovered a version of Immanuel Kant's 'perpetual peace'. Many years ago, the Czech author Milan Kundera reassured his readers that the Germans and French were now 'anthropologically' incapable of going to war against each other. Note, not economically or politically or even culturally, but *anthropologically*. In other words, war was no longer encoded in their cultural DNA.

Browse the bookshelves and you will find many authors spinning this tale. One is Steven Pinker, the author of *The Better Angels of our Nature* and *Enlightenment Now*, another John Mueller, the author of *The Retreat from Doomsday*, and then there is John Horgan, a former editor of *Scientific American* and author of a book called *The End of War*, whose title leaves you in no doubt about its conclusion. In his book *Enlightenment Now* (2017), Pinker insisted that war was now largely only of historical interest. But he also told us in the same work that because it was now much easier to identify pathogens and invent vaccines, pandemics had probably disappeared from history [2]. It is great story to tell and on the face of it, it is one that is almost too good to be true. It is easy to forget that such a phrase usually means 'not true'. Now, we are told by epidemiologists that the 21st century is likely to be the century of pandemics and global warming (the two are interlinked) in the same way that the 20th century was the century of revolution and total war (they too, were intimately interlinked).

The Ukraine war is a classic wake-up call which was long delayed. Cast your eye around the world: at Syria's broken cities, like Aleppo, whose medieval seminaries have been destroyed and its ancient citadel damaged beyond repair. Or give a thought to the global War on Terror, now over twenty years old with no end in sight. Some American soldiers who were pulled out of Afghanistan in 2021 were first-grade students on the day the World Trade Center was attacked. A depressing fault line, in fact, runs through the world dividing those regions that are at peace with themselves and those that are not. Only a few years ago, professors were even reassuring their students that there wouldn't be another Great Power war. Today, we are far less sanguine, whether the West finds itself at war with China or Russia or a medium power like Iran. The new buzzwords in the military field are 'directed energy', 'hypersonic missiles', 'space', 'cyber', and 'quantum computing', and very soon artificially intelligent machines will be waging war on our behalf, or possibly their own. Never place a loaded gun on the table, wrote Chekhov unless it is going to go off at some point in the play. It is wrong to make promises you can't keep! Eventually any weapon we invent will be used.

We forget at our peril what a tenacious hold war has on history. It can flare up when least expected, as it did in 1914, or sneak up unsuspected, as it did in Syria ten years ago. 'You may not be interested in war', Trotsky famously remarked, 'but war is interested in you.' The sentiment, though hackneyed, it is still as true as the day he said it.

The World before Ukraine

What we ignored before the war in Ukraine was the world disorder all around us. All that we escaped and then briefly in 1989 was a sub-set of war: Great Power conflict. In truth the rest of the world had not escaped war's iron grip on life. Think of the wars that were waged between 2001–2019. There were 106[1], involving more than a hundred nations [3]. Most were fought in the Middle East, West Africa, and in what the Russians like to call their Near Abroad – the periphery of the old Soviet empire. But who in the West caught a glimpse on television of the conflict in the Niger Delta, which first broke out in 2004, and what television companies provided prime-time coverage to the civil war in Chad (2005–2010)? When we switched on our TVs, we watched a series of conflicts like the war in Afghanistan, which were filtered through a particular lens, the War on Terror.

We have also seen a dramatic transformation in our understanding of war itself. Military analysts are forever declaring the onset of a new age of warfare, but perhaps in this case it has already arrived. The point is that war is a shape-shifting phenomenon; 'new' wars arise as swiftly as the old disappear. Periodic plot twists arise all the time. One way to think about war, to invoke a timely metaphor, is to regard it as a virus which produces many different variants. In the last few years academics have rebranded war as 'surrogate', 'Fourth Generation', 'irregular', 'proxy', 'hybrid', 'non-linear', 'grey zone', 'shadow', and 'vicarious'. It is in the nature of any virus to produce variants; in the case of war, they are shaped by culture and technology. Before Putin's 'special military operation' in Ukraine, hybrid warfare was probably the most discussed thanks to what happened in the Crimea in 2014, which witnessed the deployment of disinformation, botnets, military proxies, and soldiers in disguise. But old-fashioned conventional wars are still fought, as we have seen in the Ukraine. Meanwhile the Chinese and the Americans are already gaming World War 3. If you want to know what it may look like, read two recent novels: *Ghost Fleet* (2017) and *2034: A novel of the next world war* (2021).

We have also tended to ignore what was perhaps the most significant challenge of all. Whenever we think of cyber-attacks against the West every other week, most of which go unreported, or information warfare or the constant assault on our democratic systems by troll factories in Russia that you can read about in Nina Jankowitcz's book, *How to the Lose the Information War* (2009), the West may well conclude (as many commentators do) that it has been 'at war' with Russia since its cyberattack on Estonia in 2007. We all find ourselves living in what Lucas Kello calls an era of 'Unpeace', a new era of mid-spectrum rivalry which is especially visible in cyberspace [5].

It is becoming increasingly difficult these days to distinguish war from peace. For war can now be played out not only on the battlefield but in the minds of citizens at home. Our societies are becoming more vulnerable everyday thanks to the fact that we have weaponised our high-tech tools. There are at least 30 billion internet-connected devices in the world; 130 are added to the web every second. Every one of them is vulnerable to attack, as too are the servers which power the cloud, on which so much of the world's data is stored. In fact, it is becoming increasingly difficult to define the meaning of 'peace' in a digital era which denies us peace of mind.

So, What is War for?

Morality aside, some of you of course may think that asking what war is for is rather like asking a question that is popular these days: what is a corporation for? Clearly, to make a profit. But CEOs like to issue statements of purpose in which you will find that they are leery of using the word 'profit' and prefer instead to talk instead of 'corporate social responsibility'. A striking example is the French company Danome, which liked to claim that its corporate mission was bringing 'health through food'. Its former CEO, Emmanuel Faber even boasted that he had toppled the statue of Milton Friedman, but in March 2020 the shareholders toppled him – they fired him for not making enough money. These purpose statements have been hitting the headlines for some time and we should not be fooled by them. Cecil Rhodes, a former CEO, called empire-building '95% philanthropy and 5% profit'. The reality was rather different, which is why his statues have been toppled from Cape Town to Oxford.

Like our unfortunate CEO, if you come from the West, you might claim that the purpose of war is to fight for human rights as NATO did in Kosovo, the first – and probably last – 'humanitarian war' in history. One of the reasons that Putin chanced his hand in 2022 was that he believed that the West had lost the plot; it was obsessed with 'statements of purpose'. The vernacular in Afghanistan was captured by a British journalist [6] who attended a briefing in Kabul in 2009 eight years into the campaign:

> 'Agents for Change', 'Alternative Livelihoods', 'Asymmetric Means of Operation', Capability Milestones', 'Demand Reduction', 'Drivers of Radicalisation', 'Fledgling Capabilities', 'Injectors of Risk', 'Kinetic Situation', 'Light Footprint', 'Capacity Building', 'Reconciliation and Reintegration', 'Shake-Clear-Hold' and 'Upskilling'

What he claimed to have caught was not the meaning but the ambient noise or, to mix metaphors, the 'acrylic blanket' of the language of modern warfare [6]. Twelve years before its ignominious withdrawal from the country, he concluded that NATO was on no win mission. The whole mission was an attempt to produce what the US military calls 'sustained behavioural change' at the national level. In the end the US pulled out, not because its goals had been achieved but because it had given up on them. The basic assumption of the whole benighted NATO mission was based on the belief that the Afghans wanted what the West wanted for them, or what they wanted them to want. (The ultimate error, however, was thinking that you could fight a war and rebuild a nation at the same time; it has never been done before. The only examples of successful regime change by the US military [Germany/Japan 1945; Grenada/1983; Panama/1989] were undertaken after the fighting had stopped.)

But in every war the payoff is the same: winning. Winning matters and in most wars nothing else matters more. So, what – for the Russians – is the present war 'for'? War is riddled with purpose, it always involves an endgame, but different countries have different purposes and entertain different reasons for going to war. The three principal ones: fear, honour, and interest were identified by Thucydides two thousand years ago, and they remain as valid today as ever.

1. Fear

For the Russians the Ukraine war has become an existential struggle. It didn't start out that way. Like the West they saw Ukraine as a corrupt, failed state that would fold at the first push. Instead, the Ukrainians have found a purpose in the world and a unity they never enjoyed in peacetime. In her book, *Paradise Built in Hell*, Rebecca Solnit writes that an unexpected and widespread response to disaster seems to be joy, not only at having survived an ordeal but at being provided with an opportunity to put our heroic selves on display [7]. It seems that many of us also want to experience the heroic at least once in our lives. This may be because only in times of crisis do some of us feel more fully alive. Rates of anxiety, depression, and even psychosis, psychologists tell us, seem to decline when a society finds itself at war. The very act of overcoming adversity and the recognition that some of our fellow citizens are willing to sacrifice their lives for the rest of us can reinforce pride in our own humanity.

But the Russians are not going to give up the fight. They fear that if they were to lose, Russia would become a sub-optimal strategic player, a kind of Eurasian Iran. It is a centuries-old fear. The relationship between old and new, wrote Hannah Arendt, is 'more complex than it seems at first glance. The past does not always pull back but progresses forwards and contrary to what one would expect, it is the future which drives us back into the past' [8]. In his long and tedious essays on the Ukraine and its historical relationship with Russia Putin invoked the past time and again for fear that the country did not have much of a future. The essays captured both his evasive relationship to the truth but also his country's complex relationship with its own history.

Russia's past is also bound up with its supposed 'exceptionalism'. Only a few people still claim to be exceptional. One is Russia, another the United States, the oldest is of course the Chosen People, the Jews. 'We must hope God loves us as much as we love him', remarked the Jewish philosopher Spinoza, 'because there's no evidence of it in the historical record'. Russia has always aspired to be a Great Power as much out of fear as interest. Unfortunately, its capabilities have rarely matched its aspirations, except for a brief period in the 1930s, when left-wing intellectuals travelled to Moscow to see their own future. At every stage in Russia's history, the West has always been more powerful, more dynamic economically; it has also enjoyed a much greater cultural pull and built much better technology. And at every stage of its history since Peter the Great, Russia has tried to compensate for this weakness by a show of strength.

In the case of Ukraine, there may be another factor at play. War, wrote the novelist John Fowles, is 'a psychosis caused by an inability to see relationships' [9]. The sheer simplicity of this definition is seductive, but it's also highly misleading. You could argue not only that war is not a psychosis, it is still less an evolutionary maladaptation. It's intrinsically social and arises precisely from the social networks we forge. The oldest division in history is social – between the 'in-group' and the 'out'. Norms that grossly devalue out-group members can be favoured by in-group selection, as the anthropologist Joe Heinrich points out; sometimes it can inspire its members even to exterminate the competition [10]. But even in-groups can fracture. In some myths, war arose from sibling rivalry, from brother fighting brother. Think of Cain's murder of Abel after their parents were expelled from Eden, or Romulus' murder of Remus, which was the founding act of Rome. Both murders alert us to something quite disturbing: whatever brotherhood human beings may be capable of may well have grown out of fratricide [11]. Brotherhood and war are often related. Putin invaded Ukraine to 'liberate' the Ukrainians from fascism and reunite them with the Russians, their ethnic 'brothers'. It hasn't worked out that way; instead, the invasion has solidified Ukrainian national consciousness.

2. Honour

'Who are you looking at, Jimmy?' is not a question you want to be asked in a Glasgow pub on a Friday night. The Russian equivalent is *'ty menya uvazhaesh* – do you respect me, Ivan'? And there is a sound historical explanation for why you might be asked the question. In a country that has never known the rule of law or a politically accountable government, to be disrespected is to find oneself at another person's mercy. And to be respected for one's achievements rather than one's might carries no special resonance with the Russian people. Nothing has changed since the fall of communism. Don't expect any significant public opposition to the war. As Michael Burleigh wrote of the German people in the 1930s, they 'abdicated their individual critical faculties in favour of a politics based on faith, hope, hatred and sentimental collective self-regard for their own nation' [12]. The Russian people may not have much faith or hope, but they are famous for their collective self-regard.

Russia is not alone, of course. After 9/11 the United States spent $7 trillion getting back its credibility (what honour has become in a mercenary age). The defeat of Taliban was not enough, insisted Henry Kissinger who backed the invasion of Iraq as necessary to re-establish America's credibility [13]. Of the many reasons that countries go to war, *status anxiety* is one of the most important, for to lose status as Russia has done since the end of the Cold War is to find oneself in a world in which the strong do what they wish, and the weak what they must. This was expressed first perhaps in Putin's threat at the Munich security conference back in 2007 [14]: 'treat us with a modicum of respect; why do you refuse others the security you insist on yourself?' The formula is very simple: peace won't bring security, but security will produce peace.

3. Interest

In most cases of war, we are dealing with power and power involves interests, material and spiritual. War, writes the historian Tim Blanning, can be defined as the exercise of power at its most brutal [15]. Different war aims are simply varieties of power: the vanity of nationalism, the wish to export an ideology, the protection of kinsmen in an adjacent land, the desire for more territory or larger market share, the avenging of a defeat or insult, the craving for greater national strength or independence, the wish to impress allies or cement alliances. All these in very different ways represent power in different wrappings [15]. The exercise of power is probably the one irreducible reality behind any act of violence, individual or collective.

And what often impresses most is the application of power for its own sake. At the personal level this can be disastrous. The great conquerors of history like Hitler and Napoleon may well have suffered from a power psychosis. Over time power can have an addictive dopamine-boosting effect on the brain, producing behavioural changes such as a loss of empathy, grandiosity, and paranoia. Such changes in the frontal lobe of the brain can often diminish the affected person's ability to weigh up risk. Think of Alexander the Great, who would have gone on fighting until he eventually was killed in battle had his army not forced him to turn back, or Napoleon, who undid everything he had achieved by invading Russia. Two years of isolation in the Kremlin and twenty-two years of power may have had a similar effect on Putin. In Russia we are witnessing a state that is setting back its own development by decades because of the folly of a disastrous war originally intended to be fought for a very limited and apparently achievable end: to make Ukraine a client state of its larger neighbour.

But was that ambition ever rational? Putin had no need to invade Ukraine on 24 February 2022. If he had not, the country would have continued its regression into a corrupt, failed state it was well on the way to becoming on the Transparency Corruption

Index just marginally ahead of Gabon and Zambia [16]. So why did he invade? 'War is a daemonic power that shapes our lives outside the governance of reason', writes George Steiner in *The Death of Tragedy*. When governments act irrationally, we shouldn't be surprised. Unfortunately, we usually are because we still cling to the economists' mistaken view of rational man, *homo Economicus*. The rational actor model presumes that we make choices aimed at maximising material payoffs based on all the available information of the time. The model is not wrong in presuming that people do indeed try to be rational, at least most the time. The problem is that we are not as intelligent as we like to think, and often we have great difficulty identifying what is in the true interests.

Different ideas about reality also explain very different styles of behaviour. Some of us are more fearful of failure than we are of achieving success; others will be willing to take a leap of faith into the future, even at some risk to themselves. Our decisions are also often based on irrational heuristics and biases of which we are not always consciously aware. And we are frequently given to unwarranted optimism: we think we will succeed even in the face of evidence that we won't. And if one way of being rational is to learn the lessons of history, we appear to be chronically incapable of doing so.

These characteristics of human nature are no different today than they were back in the Stone Age, when our ancestors gathered round a fireplace to tell each other stories to sharpen their understanding of reality. So, is the problem with war the stories we choose to tell, or the language in which we tell them? Every grammar has rules, tenses, and conjugations that shape the way we think, though languages differ quite a lot. Classical Chinese – the language of Sun Tzu – had no syntax. Nor, for that matter did it have any tenses, so that it was possible to describe an action without revealing when it actually happened. In the Indo-European languages, this is quite impossible with one exception: the Russian language. 'Perhaps, the secret for understanding Russian history lies in its grammar', writes one Russian dissident. In Latin, English, and German the pluperfect describes an action completed. The Russian language has no such tense. It's an unfortunate grammatical loss, for nothing in Russian history ever seems to become history. Like a stubborn page in a new book, it refuses to be turned over by the reader. Everything seems to happen again and again. Tsars continue to reappear in different guises at different times, as Stalin or Putin; dissidents of all persuasions, or none (contrarians) continue to be locked up; the Russian Bear continues to menace its neighbours, and its wars are framed these days as eternal repeats of the Great Patriotic War (1941–45). The country seems to be locked into an endless 'past imperfect' [17].

Speaking to journalists in January, the Russian Foreign Minister Sergei Lavrov accused the West of putting together a coalition to deal with the Russians as Hitler had dealt with the Jews. 'They are waging war against our country with the same aim "the final solution" of the Russian question' [18]. Casting oneself as the victim of the Ukraine war is also very Russian – it was the country after all, that aided Napoleon until 1812 and Nazi Germany until 1941, only to find itself attacked. The invader now see itself as the victim of a 'demonic West' that is aiming for nothing less than its disappearance from history.

The Return of Great Power Politics

The scenes from Ukraine played out on our television screens every night look very similar to the grainy black-and-white newsreel photos from the Second World War, with a modern colour technique to bring them to life. When Hitler invaded Czechoslovakia in March 1939, he opened the eyes of the Western powers to the fact that violence had become the governing principle of European political life. As we watch the slow dismantling of Ukrainian society, the destruction of its infrastructure and economy, we are witnessing what may well turn out to be a 'system transforming' war dissolving the last illusions of a stable European order that were too quickly embraced in the immediate post-Cold War euphoria.

Who is to blame? Perhaps we are. One reason for Putin's risk-taking is that he believed the West was in terminal decline. Obama's 'red lines' were ignored in Syria. Unlike his predecessor, Trump had a strategy to win over Russia, isolate China, avoid Middle East entanglements and scale-down commitments to allies. But this regrettably projected the image of a US that was weaker than it was, and some of the commitments Trump wanted to scale down included membership of NATO. And then there is the European Union, which for too long has indulged in wishful thinking. In 2014 Angela Merkel memorably concluded, after 38 phone calls with Putin, that he was living in another world: 'I am not sure that he is in touch with reality' [19]. But she too, was living in a make-believe world of her own. One thinks of the psychologist Eric Erickson and his concept of 'maladaptive optimism', whereby the infant fails to acknowledge the bounds of the possible by being unable to register the desires of those around it and their incompatibility with its own. The EU has been in denial for years, telling itself comforting stories about globalisation and global civil society, believing that the Great Powers were permanently tied into a world of human security, hoping that 'soft' or 'smart' power would trump hard power, even claiming that the minds of dictators like Putin could be changed by argument. But all such arguments were remarkably inattentive to history, or for that matter what was happening outside the Western world.

Indeed, the West has been surprised to find itself largely on its own in this struggle in the Global South. Seventy-five percent of the planet refuses to take sides, and a large percentage support Russia [20]. The explanation, suggests the French anthropologist Emmanuel Todd, is that the West is losing its soft power by turning itself into a laughingstock, with its obsession with transgender rights, same-sex marriages, and its lack of perspective on slavery (the Russians will tell you that the largest number of people ever enslaved were not Africans but Slavs). The non-western world doesn't find Putin's anti-LGBT stance objectionable; it still thinks sex is binary; its family structure is still what it was in the western world 30 years ago: patrilineal. As Todd writes, 'for the collective non-West Russia affirms a reassuring moral conservatism'. We see this conflict as one of political values; much of the rest of the world sees it at a deeper level as one of anthropological values. To which, he adds, it is this unconscious aspect of the divide and this depth that makes the confrontation so historically seminal, and so dangerous. This really is a 'war of the worlds' [21].

And so, the war is likely to drag on. The unqualified Ukrainian victory for which the West is rooting looks doubtful.

Any negotiated settlement will simply create another frozen conflict which can be unfrozen at a time that suits Moscow. Russia will remain a spoiler, a permanent threat to neighbours like the Baltic republics, Moldova and Georgia. The likelihood is that we will be confronted with chaos. It's not something that the West likes. It doesn't do frozen conflicts; it tries to resolve crises; it likes order, but the Russians really don't. Additionally, they don't have the power of China to re-order it as they might wish. At the Valdai conference in 2021 Putin emerged from his self-exile in the Kremlin and waxed lyrical. He claimed that the Covid pandemic has revealed that life is fragile and unpredictable, that the international system is open to chaos all the time, and that liberal societies refuse to accept that war is a permanent condition of life. Chaos, not stability, is the international norm. Both Russia and China had grasped history's rules of engagement, which is why the future is theirs.

Ironically, Cold Warriors, like the author, must acknowledge that we miss the old enemy, the Soviet Union. The USSR promised order, a socialist one, of course; it even held out the vision of eternal peace, the brotherhood of the proletariat, the Socialist International. Putin's worldview is very different. The world is a Wild West, where the strong rule and the weak know their place. That is just the way it is. The challenge we face in the next few years is to prove that this is the way it isn't.

Note

[1] Total number of wars calculated from [3] and [4].

References

1. Montefiore SS. The world: A family history. London: Weidenfeld and Nicolson. 2022; p. 1257.
2. Pinker S. Enlightenment now. Penguin. 2019; p. 23.
3. List of wars: 1990–2002. In *Wikipedia, The Free Encyclopedia*. 2023 May 7 [cited 2023 May 15]. https://en.wikipedia.org/w/index.php?title=List_of_wars:_1990%E2%80%932002&oldid=1153572300.
4. List of wars: 2003–present. In *Wikipedia, The Free Encyclopedia*. 2023 May 7 [cited 2023 May 15]. https://en.wikipedia.org/w/index.php?title=List_of_wars:_2003%E2%80%93present&oldid=1153557128.
5. Kello L. The virtual weapon and international order. New Haven: Yale University Press; 2017. DOI: https://doi.org/10.2307/j.ctt1trkjd1.
6. Parris M. In the fog remember this: Victory is impossible. *The Times*. 2009 July 4; 21.
7. Solnit R. Paradise built in Hell. London: Penguin; 2010.
8. Arendt H. Between past and present. New York: Penguin. 2006; p. 10.
9. Fowles J. The Magus. New York: Vintage. 1997; p. 413.
10. Macaskill J. What we owe the future. London: One World. 2022; p. 58.
11. Arendt H. On revolution. Penguin. 1990; p. 20.
12. Burleigh M. The Third Reich: A new history. Hill and Wang. 2001; p. 236.
13. Robin C. Fear. Oxford University Press. 2004; p. 24.
14. Putin V. Speech and the Following Discussion at the Munich Conference on Security Policy. 2007 February 10 [cited 2023 May 15]. http://en.kremlin.ru/events/president/transcripts/24034.

15. Blanning T. The French Revolutionary Wars. London: Arnold. 1996; p. 77.

16. Transparency International. Corruption Perceptions Index [Accessed January 2023]. https://www.transparency.org/en/cpi/2021.

17. Pomerantsev P. In Sasha Stepanova, In memory of memory. The Spectator. 2021; p. 38.

18. Freedman L. Proxies and puppets. Comment is freed. 2023 January 21 [cited 2023 May 15]. https://samf.substack.com/p/proxies-and-puppets.

19. Foa RS, Mollat M, Isha H, Romero-Vidal X, Evans D, Klassen AJ. A World Divided: Russia, China and the West. Cambridge, United Kingdom: Centre for the Future of Democracy; 2022.

20. Todd E. La Troisieme Guerre mondial a commence. *Figaro*. 2023 January 12 [cited 2023 May 15].

21. Rohrich K. Human Rights Diplomacy Amidst "World War LGBT": Re-examining Western Promotion of LGBT Rights in Light of the "Traditional Values" Discourse. 2014 [cited 2023 May 2015]. https://humanityinaction.org/knowledge_detail/human-rights-diplomacy-amidst-world-war-lgbt-re-examining-western-promotion-of-lgbt-rights-in-light-of-the-traditional-values-discourse/.

PART 1
Russia

3. Who Supports the War? And Who Protests? The Legacies of Tzarist Social Divide in Russia

Tomila Lankina

> Although Russian studies is a thriving field, there are significant gaps in our knowledge of Russian politics and society. One of the most significant blind spots is how Russian support for the war remains apparently robust, despite the atrocities inflicted on Ukraine and the tenuous justifications that have been offered for war. I draw on my own research to make sense of social responses to autocracy and the war. Specifically, I highlight the deep and intractable social inequalities within Russia that date back to the tzarist times and that the communist project never succeeded in obliterating. The social divides help explain why there has been no mass opposition to autocracy and the war.

In May 2022 Ukraine held the first trial for war crimes in Russia's current war on Ukraine.[1] The accused was Vadim Shishimarin, a 21-year-old Russian army sergeant charged with shooting and killing a 62-year-old unarmed Ukrainian civilian. In the media, almost all of the attention was on the crime and its punishment. Did the soldier admit to committing the crime? Has he shown remorse? How long will his sentence be [4]?

As a political scientist who has studied Russia for over two decades, I saw the young soldier as the face of a society about which we know little, hardly anything. Despite the fact that Russian studies is a thriving field [5, 6], there are significant blind spots in our knowledge of Russian politics and society.

It is these blind spots that are the focus of this piece, and how gaps in our knowledge have implications for broader debates on Russia, whether in government, public policy, think tanks, or the realm of public opinion. One of the most significant blind spots is how Russian support for the war remains apparently robust despite the atrocities inflicted on Ukraine and the tenuous justifications that have been offered for war.

Within this piece, I draw on my own research, which has highlighted the deep and intractable social inequalities within Russia that the communist project never succeeded in abolishing. I consider how we are dealing with a historically bimodal society, where conventional class and social categories are meaningful only when we systematically embed them in the complexities and historical texture of Russian society.

The divide – or *chasm* as the pre-Revolutionary Russian intelligentsia aptly termed it – between the classes is a by-product of the institution of *sosloviye*. The most accurate translation of this is 'estate', as in the estates of the realm that we are familiar with from reading about the French Revolution. The pre-Revolutionary Russia's estate system rigidly divided society into the four estates: the hereditary nobility and personal nobles (equivalent to a life peer in the UK) at the very top of the social hierarchy, the clergy, the urban estate consisting of merchants, *meshchane*, and artisans, and, at the very bottom, the peasant estate. The Bolsheviks abolished the estate system in one of their first decrees. But their own policies contributed to the reproduction and even consolidation of the gulf between peasants and urban worker masses, on the one hand, and on the other, the small minority of the habitually educated estates of nobles, clergy, and those from the urban merchant-*meshchane* estates who smoothly transitioned into the so-called new Soviet intelligentsia and middle class. Superficially, the Soviet project 'levelled' society in a material sense. But the vast gulf in education between the tiny minority and the majority never disappeared. The tzarist and communist-era social inequalities also shaped the opportunities of people to adapt to the new trans-nationalised market economy during the so-called post-communist transition of the 1990s. The educated intelligentsia had the human capital – knowledge of foreign languages and specialised skills in engineering and IT, for instance – to adapt to the new market economy and take advantage of opportunities to study and work abroad. The low-skilled populations in the collective farms and the urban blue-collar workforce had fewer such opportunities. In the USSR, collective farm workers faced restrictions in access to urban residence, employment, and higher education. For many peasants, the opportunity for social mobility was to join the urban factory workforce. But equally important is the difference in the rights and citizenship of the various groups in pre-Bolshevik Russia, something that is likely to have shaped civic values, political participation, and public engagement among the respective social strata. In Russia, serfs were only emancipated in 1861. But even after emancipation, peasants remained tied to their rural commune because they owed to the state payments for the land-plots that they received.

And even after 1861, former serfs faced hurdles to become urban residents and acquire the rights of the urban estates of *meshchane* or merchants. Meanwhile the urban estates enjoyed the privileges of trading, owning property, and receiving social services in towns. The clergy and aristocracy also were more privileged than the rural estate. Unlike the vast majority of peasants, members of these estates habitually attended secondary schools and studied at university. These different opportunities to free movement, property rights, and educational access will have implications for the ease with which members of the various estates could become professionals in a modern sense. And these legacies affected how the various groups would be positioned in the Soviet class system and how they would fare in the circumstances of the market transition of the 1990s. Just like under the tzars, Russian society remains divided between a tiny minority of dynastically educated intelligentsia who are able to access high-status professions that are insulated from state pressures to conform to the regime line, and the economically vulnerable – and poorly educated – majority [31].

This is the background to the story of the majority supporting Putin or those unable to challenge the autocracy and of those vulnerable to his propaganda, on the one hand, and, on the other, of the tiny minority of active dissenters. This pattern of social divides in education and professional opportunities has been recurring through Russian history for centuries. But why did we get Russia so wrong despite these realities that are obvious to anyone with even a cursory familiarity with Russian history? Why did so many contemporary observers in the 20th century believe that there had been an egalitarian society in the USSR, and why did others believe that Russians in their mass would embrace democracy after the collapse of the Berlin Wall?

A variety of factors explain this. A focus on the urban elites and the neglect of the precariat and rural folks left behind, as well as the shallow obsessions of the mainstream media and the trade presses with Putin – a form of neo-Kremlinology – made it difficult for us to make sense of the opinions and sentiments of the broader swathes of Russian society. There are also ideological reasons for our misconceptions about Russia. During communism, Western left-leaning intellectuals embraced the narrative of Soviet propagandists about the bright new revolutionary dawn that left behind the centuries-old social injustices. After communism's collapse, the new focus was on the transition to democracy and to free-for-all market capitalism, with a strong underpinning in the prevailing ideologies of neo-liberalism. While this ideology is increasingly discredited, many seasoned western foreign policy experts now couch their discussions of Russia using the Kremlin's rhetoric.[2] Thinkers like Henry Kissinger and John Mearsheimer explain Russia's politics of uber-patriotism and war as reaction to NATO expansion, Western democracy promotion, and other such purported threats to national security. Russian society and the nuanced texture of social relationships going back to the tzarist period have been left out of these narratives.

The Face of the Soldier as the Russian Political Unknown

As Russia's full-on aggression against the Ukrainian people unfolded, a more systematic picture began to emerge that allows us to put concepts and causes to the face of the Russian war criminal. Most of the soldiers, it became clear, come from the rural communities or from small town precariat. A significant minority come from ethnic minority communities, such as in Siberia and the North Caucasus. The Russian and then Soviet colonial project has altered or destroyed their native ways of life under the banner of modernization and progress even when giving a superficial nod to native languages. The destruction of indigenous ways of life in Siberia impinged on the livelihoods of native peoples. While the privileged elite could find ways to avoid performing military service, the state can more easily pressure young men from deprived communities to enlist.

But not all Russian soldiers are conscripts. Even in towns and even among the reasonably well-off strata of society there are volunteers to fight, many of whom feel that it is their 'patriotic duty'.

In Russian and Western media commentary there has been some sympathy for the minorities disproportionately recruited; for the destitute who could not buy their way out of conscription; and for those who clearly did not know where they were going or what they were going to do. However, there has been significant derogatory commentary, on social media and elsewhere, for those who queued – voluntarily and even enthusiastically – to join the Russian forces waging war upon the people in Ukraine. They were described as *kak barany* (like sheep) [7]. Did they not know that they are going to get slaughtered? Did the perverse promise of sexual violence against Ukrainian women blind them so much to the reality that they are heading into the embrace of death? A number of studies have analysed how the state fabricates compliance with its policies, explaining how Russian propaganda works [8-10] and how it fabricates support for the war. But there is an ongoing question about why it works on some and not others.

Of course, 'pocketbook' explanations abound. An individual's personal finances and their level of education are two characteristics that explain the efficacy of conscription and a person's susceptibility to propaganda. Over the last century the trend has been for the urban educated in many states to protest against oppressive regimes globally [11]. Regardless of the country under analysis, the evidence suggests there are some people who are susceptible to spin, and some who are not [10].

Equally, while explanations of brutal repression putting a break on protest go some way towards accounting for the apparent passivity of the populace, there is the unsettling picture of thousands of women, men, and children resisting the regime in Iran. There has been a more muted response in Russia. Both populaces faced the risks of brutal repression, yet Iran's rebelled, while Russia's acquiesced. And of course we have the example of Ukraine, which has experienced far more sustained mobilization in 2004, and then again in 2013-2014, and its citizens are mobilising to fight and otherwise bravely resist aggression – amidst violence far more horrific than anything that Russian protesters have ever experienced over the course of Putin's rule. What is it that motivates acquiescence or inhibits rebellion?

Rethinking Russian Society: Bringing the Historical Social Divide In

There is a puzzling variation in support for democracy among various social groups and in various Russian regions. Siberian regions and cities like Tomsk or Omsk tend to be more democratic than the so-called Black Earth 'red belt' territories that stubbornly voted communist or endorsed the pro-Kremlin party of power, United Russia. This determination was present even in the face of opposition activists like Alexei Navalny, who branded it as the party of 'crooks and thieves'. It is also why, even now, citizens in some regions actively protest against the war while others are heavily contributing conscripts and volunteers.

History matters, and there are historical drivers of these variations going beyond even the communist period. In my book, *Estate Origins of Democracy in Russia*, I discuss the significance of the tzarist division of society into *sosloviya*. I point out how when the Bolsheviks took power, they ended up reproducing the tzarist social divisions. We all know about the high-profile regicide and witch-hunts against the extended royal family and the bourgeoise. Less is known about the fate of the wider swathes of educated nobles, clergy, and urban groups. In my book, I trace the process of transformation of the cultivated members of tzarist society into the Soviet middle class. I also discuss how the Bolsheviks trapped the peasants in collective farms and limited their possibilities for escape into towns and especially Moscow and Leningrad, where the prestigious universities and jobs were concentrated. Different regions had variable constellations of *sosloviya*, and the prevalence of serfdom also varied across Russia. Accordingly, the local economies developed in different ways and citizens did not have the same opportunities to obtain higher education and become professionals in high status occupations where state pressures to conform are less severe than in public sector jobs. But political scientists studying the social consequences of the market and 'democratic' transition of the 1990s paid scant attention to these legacies of tzarist and communist Russia.

The *sosloviya*, a relic of the bygone times, had no place in the then-fashionable intellectual paradigmatic frameworks. What made this more complex was that communism as a paradigm had programmed both those outside *and* inside Russia to think about Soviet society as the 'great leveller' [12], as did the celebrated Marxist and other left-leaning thinkers past [13] and present [14]. We have tended to couch the new inequalities with reference to the apparatchiks or Komsomol functionaries who became oligarchs, and the rest of the population we labelled the 'middle class' and 'workers' who lost their Soviet-era social safety nets and were cast adrift into the wild free-for-all of the catastrophically executed market transition.

The problem with the communism paradigm is that while it accepts that there had been a layer of citizens more equal than others, there is the general notion that the Bolsheviks inflicted death upon the old pre-Bolshevik order and the social baggage that it carried. These assumptions persist among social scientists even though new historical research is beginning to question them. Sheila Fitzpatrick wrote about the adaptation of the bourgeoisie in Soviet Russia [15, 16]. New ethnographic work is suggestive of the layering of religious and other sensibilities from the bygone era upon experiences intrinsic to communism [17]. Together, these works ought to have steered us towards a rethinking of the nature of Russia's social relations.

Nor do categories from comparative politics, even if taken from contemporary autocracies, help clarify the nature of Russian society and its resilience (or lack thereof) against autocratic government. In the traditional language of political science, autocratic government is divided into: (i) the autocrat; (ii) the elites; and (iii) the masses, sometimes disaggregated into the 'middle class' and the 'working class'. We have individuals with 'tertiary' education and those with none. The reality is that education is an unreliable predictor of democratic inclinations. Autocracies have shorn the concept of the middle class of its rosy modernization paradigm-inspired premise, for huge chunks of the middle classes in autocratic strongholds like Russia or China are state dependent [18]. Put simply, educated middle-class Russians do not always behave as predicted or as their counterparts do in other post-socialist countries and beyond.

Understanding the nature of the transition was further complicated by the fact that the first post-Soviet decade was dominated by survey research in an attempt to depart from Kremlinology and 'area studies'. Valuable as the insights were, the mega cross-national projects to study public opinion in 'countries in transition' [19] left little room for the insertion of context-rich nuance that would allow for greater insight into the existing social divides and their likely impact on the political realm. This was evident as late as in 2017, when I, with my collaborators, attempted to survey respondents on the basis of their *sosloviye* ancestry [20]. No previous academics or pollsters had examined this factor. The deep historical divisions in Russian society apparently had no place in survey work. This situation is not an indictment on the method per se. Instead, it illuminates how we have not embedded ourselves sufficiently in the *sui generis* texture of social relations that still bear strong echoes of the more distant, pre-communist past. We have, in other words, failed to move beyond the paradigm of *post-communism*.

The Russian *Sosloviye* and Why it Matters for Politics now

To understand Russian social divides that explain the motivations of different social groups to support or challenge autocracy and Putin's war, we need to go back to the *sosloviye*. The Russian historian Boris Mironov defines estate (*sosloviye*) as 'a juridically circumscribed group with hereditary rights and obligations'. It was a term that became widespread in Russian jurisprudence by the second quarter of the nineteenth century [21 p334]. The legal underpinnings of the *sosloviye* were enshrined in the 1835 Code of Laws of the Russian Empire (*Svod zakonov Rossiyskoy imperii*). This Code was modified over time but remained in place until the Bolshevik Revolution. Within the Code, there were four main estates of: (i) nobles (*dvoryane/dvoryanstvo*), the service estate, which is also often referred to as 'gentry' [22]; (ii) the clergy (*dukhovenstvo*); (iii) town dwellers (*gorodskiye obyvateli*); and (iv) rural dwellers (*sel'skiye obyvateli*), which included serfs (before emancipation) and other categories of peasants, such as state peasants, who had greater freedoms. Russian laws distinguished between the various categories even within one estate designation, for instance, hereditary and personal nobility [23]. The Great Reforms of the 19th century helped undermine the estate division, not least because many nobles became less wealthy after losing serf ownership, while former serfs acquired rights they never had before. But this does not mean that the 'the four-estate paradigm' ceased to be relevant. Rather, it affected both the rights that different categories of citizens had and their obligations towards the state, and, in a cognitive sense, how they perceived others.

The Bolsheviks inadvertently contributed to the preservation of the estate divides. After the Revolution, there was an exodus of peasants from the countryside into large cities, notably Moscow, over the course of the 1920s and 1930s. Russian urban society became 'peasantifed' during and immediately after collectivization in the late 1920s through early 1930s [24]. Collectivization worsened the conditions after the Bolshevik Revolution, whether in terms of food supply or health. Many peasants fled into cities while they still could, in search of a better life. Of course, in the last decades of the Romanov dynasty, peasants had been also increasingly moving to cities, and this process accelerated after serf emancipation in 1861. The process of urbanization was not a straightforward one. The urban corporations (*soslovnyye obshchestva*) sought to restrict peasant entry into towns. Even after serfs were emancipated, they could not easily attain the status of urban citizens with the same rights as merchants or *meshchane*. Many peasants living in towns retained their peasant estate and maintained a foothold in villages. Peasant assimilation in cities as full urban burghers had been protracted and piecemeal. As Alison Smith writes in her book on estates in late Imperial Russia, the process sometimes took several generations, and often it took a long time before the peasant swapped the rural estate for an urban one with full urban citizenship rights [25].

But after the Bolshevik Revolution, the pace of urbanization dramatically accelerated. The new peasant entrants into towns confronted severe prejudice from established urbanites. The

Bolsheviks made the chasm worse when, faced with peasant resistance to collectivization, they adapted draconian laws which had the effect of trapping, in the new collective farms, peasants who had not escaped or were not exiled or otherwise repressed. These restrictions lasted well into the 1950s–1960s. Because peasants were deprived of passports and could not easily leave the village without permission from the local soviet and collective farm managers, they were deprived of the rights and opportunities that urban citizens enjoyed in the Soviet Union. Among these possibilities were obtaining education in prestigious universities and joining the elite professions that allowed travel abroad and access to foreign periodicals, newspapers, and other sources of information alternative to Soviet propaganda.

The Bolshevik policies thus overall consolidated the chasm that had existed for centuries, still separating a small minority of educated elites from the vast majority denied such opportunities because of the *sosloviye* system or the imperatives to keep peasants in their collective farm. Even as the 1950s–1960s atmosphere of political liberalization in the period after Stalin's death and the lifting of restrictions for peasant movement encouraged greater numbers of the *kolkhozniki* (collective farm workers) to move to towns and cities, the rural communities faced serious barriers to social mobility [5].

The consequence of this was that at the end of the 20th century, Russia was still a less-urbanised country. Anatoly Vishnevsky, the social demographer, points out that in 1990, urbanization stood at 66% in the USSR, a significantly lower percentage than the UK or the USA, where it stood at about 78%. But more importantly, a large chunk of the urban population that is included in the urbanization statistic had not even been born in cities. Vishnevsky estimates that among those aged 60, only approximately 15–17% had been born in the city (*korennyye gorozhane*); roughly 40% of those aged forty; and only among those aged twenty and younger, there were over 50% who were native urbanites, and this group formed only 37% of the population [26].

The new urbanites did not have the same opportunities as the established urban professionals when it comes to access to education and the high-status professions. And like in tzarist Russia, in the USSR, the new urban citizens kept strong ties to the countryside. Many had either moved to cities from their villages in adulthood or, even if born in a town, had parents and grandparents who did manual labour in the collective farms for a living. Scores of the new urbanites joined the bloated public sector and became clerks, schoolteachers, or social workers highly dependent on the state for pay and perks. These latter-day rural and new urban workers fared poorly in the context of market transition. As Vishnevsky wrote:

> By the time of the USSR's collapse, one could not contend that Soviet society became a solidly and overwhelmingly urban society. The USSR citizens in their majority remained urbanites in the first generation, with half to three quarters comprised of urbanites and half or a quarter of peasants – bearing the stamp of transient status, of marginality. To a certain extent, this stamp will be inherited by their children [26].

Why did collective farm workers find it so hard to integrate into the Soviet urban society? The Soviet state set up the *propiska* system of residential registration that made it difficult for citizens to move into prestigious cities like Moscow and other large regional hubs. For many citizens, geographic and social mobility meant moving from their village into the nearby regional centre, often with few opportunities for higher education and high-paying jobs. Russia has many medium-size towns that used to be company towns where workers have remained dependent on one or a handful of factory employers for jobs and social welfare. The collective farm workers who were lucky to gain a foothold in the larger cities often congregated in the micro-*rayony* (micro-districts) with low social prestige on the outskirts in the sprawling suburbia of faceless tower blocks. Yekaterina Gerasimova and Sofya Tchuikina powerfully describe how these communities re-enacted their rural lives and re-created a kind of rural microcosm, which remained separate from the cultural influences of the urbanites living in the more prestigious elite districts [27].

As the public sector under Putin's autocracy expanded, the historically marginalised rural and urban citizens coveted the service jobs in the increasingly vast public sector, including in the police and national guard (*Rosgvardiya*), viewing them as a means to improve their social standing.

We have yet to paint a systematic social portrait of the urban public sector workforce that includes joiners of Putin's vast repressive machinery. But we can examine the biographies of prominent Putin opponents in the prestigious and high-status positions; these are easily available from Wikipedia and other public sources. Take TV Rain, the independent news channel that became an eyesore for Putin because of its critique of the war and as an outlet that routinely gives a platform to the political opposition. The Putin regime has branded the channel a 'foreign agent' in the context of witch-hunts against the opposition and liberal NGOs and press; it is now broadcasting from the Netherlands. The journalists employed on this channel, including the editor-in-chief Tikhon Dzyadko and Anna Mongait, another prominent journalist, come from families of dynastic intelligentsia who were already privileged or well-educated before the Revolution and joined the academic, artistic, and other professional elite in Soviet Russia. As I write elsewhere,

> The probability of a peasant *otkhodnik* [seasonal urban worker] ascending into the prestigious and autonomous *Soviet* professions with the pedigree of Dzyadko or Mongait's family was extremely low... the pathway to becoming a Soviet dissident and post-Soviet Russian public intellectual openly challenging Russia's war against Ukraine does not lie via the peasant route to social mobility [5].

Timothy Frye and his collaborators have researched 'workplace dependencies' whereby enterprise managers pressurise vulnerable and dependent employees to support and cast their vote for incumbents or incumbent-supporting parties during elections [28]. And Bryn Rosenfeld shows how being socialised within the public sector of autocratic regimes engenders pro-regime sentiments and orientations [18]. But we are still left with the question of why an Anna Mogait or a Tikhon Dzyadko are able to avoid employment with the state-dependent enterprises or public sector. What does it take for someone to be able to join the independent media on a trendy news channel, one of the few islands of open challenges to the regime whether in Russia or in exile?

The reality is that the 'communism as a great social leveller' narrative does not capture the persistent divide between the peasant estate on the one hand and, and on the other, the descendants of the educated *sosloviye*, a stratum that together with a sprinkling of the upwardly mobile educated peasants comprised a minority of the Imperial population.

Habitually literate and educated, many, though of course not all, from among the educated and privileged estates were in the best position to withstand the ideological onslaught of Bolshevism, and their descendants now are better able to scrutinise and resist Putin's propaganda machinery. They form the bulwark of anti-Putinism. The minority's democratic inclinations are not so much because of deeply internalised democratic values, though many of course share them. Rather, this small minority of Russian society are able to resist because these groups have habitually colonised the professions where independent thought thrived and where there is greater access to alternative sources of information. They were also desperate to safeguard their identities as cultivated Russian nobility and the bourgeoisie, distinct from the rural mass with which they never identified and for which many had disdain even as they pursued 'done with illiteracy!' and other progressive causes. Their preoccupations were not so much public as they were corporate and in-group. But corporate autonomy also provides those with a moral core with the resources to resist or to flee. The Soviet dissidents came from this milieu, and in Russia now it is the cultural and scientific intelligentsia and people in the spheres of independent journalism, academia, and the arts who are in the anti-Putin vanguard.

The second prong of the bimodal society has neither the imperative nor the resources to resist in the same way. This does not mean that the marginalised people – the majority actually – in Russian society do not resent authority, autocracy, and atrocity. They do. But their resentment is also about the big chasm and their failure to identify with the small minority of the habitually privileged intelligentsia. Understanding how Russians perceive Putin and the war requires factoring the triadic nature of this attitudinal phenomenon. It's not just about how the 'masses' perceive the 'autocrat'; it's more about how perceptions of the autocrat are filtered through attitudes vis-à-vis those who resist him – the historically and intergenerationally privileged minority. The underprivileged will not join the protest, because they do not identify with the people who stage it.

Vladimir Putin's life story too illustrates the different family trajectories and sentiments of individuals from distinct social backgrounds in Russia. It is well known that Putin grew up in the city of Leningrad (renamed now again St Petersburg), where he was born into a family of workers of peasant origin. Putin's grandfather famously was a chef to Stalin; and Putin's father was a Navy conscript, while his mother was a factory worker. Tchuikina and Gerasimova and Tchuikina found that social divisions in Soviet Leningrad derive from tzarist times, when aristocrats colonised central districts of the city; they continued to do so discreetly in the Soviet period, while the un-prestigious Soviet suburbs, the *mikrorayony*, remained plebeian and overwhelmingly concentrated factory workers of peasant origin, mirroring the predicament of the peasant *otkhodniki* in tzarist times [27, 29].

Putin would have acutely felt his underprivileged position in the Soviet Union where the tzarist-era intelligentsia continued to look down upon the peasants and 'proletariat' overwhelmingly of peasant origin. Behind Putin's lashing out against a new liberal Russia and the Western-oriented intelligentsia there may well be the generations of accumulated marginality that began with his peasant ancestors and ended in the St Petersburg *kommunalka* (communal apartment). Like scores of others of his group, Putin would never wash off the stigma of the downtrodden in Russian Imperial and then Soviet society. While the descendants of aristocrats, merchants, clergymen, and *meshchane* with a sprinkling from the peasant estate – the core of the so-called *Soviet* middle class – colonised the elite professions, the media, and the arts, the likes of Vladimir Putin had to bury their resentments in the backstreets of his shabby dwelling.

Conclusion

The example of the soldier that I gave at the start of this essay ought to make us reconsider how we study Russia and how we make sense of it. What do we know about the social predicament of this young man? How does his upbringing differ from that of the small intelligentsia in large cities who are not fighting in this war and perhaps are even protesting against it? What imprint does he have of the values of his grandmother? Has his family been repressed by Stalin? Were they peasants before the Revolution? What parallels can we draw between his life and that of one Vova

(Vladimir) Putin growing up in Leningrad? Does he feel the same kind of anger about the cultivated neo-aristocracy of museum workers, art historians, physicists – people with whom he will never identify? What role for social identity in constructing a social consensus against the war? Does his faith matter?

The research that I have carried out recently for my new book, *Estate Origins*, tells me that the dissenting minority in Russia can be best understood in a historical sense. My Ukrainian colleagues and fellow scholars of Central and Eastern Europe are rightly calling attention now to the differences in civic culture between Russians and Ukrainians [30]. This is an important argument that also deserves careful historical study. But I here present a complementary angle that shows that if there is a 'civicness' in Russia, it has been limited to much smaller segments of society (and now, with the exodus of the educated and opposition-minded citizens, it is shrinking too) than in the countries of Central Europe with very different historical trajectories, a record of organising to resist the colonial empire, and more limited experience of serfdom. Throughout Russian history, only a small minority of citizens had the education, freedoms, and autonomy to resist the pressures of the autocratic state to conform – whether tzarist, Soviet, or post-Soviet. Understanding this reality of a deeply divided society should help us not only make sense of the drivers of social support for or challenge to Putinism, but to anticipate what might happen after Putin exits the stage.

Acknowledgements

The author acknowledges support from the Research Infrastructure Investment Fund grant, LSE International Relations Department.

Notes

[1] An earlier draft of this paper was presented at the Workshop on Political Ethnography of the State in the Post-Soviet Contexts, held on December 9-10, 2022, at the East European and Eurasian Studies Program of the Yale MacMillan Center, New Haven. This essay also develops some of the themes I discussed in my new book on the Russian social divisions and support for democracy/autocracy [1]. I also draw on my contribution to the special issue of the journal Post-Soviet Affairs that I guest edited, on the logic of 'fractals' in Russian studies [2]. The title of my PSA essay reflects the sociologist Andrew Abbott's discussion of the propensity of fields and sub-fields of knowledge to divide along disciplinary, epistemological, and other fault-lines; 'fractal' captures the self-replicability of broader disciplinary divisions within the sub-divisions, for instance, between positivists and non-positivists; Marxists, feminists, and others, etc. [3].

[2] See: https://www.newyorker.com/news/q-and-a/why-john-mearsheimer-blames-the-us-for-the-crisis-in-ukraine, https://www.ft.com/content/2d65c763-c36f-4507-8a7d-13517032aa22, https://thehill.com/opinion/international/3838012-kissinger-admits-he-was-wrong-on-ukraine-what-about-taiwan/, https://www.spectator.co.uk/article/there-are-three-possible-outcomes-to-this-war-henry-kissinger-interview/.

References

1. Lankina TV. The estate origins of democracy in Russia: from imperial bourgeoisie to post-communist middle class. Cambridge: Cambridge University Press; 2022. DOI: https://doi.org/10.1017/9781009071017.

2. Lankina T. Branching out or inwards? The logic of fractals in Russian studies. *Post-Soviet Affairs*. 2023; 39(1–2): 70–85. Special Issue: Conversations within the Field: Russia's War against Ukraine and the Future of Russian Studies. Guest Editor: Tomila Lankina. DOI: https://doi.org/10.1080/1060586X.2022.2147382.

3. Abbott A. Chaos of disciplines. Chicago: University of Chicago Press; 2001.
4. Myre G. Ukrainian judge hands down a sentence in the first war crimes trial in that conflict. In: Inskeep S. Heard on Morning Edition; 2022.
5. Lankina T. Branching out or inwards? The logic of fractals in Russian studies. *Post-Soviet affairs*. 2022; ahead-of-print(ahead-of-print): 116. DOI: https://doi.org/10.1080/1060586X.2022.2147382.
6. La Lova L. Methods in Russian studies: overview of top political science, economics, and area studies journals. *Post-Soviet Affairs*. 2022; 39(1–2): 70–85. Special Issue: Conversations within the Field: Russia's War against Ukraine and the Future of Russian Studies. Guest Editor: Tomila Lankina. DOI: https://doi.org/10.1080/1060586X.2022.2162293.
7. Kharatyan K. Barany i soldaty (sheep and soldiers). *The Moscow Times*. 2022 September 30.
8. Lankina T, Watanabe K, Netesova Y. How Russian media control, manipulate, and leverage public discontent: framing protest in autocracies. In: Koesel KJ, Bunce VJ, Weiss JC, (eds.), Citizens and the state in authoritarian regimes: comparing China and Russia, 137–64. Oxford: Oxford University Press; 2020. DOI: https://doi.org/10.1093/oso/9780190093488.003.0006.
9. Lankina T, Watanabe K. "Russian Spring" or "Spring Betrayal"? The media as a mirror of Putin's evolving strategy in Ukraine. *Europe-Asia Studies*. 2017; 69(10): 1526–56. DOI: https://doi.org/10.1080/09668136.2017.1397603.
10. Guriev S, Treisman D. Spin dictators: the changing face of tyranny in the 21st century. Princeton: Princeton University Press; 2022. DOI: https://doi.org/10.1515/9780691224466.
11. Beissinger MR. The revolutionary city: urbanization and the global transformation of rebellion. Princeton, New Jersey:

Princeton University Press; 2022. DOI: https://doi.org/10.1515/9780691224756.

12. Scheidel W. The great leveler: violence and the history of inequality from the Stone Age to the twenty-first century. Princeton, New Jersey: Princeton University Press; 2017. DOI: https://doi.org/10.1515/9781400884605.

13. Webb S, Webb B. Soviet communism: a new civilization. Third ed. London: Longmans, Green; 1947.

14. Piketty T. Capital in the twenty-first century. Cambridge, Massachusetts: The Belknap Press of Harvard University Press; 2014.

15. Fitzpatrick S. The two faces of Anastasia: narratives and counter-narratives of identity in Stalinist everyday life. In: Kiaer C, Naiman E, (eds.), Everyday life in early Soviet Russia: taking the revolution inside, 23–34. Bloomington, Indiana: Indiana University Press; 2006.

16. Fitzpatrick S. Tear off the masks! Identity and imposture in twentieth-century Russia. Princeton, New Jersey: Princeton University Press; 2005. DOI: https://doi.org/10.1515/9781400843732.

17. Rogers D. The old faith and the Russian land: a historical ethnography of ethics in the Urals. Ithaca, New York: Cornell University Press; 2009.

18. Rosenfeld B. The autocratic middle class: how state dependency reduces the demand for democracy. Princeton, New Jersey: Princeton University Press; 2021. DOI: https://doi.org/10.1515/9780691209777.

19. Barometer Surveys: The University of Strathclyde. https://www.cspp.strath.ac.uk/catalog13_0.html.

20. Lankina T, Libman A, Tertytchnaya K. State violence and target group adaptation: maintaining social status in the face of repressions in Soviet Russia. *The Journal of Peace Research*. Forthcoming.

21. Mironov BN. Sotsial'naya istoriya Rossii perioda Imperii (XVIII–nachalo XX v.). Genezis lichnosti, demokraticheskoy sem'yi, grazhdanskogo obshchestva i pravovogo gosudarstva. Revised third ed. St Petersburg: Dmitriy Bulanin; 2003.

22. Reyfman I. How Russia learned to write: literature and the imperial table of ranks. Madison: The University of Wisconsin Press; 2016.

23. Mironov BN. Rossiyskaya imperiya: Ot traditsii k modernu. St Petersburg: Dmitriy Bulanin; 2014.

24. Hoffmann DL. Peasant metropolis: social identities in Moscow, 1929–1941. Ithaca, New York: Cornell University Press; 1994.

25. Smith AK. For the common good and their own well-being: social estates in imperial Russia. New York: Oxford University Press; 2014. DOI: https://doi.org/10.1093/acprof:oso/9780199978175.001.0001.

26. Vishnevsky A. Serp i rubl': Konservativnaya modernizatsiya v SSSR. Second ed. Moscow: State University Higher School of Economics; 2010.

27. Gerasimova Y, Tchuikina S. Ot kapitalisticheskogo Peterburga k sotsialisticheskomu Leningradu. Izmenenie sotsial'no-prostranstvennoy struktury goroda v 1930-e gody. [From capitalist St Petersburg to socialist Leningrad: Changes in the socio-spatial structure of the city in the 1930s]. In: Vihavainen T, (ed.), Normy i tsennosti povsednevnoy zhizni [Norms and values of everyday life], 27–72. St Petersburg: Neva; Letniy Sad; 2000.

28. Frye T, Reuter OJ, Szakonyi D. Political machines at work: voter mobilization and electoral subversion in the workplace. *World Politics*. 2014; 66(2): 195–228. DOI: https://doi.org/10.1017/S004388711400001X.

29. Tchuikina SA. Dvoryanskaya pamyat': "Byvshiye" v sovetskom gorode (Leningrad, 1920-30-e gody). St Petersburg: European University at St Petersburg; 2006.

30. Hale HE, Onuch O. The Zelensky Effect. London: Hurst Publishers; 2022.
31. Lankina TV. The estate origins of democracy in Russia: from imperial bourgeoisie to postcommunist middle class. Cambridge: Cambridge University Press; 2022. DOI: https://doi.org/10.1017/9781009071017.

4. Rewriting History and 'Gathering the Russian Lands': Vladimir Putin and Ukrainian Nationhood

Björn Alexander Düben

While the causes of Russia's war against Ukraine are often discussed in terms of geopolitics, another factor that seems to have been an important part of Vladimir Putin's rationale for launching the invasion in February 2022 is his nationalist vision of Ukraine – or significant portions of it – as a historic part of Russia. In the years leading up to the invasion, Putin wrote and spoke at great length about Ukrainian history, establishing a narrative centred around the denial of Ukraine's historic state- and nationhood, presenting Ukrainians and Russians as a single people, and laying claim to large swathes of Ukrainian territory as 'primordial' Russian lands. While analysts have long struggled to adequately assess it, Putin has used this narrative to justify the invasion of Ukraine to a domestic audience, and it appears to have influenced the Kremlin's war aims and the conduct of Russian troops on the ground. There is much to suggest that Putin's invocation of such nationalist and irredentist themes, rather than being a purely tactical move, reflects his genuine convictions. In addition to analysing how and why Putin has been (mis)interpreting Ukrainian history and denying Ukrainian

> nationhood, this chapter examines how this narrative has affected the Russian war effort and how far Putin's territorial claims in Ukraine extend.

One of the most surprising aspects of Russia's full-scale invasion of Ukraine in February 2022 was how many international analysts and policymakers were surprised by it. By the time the Kremlin's 'special military operation' commenced, its contours had been visible for months. Moscow had clearly laid the logistical, administrative, and informational foundations for a complex military offensive, and each operational step of Russia's armed forces had been minutely predicted and documented by American and British intelligence. Indeed, the assault in 2022 was not even an entirely new conflict but the escalation of a hybrid invasion that had begun in 2014. One likely reason why the invasion caught so many observers by surprise was their proclivity to regard Vladimir Putin's motivations through a predominantly realist lens. Russia's president was seen as a rational, non-ideological practitioner of realpolitik – an image that appeared at odds with the reckless and strategically misguided nature of the campaign. In countless speeches and discussions in the months prior to the invasion, Putin had constantly spoken about Ukraine under its post-Maidan government as a geopolitical threat to Russia, particularly in light of Kyiv's aspirations to join NATO. Those who viewed Putin as a quintessential realist and prudent strategist were inclined to regard the massing of Russian troops on Ukraine's borders as a deterrent measure and a geopolitical bargaining chip. They generally did not – or refused to – see it as preparations for an imminent attack against a much weaker neighbour that posed no immediate threat.

It is very likely that the geopolitical grievances and concerns that Putin repeated in the months leading up to the invasion were one of his main motivations for launching the attack on Ukraine. But another motivation seems to have been equally relevant for cementing Putin's conviction that Russia needed to seize and control Ukraine, even at the risk of triggering a major war: his nationalist, irredentist perspective on Russian and Ukrainian history, culminating in his repeated claims that Ukraine has no state- and nationhood of its own and is essentially a historic part of Russia.

This chapter seeks to analyse this aspect of Putin's reasoning and is structured as follows: It first outlines what Putin has stated about Ukrainian history and Ukraine's historic statehood, and it examines how this is related to the Russian-Ukrainian war. Second, it considers whether Putin is promoting these views for tactical reasons or out of genuine conviction, and it assesses whether they are historically (in)correct. Lastly, to the extent that Putin acknowledges Ukraine's statehood at all, the chapter examines which parts of its territory he views as 'historic Russian lands' which he aims to 'restore' to Russia, and it assesses how plausible these territorial claims are.

Lessons from Russia's Historian-in-Chief

For many observers, this nationalist and irredentist part of Putin's mindset regarding Ukraine first became clearly visible in a speech he gave on 21 February 2022. This was the day he formally dispatched Russian troops into the separatist 'republics' in eastern

Ukraine's Donets Basin (Donbas) in preparation for the all-out invasion of Ukraine three days later. While Putin repeated the same geopolitical talking points he had been voicing for months, he surprised his audience by devoting around a third of the hour-long speech to expounding his idiosyncratic interpretation of Ukrainian history. Addressing Ukrainians as 'our compatriots', he proclaimed that Ukraine was a part 'of the historical Russia' and that 'Ukraine is not just a neighbouring country for us. It is an inalienable part of our own history, culture and spiritual space' [1]. Among his most memorable claims, Putin asserted 'that Ukraine actually never had stable traditions of real statehood'. Instead, 'modern Ukraine was entirely created by Russia or, to be more precise, by Bolshevik, Communist Russia'. In Putin's view, it 'can be rightfully called "Vladimir Lenin's Ukraine." He was its creator and architect.' What's more, 'Lenin and his associates did it [creating Ukraine] in a way that was extremely harsh on Russia – by separating, severing what is historically Russian land' [1]. Putin condemned the Bolsheviks for having transferred territory to Ukraine and other Soviet republics: 'vast territories that had nothing to do with them … were transferred along with the population of what was historically Russia'. In particular, this included the 'Donbass, which was actually shoved into Ukraine', and 'the lands of the Black Sea littoral', formerly known as 'Novorossiya (New Russia)'. Putin left no doubt that he regarded 'the disintegration of our united country' and the formation of Ukrainian statehood as a series of 'historic, strategic mistakes' that ran against 'the historical destiny of Russia and its peoples' [1].

Putin's lengthy lecture about Ukrainian history may have seemed out of sync with his previous Ukraine-related statements directed at international audiences. But his spotlighting of Ukrainian history and his denial of Ukraine's historical statehood was in fact nothing new. As early as April 2008, on the sidelines of a NATO summit in Romania, Putin had reportedly told then-US President George W. Bush that 'Ukraine is not even a state! What is Ukraine? A part of its territory is [in] Eastern Europe, but a[nother] part, a considerable one, was a gift from us!' [2]. On the same occasion, Putin also went on the record with the comment that

> Ukraine is a very complicated state. Ukraine, in the form it currently exists, was created in the Soviet times. ... It received huge territories from Russia in the east and south of the country. It is a complicated state formation. ... Well, seventeen million Russians currently live in Ukraine. Who may state that we do not have any interests there? South, the south of Ukraine, completely, there are only Russians. [3]

At a conference in Kyiv in July 2013, Putin spoke about Ukraine's 'reunification with Russia' from the 17th century onwards and referred to Ukrainians, Belarusians, and Russians as 'a single people' [4].

While Putin's public denial of Ukraine's historical statehood was initially subtle and implicit, it became increasingly explicit in later years, particularly following the ouster of Viktor Yanukovych's pro-Russian government in Kyiv in early 2014 and Russia's subsequent annexation of Crimea. In his speech marking the annexation on 18 March 2014, Putin proclaimed that Russians and Ukrainians

> are not simply close neighbours but, as I have said many times already, we are one people. Kiev is the mother of Russian cities. Ancient Rus is our common source and we cannot live without each other. [5]

In subsequent years, Putin went on to make similar assertions. In February 2020, for instance, he stated in an interview that Ukrainians and Russians 'are one and the same people', and he insinuated that Ukrainian national identity had only emerged as a product of foreign interference [6] – claims which he repeated in his annual marathon press conference in June 2021 [7].

Meanwhile, some of Putin's closest associates went considerably further in their public derision and denial of Ukrainian state- and nationhood. Vladislav Surkov, for instance, formerly one of Putin's top advisers and his point man on Ukraine prior to 2020, stated in February of that year that

> there is no Ukraine. There is Ukrainian-ness. That is, a specific disorder of the mind. An astonishing enthusiasm for ethnography, driven to the extreme. ... But there is no nation. [8]

Throughout the last decade, Putin has shown a remarkable interest in historical themes, taking time out of his presidential schedule to write lengthy treatises on historical topics. In June 2020, he published an article in *The National Interest* which tried to revise the academic narrative about the outbreak of the Second World War by justifying the 1939 Molotov-Ribbentrop pact and its secret protocol [9]. The article was roundly dismissed by foreign historians as unprofessional and poorly researched.

But few historical topics appear to have preoccupied Putin as much as the history of Ukraine. This became particularly evident in July 2021, when he published a 6900-word article titled 'On the Historical Unity of Russians and Ukrainians'. Providing a sweeping (but extremely selective) account of Ukrainian history stretching back to the early Middle Ages, Putin tried to make the case that Ukrainians and Russians – along with Belarusians – form 'a single large nation, a triune nation', and that they are essentially 'one people – a single whole. ... It is what I have said on numerous occasions and what I firmly believe.' According to Putin, it has been Moscow's historical mission to be 'the center of reunification, continuing the tradition of ancient Russian statehood [and] gathering the Russian lands' [10].

In Putin's historical account, Ukrainians always thrived most when they were under Moscow's rule, and the common people in Ukraine consistently wished to remain close to Russia. By contrast, whenever there had been manifestations of 'the idea of Ukrainian people as a nation separate from the Russians' (an idea for which 'there was no historical basis'), these were merely the aberrant schemes of self-serving, detached elites, usually acting at the behest of manipulative foreign powers that wished 'to divide and then to pit the parts of a single people against one another'. These historical villains ranged from 18th-century anti-Muscovy Cossack leader Ivan Mazepa, 'who betrayed everyone' to Lenin's Bolsheviks, who, according to Putin, instigated the consolidation of the Ukrainian language and identity in the early 20th century. The ultimate result of these misguided policies was that 'in 1991, all those territories, and, which is more important, people, found themselves abroad overnight, taken away ... from their historical motherland' [10]. In his article, Putin also repeatedly claimed that, historically, 'people both in the western and eastern Russian lands spoke the same language'. While not explicitly denying the development of a separate Ukrainian language, he implied that it was a mere outgrowth of 'regional language peculiarities, resulting in the emergence of dialects' which remained virtually indistinguishable from Russian. To Putin, the works of Ukrainian writers 'are our common literary and cultural heritage' which must not 'be divided between Russia and Ukraine' [10].

Putin's July 2021 article, which was made required reading in Russian military academies shortly after its publication [11], provides the most exhaustive summary of his views on the history of Ukraine and Ukrainian statehood, which he has voiced in a more piecemeal fashion on countless other occasions. Since the start of Russia's 'special military operation', Putin has frequently repeated and reaffirmed these views. When asked at a plenary session in October 2022, for instance, if he had changed his mind about whether Ukrainians and Russians 'are one people', Putin responded,

> No, of course not. And how can this be changed? This is a historical fact. Russian statehood became established on our territories in the 9th century, first in Novgorod, then in Kiev, and then they grew together. It is one nation.

Putin went on to claim that it is 'a historical fact that Russians and Ukrainians are essentially one ethnicity' and that 'the nation that we now call Ukrainians' only emerged 'because some of Old

Russian lands in the west became parts of other states' which then 'started making attempts to divide the united Russian nation'. He concluded that 'Ukraine, of course, is an artificially created state', and, 'in fairness, Russia, which created today's Ukraine, could have been the only real and serious guarantor of Ukraine's statehood, sovereignty, and territorial integrity' [12].

Putin's constant denial of a Ukrainian state- and nationhood separate from Russia appears to resonate with large parts of the Russian population. Since February 2022, Putin's rhetoric has served as a catalyst for radical anti-Ukrainian and ultra-nationalist views, which previously were commonly found on the fringes of public discourse in Russia, to become fully accepted in mainstream discussion and debates. Other Russian senior officials, such as former President Dmitry Medvedev, are now referring to Ukraine as 'the Kyiv province of our native Malorossiya' [13] (Little Russia) – the latter being an obsolete way of referring to the Ukrainian lands as a province of the tsarist empire. In Russia's official and media narrative, it has become an article of faith that the territories being fought over in Ukraine are and always have been Russian lands. Most commentators in Russian state media, including lawmakers and senior officials, now routinely speak about the war as a reclamation of 'historical territories', claiming that Ukraine is not a nation in its own right and that the Ukrainian language is merely a Russian dialect.[1]

Since the war in Ukraine failed to progress as originally planned, the nationalist narrative of Ukraine being a historical Russian land has played an important role in the Kremlin's attempts to justify and promote the invasion domestically. This narrative has become firmly established as part of a trifecta of official justifications for the invasion – the other two being the alleged 'genocide' of Russian speakers in eastern Ukraine and the existential geopolitical threat posed by NATO and the 'Anglo-Saxon' West. The government-sponsored narrative of Ukraine's historical nonexistence as a state also appears to have left an imprint on Russia's actual conduct in occupied parts of the country, where towns have been renamed with Russian or Soviet (rather than Ukrainian) names, Ukrainian street signs have been systematically replaced, Ukrainian-language libraries and archives have been closed or destroyed, and Ukrainian-language curricula have been cancelled in many schools and universities, with the apparent aim of thoroughly 'Russifying' all conquered territories in Ukraine. An investigation by UN Human Rights Council special rapporteurs in Ukraine condemned the Russian occupation authorities'

> severe targeting of Ukrainian cultural symbols. Cultural resources – such as repositories of Ukrainian literature, museums, and historical archives – are being destroyed, and there is a widespread narrative of demonisation and denigration of Ukrainian culture and identity promoted by Russian officials. [14]

The report added that

> Efforts are being made to erase local culture, history, and language in cultural and educational institutions and to forcibly replace them with Russian language and with Russian and Soviet history and culture. [14]

Fact-Checking Putin's Historical Narrative

One of the central questions regarding Putin's nationalist, irredentist historical claims vis-à-vis Ukraine is whether they reflect his genuine beliefs and convictions or whether they are tactical, serving to motivate the Russian public to support the war and its sacrifices and to convince Ukrainians of the legitimacy of their 'reintegration'. This question cannot be conclusively answered, but it appears unlikely that his use of these narratives has been purely tactical. Putin's intense preoccupation with historical themes (particularly those that intersect with Russian nationalist narratives) suggests that these themes do reflect his genuine beliefs. The same can be said about his propensity for comparing himself with historical rulers like Peter the Great, as well as his self-professed affinity for the works of nationalist philosophers, such as the fascist-leaning Ivan Ilyin, whose views on Ukraine largely prefigured Putin's own [15] (and whom Putin quoted when he signed the accession treaties for four occupied Ukrainian provinces in September 2022 [16]).

Putin's views on Ukraine's historical state- and nationhood are essentially reiterations of a nationalist narrative that was already widespread in imperial Russia in the 19th century, but they do not stand up to any serious scholarly scrutiny. The roots of Ukraine's spiritual appeal to Putin and many of his compatriots lie in the fact that the Kyivan Rus' – a medieval state that came into existence in the 9th century and was centred around present-day Kyiv – is commonly regarded as a joint ancestral homeland that laid the foundations for both modern Ukraine and Russia. But from the time of its foundation to its conquest by the Mongols in the 13th century, the Rus' was an increasingly fragmented federation of principalities. Its southwestern territories (including Kyiv) were conquered by Lithuania and Poland in the early 14th century. For roughly four centuries, these lands, encompassing most of present-day Ukraine, were formally ruled by Poland-Lithuania, which left a deep cultural imprint on them. During this time, the Orthodox East Slavic population of these territories gradually developed an identity distinct from that of the East Slavs remaining in the territories under Mongol and later Muscovite rule (although some degree of cross-border contact between both East Slavic communities continued). A distinct Ukrainian (Ruthenian) language had already begun to emerge around the time following the disintegration of the Kyivan Rus' (notwithstanding Putin's incorrect assertion that 'the first linguistic differences [between Ukrainians and Russians] appeared only around the 16th century' [6]). Once present-day Ukraine had come under Lithuanian and Polish rule, the Ukrainian language evolved in relative isolation from the Russian language. At the same time, religious divisions developed within Eastern Orthodoxy, and from the mid-15th to the late 17th centuries, the Orthodox churches in Kyiv and in Moscow developed as separate entities.

Most of what is now Ukraine was formally governed by Lithuanian and Polish nobility prior to the 18th century, but these lands were predominantly inhabited by Orthodox East Slavs. Striving to escape the strict confines of serfdom, many of them began to form semiautonomous (and ethnically diverse) hosts of peasant warriors – the Cossacks – in the vast steppes on either side of the Dnipro river from around the 15th century. Most of them felt a cultural and religious affinity for Muscovite Russia but had no particular desire to be a part of the Muscovite state. In the 16th through 18th centuries, the Cossacks in present-day Ukraine formed their own de facto self-governed statelets, the 'Zaporizhian Sich' and the Cossack 'Hetmanate'. They staged a major uprising against their Polish overlords in 1648 and signed a treaty of allegiance with the expanding Tsardom of Russia in 1654. Notwithstanding this temporary turn towards Moscow, the Cossacks also explored other options. In the abortive Treaty of Hadiach with Poland-Lithuania in 1658, they were briefly on the verge of becoming a fully fledged constituent member of the Polish-Lithuanian Commonwealth. Internal disagreements about whether to side with Poland or Russia contributed to a series of civil wars among the Cossacks in the late 17th century. Their leaders frequently shifted their allegiance between Russia, Poland, and the Ottoman Empire, with the ultimate aim of preserving some degree of autonomy from all sides.

In 1667, Poland-Lithuania had to cede to Russia formal control of Kyiv and the territories east of the Dnipro river (Left Bank Ukraine). The Cossack statelet in the eastern territories was gradually reduced to a Russian vassal state, but its relationship with the tsarist government was often rife with conflict. Sporadic Cossack uprisings were now directed against the Russians as well as the Poles. In 1708, for instance, the Cossacks' leader Ivan Mazepa (whom Putin, in his 2021 article, singled out as a national traitor) allied himself with Sweden and unsuccessfully fought against Russia in the Great Northern War. In 1775, the Zaporizhian Sich was razed to the ground by Russian forces, and the Cossacks' institutions of self-governance were liquidated. Following the final partitions of Poland in the 1790s, the Russian

Empire absorbed the remainder of modern-day Ukraine – apart from its westernmost regions, which were annexed by Austria. Most of present-day Ukraine remained a part of the Russian state for the next 120 years. Nonetheless, a distinct Ukrainian national consciousness emerged and consolidated in the course of the 19th century, particularly among the elites and intelligentsia, who made countless efforts to further cultivate the Ukrainian literary language. The strength of the budding Ukrainian nationalism was such that Russia's imperial authorities perceived it as a serious threat, leading them to systematically suppress expressions of Ukrainian culture and the Ukrainian language. In his 2021 article, Putin tried to downplay and justify these repressive measures, which included the Valuyev Circular of 1863 and the Ems Ukaz of 1876, falsely asserting that these tsarist decrees merely 'restricted the publication and importation of religious and socio-political literature in the Ukrainian language' [10]. In actual fact, the Ems Ukaz in particular almost completely prohibited the usage of the Ukrainian language (which it labelled the 'Little Russian dialect') in open print, in lectures, theatre, and other performances.

When the Russian Empire collapsed in 1917, the Ukrainians declared a state of their own. However, after several years of quasi-independence, involving multiple abortive state entities plagued by foreign military interventions, Ukraine was once again partitioned between the nascent Soviet Union and newly independent Poland, Czechoslovakia, and Romania. From the early 1930s onwards, nationalist sentiments were rigorously and violently suppressed in the Soviet parts of Ukraine, but they remained latent and gained further traction through the traumatic experience of the 'Holodomor', a disastrous famine brought about by Joseph

Stalin's agricultural policies in 1932–1933 which killed around four million Ukrainians. Ultimately, it was only with the collapse of the Soviet Union in 1991 that Ukraine gained lasting independent statehood of its own. But strong sentiments of Ukrainian nationhood and Ukrainian de facto political entities struggling for their independence had already existed long before that.

Questions of historical state- and nationhood are inherently fraught with ambiguity. In contrast to Putin's essentialist understanding of a nation as a historical entity that exists as an objective fact over hundreds or perhaps thousands of years, scholars commonly understand nationhood as a relatively modern concept that is, in essence, socially constructed and malleable. Benedict Anderson, one of the foremost scholars of nationalism, described nations as 'imagined communities': large groups of people with a strong sense of commonality, which are far too big to allow for direct personal relations among all their members and could only develop in conjunction with certain socioeconomic processes linked with modernity (such as the emergence of print capitalism and the spread of literacy) [17]. Irrespective of how constructed and 'imagined' the nation as a sociopolitical principle is, however, conceptions of nationhood do not typically emerge out of thin air but are usually formed around pre-existing, relatively objective and recognisable sociocultural markers, such as a distinct language or religion, or a socially meaningful shared history.

In the case of the Ukrainian nation, it clearly does possess certain objective and conspicuous markers of nationhood, first and foremost a distinct Ukrainian language. Being under constant pressure from its more powerful (and often predatory) neighbours, it took until the 20th century for Ukraine to appear on the map of Europe

Figure 4.1: Graphic from 1926 Soviet population census report depicting percentage of ethnic Ukrainians

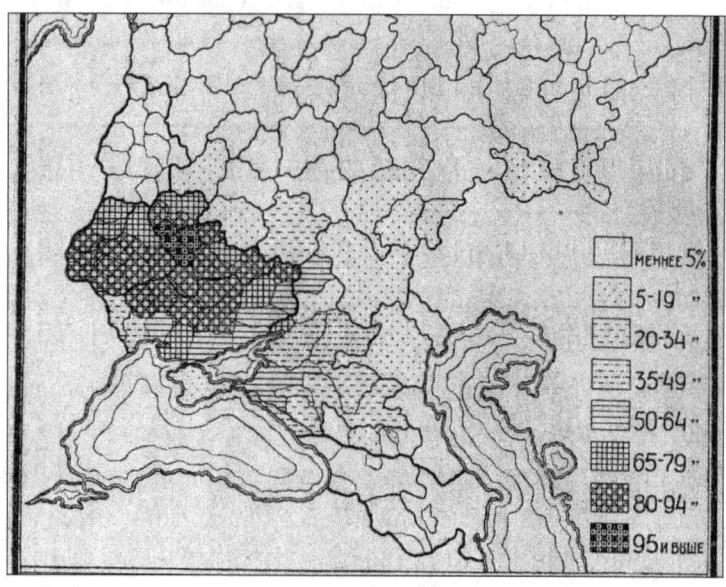

Source: Central Statistical Administration of the USSR [23] Original graphic from the 1926 Soviet population census report, depicting the distribution of ethnic Ukrainians in the south-western districts of the Soviet Union. For each district, the shading/pattern illustrates the relative percentage of ethnic Ukrainians among its total population (ranging from 'less than 5%' to '95% and higher', see bottom right). As is visible here, there were ethnic Ukrainian majorities in all districts of eastern Ukraine (UkrSSR), but also in several districts of southern Russia (RSFSR).

as an independent state (notwithstanding the centuries-long history of segments of Ukrainian society struggling for some form of independent statehood) – a fate that Ukraine shared with many other modern nation-states, both inside and outside of Europe.

The Territorial Question

Besides questioning Ukraine's historic state- and nationhood in toto, Putin also very clearly claimed in his historical treatises that, to the extent that Ukraine as an entity exists at all, its internationally recognised borders are artificial, and much of its present-day territory historically belongs to Russia but was accidentally 'lost' to Ukraine in the upheavals of the 20th century. The question he raised is thus not only whether Ukraine is a nation in its own right but also where its historic borders lie and whether Russia might have a claim to large swathes of its sovereign territory. This question directly relates to the presumed goals of the Kremlin's war effort.

What Putin's precise objectives are remains nebulous. It is unclear whether his aim is to erase Ukraine as a sovereign entity altogether or to retain a 'rump' Ukrainian state with a Moscow-friendly puppet government (similar to neighbouring Belarus), and if the second, how large such a semi-sovereign 'rump Ukraine' would then be. What we do know is that Putin's aim has been to annex and formally incorporate large parts of Ukraine's sovereign territory into Russia. In September 2022, he announced the formal annexation of four Ukrainian administrative regions: Donetsk and Luhansk Oblasts in eastern Ukraine (which together form the Donbas) and the Kherson and Zaporizhzhia Oblasts in southern Ukraine [16]. But it is doubtful that this represents the full extent of Putin's territorial ambitions, and it remains unclear how much more Ukrainian territory he ultimately seeks to place under Moscow's direct control.

Throughout his observations on Ukraine, Putin's explanations as to Russian territorial entitlement remained inconsistent and sometimes self-contradictory. Naturally, these claims include the Crimean Peninsula, which Russia formally annexed in 2014 and which Putin described as having 'always been an inseparable part of Russia' [5]. Putin has also left little doubt that he lays claim to the entire east and south of Ukraine. Since 2014, he has constantly referred to these parts of Ukraine as 'Novorossiya', an administrative name dating from the time when Ukraine was a part of the tsarist empire [18, 19]. 'Novorossiya' is an ambiguous concept, but it historically referred to a governorate of the Russian Empire that was created in the late 18th century and encompassed the bulk of southern Ukraine, including most of its Black Sea and Azov Sea coastlines and major cities like Odesa, Dnipro, Zaporizhzhia, Mariupol, Mikolayiv, and Kherson.

Putin, however, appears to be embracing a more expansive and ahistorical definition of 'Novorossiya' that also encompasses large areas of northeastern Ukraine. At an April 2014 press conference, he stated

> that what was called Novorossiya (New Russia) back in the tsarist days – Kharkov, Lugansk, Donetsk, Kherson, Nikolayev and Odessa – were not part of Ukraine back then. These territories were given to Ukraine in the 1920s by the Soviet government. Why? Who knows.' [20]

Judging from this and similar statements,[2] in addition to the territories of the former Novorossiya governorate and of Donbas (only parts of which had been within the boundaries of historic Novorossiya), Putin also considers the area around the country's second-largest city, Kharkiv, in northeastern Ukraine a historic Russian land.

Somewhat confusingly, there are other passages and statements in his speeches and historical treatises which suggest that Putin may have a very different understanding of where the 'historically correct' border between Ukraine and Russia ought to be. In his July 2021 article on Ukraine, for instance, he quoted his own political mentor, Anatoly Sobchak, the former mayor of Saint Petersburg, as having stated that

> the republics that were founders of the [Soviet] Union, having denounced the 1922 Union Treaty, must return to the boundaries they had had before joining the Soviet Union. All other territorial acquisitions are subject to discussion, negotiations, given that the ground has been revoked. In other words, when you leave, take what you brought with you. This logic is hard to refute. [10]

But it is unclear what exactly Putin thinks such a logic implies. Following this principle, Crimea would have been a part of Russia after 1991, but several now-Russian territories would not. Donbas and 'Novorossiya' would still be part of independent Ukraine, since they were within the borders of the Ukrainian Soviet Socialist Republic (UkrSSR) in 1922, as well as large swathes of territory around the cities of Taganrog and Shakhty, which were transferred from the UkrSSR to the Russian Soviet Federative Socialist Republic (RSFSR) in 1924.

In contrast to this, various other statements from the 2021 article and from Putin's speeches indicate that his territorial pretensions vis-à-vis Ukraine extend considerably further. In his February 2022 pre-invasion speech, Putin claimed that

> since time immemorial, the people living in the southwest of what has historically been Russian land have called themselves Russians and Orthodox Christians. This was the case before the 17th century, when a portion of this territory rejoined the Russian state, and after. [1]

He thereby asserted that the Ukrainian territories annexed by tsarist Russia in the 17th century – that is, most of the lands east of the Dnipro river (Left Bank Ukraine), as well as the capital of Kyiv – are integral parts of historic Russia. But he also implied that, to his mind, they merely constituted 'a portion' of Russia's historic southwest, which was evidently meant to encompass western (Right Bank) Ukraine as well. This is underscored by claims he made in his 2021 article. Ultimately, Putin has effectively described the entirety of Ukrainian territory as 'historically Russian lands'. His use of words like '*re*joined/*re*united' (воссоединилась) and '*re*gained' (возвратила) with reference to Russia's territorial conquests of the late 17th and 18th centuries (which involved territories that had never actually been under Muscovite/Russian rule before) demonstrates that his concept of 'historically Russian lands' appears to encompass, at a minimum, all the former territories of the medieval Kyivan Rus' (and, by implication, all of present-day Ukraine).

What makes the extent of Putin's territorial claims vis-à-vis Ukraine particularly difficult to assess is the fact that he appears to have formulated them with no serious consideration of the historical and demographic realities in the Ukrainian borderlands. It is undeniable that the historic borders of Ukraine, particularly in the country's east and south, are difficult to pinpoint. In the days of the Kyivan Rus', control of what is now southern Ukraine was at best sporadic, and it never extended to the east, which was ruled by Turkic tribes. During Polish-Lithuanian rule, the vast plains of present-day eastern and southern Ukraine became known as the 'Wild Fields' – a sparsely populated no-man's-land that was constantly threatened by Tatar raids. By the early 17th century, the Zaporizhian Cossacks had established a modicum of control over these territories, and they also settled in some regions that extend far into southern Russia. When most of present-day eastern Ukraine came under formal Russian control in the late 17th century, the Cossacks' rule there initially remained largely autonomous. Meanwhile, Ukraine's southern coastal territories (including Crimea) remained in Tatar and Ottoman hands until the late 18th century. Following Russia's conquest of eastern and southern Ukraine, the tsarist authorities established various cities there, usually at the sites of pre-existing Cossack or Tatar settlements. Nonetheless, substantial settlement of these vast territories did not begin until the early 19th century, and they remained very ethnically diverse and multicultural. The eastern borders of Ukraine were formally drawn in 1919–1924 as the boundaries of the UkrSSR. Putin has vigorously condemned this process on many occasions, for instance in his 18 March 2014 address to the Russian parliament, when he claimed that

> after the revolution, the Bolsheviks, for a number of reasons – may God judge them – added large sections

of the historical South of Russia to the Republic of Ukraine. This was done with no consideration for the ethnic make-up of the population, and today these areas form the southeast of Ukraine. [5]

At a January 2016 speech, he similarly lamented that the Soviet Union's internal borders had been 'established arbitrarily, without much reason' and called the inclusion of Donbas in the UkrSSR 'pure nonsense' [21]. During a press conference in December 2019, he complained that

> when the Soviet Union was created, primordially Russian territories that never had anything to do with Ukraine (the entire Black Sea region and Russia's western lands) were turned over to Ukraine. [22]

As outlined above, Putin also repeated these claims at length in his July 2021 article and in his pre-invasion speech in February 2022.

But Putin's historical claims are wrong on two counts: Firstly, the assertion that present-day eastern or southern Ukraine should have been considered part of 'the historical South of Russia' or 'primordially Russian territories' in the 1920s is preposterous since there had been no substantial Russian demographic presence in these territories at any time prior to the 19th century. Even Crimea, the region of Ukraine with the highest concentration of Russian speakers, had only become Russian territory in 1783. Ethnic Russians constituted less than half of Crimea's population until the 1940s, when the Stalinist mass deportation of the entire Crimean Tatar population, as well as smaller populations of ethnic Armenians, Bulgars, and Greeks, changed the demographic make-up of the peninsula forever.

Secondly, Putin's assertion that Ukraine's southeastern borders were established 'with no consideration for the ethnic make-up of the population' is false. The first Soviet census, conducted in 1926, a few years after the eastern borders of the UkrSSR had been finalised, showed that in all territories of Ukraine, including the border regions with Russia, the Donbas, and southern Ukraine, ethnic Ukrainians still far outnumbered ethnic Russians (especially outside of the major cities) [23]. While the census figures on Ukrainian or Russian ethnicity ('nationality') were based on the respondents' self-identification, the 1926 census also separately recorded the respondents' native language. Native Ukrainian speakers outnumbered native Russian speakers (who tended to be clustered in the major cities and also included various Russian-speaking minority groups) in all but four districts of the UkrSSR, out of a total of 41 districts: Hlukhiv, Luhansk, Stalino (present-day Donetsk), and Odesa (in the latter two districts, the number of Ukrainian speakers and Russian speakers was almost identical). In most of Donbas, almost all of the historic 'Novorossiya', and almost the entire northern Ukrainian border region with Russia (including Kharkiv), the number of native Ukrainian speakers far exceeded the number of native Russian speakers. What's more, in several districts of the RSFSR (especially parts of present-day Rostov Oblast and Krasnodar Krai in Russia), the number of (self-identifying) ethnic Ukrainians exceeded the number of ethnic Russians, and in two of these districts the number of native Ukrainian speakers exceeded the number of native Russian speakers [23]. What ultimately changed the demographic composition of eastern Ukraine and southwestern Russia, as it had been recorded in the 1926 census, was the devastation wrought by Stalin's agricultural genocide, the 'Holodomor', in the 1930s, which decimated the local populations, particularly in the Ukrainian-speaking countryside.

Conclusion

In order to properly assess the causes of the Russian-Ukrainian war, we must try to understand the motivations of the man who instigated it. While any attempt to analyse Vladimir Putin's reasoning risks being overly speculative, his statements and writings do give us certain pointers as to his aims and convictions regarding Ukraine. It is likely that Putin's complex calculus for launching the invasion combined a variety of different motives, including geopolitical concerns about systemic threats to Russia's national security and domestic considerations of shielding his own authoritarian regime against potential pro-democratic 'spill-over' from across the border. But there is much to suggest that Putin's personal readings of Ukrainian and Russian history, combined with deeply held ethno-nationalist and irredentist beliefs, have been one of the core factors motivating his decision to unleash a full-scale military assault against Kyiv.

In his communication with foreign leaders and international audiences, Putin has typically framed his justifications for the invasion in geopolitical terms, claiming that the prospect of further NATO expansion, which is itself part of a US-led scheme to diminish or destroy Russia and prevent it from being a challenge to US hegemony, left Moscow no choice but to launch a pre-emptive attack against Ukraine. This geopolitical narrative has also featured heavily in the Kremlin's efforts to justify the war to *domestic* audiences within Russia, especially as it has tried to explain its consistent military failures in Ukraine by asserting that it is now engaged in an existential conflict against all of NATO. But in its domestic messaging, the geopolitical account has been constantly intermixed with nationalist and irredentist claims that Moscow went to war to recover historic Russian lands – claims which are largely absent when addressing international audiences.

It is impossible to ascertain how much of his own geopolitical narrative – that NATO expansion and Ukraine's westward turn have posed an existential threat to Russia's security – Putin actually believes. But his belief in the *nationalist* narrative of Ukraine being a historic Russian territory, rather than a nation-state of its own, appears to be genuine and deep-seated. Putin is embracing a neo-imperialist account that exalts Russia's centuries-long repressive rule over Ukraine, while simultaneously presenting Russia as a victim of 'US imperialism' and a champion of the worldwide anti-colonial cause. There is much to suggest that, in Putin's mind, the various different arguments advanced to justify the war, incongruous though they are, have been fused together into a hybrid ethno-realist grand narrative: The Ukrainians are really Russians, but they have constantly been turned against Moscow by hostile foreign powers who used them for their own geopolitical schemes, with the primary aim of weakening Russia. Today's hostile foreign power is the US-led 'collective West', and it is repeating history once more by turning Ukrainians against Russia and thus using Ukrainian statehood as a geopolitical weapon against Moscow.

Throughout the last decade, Putin has written and spoken at great length about Ukrainian history, leading him to deny Ukraine's historic state- and nationhood and to essentially claim that present-day Ukraine, or at least a very large portion of it, ought to rightfully be considered a historic part of Russia. That Putin has developed such a fixation on historical scholarship is regrettable, not least since he is in fact very bad at it. At a press conference in May 2005, where he discussed the 1939 Molotov-Ribbentrop pact, the Soviet occupation of Estonia, and, very briefly, a potential return of Crimea to Russia, Putin stated in jest that perhaps he did not study well at university since he spent his free time 'drinking a lot of beer' [24]. Fast-forward to the present and Putin has nonetheless assumed the role of Russia's historian-in-chief, and he seems convinced (in the words of his spokesman Dmitry Peskov) that he 'has an absolutely phenomenal knowledge of history' [25].

In practice, Putin's understanding of Ukrainian state- and nationhood and the history of Russian-Ukrainian relations is confused and inadequate. His treatment of historical developments has been extremely selective and imbued with nationalist irredentism. As a consequence, he has reproduced a narrative already popular in Russian nationalist circles since the 19th century, which propagates a mythical 1000-year continuity of the Russian nation and systematically ignores all manifestations of the historic growth of a distinct Ukrainian nationhood. In Putin's mind, to the extent that Ukraine as an entity exists at all, it ought to renounce most of its territory to Russia – irrespective of the fact that Russia neither has a strong *historical* claim to these lands (including Donbas, 'Novorossiya', and even Crimea), nor a *demographic* one, since the preponderance of Russian speakers in certain parts of Ukraine is not only a legacy of Russian imperial rule and colonisation but also a cruel consequence of Stalinist ethnic cleansing.

Regrettably, the fact that Putin's historical claims do not hold up to serious academic scrutiny appears to be of little practical relevance. What matters for the course of events in Ukraine is not so much objective scholarship but the version of history that exists in Putin's mind. There is every indication that Russia's president firmly believes what he has been postulating about Ukrainian history and statehood (or lack thereof). In Russia's increasingly closed authoritarian political system, there are practically no opportunities left for an open, critical discourse about Putin's claims, since historical statements and research that contradict the official narrative have increasingly been criminalised [26]. For this reason, and due to the fact that it has fallen on a fertile soil of pervasive nationalist and neo-imperialist grievances among large parts of Russian society, Putin's claim that Ukraine is not a nation in its own right but should be considered a historical part of Russia appears to have become the commonly accepted default narrative in Russian public discourse today. As such, it has served as an additional powerful and resonant narrative justifying Russia's devastating war against Ukraine to a domestic audience.

It is harder to assess to what extent the Russian president's historical convictions have had a concrete impact on Russia's *conduct* of the war. Putin's nationalist mythmaking has been infused with assumptions about the supposed wishes and desires of the Ukrainian people, paired with an outright refusal to acknowledge their own agency (and their democratic political choices), presenting them instead as perpetual pawns of malevolent foreign powers who have always quietly striven to be under Russian rule. It seems likely that this conviction played a role in Putin pursuing what in retrospect appears to have been an utterly unrealistic invasion plan in February 2022, in the apparent expectation that most Ukrainians would swiftly abandon their own elected government and greet Moscow's troops as liberators.

While it is probable that Putin's ultimate aim in this war is to gain some form of control over the entirety of Ukraine, it remains unclear how much of Ukraine's territory he is planning to annex to Russia. In this context, it is insightful to revisit Putin's oft-quoted statement that the breakdown of the Soviet Union was a 'geopolitical catastrophe': There is little to suggest that Putin had much affinity for the Soviet system, its leadership, or its ideology, but he seems to regard the Soviet Union as a political and spatial continuation of the 'historical Russia' of the nationalist imagination, which included the entirety of what he has termed the 'Russian World' and which then tragically splintered into a multitude of independent states. Putin might well be seeing himself as a 'gatherer of historic Russian lands', but based on his writings and statements, it is hard to deduce exactly how far his territorial ambitions extend. Incidents such as Putin's explicit denial of neighbouring Kazakhstan's historical statehood in August 2014 [27], barely half a year after the annexation of Crimea, serve as reminders that this question is not only relevant with regard to Ukraine but could have significant ramifications for Russia's future relations with all other states in the post-Soviet space as well.

Notes

¹ For a selection of some of the more egregious examples of such statements (some of which essentially amount to calls for genocide), see [28].

² Later that year, during a meeting with academics, Putin used an identical definition of the 'land that historically always bore the name of Novorossiya. … This land included Kharkov, Lugansk, Donetsk, Nikolayev, Kherson and Odessa Region' [29].

References

1. The Kremlin: Address by the president of the Russian Federation. 2022 February 21. http://en.kremlin.ru/events/president/news/67828.
2. Allenova O, Geda Y, Novikov V. Blok NATO razoshelsya na blokpakety. *Kommersant*. 2008 April 7. https://www.kommersant.ru/doc/877224.
3. Unian: Text of Putin's speech at NATO summit. 2008 April 18. https://www.unian.info/world/111033-text-of-putin-s-speech-at-nato-summit-bucharest-april-2-2008.html.
4. The Kremlin: Orthodox-Slavic values: The foundation of Ukraine's civilisational choice conference. 2013 July 27. http://en.kremlin.ru/events/president/news/18961.
5. The Kremlin: Address by president of the Russian Federation. 2014 March 18. http://en.kremlin.ru/events/president/news/20603.
6. TASS: 20 voprosov Vladimiru Putinu – part 2. 2020 February 20. https://putin.tass.ru/ru.
7. The Kremlin: Direct line with Vladimir Putin. 2021 June 30. http://en.kremlin.ru/events/president/news/65973.

8. Chesnakov A. Surkov: Mne interesno deystvovat' protiv real'nosti. *Aktual'nyye Kommentarii*. 2020 February 26. https://actualcomment.ru/surkov-mne-interesno-deystvovat-protiv-realnosti-2002260855.html.

9. The Kremlin: The real lessons of the 75th anniversary of World War II. *The National Interest*. 2020 June 18. https://nationalinterest.org/feature/vladimir-putin-real-lessons-75th-anniversary-world-war-ii-162982.

10. The Kremlin: Article by Vladimir Putin 'On the historical unity of Russians and Ukrainians'. 2021 July 12. http://en.kremlin.ru/misc/66182.

11. Kanayev P, Filipenok A. Shoygu obyazal voyennykh izuchit' stat'yu Putina ob Ukraine. *RBK*. 2021 July 15. https://www.rbc.ru/politics/15/07/2021/60f0475d9a7947b61f09f4be.

12. The Kremlin: Valdai international discussion club meeting. 2022 October 27. http://en.kremlin.ru/events/president/transcripts/statements/69695.

13. Moscow Times: Russia ramping up production of 'most powerful' weapons: Medvedev. 2022 December 11. https://www.themoscowtimes.com/2022/12/11/russia-ramping-up-production-of-most-powerful-weapons-medvedev-a79664.

14. Xanthaki A, Shaheed F, Ghanea N. Targeted destruction of Ukraine's culture must stop: UN experts. *UN Human Rights Council*. 2023 February 22. https://www.ohchr.org/en/press-releases/2023/02/targeted-destruction-ukraines-culture-must-stop-un-experts.

15. Laruelle M. The intellectual origins of Putin's invasion. *UnHerd*. 2022 March 16. https://unherd.com/2022/03/the-brains-behind-the-russian-invasion/.

16. The Kremlin: Signing of treaties on accession of Donetsk and Lugansk people's republics and Zaporozhye and Kherson regions to Russia. 2022 September 30. http://en.kremlin.ru/events/president/transcripts/statements/69465.

17. Anderson B. Imagined communities: Reflections on the origin and spread of nationalism. London: Verso; 1983.

18. Taylor A. 'Novorossiya,' the latest historical concept to worry about in Ukraine. *Washington Post.* 2014 April 18. https://www.washingtonpost.com/news/worldviews/wp/2014/04/18/understanding-novorossiya-the-latest-historical-concept-to-get-worried-about-in-ukraine/.

19. Sonne P. With 'Novorossiya,' Putin plays the name game with Ukraine. *Wall Street Journal.* 2014 September 1. https://www.wsj.com/articles/with-novorossiya-putin-plays-the-name-game-with-ukraine-1409588947.

20. The Kremlin: Direct line with Vladimir Putin. 2014 April 17. http://en.kremlin.ru/events/president/news/20796.

21. The Kremlin: Meeting of the Russian Popular Front's (ONF) interregional forum. 2016 January 25. http://en.kremlin.ru/events/president/news/51206.

22. The Kremlin: Bol'shaya press-konferentsiya Vladimira Putina. 2019 December 19. http://kremlin.ru/events/president/news/62366.

23. Central Statistical Administration of the USSR – Census Department: Vsesoyuznaya perepis' naseleniya 17 dekabrya 1926 g. – issue 4. 1928. https://ia804700.us.archive.org/34/items/perepis_naseleniia_1926/vyp.%204%20(RAW).pdf.

24. The Kremlin: Press-konferentsiya po itogam vstrechi na vysshem urovne Rossiya – Yevropeyskiy soyuz. 2005 May 10. http://kremlin.ru/events/president/transcripts/22967.

25. Cole B. Vladimir Putin gets corrected by schoolboy about Russian history. *Newsweek.* 2021 September 2. https://www.newsweek.com/vladimir-putin-history-student-poltava-battle-northern-war-corrected-1625442.

26. Hirsch F. Putin's memory laws set the stage for his war in Ukraine. *Lawfare.* 2022 February 28. https://www.lawfareblog.com/putins-memory-laws-set-stage-his-war-ukraine.

27. Lillis J. Kazakhstan celebrates statehood in riposte to Russia. *Eurasianet.* 2015 January 6. https://eurasianet.org/kazakhstan-celebrates-statehood-in-riposte-to-russia.

28. Apt C. Russia's eliminationist rhetoric against Ukraine: A collection. *Just Security.* 2023 May 8. https://www.justsecurity.org/81789/russias-eliminationist-rhetoric-against-ukraine-a-collection/.

29. The Kremlin: Meeting of the Valdai international discussion club. 2014 October 24. http://en.kremlin.ru/events/president/news/46860.

5. The Securitised 'Others' of Russian Nationalism in Ukraine and Russia

Eleanor Knott

In trying to analyse and understand Russian nationalism, most scholars focus on what Russian nationalism is as an ideology. But to understand Russia's war in Ukraine we also need to understand what Russian nationalism *does*. This chapter explores how Russian nationalism has increasingly securitised and repressed three groups: Muslim minorities living in Russia as internal 'others', Ukrainian citizens as external 'others', and Crimean Tatars, as 'others' in between. Overall, I argue that we need to understand the breadth and depth of the repression against these 'others' of Russian nationalism, which now extends to Russia's desire to legitimise its genocide in Ukraine. This argument is also important in terms of policy: as Russia's war against Ukraine continues, there is a real risk that some western actors will listen to or repeat Putin's narrative that Russia is the victim and allow Putin to set the terms of ending war in Ukraine through the idea that Russia is the victim and not the aggressor.

Russia's full-scale invasion of Ukraine and war against Ukraine has ethnic, imperial, and civilisational overtones. Most fundamentally, however, Russia's war poses an existential threat to Ukraine [1]. Russia is seeking to deny agency and sovereignty from Ukraine as a nation, as a state, and as a community of citizens. Alone, the ethnic, civic, imperial, and civilisational consequences are insufficient for exploring how, let alone why, Russia has brought conflict to Ukraine since 2014 and launched a full-scale invasion of Ukraine in 2022. An existential perspective is necessary, where we recognise how Russia is instrumentalising war as a tool to insist that Ukraine and Ukrainian sovereignty remain tethered to Russia's vision of it. In line with this, Russia acts as if it has the right to veto Ukrainians' interpretation of history; as if Russia has the right to insist that Ukraine has been over-run by 'Nazis'; and as if Russia – not Ukraine – can determine who are 'Nazis' in the first place.

In previous research, I introduced the concept of existential nationalism to capture the stakes of Russia's war against Ukraine, where Ukraine is fighting for its existence, while Russia is fighting for a non-consensual version of Ukrainian existence, where Russia has veto power. Put simply, existential nationalism is 'Russia's motivation to pursue war, whatever the costs, and Ukraine's motivation to fight with everything it has' [1 p46]. In this piece, I want to consider the broader context and effects of existential forms of Russian nationalism.

Similar to Laruelle [2], who argues for viewing Russian nationalism not through its 'contents', but through its 'actors' (state, para-state, and non-state), I argue for analysing Russian nationalism less through its contents or function. Rather, just as the Russian regime has become increasingly repressive, authoritarian, and violent, I focus on groups who are deliberately securitised as 'others' of Russian nationalism. By securitised, I mean groups that are targeted as security threats to the nation. The result of this securitisation is framing groups as 'others', by which I mean groups constructed as deviant because they deviate from Russia's racial, ethnic, political, and/or social norms and construed as security threats because of this deviation.

Scholars tend to focus on what Russian nationalism *is*, ideologically. But we also need to examine what Russian nationalism *does* within an increasingly repressive, authoritarian, and violent regime. Therefore, we need to determine whom Russian nationalism is instrumentalised against.

This lens is as important academically as it is in terms of politics and of policy. There is a real risk that as Russia's war continues, and continues to terrorise Ukrainian civilians, that western actors will begin to listen to, absorb, and repeat Putin's narrative that Russia is the victim. From here, it might be possible for Putin to set the terms of ending war in Ukraine through the idea that Russia is the victim and not the aggressor. These claims might seem far-fetched. But Emanuel Macron, in the shadow of Russia committing war crimes in Ukraine, has claimed that Russia – rather than Ukraine – needs security guarantees as an outcome of war [3], as if Russia is the victim and acted defensively rather than aggressively in invading another state.

By supplementing the study of what Russian nationalism *is* with a focus also on what Russian nationalism *does* forces us to see the increasing array of securitised 'others' of Russian nationalism that face repression inside and outside of Russia. Internally, primarily, it is Russia's Muslim minorities, who are problematised and 'othered'. The Russian state projects an image of the minorities as outsiders, as people who are not legitimately Russian, and whose repression is justified on this basis. Externally, it is groups like Ukrainian citizens (albeit only those who do not accept Russia's hegemony/patrimony) who are portrayed as 'others', if not the Ukrainian state as an entity. For Russia, a legitimate Ukrainian accepts that Ukraine has a primordial and biological connection to Russia. An illegitimate and othered Ukrainian rejects this connection. It is these Ukrainians – likely the majority of Ukrainian citizens – who Russia wants the world to believe are Nazis. Finally, there are the others on the periphery that fall between these external and internal stools, such as Crimean Tatars who reside in Crimea, a de jure part of Ukraine, but under de facto Russian rule since annexation in 2014.

This piece considers these three groups of securitised 'others' and situates them with existing discussions of Russian nationalism. Such an endeavour is not one of moral relativism or comparative trauma. I do not suggest that the nature and extent of repression and violence are the same across these three groups. Rather, I demonstrate that we need to speak plurally about who Russian nationalism represses and securitises, and understand its variegated nature across external 'others', internal 'others', and 'others' in between. Doing so also speaks to more a intersectional and reflexive analysis of Russia that seeks to challenge, rather than reflect, powerful narratives within the Russia regime that has 'systematically suppressed ethnic minority voices and concerns' [4 p2].

The Ideology of Russian Nationalism

In studying Russian nationalism, while also reflecting broader debates in studying nationalism, we can divide approaches between those who are state-centred and those who are more society-centred. State-centred approaches tend to be more top-down and supply-side, focusing on how elite political actors within the regime create nationalism policy, and create a vision of the Russian nation that diffuses top-down out of the state. Meanwhile, society-centred approaches are more bottom-up, that is, they focus on society rather than the state, and explore how Russian nationalism is articulated, given meaning, and practised within everyday life in Russia.

Across this cleavage in how to approach Russian nationalism, and more importantly how to approach the study of Russian nationalism, there is significant debate in how to categorise and conceptualise Russian nationalism. Is the Russian nation, for example, a civic nation – more political than cultural, where a multi-cultural and multi-ethnic Russia state and society can agree around a set of political more than cultural norms? Or is the Russian nation an ethnic nation – where to belong to the Russian nation you must identify as ethnically and culturally Russian, as well as speak Russian?

Since Putin returned to the presidency in 2012, and Russia annexed Crimea and brought conflict to Donetsk and Luhansk oblasts in 2014, this debate on how to conceptualise and categorise Russian nationalism has become even more prescient. Most scholars agree that Russian nationalism *has* shifted in this period. Scholars also largely agree on the function of Russian nationalism – regime survival and legitimation [5–7], and as something to be instrumentalised to unify the Russian population during crises [8 p223]. Where they disagree is on how to conceptualise these shifts in Russian nationalism, in particular under Putin.

One of the challenges of such a conceptualisation is the deliberately ambiguous nature of Russian nationalism in the post-Soviet period [2, 8–10]. As Laine argues, there is a clear 'contradiction' between a state that officially represents itself as 'multi-ethnic' while also trying to establish an ethnic category of 'Russian' [8 p226].

For Goode, Russian nationalism had been civic in orientation. But after the failure of civic nationalism, shifted to a more ethnic orientation. This shift occurred because of 'institutional instability and personalist dynamics of hybrid regime politics in the 1990s' [11 p141]. As a consequence, Putin's increasingly authoritarian and populist regime sought to transform an 'ambivalent civic nationhood' – that never really resonated with Russian society – by filling it 'with more popular ethnic content' [11 p154].[1]

Other scholars argue that Russian nationalism has shifted from civic to civilisational. Both from a top-down elite perspective and bottom-up societal approach, scholars remark on how belonging to the Russian nation is imagined and mythologised, such as via multi-ethnic discourses, and how this demonstrates its civilizational components [12, 13]. However, Blakkisrud argues that while Russian nationalism might appear civilisational, it is still ethnic in content [14]. For example, while civilisational rhetoric is frequently anchored in ethnocultural terms and appeals, as the Russian regime's rhetoric towards Crimea (e.g., '*KrymNash*' / 'Crimea is ours') demonstrates [14].

Others argue, as Kuzio does, that Russian nationalism is firmly imperial [15]. For example, Kuzio argues that the extent of Russia's war against Ukraine 'can only be explained by the growth of imperial nationalism and dehumanizing discourse on Ukrainians' [15 p3]. However, Laruelle problematises the distinction between imperial and ethnic as 'artificial' [2 p90]. Citing evidence of how Putin referenced Russia as a 'divided nation' when annexing Crimea, Laruelle remarks how it is not only 'ideologists' of Russian nationalism that exhibit *both* imperial and ethnic nationalism but also Putin [2 p90].

As Blakkisrud [14] and Aksiumov and Avksentev [16] identify, the problem is that neither civic/ethnic nor nation/empire dichotomies work for understanding Russian nationalism. The contemporary Russian Federation is an heir both to the Soviet Union *and* the Russian Empire, while other post-Soviet states are not. Rather these scholars dissect Russian nationalism into its different civic, multicultural, imperial, and civilisational components [16], and in terms of whether Russian nationalism is oriented towards the status quo or revision of borders, and state-centred or ethnically focused [14].

What is left out of all these accounts is a consideration of race within Russian nationalism, just as race is often left out when studying Russia more broadly [17, 18]. But how race and racialisation are invoked when Russia is a mythologised multi-ethnic state should not be overlooked. For Zakharov, the 'ethno-racial understanding of Russianness' is not an extreme or abnormal position but something mainstream in Russia, whether on the 'left, right, or liberal' dimensions of politics [18 p128]. 'Synonyms for racial whiteness' include, for example, biological or primordial understandings of the Russian nation, by attempts to 'deduce a person's origin from their physical appearance', and constructions of Russia as a 'civilized nation' via anti-western rhetoric [18 p129]. In other words, race is an implicit part of how Russian nationalism is articulated.

What Russian Nationalism Does: The Securitisation of 'Others'

Shifting from debates over what Russian nationalism is, ideologically, I pivot to consider what Russian nationalism does. Arguing that Russian nationalism understands itself through the lens of an existential threat, we need to understand how each group – the internal others (Muslim minorities), the external others (Ukrainians), and the others in between (Crimean Tatars) – is constructed as a threat to Russia. While each group experience varying degrees and forms of repression and violence, extending to war and genocide in Ukraine, such repression and violence is legitimised through an increasingly securitising rhetoric towards these 'others' of Russian nationalism.

Internal Securitised 'Others' and Russian Nationalism

Above, I described the link between Russian nationalism and anti-western rhetoric and the racialised tropes that this performs within Russia. In recent years, the construction of 'others' has turned inwards towards Russian citizens, particularly Muslim communities such as the Tatars [19 p724]. As Prina comments [20], inter-ethnic relations between ethnic Russians and the Russian state and non-Russian minorities are increasingly securitised in Russia. Muslim minorities are presented as security threats [21], facing not only political and police repression but also cultural repression. Their rights are decreased not because of legal changes but because of how the law on the rights of minority languages is now interpreted [21], demonstrating the contingent and discretionary nature of Russian law as instrumentalised by the state.

Moreover, non-Russian minorities, and Muslim minorities in particular, have been disproportionally targeted by Russian draft notices to fight in Ukraine [22]. This disproportional targeting includes Crimean Tatars, as I explore below. This disproportional drafting does not signify a contradiction in policy between framing Muslim minorities as a national threat and a security necessity during war. Rather, disproportionally drafting Muslim minorities represents a continued, and extended, use of repression of non-ethnic Russians in Russia during wartime. At best, it represents an extended instrument of control, by denying agency and implicating society-at-large in war efforts, making Muslim minorities complicit in atrocities. At worst, and in the case of Crimean Tatars, it represents an instrument of elimination via war.

Currently, there are many questions around why protests in Russia against the war in Ukraine are so limited and small in scale. In particular, observers ask why Muslim minorities are not protesting against the war or against their repression. But rights to protest are not equal. Ethnic Russians face harsh consequences for protest. Non-ethnic Russians, or those read or presumed not to be non-ethnic Russians (because of biological and primordial understandings of Russianness), do not have the capacity to take the same chances, when existing in an even more extreme and repressive politics of fear [21]. But the absence of protest is not the same as the absence of resistance: 'repressive contexts only make dissent and resentments that stem from cultural marginalisation acquire hidden forms' [4 p2].

In asking why the Putin regime has taken this course, it is important to understand the perceived benefits of such action: forging internal cohesiveness among ethnic Russians, as well as between ethnic Russians and the Russian state and Putin regime [19 p724]. Just as ethnicization of Russian nationalism can be explained as regime legitimation, the consequences of ethnicisation – repression of Muslim minorities in Russia – can equally be explained by regime legitimation. Specifically, such repression offers and ensures the promised order and 'stability' by constructing, and repressing, as threats anything that might undermine such aims [6].

Just as Russian authorities have turned more repressive towards Muslim minorities, so too have they sought to control narratives of nationalism. Radical nationalists also face repression in Russia to allow for a singular version of history to be stage managed by the regime. While radical nationalists do not face the same extent and nature of repression as Muslim minorities, alongside increasing popular xenophobia, the Russian regime is increasingly unwilling to 'share societal space' with them since 2014, and instead chooses to adopt their narratives while pushing them to the political margins [8]. Concurrently, Russia is 'securitizing historical interpretation' by constructing the idea that a 'good Russian' does not interpret history differently from the government [7 p1074].

The Securitised 'Others' in between: Crimean Tatars and Russian Nationalism

Following from the increasing repression of Muslim minorities in Russia, I want to zoom into a particular Muslim minority:

Crimean Tatars. This largely secular and pacifist Muslim minority community resides in Crimea and considers Crimea to be their native homeland, and themselves indigenous to Crimea [23]. Crimean Tatars are now securitised 'others' in between: existing in territory illegally annexed by Russia in 2014, functionally residing in Russia de facto since 2014, that de jure is Ukrainian (though many now live in exile in mainland Ukraine *due to* repression). Moreover, Crimean Tatars imagine themselves as separate from other Tatar groups residing in Russia, for example, Volga Tatars. They were and remain the biggest supporters of Crimea as Ukrainian territory. Hence they were immediately treated with suspicion and repression by Russian authorities following its annexation.

Crimean Tatars were brutally deported by Soviet authorities in 1945 to Siberia and Central Asia due to false claims they were 'Nazi collaborators', with many dying as a result.[2] Therefore, Crimean Tatars have been framed as a threatening 'other' not only by the contemporary Russian regime. For example, Soviet authorities sought to instrumentalise the coincidence of distrust towards non-Slavic communities and mobilisation of Soviet troops to set about eradicating non-Slavic 'ethnies', like Crimean Tatars, deemed to be untrustworthy by the Soviet regime" [24 p358].

Living in exile, what bound Crimean Tatars together was their shared and inter-generational grief over deportation and a longing to return to Crimea [24, 25]. Crimean Tatars were only able to return to Crimea in the late Soviet period, in the late 1980s, during perestroika. In post-Soviet Ukraine, prior to Crimea's annexation, Crimean Tatars experienced improving conditions. But they also experienced unsettled questions, for example pertaining to land rights and registration of community organisations like the Mejlis, Crimean Tatars' representative body [26].

The situation for Crimean Tatars immediately deteriorated after annexation in 2014. The Mejlis was labelled as an extremist group and banned. Crimean Tatars were exposed to rising and brutal repressions including arrest, censorship, torture, kidnapping, 'extra-legal prosecutions', and murder, 'cynically justified by rhetoric of anti-extremism and counterterrorism' [27 p29]. The options for Crimean Tatars were, and remain, exceptionally limited. Russia offers the option of co-optation or repression for those it considers 'extremist'. But we can also view Crimean Tatars' 'compliant behaviors' as 'tactics of resistance' [28 p80]. Such tactics include 'displays of politeness and compliance' to 'subvert the Russian regime's stereotyped picture' of Crimean Tatars as 'terrorists' [28].

But, in 2022, like other non-Russian minorities residing in de jure Russia, Crimean Tatars residing in illegally annexed Crimea also face disproportional draft notices. For Crimean Tatars being drafted is even more sinister since they are being forced to fight in a war against their state of Ukraine, while Russia is able to pursue a strategy of 'getting rid of undesirable people' in Crimea and Russia [29].

Exploring and explaining why the Russian regime has repressed Crimean Tatars, and why Russian nationalism views Crimean Tatars as a securitised 'other', it is necessary to view the Russian regime through the lens of 'settler nationalism' [30]. The Russian regime seeks to erase Crimean Tatars claims to indigeneity and to remove 'human and physical evidence' of

Crimean Tatars as a 'predecessor population' [23 p842]. Rather, the Russia regime seeks to reframe ethnic Russian 'settlers', including those who moved to Crimea after annexation, as the 'historic population' [23 p843]. Thus, Russia views claiming indigeneity to Crimea as a perceived threat. Russia acts to 'protect Crimea's ethnic Russians and Russian speakers' by repressing Crimean Tatars, as the central opposition to annexation, so the regime can 'maintain its grip of territory seized illegally' from Ukraine [27 p47].

External Securitised 'Others': Ukrainians and Russian Nationalism

The third securitised 'other' is Ukraine and its citizens. Here, we have to explore the contradiction between the claims advanced by the Russian regime that Ukraine is an artificial nation and inseparable from Russia, and the claims advanced by the Russian regime that Ukraine is 'other'. An unanswered question is how to explain these contradictions. Since 2014, Russia has securitised ethnic Russians and Russian speakers in Ukraine (e.g., in Crimea, Donetsk and Luhansk) since 2014, legitimising violence to 'protect' these communities (whether they asked for or consented to protection). In 2022, Russia used violence to commit a brutal war that indiscriminately targets Ukrainian military and civilians alike, regardless of whether they are Russian speakers, are Ukrainian speakers, or identify as ethnic Ukrainians or ethnic Russians.

On the one hand, Russia has a specific vision of Ukraine. Putin has claimed many times that Russians and Ukrainians are 'one people' [31, 32]. He has also claimed that Ukraine's 'true sovereignty' is only possible 'in partnership with Russia' [32]. For

Putin, Ukraine is an 'artificial' nation, and 'artificially' separated from Russia [32]. In these assertions, Ukraine and its citizens are allowed neither agency nor to divert from Russia's claims.[3] Any diversion is, for the Russian regime, an expression either of false consciousness or association with Nazis. For Russia, Ukraine must stay permanently tethered to Russia, to have its sovereignty protected, and permanently tethered to Russia's vision of what Ukraine is and can be. For Russia, this relationship is not of equals; rather, Ukraine must exist – and not resist – being in a non-consensual relationship of subservience to Russia.

On the other hand, and temporally stretching back to Russia's annexation of Crimea (if not before), Russia has been shoring up 'boundaries between the Russian and Ukrainian nations' [33], via creating a Ukrainian 'other'. Russia's rhetoric around annexing Crimea hinged on 'recasting' in an unprecedented way how Russia understood Ukraine, 'as Russia's main other, against which Russian national identity was constructed' [33 p379]. Russia blames, for example, 'contemporary Ukrainian nationalists [...] for dividing Ukraine and Russia' who seek to 'sell' Russophobia [34]. As a pretext for Russia's war against and invasion of Ukraine, Putin claimed that 'neo-Nazis' had seized power in Ukraine [35].

Of course, Zelenskyy could not be further from a 'neo-Nazi', as a Jewish Russian speaker who lost family in the Holocaust [36]. As Pisano [37] argues, Zelenskyy has offered a radically different vision of Ukraine to the 'two Ukraines' trope that has presented a vision of a divided and contested Ukraine that is far from many citizens' lived experience. Rather, Zelenskyy has put forward a plural, multi-ethnic, multi-lingual vision where Russophone

Ukrainians are as much a part of Ukraine as Ukrainian speakers. This plural inclusive vision did not emerge in response to Russia's war in Ukraine, or in Zelenskyy's presidency before 2022. Instead, it emerged via his comedy career in Studio Kvartal-95, during which he performed predominantly in Russian for 'russified Ukrainians' and created 'a space in which Ukrainians could find an idea of multicultural patriotism and community'. In other words, Zelenskyy has for a long time offered a different vision of Ukraine to academic accounts within and beyond Ukraine, and Russia's vision of Ukraine. As much as offering a different vision in terms of identity politics, Zelenskyy has offered a radically different anti-oligarchic vision of Ukraine for domestic and international audiences. A Ukraine dominated by identity debates and oligarchic politics was predictable for Russia; an alternative challenged Russia both in terms of identity, geopolitics, and a political economy where Ukraine was more easily readable and controllable by Russia.

Russia seeks either to control Ukraine or 'other' Ukraine. This contradiction is best explained by Russia's greater non-consensual vision for Ukraine that is fundamental for Russia: to be an empire, Russia needs Ukraine to be subordinate [33]. Control over Ukraine, and its subservience to Russia, are themselves an 'existential imperative' for Russia [38]. Russia sees those seeking to sow divisions between Ukraine and Russia as wanting to prevent the 'emergence of a rival, a global rival for Europe and the world' [34]. In other words, Russia frames Ukraine's Europeanisation as responsible for both the division between Ukraine and Russia and for creating a Ukraine that Russia seeks to 'other'.

This othering is classic victim blaming as Ukraine seeks to express its right to disentangle itself from a non-consensual and imperial relationship of subordination. What Russia fears is less Ukrainian nationalists and more Russian speakers, like Zelenskyy, that offer a new plural, multi-cultural, multi-ethnic, Europeanised, and democratic vision for Ukraine. Russian speakers in Ukraine can now clearly communicate a vision for these ideals within Ukraine. But they also pose a risk, in Putin's eyes, for the Russian state – threatening to offer not only a different vision for how Ukraine can interact with Russia (and oligarchs), but also a different vision for how Russian citizens can interact with Russia.

The Policy Implications of Understanding the Securitisation of 'Others' of Russian Nationalism

While the nature of repression differs between these three 'others' of Russian nationalism, what ties them together is how Russia views them all as a risk. Securitisation of these 'others' therefore serves the function of reducing perceived threats to the Russian regime under Putin.

Muslim minorities, whether in Russia or Crimean Tatars, have been targeted by old and new Russian regimes alike as convenient weapons through which to sow distrust. The othering of Ukraine is more recent, as a multi-ethnic and Europeanising state led by Zelenskyy has offered a different vision to Russia's approved version prior to and in response to Russia's annexation of Crimea and stoking of conflict in Donetsk and Luhansk. The irony is that Russia's targeting of violence towards Ukraine has shored up a vision of Ukraine that it finds increasingly contentious and threatening. Russia's indiscriminate violence towards Ukraine and its citizens via war and invasion since 2022 will only serve to shore up these processes even further.

That is why it is so dangerous for western actors, like the French President Emanuel Macron, to suggest that Russia needs security guarantees as an outcome of their war against Ukraine [3]. To do so, it is to legitimise the very threats that Russia uses as a pretext to commit war crimes and genocide, as EU and NATO member-states bordering Ukraine and Russia have echoed [39]. To allow Russia to see security guarantees as a route to peace is to allow Russia to shore up its 'trap' that Ukraine is responsible for Russia's actions because Russia is an 'innocent victim' [39]. Such guarantees will also not lead to the end of the war. Ukraine is the victim and is setting the clear terms of what the end of the war looks like: war tribunals, criminal convictions, reparations, and withdrawal of Russian troops from the entirety of Ukraine [40].

That is why it is necessary, academically and in terms of policy, to supplement debates around what Russian nationalism is, with a focus on Russian nationalism does: who it securitises and positions as a threat.[4] Russia seeks to cast itself as the victim while increasingly repressing Muslim minorities in Russia de jure and de facto, including Crimean Tatars. The Russian regime increasingly controls all aspects of political and social life, including Russian nationalists and diverting interpretations of Russian history. All are viewed as threats. But Russia is not the victim. Russia is the repressive antagonist repressing Muslim minorities in Russia, committing human rights abuses against Crimean Tatars in Crimea, and committing war crimes and genocide in mainland Ukraine.

Notes

[1] As markers of such popular ethnic content, Goode [11] identifies 'traditional Russian values, Orthodox religion, and Russian language, together with anti-Westernism and Soviet-era nostalgia'.

[2] Williams demonstrates how 20,000 Crimean Tatars served in the Wehrmacht, but many were captured as prisoners of war by the German army in 1941 and 1942; an equal number of Crimean Tatars fought in the Soviet army [24 p259].

[3] It is worth remembering also that Russians have decreasing space to interpret history differently from regime-endorsed historical narratives [7].

[4] We could, for example, also view the 'West' – whether actors in the European Union or NATO – as also securitised 'others' by the Russian regime. This article does not focus on this fourth or supplementary group since western actors, states, and societies only peripherally and indirectly experience Russia's war and Russian nationalism. My intention in this article was to focus on the three most significant, and directly affected, groups of securitised 'others' vis-à-vis Russian nationalism.

References

1. Knott E. Existential nationalism: Russia's war against Ukraine. *Nations and Nationalism*; 2023; 29(1): 45–52. DOI: https://doi.org/10.1111/nana.12878.

2. Laruelle M. Is nationalism a force for change in Russia? *Daedalus*. 2017; 146(2): 89–100. DOI: https://doi.org/10.1162/DAED_a_00437.

3. EurActiv. Macron says new security architecture should give guarantees for Russia. 2022 [cited 2022 Dec 5]. https://www.euractiv.com/section/europe-s-east/news/macron-says-new-security-architecture-should-give-guarantees-for-russia/.

4. Yusupova G. Critical approaches and research on inequality in Russian studies: The need for visibility and legitimization. *Post-Soviet Affairs*. 2022; 1–7. DOI: https://doi.org/10.1080/1060586X.2022.2156222.

5. Goode JP. Becoming banal: Incentivizing and monopolizing the nation in post-Soviet Russia. *Ethnic and Racial Studies*. 2021; 44(4): 679–97. DOI: https://doi.org/10.1080/01419870.2020.1749687.

6. Malinova O. Legitimizing Putin's regime: The transformations of the narrative of Russia's post-Soviet transition. *Communist and Post-Communist Studies*. 2022; 55(1): 52–75. DOI: https://doi.org/10.1525/j.postcomstud.2022.55.1.52.

7. McGlynn J. United by history: Government appropriation of everyday nationalism during Vladimir Putin's third term. *Nationalities Papers*. 2020; 48(6): 1069–85. DOI: https://doi.org/10.1017/nps.2020.20.

8. Laine V. Contemporary Russian nationalisms: The state, nationalist movements, and the shared space in between. *Nationalities Papers*. 2017; 45(2): 222–37. DOI: https://doi.org/10.1080/00905992.2016.1272562.

9. Shevel O. Russian nation-building from Yel'tsin to Medvedev: Ethnic, civic or purposefully ambiguous? *Europe-Asia Studies*. 2011; 63(2): 179–202. DOI: https://doi.org/10.1080/09668136.2011.547693.

10. Fediunin JS. Russian nationalism. In: Gill G (ed.), Routledge Handbook of Russian politics and society. 2nd ed. London: Routledge. 2022; p. 437–48. DOI: https://doi.org/10.4324/9781003218234-42.

11. Goode JP. Russia's ministry of ambivalence: The failure of civic nation-building in post-Soviet Russia. *Post-Soviet Affairs*. 2019; 35(2): 140–60. DOI: https://doi.org/10.1080/1060586X.2018.1547040.

12. Hale HE, Laruelle M. Rethinking civilizational identity from the bottom up: A case study of Russia and a research agenda. *Nationalities Papers*. 2020; 48(3): 585–602. DOI: https://doi.org/10.1017/nps.2019.125.

13. Blackburn M. Mainstream Russian nationalism and the 'state-civilization' identity: Perspectives from below. *Nationalities Papers*. 2021; 49(1): 89–107. DOI: https://doi.org/10.1017/nps.2020.8.

14. Blakkisrud H. Russkii as the new Rossiiskii? Nation-building in Russia after 1991. *Nationalities Papers*. 2022; 1–16. DOI: https://doi.org/10.1017/nps.2022.11.

15. Kuzio T. Imperial nationalism as the driver behind Russia's invasion of Ukraine. *Nations and Nationalism*; 2023; 29(1): 30–8. DOI: https://doi.org/10.1111/nana.12875.

16. Aksiumov B, Avksentev V. Nation-building in contemporary Russia: Four vectors of political discourse. *Nationalism and Ethnic Politics*. 2022; 28(2): 186–205. DOI: https://doi.org/10.1080/13537113.2021.2001206.

17. Yusupova M. The invisibility of race in sociological research on contemporary Russia: A decolonial intervention. *Slavic Review*. 2021; 80(2): 224–33. DOI: https://doi.org/10.1017/slr.2021.77.

18. Zakharov N. The politics of race, racism, and antiracism. In: Wengle SA (ed.), *Russian politics today: Stability and fragility*. Cambridge: Cambridge University Press. 2022; p. 128–48. DOI: https://doi.org/10.1017/9781009165921.008.

19. Teper Y, Course DD. Contesting Putin's nation-building: The 'Muslim other' and the challenge of the Russian ethno-cultural alternative. *Nations and Nationalism*. 2014; 20(4): 721–41. DOI: https://doi.org/10.1111/nana.12078.

20. Prina F. Constructing ethnic diversity as a security threat: What it means to Russia's minorities. *International Journal on Minority and Group Rights*. 2020; 28(1): 1–35. DOI: https://doi.org/10.1163/15718115-bja10002.

21. Yusupova G. How does the politics of fear in Russia work? The case of social mobilisation in Support of Minority Languages.

Europe-Asia Studies. 2022; 74(4): 620–41. DOI: https://doi.org/10.1080/09668136.2021.1965094.

22. Mackinnon A. Russia is sending its ethnic minorities to the meat grinder. *Foreign Policy.* 2022 Sep 23 [cited 2022 Dec 15]. https://foreignpolicy.com/2022/09/23/russia-partial-military-mobilization-ethnic-minorities/.

23. Wilson A. Imagining Crimean Tatar history since 2014: Indigenous rights, Russian recolonisation and the new Ukrainian narrative of cooperation. *Europe-Asia Studies.* 2021; 73(5): 837–68. DOI: https://doi.org/10.1080/09668136.2020.1867709.

24. Williams BG. Hidden ethnocide in the Soviet Muslim borderlands: The ethnic cleansing of the Crimean Tatars. *Journal of Genocide Research.* 2002; 4(3): 357–73. DOI: https://doi.org/10.1080/14623520220151952.

25. Uehling G. Squatting, self-immolation, and the repatriation of Crimean Tatars. *Nationalities Papers.* 2000; 28(2): 317–41. DOI: https://doi.org/10.1080/713687470.

26. Wilson A. The Crimean Tatar question after annexation: A prism for changing nationalisms and rival versions of Eurasianism. *Journal of Soviet and Post-Soviet Politics and Society.* 2017; 3(2): 1–45. DOI: https://doi.org/10.24216/97723645330050302_01.

27. Coynash H, Charron A. Russian-occupied Crimea and the state of exception: Repression, persecution, and human rights violations. *Eurasian Geography and Economics.* 2019 Jan 2; 60(1): 28–53. DOI: https://doi.org/10.1080/15387216.2019.1625279.

28. Shynkarenko M. Compliant subjects? How the Crimean Tatars resist Russian occupation in Crimea. *Communist and Post-Communist Studies.* 2022; 55(1): 76–98. DOI: https://doi.org/10.1525/j.postcomstud.2022.55.1.76.

29. Hyde L. 'A kind of murder': Putin's draft targets Crimea's Tatars. *Politico*. 2022 Oct 4 [cited 2022 Dec 15]. https://www.politico.eu/article/murder-putin-draft-target-crimea-tatars/.

30. Yekelchyk S. The Crimean exception: Modern politics as hostage of the imperial past. *The Soviet and Post-Soviet Review*. 2019; 46(3): 304–23. DOI: https://doi.org/10.1163/18763324-04603005.

31. President of Russia. *Meeting of the Valdai International Discussion Club*. 2013 [cited 2022 Mar 30]. https://web.archive.org/web/20220327135245/http://en.kremlin.ru/events/president/news/19243.

32. President of Russia. Article by Vladimir Putin 'On the historical unity of Russians and Ukrainians'. 2021 [cited 2022 Mar 30]. https://web.archive.org/web/20220321072605/http://en.kremlin.ru/events/president/news/66181.

33. Teper Y. Official Russian identity discourse in light of the annexation of Crimea: National or imperial? *Post-Soviet Affairs*. 2016; 32(4): 378–96. DOI: https://doi.org/10.1080/1060586X.2015.1076959.

34. Team of the Official Website of the President of Russia. Ukraine (Interview to TASS News Agency). *President of Russia*. 2020 [cited 2022 Dec 6]. http://en.kremlin.ru/events/president/news/62835.

35. President of Russia. *Address by the President of the Russian Federation*. 2022 [cited 2022 Mar 25]. https://web.archive.org/web/20220221215128/http://en.kremlin.ru/events/president/news/67828.

36. Onuch O, Hale HE. The Zelenskyy effect: Why Ukraine's "Ze" is defeating Russia's "Z". *The Toronto Star*. 2022 Mar 26 [cited 2022 Mar 30]. https://www.thestar.com/opinion/contributors/2022/03/26/the-zelenskyy-effect-why-ukraines-ze-is-defeating-russias-z.html.

37. Pisano J. Volodymyr Zelenskyy's vision of Ukrainian nationhood. *Journal of Peace and War Studies*. 2022; 4(October 2022): 187–98.

38. Bogomolov A, Lytvynenko O. A ghost in the mirror: Russian soft power in Ukraine. *Chatham House*. 2012 [cited 2012 Jun 2]. https://www.chathamhouse.org/sites/default/files/public/Research/Russia%20and%20Eurasia/0112bp_bogomolov_lytvynenko.pdf.

39. Brzozowski A. Macron's idea of 'security guarantees' to Russia faces backlash. *EurActiv*. 2022 [cited 2022 Dec 5]. https://www.euractiv.com/section/europe-s-east/news/macrons-idea-of-security-guarantees-to-russia-faces-backlash/.

40. Mikhaylo Podolyak [@Podolyak_M]. Civilized world needs 'security guarantees' from barbaric intentions of post-Putin Russia...It will be possible only after tribunal, conviction of war authors and war criminals, imposition of large-scale reparations and bloody clarification of ru-elites 'who is the one to blame?'. *Twitter*. 2022 [cited 2022 Dec 5]. https://twitter.com/Podolyak_M/status/1599356603257364481.

PART 2
Ukraine

6. The Making of Independent Ukraine

Serhy Yekelchyk

> The political and social developments in Ukraine during the last years of the Soviet Union (1988–1991) can be seen as an unfinished revolution. The proclamation of independence in 1991 marked a compromise between national-democratic forces and the republic's old Soviet elites, which slowed down democratic transformations and kept the Red directors in power. The emergence of a mass opposition movement during the early 2000s represented a return to the unfinished agenda of the revolution. The Orange Revolution (2004–2005) and the Revolution of Dignity (2013–2014) re-established the connection between the civil society's struggle for democracy and the rights of the Ukrainian language and culture, which had first developed in the late 1980s. The emergence of a new Ukrainian political nation provoked an aggressive response from Putin's Russia, but its all-out invasion of 2022 only served to consolidate a modern Ukrainian identity as separate from Russia both politically and culturally.

On 1 December 1991, the Ukrainian Soviet Socialist Republic held its referendum on national independence. The result was emphatic: 90.3% voted for independent statehood, with a participation rate of 84.2%. Even more remarkably, only one region produced an approval rate of under 80% – the Autonomous

Republic of Crimea, which voted 54.2% in favour and had by far the lowest participation rate – 67.5%. In the east, the two oblasts (provinces) of the Donbas, which had a Russophone majority, voted solidly in support of Ukrainian independence. These data portrayed the republic as united around the political choice of becoming an independent nation-state. What the people did not want was a salvaging of the Soviet Union in some form, or the creation of a more narrow federation comprised of the three East Slavic republics and Kazakhstan, which had been Mikhail Gorbachev's last-ditch effort as Soviet president.

Anyone who had paid attention to a referendum held only months before would have not expected such a landslide. On 17 March 1991, the Soviet Union held a national referendum on its preservation as a federal state. In the Ukrainian SSR, 70.2% of its residents – not yet citisens – supported the continued existence of the Soviet Union as a 'renewed federation of equal and sovereign republics'. That time, the lowest number of 'yes' votes was registered in the three western oblasts that had never been part of the Russian Empire and had been annexed by Stalin in 1939: Lviv (16.4%), Ivano-Frankivsk (18.2%), and Ternopil (19.3%) [1].

Today, more than thirty years later, what can we make of this seeming contradiction in Ukraine's national choice in 1991? Regional political differences are obvious, but they should not be seen as primordial or unchanging: The Donbas did not stand out in the way the Crimea did. Terminology itself also evolved that year. 'Sovereignty', understood as the republic's rights within a federation became 'the right to proclaim independence'. But perhaps the most important observation would be the presence of a new political unity built on a larger foundation than that of ethnic solidarity. Independence became possible when the population at large, including a significant share of national minorities and Ukrainians assimilated into Russian culture, embraced the notion of an independent and democratic Ukraine.

That moment of national unity did not last long during the early 1990s, but Ukrainian society has recovered it more than once since that decade. There was the emergence of a mass oppositional movement in 2001, the Orange Revolution (2004–2005), and the Revolution of Dignity (2013–2014). This new Ukrainian identity remains on full display now, with the mass mobilisation of Ukrainian society defending their country against the Russian Federation's full-scale invasion.

It is possible to argue that the entire history of independent Ukraine resembles this two steps forward, one step back type of progress. There has been a gradual, stop-and-go development of an assertive civil society identifying with Ukraine's democratic choice and acknowledging the importance of the Ukrainian language and culture for the republic's sovereignty.

A second argument, which is interconnected with the first one, can be that this struggle for a democratic Ukraine was from the very beginning a revolution, albeit an unusual one. The Ukrainian case study allows us to rethink the traditional understanding of social forces and political elites in a revolution, as it demonstrates the society's remarkable ability to self-organise politically.

The Soviet Legacy

The emergence of an independent Ukraine from the Ukrainian SSR determined many trends during the post-independence period. Soviet Ukraine had been the Bolshevik response to the existence in 1917–1920 of the Ukrainian People's Republic (UNR), a socialist non-Bolshevik state emphasising national independence as the right of the Ukrainian people and as the only way of overcoming the Russian colonial legacy. The brief period of Ukrainisation in the 1920s, when the Soviet state implemented affirmative-action programs for ethnic Ukrainians and their culture, ended in the 1930s, after Stalin's famine-genocide, the Holodomor (1932–1933). With the Ukrainian peasantry and intelligentsia crushed, the dictator saw no further need for such concessions to Ukrainians. Yet, during the late 1930s, the Ukrainian question remained an important foreign-policy instrument that could prove useful in justifying territorial annexations from the Soviet Union's neighbours to the west, which had a significant Ukrainian population. Once the Red Army forcibly restored between 1939 and 1945 the unity of Ukrainian ethnolinguistic territories that the UNR had previously proclaimed, the republic's Ukrainian identity came under a full-scale attack, including an assimilationist drive. At the same time, beginning in the mid-1930s, the Soviet state progressively scaled down the Ukrainian culture to a safe ethnographic mode, implicitly locating it in the past, while associating modernity with the Russian culture.

Although Khrushchev undid many of Stalin's policies, assimilation dovetailed perfectly with his agenda of building 'communism' in the Soviet Union. The state used many mechanisms for encouraging Russification. In the absence of a Ukrainian school nearby, urbanites had no choice but to send their children to Russian ones; the last Ukrainian school in the city of Donetsk in the Donbas was closed down in 1964. But even when given a choice, more and more Ukrainian parents, especially by the 1970s, felt that Russian was safer and better in terms of career prospects. The number of ethnic Russians in Ukraine, primarily living in big cities, also increased thanks to in-migration. Khrushchev's much-discussed 'gift' of the Crimea to Ukraine in 1954 can be seen in this light. The UNR intentionally did not claim the peninsula, reserving it for a Crimean Tatar polity, but Khrushchev transferred to the Ukrainian SSR the Crimea that had been purged by Stalin in 1944 of the 'traitorous' Crimean Tatar nation and other non-Slavic groups. In addition to the economic rationale of bringing the peninsula and the adjacent mainland into the same administrative unit, Khrushchev may have been thinking of balancing the unreliable 'nationalistic' western Ukraine with the Crimea, which became a majority-Russian territory after the genocidal deportations of 1944.

There was, however, a notable exception to the general assimilatory trend in postwar Soviet Ukraine. Because of the nationalist anti-Soviet insurgency, which lasted in the westernmost regions until the early 1950s, Stalinist ideologists permitted the continued existence of Ukrainian-language education and media in these western Ukrainian oblasts. Beginning in the late 1950s, when the new generation of students and workers moved from villages to Lviv and other western Ukrainian cities, they did not switch to Russian but established a Ukrainophone urban environment, which the state had to tolerate. Modernity spoke Ukrainian in Lviv, but in the Ukrainian capital of Kyiv, speaking Ukrainian on the streets while not looking like a peasant could raise suspicions about one's political loyalty.

This essentially colonial situation of culturally alien cities, which was familiar to Ukrainians from the times of the Russian Empire, was not created without a fight. During the late 1950s and 1960s, eastern and central Ukrainian cities also saw a mass influx of new workers and students coming from the surrounding Ukrainophone countryside. While some assimilated eagerly, others held a grudge and others spoke in defence of their culture. The sociologist Bohdan Krawchenko noted perceptively that, for the postwar generation of Ukrainians, the status of the Ukrainian language also served as a symbol of wider social and economic problems [2]. Fighting for the rights of the Ukrainian culture thus meant championing the rights of Ukraine in other spheres—and the KGB indeed saw cultural resistance as political nationalism.

Due to the Soviet system's suppression of nonconformist political expression, writers, literary critics, and artists in Ukraine and other republics came to speak for society in general. They tested the limits of the possible, and many eventually crossed the line into open political dissent. Known in Ukrainian as *shistdesiatnyky* ("sixtiers"), these young Ukrainian patriots of the 1960s worked closely with some representatives of the previous generation, who had seen fighting in World War II, most notably the distinguished novelist Oles Honchar. Some sixtiers saw themselves as the successors of the Ukrainian radical nationalists, but the majority criticised the system from within, urging a return to the 'Leninist' line on Ukrainian culture, which for them meant renewed Ukrainisation. The sixtiers did not subscribe to the exclusivist notion of Ukraine for Ukrainians; in 1966, the movement's leading figure, Ivan Dziuba, gave an important talk against antisemitism at an unauthorised meeting at the largest Holocaust site in Ukraine, Babyn Yar in Kyiv. He came to this memorial site together with the prominent Russian writer and dissident Viktor Nekrasov, who was living in Kyiv [3]. The main organisation of the Ukrainian dissident movement, the Ukrainian Helsinki Group (1976–1981), included Jewish and Baptist activists; it also collaborated with a similar group in Moscow.

By the early 1980s, Soviet Ukraine was a modern, urbanised society with a highly educated population. Proponents of modernisation theory saw such social changes as a precondition of democratisation, but the Soviet case did not fit the general model because of the absence of a middle class in its traditional understanding. Rather than being independent of the state, Soviet intellectuals and professionals depended on it; most of them worked for state institutions and enterprises [4]. This meant that when the revolution arrived in the late 1980s, it came from within.

The Revolution Betrayed

The declaration of independence on 24 August 1991 caught Ukrainian society in the middle of a transition. The Gorbachev reforms and the revolution from below that they had unleashed challenged the political, economic, and social order of the late Soviet period, but did not overcome it – yet. Indeed, one can argue that it took decades and two revolutions to bring Ukraine's post-Soviet period to a close, and that some traces of Soviet path-dependency are still evident today.

When we speak of the Soviet 'collapse', this terminology obscures the fact that a mass political mobilisation in support of democratic reforms began during the late 1980s. In Ukraine, where the Chernobyl disaster took place, the environmental association Green World was the first non-official organisation to emerge in 1987. The first unauthorised mass rally took place in Lviv in June 1988, when the authorities tried to prevent the establishment of another mass civic organisation, the Taras Shevchenko Ukrainian Language Society. In February 1989, the newspaper of the Writers' Union, *Literaturna Ukraina* (Literary Ukraine), published the statute of the new civic organisation, the Popular Movement of Ukraine for Perestroika, which became known simply as Rukh, the Ukrainian word for 'movement'. The conservative Ukrainian Communist Party leadership only allowed its registration in September, after Gorbachev's intervention. Although led by Ukrainian writers and former dissidents, Rukh represented the interests of the wider society and contained a significant representation of Ukraine's other ethnic groups. Rukh quickly became a mass popular front, a political catch-all movement, which by the fall of 1990 had 633,000 members. Also in the fall of 1990, a students' hunger strike in the centre of Kyiv caused the resignation of the prime minister, demonstrating the growing power of civil society.

Yet, when the elections to the Ukrainian legislature took place in the Republic in March 1990, large swaths of the country were still controlled by Soviet political elites. In the absence of registered political parties other than the Communist Party, Rukh became the nucleus of the Democratic bloc, which won in the four western oblasts and in Kyiv city and oblast, as well as in many other large cities. However, the ruling elite could still manipulate the elections in the countryside and smaller towns in central and eastern regions. The nature of the deputy corpus that these elections produced determined the outcome of what could be called the Ukrainian revolution of 1988–1991. Soviet functionaries, factory directors, and the token 'worker' and 'peasant' deputies whom they controlled together constituted a majority known as the Group of 239. Although they endorsed the slogan 'For a Soviet, sovereign Ukraine', the majority really focussed on limiting the extent of democratic reforms. The opposition held only 125 seats, and the third force in the parliament, a group of democratic socialists still affiliated with the Communist Party, 41 seats.

This legislature served until 1994, in the process declaring independence in August 1991 and upgrading itself to the parliament of the independent state. It determined the nature of the Faustian bargain that the Ukrainian democrats had to make in 1991. In the short term, it set up for failure the project of creating a prosperous democratic Ukraine built on the foundation of Ukrainian ethnic identity, but constructed as a civic multicultural society. It also produced rampant corruption and extreme social inequality.

Celebrated as a major milestone in Ukrainian history, the declaration of independence on 24 August 1991 was seen at the time as a problematic compromise between the democratic opposition and Soviet-era functionaries. From the distance of three decades, it appears as the moment when the social and political revolution in Ukraine was cut short. Seeing that the Soviet centre caved in after the abortive conservative coup in Moscow, the Group of 239 achieved an impressive turnaround, going from supporting some form of a union state to embracing full independence. In return, they preserved the political and economic domination of the country for their class.

A political pirouette like that required a competent go-between to deal with the opposition, and the Soviet Ukrainian elites found him in the person of Leonid Kravchuk. A second secretary of the party's Central Committee, he became the speaker of the legislature because the first secretary had not been an effective communicator, even less so in Ukrainian. In his new position, Kravchuk excelled as a negotiator and as a facilitator of compromise; he had been assigned to work with the Rukh before the movement even took off. However, he was neither a revolutionary nor a reformer – even if this was exactly what the Group of 239 wanted.

In the presidential election held on the same day as the independence referendum on 1 December 1991, Rukh ran its own candidate, the respected former dissident Viacheslav Chornovil; but Kravchuk won easily in the first round, with 61.6% against Chornovil's 23.2%. Chornovil won only the three western oblasts, which had rejected the preservation of the Soviet Union in the March 1991 referendum. With Kravchuk as a popularly elected president, the existence of a compromise became more apparent. The 'national-democratic' opposition (so called to distinguish it from the pro-Soviet opposition soon to emerge) supported Kravchuk's efforts at state and nation building, while accepting that there would be neither a lustration of Soviet officials nor market reforms removing economic power from the hands of the Red directors [5].

Kravchuk spent his presidency (1991–1994) developing the embryonic political institutions of Soviet Ukraine into proper state structures of an independent state. State building also involved some disassembling, with the joint Soviet army dismantled and the financial system reconstructed. In foreign policy, he focussed on gaining international recognition for the young state and establishing diplomatic relations with neighbour countries and key global players. Kravchuk intentionally downgraded Ukraine's participation in the Commonwealth of Independent States, trying to distance Ukraine from Russian governance, which was trying to use the Commonwealth as an instrument for preserving its domination of the post-Soviet political and economic space. He spoke about a Western path for Ukraine, but the reality was different. The West was more interested in Russia, and saw it as a crucial partner in the post-Soviet political space, setting aside little time for Ukraine. When it finally did become engaged, it was all about the need for Ukraine to surrender its large but decaying nuclear arsenal inherited from the Soviet Union. The 1994 Budapest Memorandum between Ukraine and all the major nuclear powers finalised this decision, promising guarantees of Ukraine's sovereignty and territorial integrity.

Internally, Kravchuk struggled. Rather than reforming Ukraine's large, non-competitive Soviet-style industry that had close links to Russia and its military orders, he subsidised industrial enterprises in the hopes of preventing a jump in unemployment and social tensions. The power of the Red directors remained largely intact; they, too, preferred thriving on subsidies to risking venturing into the free market. Because the national democrats supported Kravchuk's state-building program, they could not benefit from the protest vote. It went instead to the revived opponents on the left; the trouble was that, for much of the 1990s, it was still a Soviet-style Left led by former Soviet functionaries. Indeed, its influence was due to widespread nostalgia for the Soviet welfare model, which looked so appealing in those gloomy years of economic collapse and massive impoverishment.

Yet the nature of politics also changed, checking the Left's revival. The simultaneous fragmentation of political life and mass disillusionment with the outcomes of political activism led to leading politicians and powerful regional bosses campaigning as independents. When a major miners' strike and a conflict between the president and the parliament forced early parliamentary and presidential elections in 1994, their results revealed the new political reality. Independents became the largest group in the new parliament (168 seats), with the Communist Party winning 86 seats and Rukh, 20. In the majoritarian electoral system, with 450 districts each electing a single candidate, the regional economic elites proved the biggest winner. Because of the 50% participation threshold, many seats remained unfilled for years, with low public interest stymying repeated attempts to hold valid elections. Stunningly, these included 13 of 23 seats allocated to Kyiv.

The power of the regional kingpins, who liked the immunity granted to them as parliamentarians, also translated into a new type of political sloganeering. With Kravchuk focussing on the Ukrainisation of education and administration, their spokespersons – supported in this case by the Communist Party – tried to link Ukrainian patriotism to economic mismanagement and widespread poverty. Rather than being a contest about burning social issues, the presidential election of 1994 turned into a debate about the role of the Ukrainian and Russian languages and the importance of links with Russia, which could allegedly bring prosperity. The 1994 election became the first to produce the electoral map that has been replicated many times since, with the western half of Ukraine voting for a national-democratic candidate and the eastern half a pro-Russian one. Kravchuk, who ran as an independent, lost 45.2% to 52.3% to Leonid Kuchma, his former prime minister. As the former head of the largest rocket-building plant in the Soviet Union (in Dnipropetrovsk, now Dnipro), he was a good representative of the Red directors' march into politics.

As president, Kuchma reneged on his electoral promises to make Russian the second state language and restore closer ties to Russia. In foreign policy, too, he balanced skilfully between Russia and the West, which by then had finally discovered Ukraine's strategic importance next to an increasingly revisionist and unreliable Russia. It was Kuchma who managed to remove the populist, self-proclaimed Crimean 'president' Yuri Meshkov without causing a stir in Russia. Kuchma, he who courted NATO, also nudged Boris Yeltsin's Russia into signing the comprehensive Treaty on Friendship, Cooperation, and Partnership (1997). This agreement finalised the division of the Black Sea Fleet and confirmed Russia's recognition of Ukrainian borders, including the Crimea.

Domestically, Kuchma focussed on fixing the economy in a way that reflected the interests of his class. This included the introduction of a stable currency, the hryvnia (1996), and the privatisation of industry. The Red directors became the greatest beneficiaries of the latter process; after snapping up for mere pennies the privatisation certificates distributed to workers, the bosses proceeded to modernise these enterprises and to explore foreign markets. Kuchma-era privatisation also produced the so-called oligarchs – uber-wealthy business people who usually owed their fortunes to some political connection, and who used their money to maintain considerable political influence.

A Society Reborn

The economic revival of the late 1990s, even if interrupted briefly by the aftershocks of the Russian financial crisis of 1998, led to the development of a Ukrainian middle class. Professionals and small business owners became more confident about their future and, at the same time, more concerned about the country's direction. The presidential election of 1999, which granted Kuchma his second term, marked the high point of 'old' politics, in which the presence of convenient nationalistic and communist scarecrows served to persuade voters into supporting 'effective managers', who declared (always at election time) their special feelings for the Russian culture. This election was also a high point for the traditional pro-Soviet Left, which subsequently went into a steep decline, in part due to demographic change.

Kuchma's advisers understood that social discontent, with grand corruption, unfair privatisation, and the emergence of the oligarchs, undermined their candidate's chances. They hired so-called 'political technologists' from Russia, who helped manipulate the public into seeing Kuchma as the safest choice. They determined that their success depended on ensuring that in the run-off their boss would face the backward-looking and uncharismatic Communist Party chief Petro Symonenko. To achieve that – and the incumbent's subsequent victory in the run-off – the

Kuchma administration employed all kinds of manipulative strategies and, according to some scholars, electoral fraud [6]. Kuchma duly defeated Symonenko with 57.7% against 38.8%.

The late 1990s also saw the decline of the national-democratic forces in the form in which they had emerged a decade earlier. Rukh, as a smaller political party that came into being after the disintegration of Rukh as a large popular front in the early 1990s, had its greatest success during the parliamentary elections of 1998, when it came second after the Communists with 9.4% of the vote, securing 46 seats. (These elections inaugurated the principle of party lists, which determined 50% of the seats.) But Rukh's widely respected leader, Viacheslav Chornovil, was killed in a car crash – seen by some as suspicious – before he could put forward his bid for the presidency in 1999. None of his successors could reverse the party's decline.

Social and political trends of the late 1990s suggested the possibility of a new beginning, but it took public outrage at President Kuchma's corrupt administration to reimagine Ukrainian politics. In the fall of 2000, a leading opposition journalist named Georgiy Gongadze disappeared; his headless body was later found in a forest. Gongadze had been a pioneer of Internet journalism in Ukraine, but his online newspaper *Ukrainska Pravda* (Ukrainian Truth) acquired a mass national following only after his disappearance and the subsequent political scandal. Two months after Gongadze's murder, Oleksandr Moroz, the speaker of the parliament and leader of the Socialist Party, announced that he was in possession of recordings connecting President Kuchma to this criminal case. Mayhem ensued. The hundreds of hours of recordings leaked on the Internet portrayed the president as a thoroughly corrupt leader, and not just because of his recorded hints to police bosses that it would be good if someone silenced Gongadze.

Shocked by these revelations, Ukrainian society responded with spontaneous mass rallies in downtown Kyiv, which featured, for the first time since 1990–1991, tents intended for a longer 'occupation' of the Maidan, the capital's main plaza. The protest actions continued into 2001, when the brewing mass opposition movement acquired two charismatic leaders: recently dismissed Prime Minister Viktor Yushchenko, a Ukrainophone banker with a reputation for resisting the pecuniary temptations of high office, and his former deputy, Yulia Tymoshenko, a firebrand critic of the oligarchical system, which she knew from within. With the traditional Left and the traditional national-democratic Center-Right in decline, the time was ripe for a new catch-all protest movement. The arrival of the Internet and cell phones made recruiting and coordinating much easier. Shunned by the West, the wounded Kuchma also made things worse for himself by turning more to Russia. The new opposition movement called itself 'Ukraine without Kuchma', and it spread like wildfire. Yushchenko also made the smart choice not to focus on the rights of the Ukrainian language per se, but to discuss important social issues in Ukrainian. This served to link the Ukrainian ethnic identity to civic protest and the promise of a new Ukraine.

However, the united opposition faced a new pro-government camp. In the old tradition, Kuchma did not bother to create his own political party, but the decline of the Left allowed a new political force to reclaim the traditional electorate of the Communist and Socialist parties in eastern and southern Ukraine. This force, the Party of Regions, established in 2000, picked up the Left's message about the good old Soviet days, but emphasised the rights of Russian language and culture rather than social equality, which had also been present in the Left's program. The Party of Regions soon established its political domination in the Donbas, a majority Ukrainian but Russophone-depressed mining region, and in the Crimea. It also had a significant presence elsewhere in eastern and southern Ukraine. In 2002, the Party of Regions managed to impose on the reluctant Kuchma its own prime minister, Viktor Yanukovych, who was a native of the Donbas with two criminal convictions from his youth. That year, Yushchenko transformed 'Ukraine without Kuchma' into an electoral bloc called 'Our Ukraine', which received the majority of the party-list votes in the parliamentary elections of 2002.

The showdown between the two forces took place during the presidential elections of 2004. The Party of Regions acted in its usual corrupt and heavy-handed way, a move that was bound to spark mass protests. First, Yushchenko was poisoned with a huge amount of dioxin, which caused temporary organ failure and covered his body and face in lesions. (He eventually recovered; the perpetrators were never identified.) Then the Central Electoral Commission made its server available to the techs sitting in the Party of Regions' headquarters, who proceeded to input skewed reports from the oblasts. However, the opposition was prepared for anything and had also illegally tapped the phones at the headquarters. It thus acquired proof of electoral fraud that was inadmissible in court but that was highly effective in the court of public opinion. As soon as the Central Electoral Commission announced the predictable preliminary results giving a victory to Yanukovych on 22 November 2004, crowds of protesters headed to the Maidan, where 'Our Ukraine' had already installed large television screens. The Orange Revolution, named after Yushchenko's freshly designed campaign colour, began. Unlike the government side, the Orange revolutionaries also used the Internet widely for mobilising support and coordinating political actions [7].

During the tense winter of mass protests and permanent occupation of the Maidan, professionals and small business owners were the backbone of the revolution, while students – the generation that did not remember Soviet regimentation – led the way at decisive moments. In the end, it was Kuchma's indecision that ensured a peaceful resolution. With foreign affairs, the army, and internal affairs within the purview of Ukrainian presidents, any violent crackdown would have had to be Kuchma's decision, and all he wanted was a peaceful retirement with either formal or informal immunity from prosecution. In the end, he chose to listen to Western mediators. The infamously corrupt Supreme Court suddenly made the decision to hold a new run-off, which Yushchenko duly won.

He did not win by a large margin, however; the result was only 51.2% to 44.2% for Yanukovych. But, the geographical distribution of votes was significant. In the re-run that was judged to be free and fair, the same east-west regional divide that the Party of Regions was trying to solidify and exploit failed to produce expected results. Parts of central Ukraine sided with the western regions by connecting the notions of democracy and rule of law with the revival of the long-oppressed Ukrainian culture. On the Maidan, democracy spoke Ukrainian, or, at least, the supporters of the revolution acknowledged the Ukrainian language's symbolic importance in their struggle for the new Ukraine [8]. In a way, this was a response to the Party of Regions, which combined its rhetoric about the rights of Russophones with its bosses' increasing admiration of the political and economic regime that Putin was building in Russia.

To the Maidan, Again

With the revolution accomplished, in January 2005 the Orange revolutionaries went home, both literally – by vacating the Maidan – and politically. They left it up to Yushchenko and Tymoshenko to create a new Ukraine with the help of traditional political parties and the existing state apparatus. There were also some oligarchs who supported the revolution, including the young Petro Poroshenko.

However, Yushchenko and Tymoshenko proved less effective in power than they had been as leaders of a mass protest movement. The president, now a celebrity in the West, was welcome there, but he had little understanding of his portfolio, which included the army and foreign affairs. Ukrainians quickly grew disappointed with his long-winded speeches and lack of a coherent policy agenda. A scandal around his son's expensive car revealed that Yushchenko and his family felt comfortable with the old corrupt system of symbiosis between big business and politics, which he had promised to dismantle. As prime minister, Tymoshenko demonstrated that her fiery speeches while in the opposition translated into equally loud but inefficient populist measures, such as trying to control the price of meat and fuel. As if these failures were not enough, a conflict between

Tymoshenko and Poroshenko, who became head of the National Security and Defence Council, resulted in a falling-out between the president and the prime minister. The dynamic Yushchenko-and-Tymoshenko duo was no more, and the revolutionary dream was shattered.

In 2006–2007, an unthinkable configuration emerged in Ukrainian politics when Yushchenko was forced to accept as prime minister his arch-rival Yanukovych – the loser of the Orange Revolution. This happened not as the result of elections, but because of the splits in the Orange camp. By the time the 2010 presidential election rolled around, Yushchenko's approval rating slipped into single digits. In order to maintain any political base at all, he began awarding prestigious medals posthumously to radical Ukrainian nationalist leaders from the mid-twentieth century – a decision welcomed in the westernmost oblasts, but extremely controversial elsewhere in Ukraine. His actions hurt Tymoshenko's cause and could well be the reason for her electoral defeat in 2010.

In the first round Yushchenko, received his 5.5% of the vote, but the presidential election of 2010 became a contest between Yanukovych and Tymoshenko. The latter had served as prime minister again in 2007–2010, following her party's success in the parliamentary elections of 2007. But that was the period of economic stagnation and gas wars with Russia. Yanukovych won in the run-off, with 49% to Tymoshenko's 45.5%.

During the Yanukovych presidency (2010–2014), the Party of Regions also formed the government. The presidential administration gradually appointed reliable political figures from the Donbas to gubernatorial positions all over the country and supported friendly oligarchs in their efforts to expand in other parts of the country. Yanukovych busied himself building a business empire with his sons, their young friends posing as owners. Ukrainians referred to the president's fast-growing business group as the 'Family', in the Mafia sense.

In domestic politics, Yanukovych sought to build a stronger presidency. The Party of Regions used political pressure and outright bribes to force more parliamentarians to side with its position. Taking advantage of the expensive gas contract that Tymoshenko had to sign with Russia in 2009, Yanukovych had her prosecuted on questionable charges: abuse of power and embezzlement. Tymoshenko received a seven-year prison term, the outcome decried in the West as political persecution. Yanukovych's own gas deal with Russia in 2010 involved significant price discounts in exchange for political commitments that the opposition decried as compromising Ukraine's sovereignty. The most important of them was the extension of Russia's lease on the naval base of Sevastopol in the Crimea to 2042.

However, the Ukrainian oligarchs, whose interests Yanukovych represented, had no interest in seeing the uber-wealthy Russian oligarchs march in and buy up lucrative businesses in Ukraine. Ukraine's foreign trade had long been diversified, with its Russian direction representing only about a third of the total volume. If anything, they aimed for greater engagement with European markets, which went nicely with owning property in Europe and sending their children to study there. In addition to this economic rationale, the Ukrainian political elites remembered Kuchma's success during the late 1990s at playing the West and Russia against each other to the benefit of Ukraine's ruling class. These considerations were behind Yanukovych's decision to enter into negotiations with the EU about a potential Association Agreement. Such an agreement did not put the non-EU partner country on the path to accession, as it is often erroneously assumed. Rather, it involved the acceptance of the EU production standards and legislative norms in preparation for free-trade status.

But this time, Putin reacted angrily to the Ukrainian elites' attempt to balance between the two sides. Using economic leverage and political threats, he bullied Yanukovych into proclaiming a last-minute change of course. On 21 November 2013, the signing ceremony in Vilnius, Lithuania, was cancelled, and a new course on joining the Russia-led Eurasian Economic Union was proclaimed. The Ukrainian public saw this sea change as capitulation to Russia, which put Yanukovych's attempts to establish his party's control over the Ukrainian economy and political life in a new light. It is also important to understand that the notion of 'Europe' functioned in the Ukrainian political discourse and mass culture, not as reference to the real EU structures and practices, but as a metaphor for democracy, rule of law, prosperity, and the struggle against corruption. This 'Europe' also served as the symbolic opposite of Putin's Russia [9].

It was for this reason that Yanukovych's reversal of course caused a revolution. Few people knew the details of the Association Agreement, but the refusal to sign it meant taking away any hopes for a better future for Ukraine. Among many angry posts appearing on social media on 21 November, an appeal on Facebook by the Afghani-Ukrainian journalist Mustafa Nayyem stood out. He called on Ukrainians to gather on the Maidan to protest Yanukovych's capitulation to Putin. Thousands showed up that night and soon, following the police's brutal attack on protesting students, hundreds of thousands came to the city centre. The Revolution of Dignity had begun.

This revolution was a puzzle to social scientists. All the opposition parties missed its start, and only a small minority of participants identified as members or sympathisers of any party. The defence of the Maidan and the mass volunteering effort that winter relied only on ad hoc appeals broadcast on social media, but they produced impressive results. The traditional ways of measuring the strength of civil society, such as the number of NGOs per thousand people, seemed to indicate that Ukraine had a very weak civil society. Yet, its remarkable strength was obvious to any observer [10]. One possible explanation is the legacy of Ukraine's Soviet past, in which the only political party and state-controlled 'civic organisations' generated distrust in such forms of activism. Another could be the repeated disillusionment with the institutionalisation of opposition movements both during the early 1990s and after the Orange Revolution.

This time the Ukrainian authorities had a lot to lose, and Yanukovych held on until the very end, when the police killings of some one hundred protestors on 18–21 February 2014 took the struggle on the Maidan to a new level. The police themselves became frightened of the consequences and withdrew, thus forcing Yanukovych to flee to Russia. The Party of Regions disintegrated, and its deputies joined the parliamentary opposition in voting to formalise the transfer of power to an acting president. Snap presidential elections then produced a clear victory in the first round for Petro Poroshenko, who, despite his having served in 2012 as a minister in Yanukovych's government, presented himself as a descendent of the national-democratic forces from the 1990s and the early 2000s. The public saw the billionaire oligarch and experienced politician Poroshenko as best qualified to stabilise the Ukrainian state, which would presumably stop Russia's aggression in the wake of the Revolution of Dignity.

The 2014 elections also rendered hollow any Western concerns about the alleged rise of the radical right in Ukraine – incidentally, also a major point in Putin's propaganda war. The two presidential candidates from radical-nationalist organisations received only 1.2 and 0.7% of votes, respectively.

For all the hopes that Ukrainian society invested in him, while Poroshenko was in office, he struggled on the two fronts that mattered most. Despite his genuine efforts to overcome corruption and establish a truly independent judiciary and police force, he largely failed to overcome the oligarchical system, of which he himself had been part. Although Poroshenko tried to rebuild the Ukrainian army after decades of neglect and corruption, it was mostly the volunteers who stopped the Russian assault in the Donbas in 2014–2015. (The Ukrainians authorities did not try to resist the Russian army when it took over the Crimea in 2014, straight after the revolution's victory.) The peace process, which had been moderated by the leaders of France and Germany, produced several ceasefires and, following some painful military defeats in 2015, a plan of a potential peace settlement that was unfavorable for Ukraine—and unrealistic.

During the presidential elections of 2019, Ukrainians judged Poroshenko primarily based on his domestic policies, and voted overwhelmingly for a complete political novice, the charismatic 39-year-old actor and comedian Volodymyr Zelensky. He crushed Poroshenko in the run-off by getting an unprecedented 73.2% of the votes. In the parliamentary elections that followed, his brand-new political party 'Servant of the People' swept to power by obtaining, for the first time in modern Ukrainian politics, an outright majority in the parliament (254 seats out of 450).

If Zelensky came into office with vague promises to clean up the corrupt political system and rejuvenate the peace process simply by 'stopping the shooting', he soon found himself continuing many of Poroshenko's policies. He realised the impossibility of trusting Putin with anything, and began taking painful steps toward implementing major reforms in Ukraine. These included passing laws stripping parliamentarians of immunity and establishing a process for impeaching a president. In the economic sphere, Zelensky proved wrong those commentators who portrayed him as the puppet of an oligarch owner of the TV channel that had broadcast Zelensky's entertainment shows. As president, he adopted measures to undermine the influence of this businessman in particular and all oligarchs in general. Some of Zelensky's policy and personnel decisions seemed hasty and based on his trust in people whom he knew from his entertainment-industry days. Yet, he and his inner circle also demonstrated their ability to listen to the public, including reacting to popular posts on social media. In other words, they were forced to acknowledge the power of public opinion and social self-organisation.

When Zelensky emerged after the all-out Russian invasion in February 2022 as Ukraine's unquestionable wartime leader, this did not mean that Ukrainians accepted his program or vision.

Rather, he had molded himself into a perfect representative of society's drive to defend Ukraine. Many of his close political collaborators remain deeply unpopular, and corrupt motives are often suspected in their actions. But Ukrainian civil society strongly identifies with the defence of its democratic values, and it is this message that Zelensky delivers to the world on the people's behalf. The enormous scale of domestic volunteer activities in support of the Ukrainian army and humanitarian causes is such that, in many cases, informal networks of volunteers take over the state's responsibilities. This is precisely the kind of people power that makes the Putin regime so scared of Ukraine, the country that emerged from the fire of the Maidan.

In 2022, Putin decided on an all-out invasion of Ukraine in part because he fell victim to his regime's own propaganda, which alleged mass support for Russia among Ukraine's ethnic Russian and Russophone population. But the Russian army's atrocities and deliberate attacks on civilian infrastructure had the opposite effect: They destroyed whatever remained of the Soviet myth of 'fraternal' relations between Ukrainians and Russians. The war also prompted in Ukraine a rejection of Russian culture as a tool of imperial domination, complete with the removal of once-obligatory monuments to Russian writers. Putin sought to reclaim Ukraine. Instead he lost it for good.

The Ukrainian revolution, which began in the Soviet Union in 1988–91 and continued through the political struggles culminating in the Orange Revolution and the Revolution of Dignity, was bound to produce a war with Putin's Russia. For Ukraine, the war marks the end of the post-Soviet period in its history. Based on the acknowledgement of the Ukrainian language and culture as important markers of sovereignty, modern Ukrainian identity is nevertheless civic and political rather than ethnic. The very existence of democratic Ukraine is a challenge to Putin's political model and his drive to restore Russia's imperialist past. But authoritarian Russia, which has suppressed and atomised its own society, lacks the kind of social support and volunteering that Ukrainians demonstrate in defence of their country. In the fight between the army of convicts and mercenaries and the people at arms, the final victory can only be Ukraine's.

References

1. Kuzio T, Wilson A. Ukraine: Perestroika to Independence. Edmonton: CIUS Press. 1994; 159–162 and 184–191. DOI: https://doi.org/10.1007/978-1-349-23240-6.

2. Krawchenko B. Social change and national consciousness in Twentieth-Century Ukraine London: Macmillan. 1985; 198. DOI: https://doi.org/10.1007/978-1-349-09548-3.

3. Petrovsky-Shtern Y. A paradigm-changing day: The twenty-fifth anniversary of Babyn Yar and Ukrainian-Jewish relations. *Harvard Ukrainian Studies*. 2021; 38(3–4): 227–258.

4. Hough JF. Democratisation and revolution in the USSR, 1985–1991. Washington, DC: Brookings Institution Press. 1997; 11–15.

5. Wilson A. The Ukrainians: unexpected nation, 4th ed. New Haven: Yale University Press. 2015; 174–176.

6. Myagkov M, Ordeshool PC. The trail of votes in Ukraine's 1998, 1999, and 2002 elections. *Post-Soviet Affairs*. 2005; 21(1): 56–71, 65–67. DOI: https://doi.org/10.2747/1060-586X.21.1.56.

7. Wilson A. Ukraine's Orange Revolution. New Haven: Yale University Press. 2005; 131–132.

8. Yekelchyk S. Ukraine: Birth of a modern nation. New York: Oxford University Press. 2007; 214 and 218.
9. Yekelchyk S. Ukraine: What everyone needs to know, 2nd ed. New York: Oxford University Press. 2020; 93. DOI: https://doi.org/10.1093/wentk/9780197532102.001.0001.
10. Marples DR, Mills FV. (eds.) Ukraine's Euromaidan: Analyses of a civil revolution Stuttgart: Ibidem; 2015.

7. Russia's Networked Authoritarianism in Ukraine's Occupied Territories during the Full-Scale Invasion: Control and Resilience

Tetyana Lokot

> Russia's full-scale invasion of Ukraine in February 2022 has seen the Kremlin mixing its usual external cyber warfare tactics with internet control and information manipulation approaches inspired by its internal networked authoritarian regime. I argue that Russia's interventions in the information spaces and telecommunications infrastructure in temporarily occupied Ukrainian territories demand greater scrutiny from the domains of internet governance and cyber warfare studies alike. This analysis of the 'networked authoritarian' creep of Russia's censorship and surveillance tactics beyond its borders as a part of its expanding war arsenal enables a comprehensive assessment of the impacts of both kinetic attacks on communications infrastructure and informational attacks on the digital communication space in Ukraine. The analysis also summarises Ukraine's observed capability for resistance and resilience in the face of Russia's networked authoritarianism in the context of the war and discusses the implications and lessons from the events of the full-scale invasion for the future rebuilding of Ukraine and for the broader international policymaking community.

Russia's approach to governing the internet and telecommunications inside the country has seen significant scrutiny by internet governance and digital rights scholars. They, alongside internet freedom advocates, have been rightly concerned with the narrowing space for free expression and growing crackdown on digital freedoms inside Russia [1, 2]. At the same time, Russia's external cyberwarfare strategy has gained more attention in the global cybersecurity domain, with the Kremlin using cyberattacks belligerently to support conventional military incursions (e.g., in Georgia in 2008 or in Ukraine since 2014) [3, 4] or to intervene in Western political processes through a mix of hacking and information manipulation [5, 6].

Russia's full-scale invasion of Ukraine in February 2022, however, has seen the Kremlin mixing its usual external cyberwarfare tactics with approaches inspired by its internal networked authoritarian regime. I argue that Russia's interventions into the information spaces and telecommunications infrastructure in temporarily occupied Ukrainian territories demand greater scrutiny. I also contend that an understanding of the country's internal politics and its aspirations in the digital domain is necessary to assess the implications of Russia's actions and Ukraine's potential for resistance and resilience, as well as to inform appropriate and timely policy responses from the global community.

Russia's Networked Authoritarianism

The internet in Russia initially developed as a predominantly free and apolitical space alongside increasingly co-opted mainstream media. But over time, independent news outlets and opposition actors have come to rely on digital platforms and networked media to promote alternative and often critical narratives about the regime. The Kremlin grew increasingly concerned about the internet's destabilising potential following the wave of discontent in the Middle East and North Africa (MENA) region in the early 2010s and the ensuing 2011–2012 political unrest in Russia [7]. Further spooked by the Revolution of Dignity in Ukraine in 2013–2014, the Kremlin went to considerable lengths to wrest control of the digital space away from diverse private actors and to centralise internet governance, online censorship, and content regulation. Roskomnadzor, the Russian state's regulatory agency overseeing the internet, media, and telecommunications, has taken on a more prominent role in enforcing the full suite of internet controls. At the same time, state-sponsored actors also capitalised on the power of social media, building a presence for state-funded media on YouTube and Twitter and creating a number of anonymous channels to publish political commentary, conspiracy theories, and leaks on Telegram, the most popular messaging service in Russia [8]. A host of laws adopted in the decade since 2012 have consolidated this state control. With the first tranche, the government limited online freedoms, enabled pervasive surveillance, and policed and filtered online speech. More recent legislation passed since 2017 has sought to secure greater control over national internet infrastructure and to bring foreign digital platforms to heel.

To further support its goal of pervasive information control online, alongside seeking technological independence, Russia has adopted a far-reaching strategy of internet sovereignty. The strategy combines the Kremlin's desire to tightly control information flows and activity in digital domains inside the country that are viewed as posing threats to regime stability with a push for technological sovereignty, signalling the state's intention to develop and use homegrown technologies to avoid excessive dependency on foreign hardware, services, and software. To this end, over the past decade, Russia has introduced a robust legal framework and numerous regulations meant to shape its future sovereign internet, including further centralisation of online censorship mechanisms and the gradual takeover of telecommunications infrastructure and traffic exchange points.

Critics note that these steps remain mostly focused on securing greater control over citizen activity and anti-regime expressions within Russia [9]. But the state's lack of sufficient investment into domestic research, development, and production coupled with pressure from international sanctions mean the country is unable to completely decouple from the global internet and remains dependent on Western technologies in its public infrastructure and private sectors [10].

With the internet in Russia being pivotal to democratic transformations of the past decade, it is no wonder that control over digital space has also become a strategic priority for the regime. The Russian state has often taken advantage of the technologies used by people in everyday life to boost its control over its citizens and their data. The state has invested in technological innovation around e-governance services while also building extensive online censorship infrastructure, adopting restrictive data and internet regulations and enabling more sophisticated surveillance tools based on citizen data gathering and facial recognition technology. This has created a unique environment, best understood as networked authoritarianism [1], where the

Russian state is both highly supportive of technological innovation and development while being increasingly restrictive and controlling towards digital spaces and online expression [11].

Although Russia's externally facing cyber warfare efforts and information manipulation tactics are receiving growing attention in foreign policy, cybersecurity, and defence policy circles, these discussions have mostly neglected to connect activity directed at foreign states or corporate actors with the internal networked authoritarian policies. With Russia's illegal annexation of Crimea and its occupation of parts of eastern Ukraine since 2014, and especially after Russia's full-scale invasion of Ukraine in February 2022, we have been able to observe the Kremlin's overlapping efforts to use cyberattacks to target Ukrainian critical infrastructure and state communications [4, 12, 13] and to impose key tenets of networked authoritarian governance in temporarily occupied Ukrainian territories [14, 15]. Understanding the impact of this two-pronged attack style and the response of Ukrainian authorities and allies on the ground is key to the successful rebuttal of Russian interference and to the strengthening of infrastructural, political, and societal resilience of the Ukrainian state and society in the context of the full-scale war.

The Role of Digital Warfare in Russia's Invasion of Ukraine

As Boichak notes, digital technologies not only 'offer new capabilities in conducting military operations' but also bring warfare 'into the realms of communication and perception', reconstituting 'the social conditions shaping people's relationship to wars'

[16 p511]. Highlighting the expanding role of digital media in modern wars, Boichak and Hoskins [17] note that while wartime information has always been contingent upon various types of communication infrastructure, the new networked environment enables a new kind of participatory warfare [18] wherein communication about – and participation in – wars is continuously shaped 'through personalised and individualised informational feeds' [17 p2]. This technology enables large-scale participation by both military and civilian actors through smartphones, messaging apps, and social media platforms. Consequently, in this new reality of war, made vivid in the 2022 Russian invasion of Ukraine, it is crucial to understand how the invading forces not only attempt to co-opt, corrupt, or control servers, energy grids, or telecommunications infrastructure remotely or kinetically but also attempt to exert influence on the occupied Ukrainian information and communication space using domestically developed networked authoritarian approaches. In the subsections below, I provide an overview of the various Russian tactics observed in temporarily occupied territories in the first year of the war in Ukraine. Within them, I discuss both Russia's kinetic attacks and its online interference and influencing activities.

Targeting Telecommunications Infrastructure

Since it illegally annexed Ukraine's Crimean Peninsula in 2014, Russia has been targeting and weaponising internet connectivity in the Ukrainian regions under occupation. Instead of completely destroying occupied territories' internet and mobile infrastructure, Russia has instead partially subsumed it. Within Crimea and the occupied parts of the Donetsk and Luhansk regions, Russian forces have seized Ukrainian mobile base stations and internet service provider facilities, brought in domestic or newly formed mobile provider entities, and rerouted Ukrainian internet traffic through Russian exchange points. In 2014, they also laid a new undersea cable to Crimea from the Russian mainland [19].

Since February 2022, Russian invaders have similarly targeted telecommunications infrastructure in frontline areas and newly occupied Ukrainian territories, with these areas suffering partial or complete communication blackouts. According to data from Ukraine's Special Communications Service published in October 2022, over 4,000 base stations of Ukrainian telecommunications providers have been seized or destroyed by Russian troops since the beginning of the full-scale invasion, and more than 60,000 kilometres of fibre-optic internet cables have been captured or damaged by the Russians [20]. Throughout the months of the invasion of Ukraine, large-scale internet disruptions in several Ukrainian regions have been reported by Netblocks, a service monitoring online censorship and shutdowns [21]. In some areas, such as Ukraine's second-largest city, Kharkiv, or the strategic port city of Mariupol in southern Ukraine, the internet was disrupted as early as the first day of the invasion. Russian shelling and missile attacks targeted civilian infrastructure. This coincided with a suspected Russian cyberattack on Viasat satellite internet network serving Ukraine and much of Europe, which experienced a partial outage on 24 February, 2022 [21]. On 26 February, as the Russian troops besieged the capital of Kyiv, Ukraine's backbone internet provider, GigaTrans, which supplies connectivity to several other networks in Ukraine, also experienced a major disruption [21]. On 28 March, Ukraine's national internet provider, Ukrtelecom, experienced an extended nationwide network disruption following a major cyberattack that lasted for over 15 hours [22].

In the southern Kherson region, which was occupied by Russian forces for several months in 2022, Netblocks registered a near-total internet blackout at the end of April 2022 that affected multiple Ukrainian providers, including Ukrtelecom, Kyivstar, Vodafone, and Volia [21]. On 1 May 2022, regional provider Skynet (Khersontelecom) was able to partially restored access, yet metrics showed that connectivity on the network had been routed via Russia's internet instead of through Ukrainian telecoms infrastructure. Netblocks reported that the rerouting was done through Miranda Media [21], a Russian internet provider. This internet service provider (ISP) was set up by Russia to service users in occupied Crimea, where Ukrainian connections had been severed after the occupation [14]. Over the course of the current stage of the war, some areas, such as Kherson and parts of the region, have been liberated and have had Ukrainian connectivity restored. But in regions which remain under Russia's control, internet traffic is still rerouted through Russian suppliers, while they also co-opt Ukrainian mobile infrastructure, bringing in Russian phone numbers and SIM cards.

Co-opting Online Information Flows

Destroying connectivity in Ukraine has further isolated vulnerable communities in Russia-occupied areas. It has cut them off from trusted news sources and left them unable to report on instances of torture, hostage-taking, murders, and other war crimes. Reports instead only tend to emerge after areas are liberated by Ukrainian troops. An official with Ukraine's Ministry of Digital Transformation told *Time* magazine that as a result of the disconnections, 'the people living there don't know what's happening in Ukraine, they can't call family to describe the situation, they don't know whether their relatives are alive or not' [20]. At the same time, Russia's seizure of control over telecommunications infrastructure means Ukrainian civilians in occupied regions are increasingly subject to Russian internet regulations, surveillance, and censorship characteristic of the networked authoritarian regime. This means that citizens in these areas find themselves in an information ecosystem that distorts the reality of the war by spreading disinformation through anonymous pro-war Telegram channels, blocking access to Ukrainian and Western news websites and social media platforms, and feeding highly sanitised content on Russian state media. In essence, Ukrainians in Russian-occupied territories are subjected to the same networked authoritarian restrictions that distort the information reality for those living within Russia.

Punishments for Ukrainians violating the draconian Russian internet regime in occupation are similar to those habitually faced by Russians. Russia-installed authorities physically examine the smartphones of those evacuating to Ukraine-controlled territories in search of 'patriotic' Ukrainian content and have used online surveillance to identify users whom they consider to be critical of the occupying regime or collaborating with or passing information to the Ukrainians [23]. Something as innocuous as a photo of the Ukrainian flag or Ukrainian numbers listed in a smartphone's call history has reportedly led to Ukrainians across Russia-controlled regions being detained, questioned, and abused by Russian forces [24]. As evident from the cases above, control over infrastructure and influence over information flows go hand in hand in Russia's networked authoritarian logic and are also visible in the war it is waging in Ukraine. These 'hybrid' threats to both military operations and civilian connectivity are what Ukrainian authorities and citizens have been grappling with for the past year.

Ukrainian Resistance, Recovery, and Resilience

Ukraine's resistance efforts in the face of Russia's attack on networks, communications, and information platforms have taken various forms. According to a July 2022 report by Microsoft [25], the Ukrainian government has successfully sustained its civil and military operations by distributing its digital infrastructure into the public cloud, where it has been hosted in data centres across Europe, to minimise the effects of both cyber- and kinetic attacks. In addition to the governmental cyber defence measures Ukraine has been taking with international partners to resist a higher percentage of Russian cyberattacks [25], there have also been more horizontal instances of resistance by grassroots hacker groups [26]. Additionally, government cybersecurity officials have successfully rallied an informal community of IT specialists and hackers in Ukraine and abroad to target Russian state and military targets online [27].

Despite electricity shutdowns and pressure and censorship by occupying authorities, Ukrainians across the country have continued to use digital communication spaces. Within these spaces, Ukrainians have had ongoing conversations about

Ukraine's response to Russian invaders, the impact of the war on their lives, and the stories of Ukrainian resistance. Constellations of citizens mobilising into networked publics online to strategically use digital technology to support the resistance effort and propagate their ideas to broader audiences at home and abroad have played an important part in establishing state legitimacy and spreading unifying national narratives [16]. In occupied territories such as Kherson and Crimea, grassroots partisan movements such as Yellow Ribbon have been going offline to avoid digital surveillance and online censorship, instead plastering the city walls with printed posters and painting Ukrainian flags on every available surface [23]. Citizens active online have adopted anonymisation and circumvention tools, using virtual private networks and more secure messaging alternatives such as Signal. Others have resorted to deleting their messaging history and social media profiles, disguising their online identities, and protecting themselves from online surveillance and censorship.

Ukrainian authorities have reacted swiftly to disruptions in connectivity across the country. In some cases, as with the traffic rerouting in Kherson, there were successful attempts to reroute traffic back through Ukrainian channels days after the initial takeover [21]. Recognising the importance of this connectivity, in regions liberated from occupation, telecommunications and emergency workers have consistently been among the first to arrive, often risking their lives in areas close to the frontline to repair base stations and fibre-optic cables and reconnect infrastructure back to Ukrainian networks. In October 2022, Ukraine's Ministry of Digital Transformation reported that Ukrainian mobile operators had rebuilt 71 of their base stations in towns and cities liberated from Russian occupation since the beginning of the September counteroffensive [20]. From March to October 2022, Ukrainian telecommunications workers had restored 1,232 base stations in areas previously occupied by the invading army [20]. A number of international partners have provided Ukraine with assistance and support in rebuilding the country's bruised and battered infrastructure.

In liberated areas of Ukraine which bore the brunt of Russian destruction, officials have been setting up makeshift charging stations and wireless internet access spots using Starlink satellite internet technology [15]. In April 2022, Mykhailo Fedorov, Ukraine's Minister of Digital Transformation, shared an image of a crowd of locals clustered around a Starlink terminal in the village of Ivankiv, in the Kyiv region, which had been liberated from Russian control days before. 'Operation of electricity and mobile communications has not been yet restored,' Fedorov wrote, 'but Starlink came on time. Locals finally are able to tell relatives that they are alive' [28].

The longer-term recovery and resilience of Ukraine's internet connectivity and information space depends on the state and industry bolstering their technological capabilities. After the physical damage and cyberattacks, the country must rebuild its infrastructure and engage ordinary citizens in the processes of countering Russian networked authoritarian influence, control, and manipulation in online spaces. As the ongoing war in Ukraine illustrates, while there are differences between these threats, the Kremlin does not pursue them separately, nor should we place them in separate analytical categories. Investments in more modern and robust telecommunications networks should go hand in hand with further decentralisation of state and critical industry data storage and cloud infrastructure.

Sustained support from European and Western allies plays a crucial role in this. In June 2022, the EU launched a digital tech hub in Slovakia to make it easier for European companies to donate equipment to sustain and rebuild Ukraine's digital and telecommunications sector and to coordinate technical support across the EU [29]. In September 2022, the European Commission agreed to associate Ukraine to the Digital Europe Programme, bolstering funding and support for industry and state institutions in the areas of computing, AI, and digital skills [29]. The country has seen similar support from corporate giants like Amazon, which in 2022 helped Ukraine transfer critical government, business, and property databases into the company's data cloud [30]. Such intergovernmental and industry efforts need to redouble after Ukraine's victory in the war. Ukraine's battle for reconstruction and sustainable connectivity is a long-term one – and it demands working with international partners whose technologies can provide the country with stable long-term support.

To counteract Russia's networked authoritarian policies, Ukraine will benefit from strengthening international cooperation in the area of cybersecurity and defence. The country's accession to the NATO Cooperative Cyber Defence Centre of Excellence in early 2023 [31] is a good example of building alliances to support efficient responses to cyberthreats – Russian and otherwise. Continued involvement in initiatives such as the EU–Ukraine Cybersecurity Dialogue and collaboration between the Ukrainian State Service of Special Communications and Information Protection of Ukraine (SSSCIP) and the U.S. Cybersecurity and Infrastructure Security Agency (CISA) should further buttress Ukraine's cyber defence capabilities.

Ukrainian citizens, whether military or civilian, will benefit from a broadening effort to increase digital literacy, empowering them to protect their privacy and their security online and to make informed decisions about verified information sources and trustworthy digital actors. The country is making visible progress in expanding digital services and data access for Ukrainians – the government should now pay the same attention to ensuring citizens' data and identities are protected from external threats, as well as giving users more control over their privacy and information (while adhering to the universal digital rights, freedoms, and norms). This can be achieved through aligning national regulatory frameworks with the best practices and policies of the European Union and other international bodies on countering disinformation and protecting internet freedom. Equally important is that state regulators and policymakers are receptive to the interventions of local and international digital rights groups calling for more citizen agency, stronger remedy and redress mechanisms, and greater platform accountability and transparency. Such efforts will make for a more equitable, more responsible, and thus a more secure and resilient internet that will contribute to the future rebuilding and revival of Ukraine.

Future-focused plans for Ukraine call for a coordinated and comprehensive strategy to strengthen defences against the full range of cyber-destructive interventions, espionage activities, and information manipulation operations, build reliable digital infrastructure, and craft robust privacy and digital rights regulations serving the interests of citizens. Meanwhile, the country's partners would do well to learn from Ukraine's lessons and pay closer attention to the full spectrum of Russia's networked authoritarian policies and activities at home and abroad.

References

1. Maréchal N. Networked authoritarianism and the geopolitics of information: Understanding Russian internet policy. *Media and Communication.* 2017 Mar 22; 5(1): 29–41. DOI: https://doi.org/10.17645/mac.v5i1.808.

2. Lonkila M, Shpakovskaya L, Torchinsky P. The occupation of Runet? The tightening state regulation of the Russian-language section of the internet. In: Wijermars M, Lehtisaari K (eds.), *Freedom of expression in Russia's new mediasphere.* London and New York: Routledge. 2020; 17–38. DOI: https://doi.org/10.4324/9780429437205-2.

3. Deibert RJ, Rohozinski R, Crete-Nishihata M. Cyclones in cyberspace: Information shaping and denial in the 2008 Russia–Georgia war. *Security Dialogue.* 2012 Feb; 43(1): 3–24. DOI: https://doi.org/10.1177/0967010611431079.

4. Lokot T. Public networked discourses in the Ukraine-Russia conflict: 'Patriotic hackers' and digital populism. *Irish Studies in International Affairs.* 2017; 28(1): 99–116. DOI: https://doi.org/10.1353/isia.2017.0011.

5. Nakashima E. US government officially accuses Russia of hacking campaign to interfere with elections. *Washington Post.* 2016 Oct; p. 7.

6. Freelon D, Lokot T. Russian Twitter disinformation campaigns reach across the American political spectrum. *Misinformation Review.* 2020 Jan 6.

7. Gehlbach S, Lokot T, Shirikov A. The Russian media. In: Wengle S (ed.), *Russian politics today: Stability and fragility*. Cambridge: Cambridge University Press. 2022; 390–407. DOI: https://doi.org/10.1017/9781009165921.021.

8. Lokot T. Telegram: What's in an app? *PONARS Eurasia*. 2018 Nov 26 [cited 2023 Mar 1]. www.ponarseurasia.org/point-counter/telegram-whats-app.

9. Daucé F, Musiani F. Infrastructure-embedded control, circumvention and sovereignty in the Russian internet: An introduction. *First Monday*. 2021 May 1; 26(5). DOI: https://doi.org/10.5210/fm.v26i5.11685.

10. Epifanova A, Dietrich P. Russia's quest for digital sovereignty: Ambitions, realities, and its place in the world. *German Council on Foreign Relations*. 2022 Feb 21 [cited 2023 Mar 1]. https://dgap.org/sites/default/files/article_pdfs/DGAP-Analyse-2022-01-EN_0.pdf.

11. Lokot T. Unfreedom monitor: Russia country report. *Advox, Global Voices*. 2022 Aug 25 [cited 2023 Mar 1]. https://globalvoices.org/wp-content/uploads/2022/08/Unfreedom_Monitor_Russia_Country_Report_2022.pdf.

12. Greenberg A. The untold story of NotPetya, the most devastating cyberattack in history. *Wired*. 2018 Aug 22; 22.

13. Lin H. Russian cyber operations in the invasion of Ukraine. *Cyber Defense Review*. 2022 Oct 1; 7(4): 31–46.

14. Ermoshina K. 'Voices from the island': Informational annexation of Crimea and transformations of journalistic practices. *Journalism*. 2023 Jan 16. DOI: https://doi.org/10.1177/14648849231152359.

15. Boichak O, Lokot T. Billionaires won't save Ukraine's internet. *Foreign Policy*. 2022 Nov 20 [cited 2023 Mar 1]. https://foreignpolicy.com/2022/11/20/ukraine-russia-war-internet-musk-starlink-space-x/.

16. Boichak O. Digital war: Mediatized conflicts in sociological perspective. In: Rohlinger DA, Sobieraj S (eds.), The Oxford

17. Boichak O, Hoskins A. My war: Participation in warfare. *Digital War*. 2022 Dec 2; 1–8. DOI: https://doi.org/10.1057/s42984-022-00060-7.

18. Merrin W. Digital war: A critical introduction. London and New York: Routledge; 2018. DOI: https://doi.org/10.4324/9781315707624.

19. Sherman J. Cord-cutting, Russian style: Could the Kremlin sever global internet cables? *Atlantic Council*. 2022 Jan 31 [cited 2023 Mar 1]. https://www.atlanticcouncil.org/blogs/new-atlanticist/cord-cutting-russian-style-could-the-kremlin-sever-global-internet-cables/.

20. Bergengruen V. The battle for control over Ukraine's internet. *Time*. 2022 Oct 18 [cited 2023 Mar 1]. https://time.com/6222111/ukraine-internet-russia-reclaimed-territory/.

21. Netblocks. Internet disruptions registered as Russia moves in on Ukraine. *Netblocks*. 2022 Feb 24 [cited 2023 Mar 1]. https://netblocks.org/reports/internet-disruptions-registered-as-russia-moves-in-on-ukraine-W8op4k8K.

22. Vallance C. Ukraine war: Major internet provider suffers cyberattack. *BBC News*. 2022 Mar 28 [cited 2023 Mar 1]. https://www.bbc.com/news/60854881.

23. Beketova E. Behind the lines: Russia's occupation forces move to crush dissent. *Center for European Policy Analysis*. 2023 Mar 9 [cited 2023 Mar 1]. https://cepa.org/article/behind-the-lines-russias-occupation-forces-move-to-crush-dissent/.

24. Reporters Without Borders. In Ukraine's occupied zones, 'the Russians let us choose between collaboration, prison or death'. *Reporters Without Borders*. 2022 Aug 22 [cited 2023 Mar 1]. https://rsf.org/en/ukraine-s-occupied-zones-russians-let-us-choose-between-collaboration-prison-or-death.

(Note: item 16 continued) handbook of sociology and digital media. Oxford: Oxford University Press. 2020; 511–527. DOI: https://doi.org/10.1093/oxfordhb/9780197510636.013.31.

25. Smith B. Defending Ukraine: Early lessons from the cyber war. *Microsoft*. 2022 Jun 22 [cited 2023 Mar 1]. https://blogs.microsoft.com/on-the-issues/2022/06/22/defending-ukraine-early-lessons-from-the-cyber-war/.

26. Schectman J, Bing C, Pearson J. Ukrainian cyber resistance group targets Russian power grid, railways. *Reuters*. 2022 Mar 1 [cited 2023 Mar 1]. https://www.reuters.com/technology/ukrainian-cyber-resistance-group-targets-russian-power-grid-railways-2022-03-01/.

27. Schechner S. Cyberattacks don't appear to have increased in Ukraine war, EU says. *Wall Street Journal*. 2022 Mar 9 [cited 2023 Mar 1]. https://www.wsj.com/livecoverage/russia-ukraine-latest-news-2022-03-09/card/cyberattacks-don-t-appear-to-have-increased-so-far-in-ukraine-war-eu-says-mHV8L58ppVwINzQoQzpX.

28. Fedorov M. The village of Ivankiv, Kyiv region, right after RU occupation. *Twitter*. 2022 Apr 7 [cited 2023 Mar 1]. https://twitter.com/FedorovMykhailo/status/1512157048133275651.

29. European Commission. Supporting Ukraine through digital. *European Commission* [cited 2023 Mar 1]. https://digital-strategy.ec.europa.eu/en/policies/support-ukraine.

30. Mitchell R. How Amazon put Ukraine's 'government in a box' – and saved its economy from Russia. *Los Angeles Times*. 2022 Dec 15 [cited 2023 Mar 1]. https://www.latimes.com/business/story/2022-12-15/amazon-ukraine-war-cloud-data.

31. SSSCIP. Ukraine has signed an agreement on accession to the NATO Cooperative Cyber Defence Centre of Excellence. *State Service of Special Communications and Information Protection of Ukraine*. 2023 Jan 19 [cited 2023 Mar 1]. https://cip.gov.ua/en/news/ukrayina-pidpisala-ugodu-pro-priyednannya-do-ob-yednanogo-centru-peredovikh-tekhnologii-z-kiberoboroni-nato.

8. Ukraine's Decentralisation Reforms and the Path to Reconstruction, Recovery and European Integration

Tamara Krawchenko

The twin concepts of territorial cohesion and competitiveness have underpinned European integration and are fundamental to the development of robust democracies. They speak to the importance of reducing territorial inequalities and ensuring that all places deliver good livelihoods and well-being. Governments can strengthen subnational capacities to help deliver on these objectives through administrative, fiscal and political decentralisation and regional development. Driven by a strong, community-oriented social foundation, Ukraine has pursued this path. Since 2014, it has embarked on ambitious decentralisation, anti-corruption and regional development reforms, and progress has been made in a number of areas, such as service delivery, municipal finance and decision-making. Russia's full-scale invasion that began in February 2022 has disrupted the reforms and led to massive destruction, especially in Ukraine's eastern regions. Here I argue that the continuation of these reforms is critical for democracy, reconstruction, recovery and eventual European integration and that the future of the global order rests not just upon the success of countries but also on

> their constituent regions and communities. The international community has a central role to play in supporting such a place-based approach to territorial development.

Russia's invasion of Ukraine has directly challenged the rules-based international order. It violates the UN Charter and is an archetypal example of how authoritarian governments are emboldened across the globe, with the world suffering consecutive years of decline in global freedom [1]. Frustration at the rise of anti-democratic populism in democracies has increased attention on the role of interpersonal and territorial inequalities in fostering people's discontent with their government. Writing in the *LSE Public Policy Review*, Rodrigues-Pose has argued that the vote for anti-system parties is part of 'the revenge of the places that don't matter' and that their popularity stems from a mix of cultural and economic factors [2]. He and others have argued that place-based territorial investments are needed to reverse trends of decline in territories [3–5]. Others stress the importance of fostering a shared national identity based on liberal democratic values [6]. While the root causes of populism and discontent differ across countries and regions, economic inequality and a lack of government responsiveness to citizens' needs, values and identity appear to be central factors [7].

On these fronts, Ukraine is in the midst of transformation. The social movement flowing from the 2014 Revolution of Dignity demanded that Ukraine build a non-hierarchical community of fairness (*spravedlyvist*) [8]. The Euromaidan protests were sparked by student-led protests of the Ukrainian government's decision under President Yanukovych to suspend the signing of an association agreement with the European Union. Protestors were violently beaten by special units of the Ministry of Internal Affairs, leading to widespread discontent at the corrupt policies of the Yanukovych Government and its authoritarian practices and violation of human rights [9]. President Yanukovych's government killed over 100 protestors; he then fled to Russia in February 2014, the same month that Russia occupied Crimea. In August 2014, regular units of the Russian army crossed the border in eastern Ukraine and together with pro-Russian separatists occupied the Donetsk and Lugansk regions. Ukraine then held parliamentary elections, and there was a political imperative to meet the demands of the Euromaidan social movement – among these, democratic/anti-corruption reforms and territorial development.

Ukraine's 2014 decentralisation reforms took place in this context, amidst a challenging environment while parts of the country were under Russian invasion and occupation. And yet, they have been one of the most successful areas of reform to date, introduced alongside efforts to strengthen regional development [10]. Such decentralisation reflects Ukrainian social organisation and also serves to discourage or prevent regional pushes for more autonomy that could further undermine Ukraine's territorial integrity [11]. However, what some may view as a policy deterring further fracturing of Ukrainian territory, others see as supplementing Russia-sponsored separatist ideals. For example, Barbieri argues that Ukraine's decentralisation process also carries risks to Ukrainian unity. In handing greater independence to regions like the Donbas, it aids Russia's claims to sovereignty over the region, fracturing Ukraine's sense of geographic identity. The consequence of this in the Donbas was the granting of 'special status' to Donbas as part of the Minsk process, which postponed decentralisation-related constitutional amendments [12].

Russia's full-scale invasion in February 2022 disrupted the implementation of decentralisation reforms and has caused massive destruction, especially in Ukraine's eastern regions. Despite this, the continuation of these reforms is critical for Ukraine's democracy, reconstruction and eventual European integration. Discussions of the global order tend to focus on nations, their connections, interests and conflicts, but this state-centric view has recently been challenged by the world politics of *heterarchy* – 'the coexistence and conflict between differently structured micro- and meso- quasi-hierarchies' within the state [13]. From this view, policymaking is complex, multi-actor, multilevel, multi-nodal and, as such, less state-centric. This lens raises the importance of the regions and communities, their identities and their values for the future of the global order. As such, the twin concepts of territorial cohesion and competitiveness that have underpinned European integration and internal development remain as relevant as ever – decentralisation, territorial development and effective place-based policies are critical to delivering on these objectives. In Ukraine, these concepts converge with the need for a place-based approach to reconstruction and recovery, and the international community has a major role to play in supporting this process. This chapter draws in part on research conducted by the Organisation for Economic Cooperation and Development in Ukraine: the *OECD Territorial Review of Ukraine* (2014), *Maintaining the Momentum of Decentralisation in Ukraine* (2018) and *Rebuilding Ukraine by Reinforcing Regional and Municipal Governance* (2022).

Governance, Identity, Trust and the Social Fabric

In an overview of the territorial-administrative governance models of independent Ukraine, Kataryna Wolczuk notes that 'at first sight, Ukraine is custom-made for far-reaching regionalisation or even federalism' [14]. There are strong regional identities in Ukraine comprising diverse ethno-linguistic, economic, cultural and political identities – even if the boundaries of these regional identities are sometimes fluid. Yet, for much of its history, political organisation in independent Ukraine has largely been out of step with this – hierarchal and centralised, with little authority at the local levels. Following independence in 1991, Ukraine maintained aspects of the centralised governance model of the Ukrainian Soviet Socialist Republic (UkrSSR). Such a centralised model stands in contrast to Ukraine's indigenous traditions of governance that tended towards federalism and decentralisation in intellectual thought and practice [14].

In the early years of independence, there were debates about the merits of different territorial-administrative models and how to balance regional interests against the need for a unified political entity. This led to an ambiguous declaration in the 1996 constitution that the territorial structure of Ukraine 'is based upon the principles of unity (*yednist*) and cohesion (*tsilisnist*) of state territory and the combination of centralisation and decentralisation in the exercise of state power' (Art. 132). In 1997, the Law on Local Self-Government in Ukraine led to the creation of directly elected *oblast* (region) and *raion* (district) councils, but fiscal decisions remained largely centralised. Oblast and raion levels of government were not aligned with the EU Charter of Local Self-Government, which advocates an application of basic rules guaranteeing the political, administrative and financial independence of subnational authorities [15]. Moreover, the administrative regions established under the UkrSSR were retained. These bore little resemblance to historical regions, lacking meaning for the people who lived under them. At the very local level, there were many villages, towns and municipalities – many with limited administrative capacities. At the subnational level, Crimea was a special case. It was made an autonomous parliamentary republic within Ukraine, governed by the Constitution of Crimea in accordance with the laws of Ukraine.

The government's post-2014 decentralisation reforms represented a clear break with the model of centralised state authority that had flourished under Yanukovych [16]. For Ukraine, political-administrative organisation is not just a matter of recognising and accommodating regional identities but rather acknowledging governance arrangements in which the society organises itself. This organising principle was particularly apparent during the Euromaidan social movement, which was leaderless and self-organising with volunteer battalions and grassroots aid organisations [8]. These features of Ukrainian society make decentralisation and local/regional development intrinsic to its polity. Decentralisation reforms should therefore not be viewed as an outcome of the Revolution of Dignity but rather as part of the very reason that they have been successful in the first place. This civic orientation is only strengthening.

A cross-sectional survey conducted between 19 and 24 May 2022 reveals that the values of civic nationalism, democracy and civic duty are strengthening alongside an increase in pro-EU orientations which 'outpaces any ethno-linguistic identification patterns and maps onto civic identities which were already strong in the country prior to Russia's invasion' [17].

Russia's invasion has highlighted the resilience of Ukraine's social fabric and the nature of social trust, even resulting in the local civilian organisation of defence [18]. Analyses of social cohesion prior to 2022 indicated low trust in state institutions but a strong sense of belonging both at a local and a national level, as well as relatively high trust in local leaders [19]. In a nationally representative public opinion survey conducted in December 2022, the Armed Forces of Ukraine is now the most trusted social institution, followed by the president of Ukraine, volunteers and then ordinary people, respectively [20]. High trust in the president is a major reversal from the previous year (from 21% in December 2021 to 84% in 2022). Recent research has also identified the positive effects of the decentralisation reforms with respect to strengthening social cohesion in Ukraine [21]. Finally, Ukraine is increasingly committed to democratic development – 95% percent of respondents to an August 2022 nationwide poll indicated that it is 'very important' or 'important' for them that Ukraine becomes a fully functioning democracy (an increase from 76% the previous year) [22]. Democratic values, civic identity, and social trust in others and in volunteers are only strengthening. This is important to keep in mind as reforms are considered.

Ukraine's Decentralisation Reforms and Regional Development

Proponents of decentralisation argue that local and regional governments are closer to the people and are better placed to understand and respond to local needs. For example, Oates's seminal work advocates that decentralisation can lead to more cost-effective public service provision [23]. Local jurisdictions compete to attract residents and businesses, leading to more responsive and flexible governments, fewer layers of bureaucracy and greater opportunities for innovation and experimentation in public services provision [23]. Beyond this presumed allocative efficiency, decentralisation is claimed by some to promote accountability and reduce corruption in government [24].

Critics point out that shifting services to the local level can lead to the deterioration of service provision and to increased costs due to diseconomies of scale, the duplication of responsibility and services and higher administrative overheads. In practice, decentralisation is a multidimensional concept spanning political, administrative and fiscal elements, and the context in which it takes place is important. Decentralisation can entail: i) *delegation*, wherein some decision-making and administrative authority for well-defined tasks is transferred from the central government to semi-autonomous lower-level units; ii) *devolution*, wherein the central government transfers authority for decision-making, finance/taxation and administration to regional or local governments; and iii) *deconcentration*, where there is a geographic displacement of power from the central government to units based in regions (deconcentrated state services) [25]. Where decentralisation occurs without adequate resourcing, the ability of subnational governments to carry out their mandate is undermined. Thus, it is not enough to look at which level of government is tasked to deliver services. It is also necessary to consider the contexts in which they operate and the resources that they receive from higher-level governments alongside the authority capacity and power that they have in performing their duties.

Ukraine's decentralisation strategy was outlined in the 2014 *Concept Framework of Reform of Local Self-Government and the Territorial Organisation of Power in Ukraine.* The framework called for increased democratic governance at the subnational levels that spanned all three areas of decentralisation: political, administrative and fiscal [26]. The framework is being implemented through new legislation and regulation and reforms to existing legislation (e.g., budget and tax codes), and the regional development policy framework is evolving. Concurrently, Ukraine's 2015 law On the Principles of State Regional Policy established key concepts and regional development programmes and projects and introduced a set of planning instruments (e.g., the State Strategy for Regional Development, as well as oblast and municipal development strategies). In an effort to increase local capacity, voluntary municipal mergers were launched between 2015 and 2020, financial incentives were provided to amalgamate (expanded own-source revenues) and new funding was made available for regional and local development. Moreover, municipalities gained the right to negotiate annual municipal budgets with the oblast state administration. As a result of the reforms, over 4882 municipalities merged to form 1070 amalgamated municipalities (unified territorial communities) by mid 2020. A second mandatory stage of amalgamations followed. In the end, Ukraine went from a total of 10,000 municipalities to a total of 1469.

Results from a 2021 OECD survey of Ukraine municipalities demonstrate that decentralisation reforms have had a positive effect on the administrative, human resource and fiscal capacities of municipalities, as well as on service quality.[1] At the same time, many municipalities, particularly rural ones, indicate that they lack the human resource capacity to carry out key strategic planning, public investment and budgeting tasks. Implementation has not always generated municipalities with sufficient capacity to meet the challenges of decentralised local governance. Despite the reforms, there remains some confusion over the division of public service and of administration responsibilities at the subnational level, while there are inequalities in public service quality, type and access at the local level. Ongoing work is needed to clearly assign responsibilities among levels of government, strengthen centre-of-government practices and strengthen dialogue mechanisms across and among levels of government [10].

In the preceding decade, Ukraine's performance in several strands of development significantly improved. For example, between 2015 and 2019, the share of the population living below the nationally defined subsistence income level fell by over half, from 52% to 23% [27]. On other metrics, however, territorial disparities have grown, and inequalities have deepened over the past decade. For example, all but two oblasts and Kyiv City have witnessed population declines, and the national economy has become increasingly dependent on the Kyiv agglomeration, with other regions lagging behind [27]. Russia's war has only deepened the territorial disparities, with widespread destruction, urbicide (the erasure of entire cities/communities) and massive internal displacement and outmigration. In this context, local capacity and regional development take on even more critical and yet hugely challenging roles.

Immediately after the full-scale invasion began on 24 February 2022, Ukraine declared martial law and facilitated the creation of oblast, rayon and municipal military administrations. Legislation was swiftly introduced to clarify the powers and responsibilities of subnational governments under martial law, giving them additional powers to transfer funds from local budgets to the armed forces and to inspect buildings and other infrastructure damaged by the war. Local governments and communities have been actively involved in the organisation of defence through territorial defence forces, of which there are thousands of civilian volunteers. They have also supported the war effort in other ways – e.g., registering internally displaced people at administrative service centres, as well as co-ordinating the distribution of humanitarian aid. As some have commented, Russia's full-scale invasion was a test of decentralisation, and local governments have proved themselves responsive, agile and competent [28]. Despite the fact that Russia continues its war, Ukraine is already thinking about reconstruction and recovery and the path to European integration. There are robust debates among political leadership, civil society, labour unions and academia about the way forward.

Reconstruction, Recovery and European Integration

Russia's war has been brutally destructive. As of December 2022, the total amount of documented damage to Ukraine's infrastructure is estimated at USD137.8 billion (at replacement cost), and it is growing daily [29]. There are more than 8 million Ukrainian refugees in Europe, over 17 million people are in urgent need of humanitarian assistance in Ukraine and 5 million are internally displaced [34]. Some municipalities have doubled or tripled in population, while others have declined dramatically or no longer exist at all. Local leaders in occupied areas have been abducted, tortured and killed. The war is widening gaps between territories, with some municipalities administratively hollowed out and destroyed, while others face new pressures due to population displacement. Local governments are challenged to maintain functions over wartime while planning for the types of skills that the labour force will need for reconstruction efforts, now and in the future. Capacity sharing and collaboration take on renewed importance amidst these challenges.

Donor governments are already developing mechanisms to support Ukraine's rebuilding and recovery. Within the EU, the Multi-agency Donor Coordination Platform was established in January 2023 to coordinate financial resources, implementation, monitoring and accountability. The EU's plan for longer-term reconstruction notes that it will be led by Ukrainian authorities together with the EU and other partners and will include partnerships between cities and regions. A place-based approach to reconstruction and recovery will necessarily underpin this approach, and as such, Ukraine's decentralisation and regional development reforms become all the more important. Adopting a constitutional amendment that replaces oblast (region) and rayon state administrations with a system of prefects, as Ukraine has been discussing at length in parliament, would be valuable. It could help the country strengthen local administrative supervision and facilitate the coordination of national-level priorities at the municipal level. Dialogue between national and subnational levels of government has been limited, as key coordination bodies (e.g., the Inter-Departmental Co-ordination Commission for Regional Development and the Congress of Local and Regional Authorities) have either not been fully operational or lack the systematic participation of municipal governments [27].

Oversight will be particularly important during the recovery period given the expected inflow of recovery funding and the pressure on municipalities to allocate resources swiftly, efficiently and effectively. At the same time, efforts to strengthen oversight should not necessarily increase administrative control or burden and need not undermine municipal autonomy or restrain municipal decision-making. Ukrainian lawmakers are considering the creation of prefects, which could oversee the legality of municipal decisions. However, this proposed reform cannot be adopted as long as martial law is place (no constitutional amendments can be made under martial law).

Russia's invasion has deepened territorial inequalities, which can undermine democratic governance. Yet, it has simultaneously solidified Ukrainian identity as a civic nation and demonstrated the resilience of the social fabric at the community level. Reconstruction and recovery efforts should be grounded in place-based need and development goals and broader community networks that are Ukraine's strength. A regional development approach is already foundational to EU Cohesion Policy – it is how it delivers many of its objectives. As such, Ukraine's reforms in this direction are compatible with the policy and are promising as the country seeks further European integration and eventually membership. Yet, there are risks that existing territorial inequalities grow more entrenched. Cities like Lviv, which are far removed from the front line and have strong local capacity, enjoy more auspicious starting conditions for growth and prosperity, while those that have been decimated in the eastern regions may require much greater support and central government interventions. It can be easier for investments to flow where there is already local capacity and the risk of elite capture. Liberated Crimea, Donetsk and Luhansk will likely be governed under military administration for a time. How can such administrations ensure that local populations feel they are an important part of the recovery process while materially improving their lives? Rebuilding can also tend to focus on physical assets and ignore the need for social investments, which may be of equal importance.

Reconstruction and recovery will involve a multitude of actors, and Ukraine's mighty civil society and labour unions need to be involved. Since the war, civil society actors and regular people have worked through informal networks to deliver aid and other supports. As new programmes are designed, there needs to be a way for these civil society groups to converge and to adopt greater formality. This would enable them to receive government funds in support of recovery and to have formal reporting for accountability. Labour unions and workers more generally must be meaningfully involved in and benefit from reconstruction and recovery efforts. There are already concerns that Ukrainian authorities have launched privatisation programmes and dismantled labour legislation, such as rights for workers at small and medium-sized companies under wartime measures and the legalisation of zero-hours contracts [30].

Reconstruction and recovery will also involve a wide number of external actors. Municipal governments in the West have pledged assistance, as have hundreds of private companies, philanthropists and others. While bilateral and multilateral assistance will be a major source of funding, there are many other types of donors and expertise and multiple connections across scales. This too is a strength, remaking Ukraine's global connections and relations. For example, initiatives such as the 'yurts of invincibility' set up by Kazakh businessman Daulet Nurzhanov have provided warmth and refuge in cities across Ukraine – a form of private aid representing solidarity in the face of Russian colonialism.

Given that the costs of reconstruction have been estimated at around €383 billion in early 2023, there is an urgent need to strengthen subnational government capabilities to efficiently and effectively absorb and manage reconstruction funds [31]. This can be done by introducing legislative amendments to ensure open and merit-based recruitment, performance management and appraisal processes, as well as a political neutrality requirement for local civil servants. In addition, the government could establish a reconstruction and recovery training strategy for municipal civil servants, building skills in strategic planning, budgeting and financial and investment management supported by initiatives to exchange experiences, tools and methodologies among Ukrainian municipalities and with local authorities abroad.

Rebuilding civic institutions and channels to reach and engage communities in the design of new plans and programmes will be critical. Doing so helps direct resources where they can have the most impact and build trust in the reconstruction process and government more generally. Ukraine starts from a strong base: a recent survey found that Ukrainian municipalities enjoy the highest level of public trust in government, after public institutions directly responsible for security [32]. Here Ukraine could look to develop guidelines and provide training on mechanisms to inform, consult, involve, collaborate and/or empower stakeholders and make municipal budget information – including on revenues and expenditures for recovery projects – more easily accessible and understandable to the public.

Finally, Ukraine should consider building and strengthening systems to manage and monitor the use of recovery funding and tackle corruption. This will help ensure that funds, which are already being provided as part of relief and rehabilitation efforts, are well spent. This can be achieved by designing and implementing citizen-based accountability mechanisms, such as participatory budgeting and public expenditure tracking, and establishing citizen advisory boards and digital platforms to enable the public to track recovery funds and projects. In doing so, Ukraine can build on the digital infrastructure it established prior to the February 2022 invasion, in particular the mobile DIIA application and online portal that provides citizens with digital access to many government services and enables Ukrainians to engage with the government in an online one-stop shop [33].

Conclusion

Ukraine has found itself at the centre of global relations today – its flag raised in solidarity across democracies worldwide. At the same time, Ukrainian society has coalesced and strengthened around a civic national identity grounded in bottom-up social organisation. Ukrainians are paying a very high price to defend their nation, and the social contract is clear: there is no tolerance for corruption, and expectations for the government to deliver reconstruction and recovery are high. The Ukrainian government will need to deliver infrastructure, services, stability and economic development at all levels, which means working with the subnational authorities and listening to communities. There is a strong desire to join the EU and to rebuild those regions that have been destroyed. The future accession of Ukraine to the EU would be made possible, at least in part, because of the success of its decentralisation and regional development reforms, which might serve as an impetus for reinforcing local self-governance and place-based development throughout the EU. The international community has a central role to play in supporting such an approach to territorial development, and these global-local connections can be seen as part of a global politics of heterarchy that can help to strengthen democratic solidarity at a time when it seems so vulnerable.

Acknowledgements

This research has been informed by the OECD's research on regional and local government in Ukraine led by Maria Varinia Michalun, Head of the Governance and Strategic Planning Unit in the Regional Development and Multi-level Governance Division of the Centre for Entrepreneurship, SMEs, Regions and Cities (CFE), and policy analysts Stephan Visser and Geoff Upton. The author is grateful for their comments and review. All opinions, errors and omissions expressed are the author's alone.

The author is a regular consultant with the Organisation for Economic Co-operation and Development and a former OECD official (2015–2019). She was a contributing author to the 2022 OECD study *Rebuilding Ukraine by Reinforcing Regional and Municipal Governance* led by Maria Varinia Michalun, Head of the Governance and Strategic Planning Unit in the Regional Development and Multi-level Governance Division of the Centre for Entrepreneurship, SMEs, Regions and Cities (CFE), and policy analysts Stephan Visser and Geoff Upton.

Note

[1] The online survey of Ukrainian municipalities was conducted in 2021. In total, 741 municipalities, covering 119 rayons, as well as 24 oblasts and Kyiv City completed the survey, resulting in a highly representative sample (over 50%).

References

1. Freedom House. The global expansion of authoritarian rule. Freedom House. 2022 [cited 2023 March 14]. https://freedomhouse.org/report/freedom-world/2022/global-expansion-authoritarian-rule.

2. Rodríguez-Pose A. The rise of populism and the revenge of the places that don't matter. *LSE Public Policy Review*. 2020; 1(1): 1–9. http://ppr.lse.ac.uk/articles/10.31389/lseppr.4/. DOI: https://doi.org/10.31389/lseppr.4.

3. Dijkstra L, Poelman H, Rodríguez-Pose A. The geography of EU discontent. *Regional Studies*. 2019; 54(6): 737–753. DOI: https://doi.org/10.1080/00343404.2019.1654603.

4. International Monetary Fund. Closer together or further apart? Within-country regional disparities and adjustment in advanced economies. In: International Monetary Fund, World economic outlook: Global manufacturing downturn, rising trade barriers. Washington, DC: IMF. 2019; 65–88.

5. McCann P. Perceptions of regional inequality and the geography of discontent: Insights from the UK. *Regional Studies*. 2019; 54(2): 256–267. DOI: https://doi.org/10.1080/00343404.2019.1619928.

6. Velasco A. Populism and identity politics. *LSE Public Policy Review*. 2020; 1(1): 1–8. DOI: https://doi.org/10.31389/lseppr.1.

7. Lombardo R, Ricotta F. Individual trust and quality of regional government. *Journal of Institutional Economics*. 2022; 18(5): 745–766. DOI: https://doi.org/10.1017/S1744137421000801.

8. Wynnyckyj M. Unravelling the Ukrainian revolution: 'Dignity,' 'fairness,' 'heterarchy,' and the challenge to modernity. *Kyiv-Mohyla Humanit J*. 2020; 7(7): 123–140. http://kmhj.ukma.edu.ua/article/view/219663. DOI: https://doi.org/10.18523/kmhj219663.2020-7.123-140.

9. Shveda Y, Park JH. Ukraine's revolution of dignity: The dynamics of Euromaidan. *Journal of Eurasian Studies*. 2016; 7(1): 85–91. DOI: https://doi.org/10.1016/j.euras.2015.10.007.

10. OECD. Maintaining the momentum of decentralisation in Ukraine. Paris: OECD; 2018. https://www.oecd-ilibrary.org/urban-rural-and-regional-development/maintaining-the-momentum-of-decentralisation-in-ukraine_9789264301436-en.

11. Shelest H, Rabinovych M. Decentralization, regional diversity, and conflict. *Decentralization, Regional Diversity, and Conflict*. 2020; 1–378. DOI: https://doi.org/10.1007/978-3-030-41765-9_1.

12. Barbieri J. The dark side of decentralization reform in Ukraine: Deterring or facilitating Russia-sponsored separatism? *Decentralization, Regional Diversity, and Conflict*. 2020; 211–256.

https://link.springer.com/chapter/10.1007/978-3-030-41765-9_8. DOI: https://doi.org/10.1007/978-3-030-41765-9_8.

13. Cerny PG. Heterarchy in world politics. London: Routledge; 2022. https://www.taylorfrancis.com/books/9781003352617. DOI: https://doi.org/10.4324/9781003352617.

14. Wolczuk K. Catching up with 'Europe'? Constitutional debates on the territorial-administrative model in independent Ukraine. *Regional & Federal Studies*. 2010; 12(2): 65–88. https://www.tandfonline.com/doi/abs/10.1080/714004750. DOI: https://doi.org/10.1080/714004750.

15. European Commission. European charter of local self-government. Treaty No. 122; 1988 [cited 2023 April 4]. p. 1–6. https://www.coe.int/en/web/conventions/full-list?module=treaty-detail&treatynum=122.

16. Kudelia S. The sources of continuity and change of Ukraine's incomplete state. *Communist Post-Communist Studies*. 2012; 45(3–4): 417–428. DOI: https://doi.org/10.1016/j.postcomstud.2012.06.006.

17. Onuch O. European Ukrainians and their fight against Russian invasion. *Nations and Nationalism*. 2023; 29(1): 53–62. DOI: https://doi.org/10.1111/nana.12883.

18. Volodmyrovych VD, Tyshchenko M. Direct from Bucha: How self-organisation, leadership initiatives and social cohesion saves Ukraine and will lead to victory (Part 1 of 2). Mansklig Sakerhet; 2022 [cited 2023 March 25]. https://manskligsakerhet.se/2022/05/26/direct-from-bucha-how-self-organisation-leadership-initiatives-and-social-cohesion-saves-ukraine-and-will-lead-to-victory-part-1-of-2/.

19. Aasland A, Deineko O, Filippova O, Kropp S. Citizens' perspectives: Reform and social cohesion in Ukraine's border regions. *The Accommodation of Regional and Ethno-cultural Diversity in Ukraine*. 2021; 237–272. https://link.springer.com/chapter/10.1007/978-3-030-80971-3_9. DOI: https://doi.org/10.1007/978-3-030-80971-3_9.

20. Hrudka O. Trust in Ukraine's president increased three-fold in 2022; Army still most trusted institution. Euromaidan Press; 2023 [cited 2023 March 25]. https://euromaidanpress.com/2023/01/13/trust-in-ukraines-president-increased-three-fold-in-2022-army-still-most-trusted-institution-poll/.

21. Deineko O, Aasland A. Ukrainian society under conditions of war: A strong force of social cohesion. Forum for Ukrainian Studies; 2022 [cited 2023 March 14]. https://ukrainian-studies.ca/2022/04/02/ukrainian-society-under-conditions-of-war-a-strong-force-of-social-cohesion/.

22. National Democratic Institute: Ukraine: Optimism soars despite brutal war. 2022 September 19 [cited 2023 April 4]. p. 1–2. https://www.ndi.org/our-stories/ukraine-optimism-soars-despite-brutal-war.

23. Oates WE. Fiscal federalism. New York: Edward Elgar Publishing; 1972.

24. Ostrom E, Schroeder L, Wynne S. Institutional incentives and sustainable development: Infrastructure policies in perspective. Abingdon, UK: Routledge; 1993.

25. OECD. Making decentralisation work: A handbook for policy-makers. Paris: OECD Publishing; 2019. https://www.oecd-ilibrary.org/governance/making-decentralisation-work-in-chile_9789264279049-en.

26. Cabinet of Ministers of Ukraine. Concept framework of reform of local self-government and the territorial organisation of power in Ukraine. Kyiv, Ukraine: Supreme Council of Ukraine; 2014. https://zakon.rada.gov.ua/laws/show/333-2014-p#Text.

27. OECD. Rebuilding Ukraine by reinforcing regional and municipal governance. Paris: OECD Publishing; 2022. https://www.oecd-ilibrary.org/urban-rural-and-regional-development/rebuilding-ukraine-by-reinforcing-regional-and-municipal-governance_63a6b479-en.

28. Bezhin V. Країна громад в умовах війни. Яким був 2022-й для децентралізації та місцевого самоврядування [The country of communities in conditions of war. What was 2022 for decentralisation and local self-government]. Lb.UA. 2022 [cited 2023 March 26]. p. 1–5. https://lb.ua/news/2022/12/28/540561_kraina_gromad_umovah_viyni_yakim_buv.html.

29. Kyiv School of Economics. The total amount of damage caused to Ukraine's infrastructure due to the war has increased to almost $138 billion. Kyiv School of Economics; 2023 [cited 2022 July 12]. https://kse.ua/about-the-school/news/direct-damage-caused-to-ukraine-s-infrastructure-during-the-war-is-103-9-bln-due-to-the-last-estimates/.

30. Open Democracy. Ukraine passes anti-worker law 5371; 2022 [cited 2023 May 2]. p. 1–5. https://www.opendemocracy.net/en/odr/ukraine-labour-law-wrecks-workers-rights/.

31. World Bank. Updated Ukraine recovery and reconstruction needs assessment; 2023 [cited 2023 May 23]. https://www.worldbank.org/en/news/press-release/2023/03/23/updated-ukraine-recovery-and-reconstruction-needs-assessment.

32. Keudel O, Huss O. National security in local hands? How local authorities contribute to Ukraine's resilience – PONARS Eurasia. Ponars Eurasia; 2023 [cited 2023 May 23]. https://www.ponarseurasia.org/national-security-in-local-hands-how-local-authorities-contribute-to-ukraines-resilience/.

33. Ukraine.ua. Digital country; 2023 [cited 2023 May 23]. https://ukraine.ua/invest-trade/digitalization/.

34. UNHRC. Operational data portal: Ukraine refugee situation; 2022. https://data2.unhcr.org/en/situations/ukraine.

PART 3
Impact

9. Uprooting and Borders: The Digital Architecture of the Ukrainian Refugee Crisis

Myria Georgiou and Marek Troszyński

> This essay situates the Ukrainian refugee crisis within the politics of the border, and particularly its digital architecture. Increasingly, we illustrate here, decisions about the right to protection are managed digitally. From data, drones, and AI technologies that are mobilised to control territories and to only selectively allow safe passage, to media representations that symbolically regulate public conversation by making certain refugees visible and others invisible, digital technologies have become fundamental to the politics and policies of refuge. Taking the growing role of communication technologies in managing and representing forced migration and the right to protection, this analysis calls for closer attention to the digital architecture of the border. By doing so, we can better understand how technologies that enable Ukrainian refugees to seek safety, as well as to have their flight represented in the media, become crucial components of their refugee rights' realisation and their welcome in receiving countries.

Russia's invasion of Ukraine has not only devastated the country, but has uprooted enormous numbers of people. More than eight million Ukrainians, almost a fifth of the country's population, have been forced to seek refuge in Europe [1]. But recording these inconceivable numbers of displaced people only offers a partial glimpse into the vast scale of the humanitarian crisis caused by the war in Ukraine. The first months of the invasion saw over 19 million people forced to leave their homes. They sought respite in western Ukraine and in neighbouring countries. Although almost half of this population has returned, many still have no safe home to return to. The ongoing ordeal facing Ukrainian refugees is the result of war. Yet, the ways it is understood and managed is a matter of communication and the technologies that enable the circulation of information but also of safe passage.

The story of Ukrainian refugees is one of humanitarian disaster. It is also a national crisis within a global refugee crisis. Ukrainians' displacement reflects one of the most brutal faces of war, but it also represents a striking reminder of what makes (or unmakes) refugees. Not only a violent uprooting, but also decisions made about the border – who can cross and who cannot – shape what we now understand as refugee crises across the world. In fact, if we observe how national and regional policies unequally, and often conditionally, distribute the right to seek and find protection, we can see how some among those fleeing war can cross borders into safety, while many others are denied this right.

This essay situates the Ukrainian refugee crisis within the politics of the border, and particularly its digital architecture. Increasingly, we illustrate here, decisions about the right to protection are managed digitally. From data, drones, and AI technologies that are mobilised to control territories and to only selectively allow safe passage, to media representations that symbolically regulate public conversation by making certain refugees visible and others invisible, digital technologies have become fundamental to the politics and policies of refuge. Taking the growing role of communication technologies in managing and representing migration and the right to refuge, this analysis argues for the need to pay closer attention to the digital architecture of the border. By doing so, we can better understand how technologies that enable Ukrainian refugees to seek safety, as well as to have their flight represented in the media, become crucial components of their refugee rights' realisation and their welcome in receiving countries.

As every refugee knows, the right to cross territories and to find protection is not to be taken for granted. While the Refugee Convention recognises the universality of this right, policies across many western countries are currently introduced to reduce this precise universality. The essay examines how Ukrainian refugees, once uprooted, have been able to find safety, dignity, and prospective settlement in arrival countries and how their experience relates to wider systems of communication and technological control of transnational mobility. We examine this issue by identifying how the technologies of the border shape policies and public perceptions of the Ukrainian refugee crisis, but also of refugee crises more globally. Specifically, we examine the relationship between forced migration and the technologies that, on the one hand, regulate the border territorially (databases, AI technologies, drones, which aim to control who crosses across nation-states), and on the other, the technologies that regulate the border symbolically (social media and online news media that regulate refugees' access to western publics through fair representations, or denies them that access through hostile representations). As we will show, the territorial and symbolic dimensions of the border are entangled as each plays its role in regulating, respectively, bodies and perceptions on migration.

The essay is organised in two main parts. The first part focusses on the transnational and national entanglement of policymaking and of media. Together, we show that policies and particular media representations circulated across western news media and social media enable opportunities for Ukrainian refugees' protection; however, we see that these are often exceptional and contingent opportunities. This section draws on research conducted between 2015 and 2022 across Europe and discusses media narratives and technologies of cross-border mobility control [2, 3, 4]. The essay's second part moves from macro-scale processes to the micro-scale of Ukrainian refugee reception on a regional and a local level. Understanding the condition and recognition of refugees, we argue, requires the analysis of the relationship between media narratives and decision-making, as well of the experience of refugees themselves on the ground. This section draws on fieldwork that we conducted across the borders of Ukraine and Poland in spring 2022. The essay concludes by interrogating western responses to the Ukrainian refugee crisis, emphasising the need for refugee recognition beyond discriminatory and ephemeral acts of protection.

Making and Unmaking Refugee Crises: National and Transnational Digital Entanglements

The Ukrainian refugee crisis is devastating on a local and a global scale. The Ukrainians' displacement needs to be understood in the context of the war but also within the global realities of forced migration. Currently, human displacement has reached an unprecedented scale in post-war times, with more than 117 million people forced to leave their homes because of war, disaster and destitution in 2022 [1]. Among them, 29.3 million have crossed an international border and are recognised refugees, while another 5.6 million are recorded as asylum seekers [1]. Others are displaced within their country of origin (61.2 million). Many, however, receive no status at all, denied recognition as refugees or even as asylum seekers. These people still need and deserve protection, though evidence shows that many fleeing extreme violence in Sudan, Yemen, Myanmar, but also Syria and Afghanistan, are now pushed back when trying to reach Europe [5]. We are living at a time of extraordinary displacement, exacerbated by extraordinarily unequal access to protection.

The flight of Ukrainian refugees, unlike the case of many others fleeing war or who are otherwise uprooted, generated a swift response across the West. Immediately after the Russian invasion of Ukraine, and for the first time in its history, the European Union activated the Temporary Protection Directive [6], while the UK established its Home for Ukrainians scheme [7]. Both schemes, which resembled many enacted across the West, aimed to ease the migration of Ukrainians as well as to address the significant scale of Ukrainian suffering. For instance, EU measures relaxed the restrictions of the Dublin Treaty, which require those seeking asylum to do so at first point of entry – a treaty that has generated unevenness on the scale of responsibility for migrants seeking settlement across EU states. In the case of Ukrainian refugees, prioritising values of shared responsibility meant that countries in the EU, and in other western states, opened their doors to almost 19 million people. At least temporarily, those arriving from Ukraine after the start from the war benefitted from the suspension of the otherwise highly controlled territorial border and its technologies that usually deter potential migrants from crossing into the EU.

The stringent territorial border policies have been largely suspended for Ukrainian refugees. No passports are necessary for Ukrainians fleeing to leave their home country and enter a neighbouring country. But this does not mean the suspension has been unconditional or with a view to long-term strategies of reception and resettlement. Even during the early days of the war, EU countries receiving Ukrainian refugees refused to fully suspend their surveillance technologies at crossing points into the EU. The consequence of this was that thousands had to wait in freezing temperatures while authorities turned to transnational databases, passport and biometric records, to identify them as rightful or not claimants of protection [8]. Polish authorities, for example, insisted on the need to keep thorough data profiles of those crossing, arguably to avoid irregular migration. The stringent and temporary suspension of the rigid border included more exceptions: Ukrainians leaving their countries even days before the war started had no rights to the protection enabled by the EU Temporary Protection Directive, while others born in the country but without legal documentation (e.g. stateless Roma people) were also excluded. Such measures revealed 'Europe's double standards for refugees' [9] expressed in racial profiling of people seeking to cross. Also, significant discrimination against non-white people uprooted from Ukraine, including African students, was reported at the time [10]. Opening the territorial border was a decision that stood in stark contradiction to the reinforcement of military and digital surveillance that sought to deter non-Ukrainian refugees at all cost from crossing into the EU [11]. 'In the midst of conflict, racism has once again emerged as pervasive and pernicious, exacerbating Ukraine's humanitarian crisis', Bajaj and Cody Stanford have noted [12]. To sum up, it is clear that the Ukrainians' experience of being a refugee is strikingly unique. Against this exception, western governments' primary focus remains on deterring those seeking to cross from entering their territories, and increasingly do so by mobilising digital technologies, including drones and AI technologies that aim to surveil and predict people's movement and stop them even before approaching their borders. For example, the UK spent almost a billion pounds buying high-tech drone technologies to deter those who try to cross the English Channel [13].

Deterring refugees, in part through rigidly enforcing the border, now reflects a core element of migration governance across the world. The Transnational Institute reveals how 'the border industry' [14] has grown globally in recent years, promising targetted responses to what it considers as migration induced threats. Resisting widely imposed cuts in public spending across the west, Transnational Institute notes, the 'border industry' is predicted to grow annually by 7.2–8.6%, with the estimated $65 billion spending primarily directed to AI (artificial intelligence) and biometrics technologies. Such substantial investments into technological control of migration emerge as an almost inevitable response to two converging beliefs in current policy and media narratives across the west – that migration is a threat, and that technology has an answer to the problem.

In this climate, the suspension of territorial border restrictions could not have been possible without the suspension of the symbolic border [4]. The symbolic border is constituted through narratives that circulate across news platforms and social media. These narratives often activate reductive formulas of incompatible binaries, presenting the needs or demands of refugee populations as being at odds with the interests of the citizens of the country where refuge is sought [4]. These narratives include the wide and persistent construction of migration through binaries that emphasise the incompatibility of categories of 'us' (citizens) and 'them' (racialised migrants), or of 'deserving refugees' versus 'undeserving migrants'.

In the case of Ukrainian refugees, we have often seen the suspension of the symbolic, as well as of the territorial border. Against binary norms of reporting migration, we have seen complex narratives, with western media recognising newcomers' right to protection as well as their humanity. These narratives, temporarily at least, replaced established media tropes that often express suspicion or hostility towards refugees and migrants. Visual and textual narratives often represent migrants as silent and strange 'others', fundamentally different to national subjects.[15, 16] These same narratives also produced a discursive category of Ukrainian newcomers as exceptional refugees: referred to in the media as 'people like us', 'civilised' and 'blue-eyed' [17], even when the neighbouring nations share a complicated history [18].

Media narratives matter because they are important resources of information and knowledge about migration, but also because they shape public and political perceptions on migration more generally, as well as of specific migrant and refugee groups, more particularly. In fact, research shows that media are often entangled in the production of policy narratives and decision-making on migration, partly influencing and partly amplifying policy priorities [19, 20]. In the context of migration reporting, media coverage in Poland as in other European countries has repetedly reproduced narratives of suspicion towards newcomers in recent years. Rightwing press primarily but also liberal media have repeatedly reported the disadvantages of accepting refugees [21]. Through the regular reproduction of narratives of migration as a problem, media frame public conversations around a distinction between 'legitimate refugees' and 'undeserving migrants' [22].

The Ukrainian refugee crisis has thus far been an exception to the rule in terms of the broader structures of the border and the contemporary global refugee crisis. This is a case that, in fact, narratively reflects an ethics of welcome and politically decision-making driven by a commitment to shared responsibility, when humanity is affected by war. Symbolically, a politics of protection towards Ukrainian refugees has systematically been prioritised in media and policy narratives of care and respect widely circulated across digital spaces. Territorially, this politics and ethics have been expressed in openings (though not without digital controls) of the border for Ukrainians. The Ukrainian refugee story thus far is one of promise and learning: it reveals that human rights can effectively drive policy and media responses to forced migration, even when the numbers of those seeking protection are significant. Of course, the overall effective policies of protection extended to Ukrainian refugees need to continue being read in the context of exceptionality and in relation to the selective compassion towards a particular group of refugees against racialised others, as a result of a perceived similarity between those arriving and those receiving them, as well as a result of geopolitical interests driving such western responses. This is a story that is only at its early days. It is also a story, as discussed in the next section, that is not fully determined through macro-scale processes but also situated in micro-scale practices of reception. The making and unmaking of refugees involves many actors, spaces and temporalities.

Received as Refugees but Recognised as Humans? Digital Border Entanglements on the Ground

Fieldwork we conducted across the Polish/Ukrainian border in March 2022 revealed that national and transnational policies on migration trickle down into distinct locales. Migration regulation and governance, we saw, are enacted by the agents of the border, most notably border guards, the police and local authorities, but of course implicate refugees themselves who are not only on the receiving side of political decision-making but they themselves develop their own responses to those decisions. Whether or not refugees are humanised or dehumanised, or made or unmade, cannot be fully understood if we do not examine how they are treated locally – a dimension of refugee lives and fates that is rarely considered when broader refugee policy is analysed.

The first striking, but also perhaps unsurprising, observation at the territories that separate but also connect a country at war, Ukraine, and its neighbour, Poland, is that not all crossing the border are doing so because of war. This initial observation revealed that those received as refugees are not all people fleeing war. Some are selectively and conditionally recognised in their humanity, while others are not. Following the routes that many refugees take once they escape immediate danger, we travelled from the Ukrainian border town of Yavoriv (Яворів) through the Polish crossing points of Medyka and Budomierz, and into the border city of Przemyśl and regional capital of Lublin. We then followed the pathways that bring so many into Warsaw's train stations, and eventually into peripheral Polish towns and villages, such as those of Wieliszew. As we followed the refugee routes into EU territories, what became apparent is that media representations and communication networks that expand across news media but also social media shape fundamental dimensions of policy enactment and practices of refugee reception.

Specifically, our research recorded three contradictory and competing dimensions of the border's digital architecture, that is, the technologies implicated in shaping restrictions, in granting permission for crossing borders and in finding safety. These technologies, as discussed below, include digitised systems of cross point controls (e.g., passport biometrics and transnational databases); social media networks that connect different actors of the border and coordinate reception; and social media and news media representations of refugees' flight that enable publics in receiving countries to understand (or misunderstand) refugees' lives and needs. The specific realisation of the border's digital architrcture, as we observed it, is outlined below under three themes: control and exceptionalism, philanthropy and post-humanitarianism, but also, solidarity and resistance.

Control and Exceptionalism

At times of a humanitarian emergency, the complexity of border control becomes more apparent. On the one hand, national boundaries' porosity increased, with refugees and humanitarians crossing between Ukraine and Poland all the time. On the other hand, the digital systems of control and exceptionalism became yet more rigid. Specifically, when we crossed between the two countries as part of a humanitarian mission, we were reminded that, crisis or not, the border is now a digital border of inflexible passport checks and use of transnational databases that decide who can cross and who can't. Humanitarian medics' experience is one of daily scrutiny as their data profiles are constantly checked when they cross everyday between Poland and Ukraine, especially when returning to EU territories. Inflexible border governance has become most ordinary across the West, especially as it is increasingly digitally controlled, with 'firewall bordering' [22] activated through drones, thermal cameras, and transnational databases [4]. Humanitarian practice and displaced people's protection and care remain subjected to the surveilled, rigid restrictions of the border. Even at times of war and when millions of people were desperately seeking access to safety, while facing the most adverse weather conditions.

The control that states impose on the territorial border is nothing new, but there is a particularity in this case that brings racial exceptionalism and conditional hospitality together. In fact, the most striking element of the wartime border we witnessed in Poland was its exceptionalism. As previous research shows, the dominant rationale for belonging in Polish society was ethno-cultural [23].

While the Polish government has been welcoming Ukrainian refugees, it has continued to use its military and intelligence power to deter victims of other wars, such as those from Syria and Afghanistan, who remain trapped at the Belarus-Polish border [24]. From imposing no-go zones around that 'other' border so that media and activists have no access to information, to aggressive campaigns on state media that present those seeking refuge there as merely male, non-white, and threatening migrants [25], the Polish government fundamentally divides those seeking refuge into 'good refugees' and 'bad migrants'; yet even this distinction is not a simple or consistent one. Nationalist concerns are still imposed on refugees, with the Polish Minister of Education requiring Ukrainian children in Polish schools to write their school exams in Polish as the government has no intention to introduce 'privileges' [26].

Philanthropy and Post-Humanitarianism

The scale of citizen-generated humanitarian support for those arriving in Poland has been unimaginable: an incredible scale and level of fast response from the ground up supported refugees when the state was unable, or, according to some, unwilling, to help. Formal structures of reception were minuscule during the first few weeks of the war and Polish citizens were acting as first point of response, trying to manage incredible levels of need. In many cases they still do. Even now, numerous volunteer-organised warehouses across villages, towns and cities receive and distribute vast humanitarian supplies of all kinds both in Poland and in Ukraine. Citizens' effective on-the-ground humanitarianism is largely organised on social media, where volunteers have developed incredibly effective digital skills to self-organise and mobilise others, collecting huge amounts of humanitarian aid, including medication, clothing and food.

While the level of effective and digitally mediated volunteerism is impressive, it is underpinned by a mix of values and motivations. Some of the volunteers we met told us how their preconceptions of the previously suspicious neighbours have been replaced by solidarity towards those in need. Others, such as the members of a border village humanitarian campaign in Poland, told us how important it is to support Ukraine, while still telling us that Ukrainians cannot be trusted. Instead, they only trust their Polish compatriots to deliver and distribute humanitarian aid. Histories of animosity and territorial disputes around the Polish/Ukrainian border [27, 28], alongside solidarities associated with geopolitical struggles, often shape responses and conditions of refugee recognition. Many Ukrainians are often received and cared for, or not cared for, on the basis of regional histories and geopolitics, rather than on the basis of their humanity, as we have seen in the above example. Even more so, the conditionality of refugee recognition, we observed, was in many cases racially determined, even among local authorities and citizens. Some considered Ukrainians as uniquely entitled to refugee status. A Mayor of a border town told us how concerned he was to see a group of 'dark men' approaching in the early days of the war, reminding him, he said, of what he saw on television screens in 2015: certain unwelcome refugees arriving at Europe's

Mediterranean shores. On the micro-scale of the border, not unlike the macro-scale processes of media and policy narrative production, these examples show who refugees are and what rights they have remains a matter discursively and ideologically constituted.

Solidarity and Resistance

Alongside acts of philanthropism and exceptional benevolence, we also witnessed activism of solidarity, which has stubbornly defied the border regime's attempts to divide 'good refugees' and 'bad migrants'. Unlike some of the acts referred to above, which exceptionally expanded welcome to people from Ukraine alone, numbers of grassroots and activist groups have persistently emphasised in their acts and communication their unconditional welcome to all refugees. In Poland, such is the case of the grassroots Homo Faber in Lublin that has over the recent years used its social media to demand long-term strategies of welcome and resettlement, including refugee housing, and that of Grupa Granica that has been campaigning, not only in the context of the war in Ukraine, for nondiscriminatory welcome of all refugees, no matter where they come from.[29] Also the incredible activism of local and international networks of solidarity that supported refugees on both sides of the border was impressive. The most striking case we observed was that of Folkowisko 'Embassy of Freedom', a grassroots initiative at the border town of Cieszanów, which brings together doctors, activists, volunteers from across the world; day in day out, they generate from the ground-up actions that vary from book collections for Ukrainian refugee kids ('Books not Bombs') to humanitarian and medical support delivered to cities across Ukraine.

The most important actors of the border, of course, are refugees themselves. Since the beginning of the war, Ukrainian refugees have been appearing on social media and mass media screens as victims of violence and uprooting. As is often the case with media representations of war, refugees appear as silent victims, or people who only speak of their suffering. During our research, we met many Ukrainian refugees that reminded us of their complex humanity. While having experienced trauma and violent uprooting, most resisted being defined either through silent suffering, or through the west's benevolent philanthropism. Among those we met, two women told us that they were eager to get a job, knowing perhaps how conditional and ephemeral Polish state's support is. A young man showed us his Instagram profile that looked like any other teenager's social media profile, reminding us how he, like so many other young people, sought ordinariness under conditions of precarity and uprooting, at least in appearance. This complex self-representations and voices of refugees are stark reminders, not only of their humanity and diverse needs but also of the urgency to further reflect on the problematic misrepresentations and stereotyping of refugees in news media headlines and imageries, those often dividing the 'good' and the 'bad', the 'deserving' and the 'undeserving'.

Conclusion

The story of the Ukrainian refugee crisis, we argued, is one that emerges and takes its shape within the digital architectures of the border – the technologies that are mobilised territorially and symbolically to manage refugees' flight, but also to assort the bodies of those who have the right to cross territories and to seek protection, as well as their representations as deserving or undeserving of refuge. Listening to the people who are living the war and its consequences, and observing policies, narratives and practices of control but also of struggle, remind us how the stories of refugees and of humanitarianism often simplify the agency and the politics of the border. The border – in its visible and invisible structures and expressions – is a site of violence, of liminality, but also of resistance and agency, implicating locals, humanitarians and refugees themselves.

The story of the Ukrainian refugee crisis is also a story of humanity. If we consider the forces at play both across the macro and the micro level of reception, as we aimed to do in this essay, it becomes apparent that the welcome extended to Ukrainian refugees so far cannot be taken for granted in the future. Ukrainian refugees' right to protection more often than not is subjected to geopolitical priorities, with their humanity remaining subjected to conditional recognition. Narratives that turn Ukrainians into yet another group of 'others' are already surfacing, as seen in the words of the German opposition leader Friedrich Merz, who accused Ukrainian refugees of 'welfare tourism' [30]. As many Ukrainian refugees struggle to secure employment or housing [31, 32], their right to protection seems to be precariously dependent upon public opinion and political discourse. Without the west committing to the recognition of the universal right to refugee protection, beyond an ephemeral and selective application of this right, the risk of welcome turning to suspicion is real. This is a risk which affects the trajectories of Ukrainian refugee lives but also national and international authorities' long-term commitment to human rights. As the initial mobilisation in support of Ukrainian refugees has shown, it is possible to share responsibility and to protect the rights of refugees to a life of safety and dignity, even when the scale of uprooting is enormous. Ukrainian refugees' rights in the long run cannot but be understood and secured within a framework that recognises all refugees' rights. Racial, geopolitical and popularity biases have no place in determining the human right to protection, dignity and refuge.

Acknowledgements

The referenced research in the Polish/Ukrainian border was conducted within the project 'Migrants. Analysis of media discourse on migrants in Poland, the United Kingdom, Ukraine, Albania, and the Czech Republic (MAD)', financed by the Polish National Agency for Academic Exchange as part of the *International Academic Partnerships* programme (no. PPI/APM/2018/1/00019 /DEC/1).

References

1. United Nations High Commissioner for Refugees. Ukraine Emergency. 2023 [cited 2023 June 22]. https://www.unhcr.org/emergencies/ukraine-emergency.

2. Georgiou M. Does the subaltern speak? Migrant voices in digital Europe. *Popular communication.* 2018; 16(1): 45–57. DOI: https://doi.org/10.1080/15405702.2017.1412440.

3. Georgiou M, Zaborowski R. Media coverage of the refugee crisis: A cross-European perspective. Council of Europe DG1(2017)03; 2017 [cited 5 April 2023]. DOI: https://rm.coe.int/1680706b00.

4. Chouliaraki L, Georgiou M. The digital border. Cambridge: Polity; 2022. DOI: https://doi.org/10.18574/nyu/9781479830503.

5. European Parliament. Pushbacks at the EU's external border, Briefing PE 689.368. 2021 [cited 2023 June 22]. https://www.europarl.europa.eu/RegData/etudes/BRIE/2021/689368/EPRS_BRI(2021)689368_EN.pdf.
6. European Commission. Migration and home affairs: Temporary protection, 2023 [cited 22 June 2023]. https://home-affairs.ec.europa.eu/policies/migration-and-asylum/common-european-asylum-system/temporary-protection_en.
7. UK Government. Homes for Ukraine: Record your interest, 2023 [cited 2023 June 22]. https://www.gov.uk/register-interest-homes-ukraine.
8. France 24. Polish pushbacks to Belarus go on as Ukrainians welcome. AFP. 2022 April 1 [cited 2023 June 22]. https://www.france24.com/en/live-news/20220401-polish-pushbacks-to-belarus-go-on-as-ukrainians-welcomed.
9. Venturi E, Vallianatou AI. Ukraine exposes Europe's double standards for refugees. Chatham House. 2022. https://www.chathamhouse.org/2022/03/ukraine-exposes-europes-double-standards-refugees.
10. Amnesty International. Poland: Refugees face chaos, racism and risk of trafficking after fleeing Ukraine – New Research Press Release. 2022 March 22 [cited 2023 June 22]. https://www.amnesty.org.uk/press-releases/poland-refugees-face-chaos-racism-and-risk-trafficking-after-fleeing-ukraine-new.
11. The New Humanitarian. Why did we have to freeze in the forest? *The New Humanitarian*. 2022 March 15 [cited 2023 June 22]. https://www.thenewhumanitarian.org/first-person/2022/03/15/ukraine-poland-syria-refugee-welcome-forest.
12. Bajaj SS, Cody Stanford F. The Ukrainian refugee crisis and the pathology of racism BMJ. 2022; 376: o661. DOI: https://doi.org/10.1136/bmj.o661.
13. Fitri A. The UK has spent up to £1bn on drones to prevent migrant crossings. *TechMonitor*. 2022 April 4 [cited 2023 June

22]. https://techmonitor.ai/government-computing/uk-spent-1bn-drones-prevent-migrant-crossings.
14. Transnational Institute. Financing border wars: The border industry, its financiers and human rights, Boarder Warrs Briefing. 2021.
15. Arcimaviciente L, Baglama SH. Migration, metaphor and myth in media representations: The ideological dichotomy of 'them' and 'us'. Sage Open; 2018. p. 1–13. DOI: https://doi.org/10.1177/2158244018768657.
16. Pruit LJ. Closed due to 'flooding'? UK media representations of refugees and migrants in 2015–2016 – creating a crisis of borders *The British Journal of Politics and International Relations*. 2019; 21(2): 383–402. DOI: https://doi.org/10.1177/1369148119830592.
17. Bayoumi M. They are 'civilised' and 'look kike us': The racist coverage of Ukraine. *The Guardian*. 2022 March 2 [cited 22 June 2023]. https://www.theguardian.com/commentisfree/2022/mar/02/civilised-european-look-like-us-racist-coverage-ukraine.
18. Troszyński M. History and the media: historical discourse in the Polish media on the 100th anniversary of Poland's independence. In Stryjek T, Konieczna-Sałamatin J. editors. The Politics of Memory in Poland and Ukraine: From Reconciliation to De- Conciliation. Routledge; 2021. p. 169–187. DOI: https://doi.org/10.4324/9781003017349-14.
19. Boswell C, Geddes A, Scholten P. The role of narratives in migration policy-making: A research framework. *British Journal of Politics and International Relations*. 2011; 13: 1–11. DOI: https://doi.org/10.1111/j.1467-856X.2010.00435.x.
20. Moore K, Gross B, Threadgold TR. Migrations and the media. Global crises and the media. New York: Peter Lang; 2012. P. 6.
21. Troszyński M, El-Ghamari M. A great divide: Polish media discourse on migration, 2015–2018. *Humanities and Social Sciences Communications*. 2022; 9(22). DOI: https://doi.org/10.1057/s41599-021-01027-x.

22. Yuval-Davis N, Wemyss G, Cassidy K. Bordering. Cambridge: Polity Press; 2019.
23. Carmel E, Sojka B. Beyond welfare chauvinism and deservingness. Rationales of belonging as a conceptual framework for the politics and governance of migrants' rights. *Journal of Social Policy*. 2021; 50(3): 645–667. DOI: https://doi.org/10.1017/S0047279420000379.
24. Bodnar A, Grzelak A. The Polish–Belarusian border crisis and the (Lack of) European Union response. *Białostockie Studia Prawnicze*. 2023; 28(1): 57–86. DOI: https://doi.org/10.15290/bsp.2023.28.01.04.
25. Zaborowski R. Actual tweet by Polish state media: 6 differences between refugees from Ukraine and Belarus [Twitter] 2022 March 29 [cited 2023 June 22]. https://twitter.com/myredtowel/status/1508764359794864130.
26. Poland Daily Live. Ukrainian children in Polish schools will take exams with Polish colleagues say education minister [Youtube] 2022 March 30 [cited 2023 June 22]. https://www.youtube.com/watch?v=GN300HbmTxk.
27. Pasieka A. Reenacting ethnic cleansing: people's history and elitist nationalism in contemporary Poland. *Nations and Nationalism*. 2016; 22: 63–83. DOI: https://doi.org/10.1111/nana.12113.
28. Ascherson N. The war for the soul of Poland. *Prospect*. 2023 March 1 [2023 June 22]. https://www.prospectmagazine.co.uk/world/60514/the-war-for-the-soul-of-poland.
29. Pietrusińsk MJ. "People From the Forest": Discourse About Migrants in the Narratives of NGO Workers and Activists Involved in the Humanitarian Crisis at the Polish-Belarusian Border Sprawy Narodowościowe: Seria Nowa. 2022; 54: 2803.
30. Karnitschnig M. German conservative leader accuses Ukrainian refugees of 'welfare tourism'. *Politico*. 2022 September 29 [cited 2023 June 22]. https://www.politico.eu/article/german-conservative-leader-accuses-ukrainian-refugees-of-welfare-tourism/.

31. Alsaafin L. After fleeing war, hoemelessness threatens UK's Ukrainian refugees. *Al Jazeera*. 2023 February 27 [cited 2023 June 22]. https://www.aljazeera.com/news/2023/2/27/hold-the-rise-of-homelessness-among-ukrainian-refugees-in-the-uk.

32. The Economist. The desperate uncertainty of Ukrainian refugees. 2023 February 22 [cited 2023 June 22]. https://www.economist.com/interactive/international/2023/02/22/ukrainian-refugees-remain-in-limbo?utm_medium=cpc.adword.pd&utm_source=google&ppccampaignID=17551784839&ppcadID=137626460346&ppcgclID=CjoKCQiAx6ugBhCcARIsAGNmMbjeyRGMoGf_FoprzXUWP9KGlH2WrSOnQP9heqxnGjziqTDVepyBddEaAmYGEALw_wcB&gclid=CjoKCQiAx6ugBhCcARIsAGNmMbjeyRGMoGf_FoprzXUWP9KGlH2WrSOnQP9heqxnGjziqTDVepyBddEaAmYGEALw_wcB&gclsrc=aw.ds.

10. Weaponised Energy and Climate Change: Assessing Europe's Response to the Ukraine War

Robert Falkner

Russia's invasion of Ukraine has produced the biggest energy shock to Europe since the 1970s oil crises. It has also laid bare the strategic blunder at the heart of Europe's energy policy – its long-standing dependence on Russian supplies. With Moscow weaponising its dominant position in Europe's energy system, European leaders had little choice but to wean Europe off its addiction to cheap Russian gas and oil. This chapter explores the European Union's energy response to the war in Ukraine and its impact on climate policy. It addresses two questions: First, to what extent has Europe succeeded in reducing reliance on Russian fossil fuels, and at what cost? And second, how has the push for energy independence affected the continent's commitment to implementing the net zero transition? I argue that one year after the invasion, the EU's strategic decoupling from Russia has progressed to such an extent that Moscow is close to losing its energy stranglehold over Europe. Furthermore, although Europe's energy crisis is far from over, European leaders have renewed their commitment to the net zero climate agenda and accelerated investments in green energy. In the short run, the EU's pursuit

> of energy security may have temporarily set back its climate ambition. However, as Europe discovered by the end of 2022, decarbonisation is ultimately the best long-term strategy for energy security.

Russia's unprovoked invasion of Ukraine on 24 February 2022 caused the biggest energy shock to Europe since the oil crises of the 1970s. Ever since, European leaders have been grappling with the need to reduce dependence on Russian fossil fuels while softening the economic fallout from skyrocketing energy prices. Only a few weeks after the invasion, the European Union (EU) embarked on a comprehensive programme to reduce energy consumption, to replace Russian energy supplies, and to accelerate the green energy revolution. One year later, significant progress has been made in decoupling Europe's economy from cheap Russian energy. Europe has so far avoided a major energy crunch, but this has come at considerable cost. Inflation in 2022 soared above 10 percent while economic growth petered out.

The energy shock of 2022 has also turned into a moment of truth for Europe's climate policy ambition. To replace Russian energy with alternative supplies, European leaders decided to increase coal shipments from abroad while building new infrastructure for importing liquified natural gas (LNG). Both moves called into question the EU's repeatedly stated goal of accelerating the switch away from fossil fuels. Indeed, European greenhouse gas (GHG) emissions went up in the first six months of the war, mainly due to increased coal consumption. At the same time, however, European leaders reiterated their commitment to decarbonising the economy and presented the war also as an opportunity to advance energy and climate security.

This chapter examines Europe's energy and climate response to Russia's aggression and asks two questions: First, to what extent has the EU managed to counter Russia's weaponisation of Europe's energy dependence, and at what cost? And second, has Europe's drive for energy independence from Russia undermined or reinforced the continent's long-term climate strategy? It is worth noting that the answers to these questions reflect the experience of the first twelve months since Russia's invasion. They are therefore somewhat tentative, not least as the war in Ukraine looks set to drag on and the energy crisis is far from over. Nevertheless, early indications suggest that it has been possible to free Europe from Russia's energy blackmail without causing significant harm to the net zero transition. In fact, Europe's experience holds important lessons for other countries seeking to pursue energy security while pushing ahead with the net zero transition.

Europe's Strategic Blunder

Russia's invasion of Ukraine in February 2022 exposed a major strategic miscalculation on the part of Europe. After the end of the cold war, many European countries allowed themselves to become dependent on Russia as their main supplier of fossil fuel energy, mostly natural gas but also oil and coal. 90 percent of the gas consumed in the EU was imported, of which around 45 percent was of Russian origin.[1] European governments justified the deepening energy dependence on Russia on both economic and political grounds. For one, a cheap and reliable energy supply was a critical ingredient in the success of the continent's export-oriented manufacturing industries. Moreover, the creation of a vast physical infrastructure for transporting Russian gas to the EU was seen as an investment in a stable, long-term relationship with Moscow. Germany, in particular, had made a "strategic bet on a full embrace of interdependence and globalization", as Constanze Stelzenmüller from the Brookings Institution put it [2]. '*Wandel durch Handel*', the idea that the mutual gains from trade would have a transformative and pacifying effect on Russia, had been a mainstay of German foreign policy since the days of *Ostpolitik* [3].

Germany's, and indeed Europe's, strategic miscalculation is all the more troubling since various warning signs and opportunities to change course were missed. Long before Russia started to stoke secessionist tensions in Ukraine and used brute military force against its neighbour, foreign policy and energy experts had been warning that Europe's reliance on Russian energy was reaching problematic levels [4, 5]. In 2006 and 2009, disputes between Russia and Ukraine over outstanding debt and the pricing of Russian gas exports through Ukraine's territory led to temporary shutdowns of gas supplies to Europe. Both episodes could have led Europe to pull back from deepening energy ties with Russia. Instead, European countries further expanded the gas pipeline network to create new routes for Russian gas exports, not least to reduce dependence on Ukraine as the main transit territory.

Even after Moscow openly showed its revanchist ambition – when it annexed the Crimean Peninsula and supported secessionist uprisings in Ukraine's Donbas region in 2014 – Europe failed to reverse course. Despite condemning Russia's breach of international law, the German government continued to support the Nord Stream 2 pipeline project, which was to send Russian gas directly to Germany. It also allowed the Russian energy firm Gazprom to strengthen its grip over domestic gas storage facilities. Instead of reviewing its energy strategy, Europe actually allowed dependence on Russia as a major supplier of natural gas to increase after 2014: Russian imports rose from 36 percent of EU gas consumption in 2015 to 41 percent in 2018, before reaching a new plateau of 38 percent in 2020 and 2021 [6]. Repeated appeals by the American government and US sanctions against the Russian firms involved in the construction of Nord Stream 2 had little impact. The new gas pipeline through the Baltic Sea was completed in September 2021, less than half a year before Russia attacked Ukraine.

It took Russia's full-scale invasion of Ukraine finally to force a strategic rethink. By this time, all remaining hope that energy cooperation with Russia could become the basis for a political accommodation with Putin's regime had evaporated. In fact, Russia already started to weaponise its dominant position in Europe's energy market well before the outbreak of hostilities. In 2021, Gazprom reduced the flow of gas through its pipeline network, running down gas reserves and driving up energy prices across Europe. Soon after the invasion, Russia further squeezed European gas supplies. By August 2022, gas prices had reached a record 300 €/MWh, compared to price levels of around 20 €/MWh in 2020. Europe's economic growth came to a stuttering halt as inflation shot up and a cost-of-living crisis engulfed European societies [7].

European leaders thus had little choice but to seek to reduce Moscow's stranglehold over Europe's energy infrastructure.

Following the outbreak of the war, the EU began itself to weaponise its position as the largest market for Russian energy exports. After imposing a ban on coal imports from Russia, effective from August 2022, the EU introduced an embargo on seaborne Russian oil imports starting in February 2023. Together with the US, other G7 countries and Australia, the EU also imposed an unprecedented price cap on Russian oil exports to other parts of the world. Step by step, Western powers have thus sought to starve Moscow of at least some of the energy revenues that have fuelled its war machine in Ukraine. The impact of such measures has been softened by other countries (China, India, Egypt, UAE, Turkey) that increased their energy imports from Russia, but there is clear evidence that thanks to Western sanctions and lost energy revenues, Moscow has had to withdraw large sums from its sovereign wealth fund to plug a growing budget hole [6, 8, 9].

Europe's attempt to restructure its energy market and external trade raises two interrelated questions: First, to what extent has Europe managed to rid itself of its addiction to Russian energy imports, and at what cost? And second, how has this push for energy independence played into Europe's long-standing goal of eliminating energy-related GHG emissions? Early on, the EU faced an inevitable trade-off between the strategic imperatives of energy independence and climate change. One year after the invasion, how well has Europe fared on these two fronts?

Europe's Push for Energy Independence from Russia

With the launch of the REPowerEU plan in May 2022, the EU embarked on a comprehensive programme to eliminate the continent's dependence on Russian gas and make its energy system more resilient to external pressure. Time was of the essence, for the longer Europe relied on Russian energy imports the longer it helped finance the war in Ukraine. In the first six months of the conflict, Russia is estimated to have earned a total of €158 billion in revenues from fossil fuel exports, of which EU imports alone accounted for 54 percent, worth around €85 billion [8].

The EU's plan sought to achieve a two-thirds reduction in gas consumption from Russian sources by the end of 2022. It also aimed to end the EU's dependence on Russian energy exports while advancing its climate policy objectives. The measures that would deliver both objectives included an immediate focus on energy demand reduction, a diversification of energy supplies from abroad, and an accelerated push for renewable energy [10].

To contain the energy crisis, European governments had to take some politically controversial decisions early on: Germany, France, Austria, Italy and the Netherlands announced that they would extend or reactivate coal-fired power plants to replace Russian gas in electricity generation. The German government also extended the lifetime of several nuclear power plants that were set to be decommissioned. At the same time, European governments rushed to secure alternative supplies of energy, mainly from North America, North Africa and the Middle East. Given the urgency of the task, European leaders could not be choosy about where to source new energy imports from, even if it meant entering into long-term energy deals with authoritarian regimes in the Middle East.

Replacing natural gas from Russia proved more difficult than replacing oil and coal. Building new pipelines to alternative gas sources normally takes years, and several key European countries lacked sufficient terminal and storage infrastructure for importing LNG. The speed with which European governments went about addressing these bottlenecks surprised many observers. Germany, which had no existing capacity to import LNG, decided to build several port terminals from scratch. Despite the country's reputation for lengthy and bureaucratic planning processes, the first such LNG terminal in Wilhemshaven was completed in record time. Built in under 200 days, it started operating on 17 December 2022. Five more LNG terminals are still to follow [11].

Europe benefited from favourable global market conditions in 2022. Due to China's sluggish economy, Asian demand for gas shipments was relatively weak, making it easier for existing LNG capacity to be diverted to European customers, while gas imports through existing gas pipelines from Norway, Algeria and Azerbaijan could be kept at maximum levels. Furthermore, the United States had enough capacity to rapidly increase its energy exports to Europe. By the end of the year, American energy firms provided the continent with half of its LNG imports and 12 percent of oil supplies [6, 12].

To avert energy blackouts during the 2022–23 winter season, Europe could not rely on a gas replacement strategy alone, it also needed to curb energy demand across the continent. In August 2022, the EU called on Member States to set a target of 15 percent of total demand reduction for gas [13]. Companies were encouraged to find additional energy efficiencies in offices and factories, while households were advised to turn down thermostats in their homes and cut down on the use of air conditioning [14]. Although mostly voluntary in nature, these appeals eventually bore fruit. A combination of skyrocketing energy prices and solidarity with Ukraine proved to be enough of a motivating factor for firms and citizens to cut down their energy use. In fact, by early 2023, the EU managed to exceed its original savings target. In the six months from August 2022 to January 2023, gas consumption in the EU fell by 19.3 percent, compared with average consumption levels in the 2017–2022 period [15].

How much did Europe suffer economically from the weaponisation of energy in 2022? Early economic model calculations predicted a limited to moderate economic contraction in the EU mainly due to gas shortages, on a scale of 0.5 to 3 percent of GDP.[2] In the end, some industries found it relatively easy to reduce gas consumption without suffering any fall in manufacturing output, largely due to available options for improving efficiency and fuel switching. With global gas prices falling again in early 2023, fears of a protracted recession in Europe have gradually eased [16]. For some industrial sectors (e.g., chemicals, fertilisers, ceramics), however, gas remains an essential input factor that cannot be easily replaced or reduced. Faced with gas shortages and high energy prices, they have little choice but reduce output or relocate production outside Europe – a scenario that has proved particularly troubling for politicians in Germany, Europe's export-oriented manufacturing powerhouse [17, 18].

In sum, Europe's drive for energy independence from Russia has proved costly but has advanced more quickly than originally anticipated. One year after the invasion of Ukraine, oil and coal imports from Russia are down to nearly zero, while the flow of Russian gas through the pipelines network has been substantially cut. European leaders were able to overcome institutional inertia and regulatory hurdles to build new LNG terminals, sanction Russian energy exports and aggressively bid for alternative energy sources in world markets. As a consequence, Moscow has already lost much of its stranglehold over Europe's energy network and is now suffering from a ballooning fiscal deficit. Its military spending has shot up, while export losses and sanctions are beginning to bite. Concerns remain, however, about a renewed energy crisis in the winter season of 2023–24, particularly as China's economic growth and energy demand is expected to pick up again. For this reason, Fatih Birol, the head of the International Energy Agency (IEA), cautioned in February 2023 that "it would be too strong to say that Europe has won the energy battle already" [19]. Europe's struggle for energy security and independence, just like the war in Ukraine, is unlikely to end anytime soon.

What Happened to Europe's Climate Ambition?

How did the push for energy independence affect Europe's long-term climate strategy? In the first few months after the invasion, when European governments scrambled to secure alternative fossil fuel supplies, experts predicted a major setback for the EU's net zero strategy. The reopening or extension of coal-fired power plants and the building of new infrastructure for LNG imports seemed to suggest that, far from accelerating the shift away from fossil fuels, Europe was willing to delay the net zero transition in a bid to wean itself off Russian energy. Few commentators doubted the urgent need to gain strategic autonomy vis-à-vis Moscow. However, as GHG emissions began to rise again in the first half of 2022, reversing a decade-long decarbonisation trend in Europe, questions surfaced about whether Europe's climate leadership was under threat from the renewed focus on energy security [20, 21]. One commentator went as far as stating that "geopolitical confrontations and the foreign policy agenda seem to have gained the upper hand, and EU energy policy is now being adjusted to the necessities of realpolitik" [22].

One year after the invasion, such climate policy pessimism seems increasingly misplaced. A temporary increase in coal usage initially drove up emission levels, but the combination of a warm winter, effective demand management and energy savings in industry led to an overall decline of Europe's emissions. According to IEA estimates, the continent's energy-related emissions fell by 2.5 percent in 2022, with sharply reduced natural gas emissions counteracting increases in emissions from the burning of coal and oil [23].

More importantly, the Ukraine war did not reduce Europe's determination to push ahead with its net zero climate strategy. Far from it, Russia's military aggression seemed to have galvanised European policy-makers to accelerate the decarbonisation drive. In March 2022, the European Commission declared unequivocally that "[f]ollowing the invasion of Ukraine, the case for a rapid clean energy transition has never been stronger and clearer" [24]. With its 2050 net zero commitment and interim target of a 55 percent reduction of emissions by 2030, the EU had already staked out a claim for being a "climate great power" with a desire to advance the international climate agenda [25]. Europe's immediate energy response to the Ukraine war therefore posed a threat to this international leadership position, but more recent actions have reduced such concerns. Indeed, by the end of 2022, the EU was able to agree a package of measures to accelerate investment in renewable energy and energy efficiency. It also enacted overdue reforms to the EU emissions trading system, which helped drive up carbon prices in Europe [15].

There are good reasons to conclude that the search for energy independence from Russia has not derailed the EU's net zero transition. Despite the decision to reactivate coal power plants, Europe did not entrench a "return to coal" as originally feared. In fact, much of the extra coal capacity that EU countries created in 2022 remained unused. Coal-fired power generation started to fall again by the end of the year and is expected to continue to decline in future years. By contrast, investment in renewable energy has continued apace. By the end of 2022, wind and solar installations produced a record 22 percent of electricity in the EU, ahead of gas (20 percent) and coal (16 percent) [26]. If there is a trade-off between energy independence and climate policy in Europe, it exists only in the short run. In the long run, only a determined switch away from coal, oil and gas can serve both strategic objectives.

Unfortunately, the war's wider climate policy repercussions in international society have not been as benign. For one, Russia's attack on Ukraine has absorbed a lot of political attention in capitals around the world that would be better spent on advancing international climate cooperation. Moreover, amidst the energy crisis that has afflicted the global economy, many governments rolled out support programmes for households and industry that often ended up boosting high carbon energy sources. By the end of 2022, global subsidies for fossil fuels shot up to a record $1 trillion [27]. Several major GHG emitters in the Global South also snapped up cheap energy exports from Russia that Western customers had rejected. If this global demand shift continues, it is bound to lock in high-carbon energy production in key emerging economies, such as India and China, which would have an adverse impact on global emissions trends. As for Russia, its military aggression and the impact of Western sanctions have, if anything, made the country ever more reliant on future fossil fuel revenues and increased its hostility to the net zero transition. Moscow continues to engage in the international climate negotiations but increasingly acts as a recalcitrant player. At the COP27 conference in Egypt and in other forums, for example, Russia firmly opposed any agreement aimed at reducing fossil fuel use or at increasing renewable energy [28].

International climate cooperation has thus suffered several setbacks due to the war in Ukraine, although high energy prices have reinforced the importance of accelerating the green energy revolution. So far, international support for the Paris Agreement has held up, and the international climate regime is flexible enough to withstand temporary crises. The more difficult question is whether the main climate great powers can transcend at least some of their fundamental differences and carve out a niche for continued multilateral cooperation on the climate threat.[3]

Conclusions

Russia's full-scale invasion of Ukraine in 2022 exposed Europe's strategic miscalculation in having allowed itself to become dependent on Russian energy supplies. Faced with the horrors of the most devastating war on European soil since World War II, the EU decided to cut the links that had tied its economy to Russia's fossil fuel wealth. Within a matter of a few months,

Europe stopped all Russian coal imports. A year after the start of the invasion, it also imposed a comprehensive embargo on seaborne oil exports from Russia. Replacing gas imports from Russia proved more difficult, but a combination of reduced gas consumption and alternative LNG supplies have allowed Europe to dramatically cut its dependence on Russian natural gas flows.

The dramatic U-turn in Europe's energy strategy following Putin's war of aggression has proved costly and disruptive to Europe's economy, fuelling inflation and bringing economic growth to a halt. However, against expectations, the continent managed to prevent an energy crunch in the winter of 2022–23. Russia may have been able to weaponise its role as Europe's single largest fossil fuel supplier, but in doing so it lost its energy stranglehold on Europe. The energy decoupling that started in 2022 is likely to mark the biggest turnaround in Europe's relationship with Russia since the end of the Cold War.

Initially, Europe's measures to cut energy ties with Russia drove up the continent's GHG emissions. Coal use shot up and new fossil fuel supply agreements were struck. At least in the short run, Europe's push for energy independence and security threatened to undermine its climate strategy and reputation as a global climate leader. Yet, in the long run, energy security and climate policy have proved to be mutually supportive. The Ukraine war has galvanised European leaders to reaffirm their commitment to the net zero goal and accelerate their decarbonisation efforts. Driving down reliance on fossil fuels should thus be seen as the single most important tool of Europe's energy security strategy.

Notes

[1] In 2021, Russia also provided around 25% of oil imports and 45% of coal imports to EU [1].

[2] For an overview of different economic modelling results, see McWilliams [6, p.1-2].

[3] On the role of great power cooperation in tackling climate change, see Barry Buzan and Robert Falkner [29].

References

1. European Commission. Press Release. REPowerEU: Joint European action for more affordable, secure and sustainable energy. 2022 March 8. https://ec.europa.eu/commission/presscorner/detail/%5Beuropa_tokens:europa_interface_language%5D/ip_22_1511.

2. Stelzenmüller C. Putin's war and European energy security: A German perspective on decoupling from Russian fossil fuels. Brookings Institution. 2022 June 7. https://www.brookings.edu/testimonies/putins-war-and-european-energy-security-a-german-perspective-on-decoupling-from-russian-fossil-fuels/.

3. Blumenau B. Breaking with convention? *Zeitenwende* and the traditional pillars of German foreign policy. *International Affairs*. 2022; 98(6): 1895–1913. DOI: https://doi.org/10.1093/ia/iiac166.

4. Baran Z. EU Energy Security: Time to End Russian Leverage. *The Washington Quarterly*. 2007; 30(4): 131–144. DOI: https://doi.org/10.1162/wash.2007.30.4.131.

5. Dyson T. Energy Security and Germany's Response to Russian Revisionism: The Dangers of Civilian Power. *German Politics*. 2016; 25(4): 500–518. DOI: https://doi.org/10.1080/09644008.2015.1133607.

6. McWilliams B, Sgaravatti G, Tagliapietra S, Zachmann G. Can Europe survive painlessly without Russian gas? *Bruegel blog.* 2022 January 27. https://www.bruegel.org/blog-post/can-europe-survive-painlessly-without-russian-gas.

7. European Commission. Directorate-General for Energy. *New reports highlight 3rd quarter impact of gas supply cuts.* 2023 January 13. https://energy.ec.europa.eu/news/new-reports-highlight-3rd-quarter-impact-gas-supply-cuts-2023-01-13_en.

8. Centre for Research on Energy and Clean Air. Financing Putin's war: Fossil fuel exports from Russia in the first six months of the invasion of Ukraine. 2022 September 6. https://energyandcleanair.org/publication/financing-putins-war-fossil-fuel-exports-from-russia-in-the-first-six-months-of-the-invasion-of-ukraine/.

9. Reuters: Russia rainy day fund shrinks by $38 bln as government plugs deficit. 2023 January 18. https://www.reuters.com/markets/europe/russias-national-wealth-fund-148-bln-jan-1-finance-ministry-2023-01-18/.

10. Communication from the Commission to the European Parliament, the European Council, the Council, The European Economic and Social Committee and the Committee of the Regions. *REPowerEU Plan.* COM(2022) 230 final. 2022 May 18.

11. DENA. Rekordtempo bei schwimmendem LNG-Terminal ist Vorbild für weitere Zukunftsprojekte. Press release. 2022 December 16. https://www.dena.de/newsroom/meldungen/2022/rekordtempo-bei-schwimmendem-lng-terminal/.

12. Levebvre B. How American energy helped Europe best Putin. *Politico.* 2023 February 23. https://www.politico.com/news/2023/02/23/american-energy-europe-putin-00083750.

13. Council Regulation (EU) 2022/1369 of 5 August 2022 on coordinated demand-reduction measures for gas. https://eur-lex.europa.eu/legal-content/EN/TXT/?uri=CELEX%3A32022R1369.

14. European Commission. The European Commission and the IEA outline key energy saving actions. 2022 April 21. https://commission.europa.eu/news/european-commission-and-iea-outline-key-energy-saving-actions-2022-04-21_en.

15. Petrequin S. EU climate czar: Putin's war accelerated green transition. *AP News*. 2023 February 21. https://apnews.com/article/russia-ukraine-putin-politics-european-union-europe-b38199c0e8410df19274be163906b36f.

16. Sheppard D. European natural gas prices fall to 18-month low as energy crisis ebbs. *Financial Times*. 2023 February 17. https://www.ft.com/content/3bb53193-da20-4860-bed6-c2781dff1ea0.

17. Hollinger P, White S, Speed M, Dunai M. Will the energy crisis crush European industry? *Financial Times*. 2022 October 19. https://www.ft.com/content/75ed449d-e9fd-41de-96bd-c92d316651da.

18. Fuest C. Die Zukunft des Geschäftsmodells Deutschland. *ifo Schnelldienst*: 2022; 75(9): 3–7.

19. Sheppard D. Europe's energy war with Russia is not over, warns IEA chief. *Financial Times*. 2023 February 23. https://www.ft.com/content/a3649a57-122b-4418-a44e-f306c194ad74.

20. Dennison S. Green peace: How Europe's climate policy can survive the war in Ukraine. Policy Brief. *European Council on Foreign Relations*. 2022 June 27. https://ecfr.eu/publication/green-peace-how-europes-climate-policy-can-survive-the-war-in-ukraine/.

21. Pendlington J. Will Europe's green future survive Russia's war in Ukraine? Oxford Economics blog. 2022 September 27. https://www.oxfordeconomics.com/resource/will-europes-green-future-survive-russias-war-in-ukraine/.

22. Siddi M. Europe's Energy Dilemma: War and the Green Transition. *Current history*. 2023; 122(842): 83–88. DOI: https://doi.org/10.1525/curh.2023.122.842.83.

23. International Energy Agency. CO2 Emissions in 2022. Paris: IEA. 2023 March; p. 12. https://www.iea.org/reports/co2-emissions-in-2022.

24. European Commission. REPowerEU: Joint European action for more affordable, secure and sustainable energy. Press release. 2022 March 8. https://ec.europa.eu/commission/presscorner/detail/%5Beuropa_tokens:europa_interface_language%5D/ip_22_1511.

25. Biedenkopf K, Dupont C, Torney D. The European Union: A Green Great Power? In Falkner R, Buzan B, editors. Great Powers, Climate Change, and Global Environmental Responsibilities. Oxford: Oxford University Press. 2022; p. 95–115. DOI: https://doi.org/10.1093/oso/9780198866022.003.0005.

26. EMBER. European Electricity Review 2023. 2023 January 31; p. 6. https://ember-climate.org/insights/research/european-electricity-review-2023/.

27. Muta T, Erdogan M. The global energy crisis pushed fossil fuel consumption subsidies to an all-time high in 2022. IEA commentary. 2023 February 16. https://www.iea.org/commentaries/the-global-energy-crisis-pushed-fossil-fuel-consumption-subsidies-to-an-all-time-high-in-2022.

28. Davydova A. How Russia's War is Impacting the Global Environmental Agenda. Carnegie Endowment for International Peace. 2023 January 11. https://carnegieendowment.org/politika/88773.

29. Buzan B, Falkner R. Great Powers and Environmental Responsibilities: A Conceptual Framework. In Robert Falkner, Barry Buzan, editors. Great Powers, Climate Change, and Global Environmental Responsibilities. Oxford: Oxford University Press. 2022; p. 14–48. DOI: https://doi.org/10.1093/oso/9780198866022.003.0002.

11. New Dynamics, New Opportunities: Trends in Organised Crime in Ukraine After Russia's Invasion

Global Initiative Against Transnational Organized Crime

> Russia's full-scale invasion of Ukraine on 24 February 2022 reshaped the way organised crime operated within Ukraine and how it interacted with criminal interests in other countries, disrupting some forms of illicit business and generating new opportunities. This chapter will explore three key areas of change: the responses of criminal actors; the nascent illicit economy in drugs and arms trafficking at the front line, and the new trend in smuggling conscripts away from the fighting; and the changes that have occurred to illicit markets and flows in the west of Ukraine, where massive inflows of military equipment and humanitarian aid, and similarly large outward movements of refugees, have created new vulnerabilities that organised crime is attempting to exploit. This last area also discusses the risks of corruption around another imminent inflow – that of reconstruction funds.

Criminals in Conflict: Patriots or Parasites?

The Russian invasion posed an interesting conundrum to organised crime actors in Ukraine: stay or go?[1] In the early stages of the war, many chose the latter, with several Ukrainian criminal bosses (and their assets) moving abroad, although their networks and lieutenants remained. (One Odesa underworld source said that his boss had moved abroad but was still paying him to ensure his loyalty) [2]. Reported destinations for crime bosses included Turkey, the United Kingdom, Germany, Spain, Monaco, Italy, Austria, Israel, and Dubai [3–5]. But as 2022 came to an end, several major organised crime figures returned to Ukraine, perhaps judging that the security situation had sufficiently improved or that their presence was needed on the ground again.

Our fieldwork found that some high-level criminal actors were looking for 'weak points' abroad where they could redirect criminal operations to avoid the conflict: Romania (Constanza), Bulgaria, Italy (Genoa), and France (Marseille) were cited as potential options [3, 6]. There are significant Ukrainian diasporas in several Eastern European countries, especially Czechia, Romania and Poland, which could provide cover for some criminal actors to either wait out the conflict or start up new ventures. The Baltic states also offer fertile ground for Ukrainian criminals to expand their operations, given that they already have extensive ties in such places. For those who have stayed, however, the war brought opportunities – and criminals were not slow in exploiting them.

One significant area of change was in the emergence of what might be loosely termed 'patriotic' criminals. At the beginning of the 2022 invasion of Ukraine, Moscow once again turned to its 2014 toolbox, with reports of sabotage and riots in Ukraine orchestrated by criminal groups linked with Russia. However, unlike in 2014, these agitations were quickly suppressed, in part due to the efforts of local organised crime [7]. According to a law enforcement figure, the Security Service of Ukraine (SBU) asked Ukrainian criminals to help to detect Russian criminals that had been sent by Moscow to destabilise the situation. Within a few months, the source alleged, most Russian criminal actors had been either apprehended or ejected from the country.[2] 'Patriotic' criminals have also been reported patrolling the streets with the police in Odesa, which hosts a large number of suspected pro-Russian criminals, particularly thieves-in-law who had been ejected from Georgia in the mid-2000s [8]. However, the patriotic tendency of some criminals should not be taken at face value. After all, seen through a criminal lens, the conflict is a threat to both territory and profit, neatly aligning issues of patriotism and self-interest. As such, patriotism could merely be the end product of a complex calculation aimed at furthering one or both of organised crime's overriding priorities: money and power.

Organised crime may also come to benefit from patriotic fervour in a more indirect way: through the recruitment of demobilised soldiers into organised crime groups. After demobilisation, many of the hundreds of thousands of ex-soldiers may struggle to find employment, may be traumatised by their experience, or may simply miss the intense camaraderie of military life, any of which will leave them vulnerable to criminal recruitment. Add ready access to illicit weapons, and the conflict in Ukraine may be incubating a reservoir of criminal violence in the near future. There is also the risk of a Ukrainian Wagner-type group emerging from the pool of demobilised personnel. Private military companies (PMCs) are currently banned in Ukraine but they are also banned in Russia, which demonstrates that laws may pose little obstacle if the relevant interests align.[3] Groups may also operate illegally – in 2021, for example, two illegal Ukrainian PMCs were broken up [10] – or laws may change.

The Fighting Economy: Drugs, Guns and Draft Dodgers

The intense fighting and extensive territorial changes of 2022 have created a degree of uncertainty and risk that has drastically hindered much criminal business in Ukraine, especially drug trafficking from east to west Ukraine. In other aspects, though, the volatile front line has emerged as a catalyst for illicit activity.

In November 2022, during fieldwork conducted for this research, a Ukrainian soldier was encountered in Bakhmut in a state of high agitation [11]. He appeared to be under the influence of a powerful narcotic – most likely amphetamine or a similar stimulant – and he is by no means an anomaly. Kyiv is increasingly concerned about growing drug use among soldiers. In December 2022, the Verkhovna Rada (Ukrainian parliament) passed a law that authorises ad hoc testing of military personnel for drugs and alcohol [12].

That drugs are present on the front line should not be surprising: soldiers have used drugs throughout history, either as stimulants to help them fight or as ways of escaping the harrowing trauma of warfare. Seen through the eyes of organised crime, the soldiers represent merely a new and lucrative market for their drugs. At the start of the conflict, monthly pay for front line soldiers in Ukraine was increased to 100,000 Ukraine hryvnias (UAH) (US$3,400 at the time). This gave them significant spending power in a country where the official average salary in September 2022 was UAH14,500 (US$360) per month [13, 14].

What is more notable is how synthetic drugs continued to be easily available, showing how organised crime can adapt rapidly during conflict. The Russian invasion drastically disrupted heroin flows from the Donbas region and domestic production of synthetics in the eastern city of Kharkiv, while the naval blockade of Odesa and Mykolaiv also made smuggling cocaine and precursors for synthetic drugs impossible. Given this, the natural assumption would be that the supply of synthetics would diminish [15, p10].

Following an initial period of disruption in Kyiv in the early days of the war [16], illicit distribution picked up once again throughout the country by means of online stores, street dealers, and the postal system [17, 18]. Traffickers may be drawing more heavily from sources in western Europe to make up for the drop in supply from eastern Ukraine, but local production also appears to be robust. Police busts of synthetic drug labs in central and western Ukraine in 2022 have continued, with INTERPOL reporting that, according to their upstream and downstream monitoring, flows appeared to be continuing almost unabated [19].

According to the Ukrainian State Bureau of Investigation, synthetic drugs are being sold in all regions of Ukraine, and on the front line [20]. In the first six months after the invasion, Ukrainian law enforcement launched more than 270 investigations into drug trafficking at the front line [20]. In military units where drug use was witnessed, cannabis was overwhelmingly the most-used drug by soldiers, although synthetic drugs were readily available. According to sources close to law enforcement, a major player in the front line drugs trade is Khimprom, a transnational organised crime group that has a long-standing presence in both Russia and Ukraine, and which has resisted repeated efforts to dismantle it.

The huge influx of weapons into Ukraine since February 2022 has also been a prominent concern for analysts of criminal activity. Given Ukraine's history of arms trafficking (rated as the country's most pervasive criminal market, according to the GI-TOC 2021 Global Organized Crime Index), the risk of weapons trafficking was flagged in the early days of the war by Europol and others [21]. Asd of January 2023, it appeared that the worst case scenario had not happened, and that the diversion of arms had been more limited than was initially feared. Of the billions of dollars' worth of weapons that the West sent to help Ukrainian armed forces in 2022 [22], there have been few reports of missing weapons, with the US reporting only one verifiable instance of weapons in the period to October 2022 [23]. In the main, this has been due to a high degree of awareness of the risks of arms trafficking, and the implementation of mechanisms to counter it [23–25]. The types of weapons involved may also have had a bearing on leakage risks: in the early days of the war small arms formed a substantial element. As the war progressed, the arms in question have become larger systems and spare parts that are less suitable for illegal diversion. The intense nature of the fighting is also likely to have a dampening effect on leakages, with significant quantities of weapons and ammunition being deployed by fighters as soon as they reach the front. For the most part, the allegations of trafficking Western weapons are unsubstantiated or appear to be the result of Russian disinformation [26, 27].

Where the leakage is most likely on the Ukrainian side is in the form of 'bad apples' – units or commanders who misappropriate weapons under the fog of war. Some units of the International Legion have seen claims of misappropriation: in December, a returning British mercenary who had served in the Legion alleged that two trucks of Western-supplied weapons and ammunition – including Javelins – had 'disappeared' from his convoy. Although this information has not been verified, other allegations of stolen arms have been reported in the Legion [28, 29]. Sources also reported that weapons from a stockpile used by an International Legion unit were moved in civilian vehicles from a city in the south to an undisclosed destination [30]. It is also possible that weapons are being hidden in caches around the front line, to be collected and sold on the black market at a later date, as happened during the 2014–2022 Donbas conflict [31].

The situation is starkly different when it comes to Russian materiel, which has been abandoned in huge quantities during the conflict. These 'trophies' have driven the emergence of what one Ukrainian soldier described as 'a simplification of bureaucracy'. Here, captured Russian materiel is exchanged among some Ukrainian units for other military equipment, with swaps negotiated using Telegram, a mobile messaging service. Although no evidence of leakage to the illicit market has been reported, an analyst for Small Arms Survey highlighted that this type of unofficial exchange could undermine stockpile management procedures, potentially increasing the supply of untracked weapons that could later enter the illicit market [32].

Soldiers are not necessarily the first to scour the battlefield. Villagers have been reported collecting abandoned weapons and ammunition and storing them at home, with some accounts of tanks being stored in barns. Many of these 'grey' stockpiles are turned over to the Ukrainian army, but there have been isolated incidents of people picking up 'trophies' around the front line and selling them on the black market. Tellingly, the domestic arms market has continued to function throughout the war, with reports of domestic arms dealers selling hand grenades, explosives, machine guns, ammunition, and anti-tank RPGs [33, 34]. It is also salient to reflect that given the prevalence of checkpoints in Ukraine since the war started, these weapons could not have moved unless the traffickers were operating as military personnel, or with the collusion of corrupt checkpoint guards.

Collectively, this rise in untracked, misappropriated and found weapons will play into the hands of criminals that are assembling illicit stockpiles for exploitation at a later date, when the fighting is less intense and the ambit for arms trafficking has expanded, as occurred when the fighting in 2014 settled into a stalemate.

The smuggling of Ukrainian conscripts, by contrast, provided a clear example of an illicit market connected with the fighting that immediately flourished in 2022. On 24 February 2022, President Zelensky ordered the mobilisation of Ukraine's adult male population between the ages of 18 and 60; all those eligible for service were unable to leave the country [35]. For human smugglers, this created a whole new clientele, and business has been brisk: between February and October 2022, more than 8000 conscripted men were caught attempting to cross the border, with 245 recorded attempts to bribe border guards [36] – but many more are likely to have succeeded. Moldova and Poland are the preferred exit routes, with small groups of people crossing at a cost of between €5000 and €10,000 each [37]. Such is the demand and revenue on offer that some smugglers of alcohol and tobacco have reportedly switched to smuggling conscripts. There have also been reports of actors with no prior criminal background setting up sophisticated smuggling schemes [38].

Corrupt professionals, including lawyers and doctors [39, 40], have facilitated the market by forging official statements, including 'fictitious documents' about the removal of conscripts from the military register and 'letters from state authorities to the State Border Service' [41]. In 2022, a counterfeit certificate of unfitness for military service cost approximately US$2000 [42]. In January 2023, the Ministry of Internal Affairs reported that Ukrainian border guards had discovered almost 3800 forged documents at checkpoints since martial law had been imposed, most around the border with Poland and Hungary [43].

The Global Initiative Against Transnational Organized Crime (GI-TOC) also received information that much more sophisticated fake documentation was in use, such as with corrupt officials inserting fake information into official databases [44]. The National Agency on Corruption Prevention (NAZK) reported a scheme in which a fake charitable organisation was set up to enter fraudulent information in the Shlyah database to enable it to register conscripts as carriers of humanitarian aid. (The Shlyah system allows those transporting humanitarian aid, medical supplies or cars for the armed forces to travel outside Ukraine for a maximum of one month.) [41, 42, 45] The head of one charity fund in Lutsk was accused of helping approximately 300 men of draft age to go abroad by offering them roles as 'drivers' of humanitarian cargo [46].

New Vulnerabilities: People, Smuggling, Reconstruction

For organised crime, the opportunities surrounding the vast number of Ukrainians displaced by the conflict – and the EU's response to the crisis – are manifold [47]. The conflict in Ukraine precipitated the swiftest and largest refugee migration in Europe since World War II, and, coupled with millions of internally displaced persons (IDPs), has created a large pool of human vulnerability [48]. Ukrainian traffickers were well placed to exploit these vulnerabilities, given that human trafficking was deeply entrenched in Ukraine before the Russian invasion of 2022.[4]

Many observers raised the alarm over the increased risk of human trafficking [50, 51], but the extent to which these fears were realised in 2022 remains unclear. At the time of writing, data was scarce, both on internal trafficking dynamics within Ukraine and among Ukrainian refugees. However, this should not be taken to indicate a lack of criminal activity, especially for human trafficking, which by its nature deprives its victims of voice and agency, and so reduces capacity for detection.

Within Ukraine, it appears likely that several forms of human trafficking, especially sexual exploitation, have continued with little interruption and may have even expanded, although the curfew may have forced brothels and other sites of exploitation to alter their hours of operation. According to GI-TOC research, online listings of sexual service providers in Ukrainian cities have begun appearing in English as well as in Russian and Ukrainian, indicating an expanding client base drawn from the diverse international actors now in-country. Some foreign fighters have reportedly used the opportunity of being in Ukraine to seek sexual services, a significant proportion of which will be rendered by women in exploitative situations [52].

As the war continues, it is likely that human trafficking within Ukraine will expand as poverty and hardship increase. In July 2022, Ukrainian officials arrested a Kyiv-based ringleader accused of orchestrating a trafficking ring that sent women recruited on Telegram to work as escorts in Turkey, where they were sexually exploited. One of the intercepted women was a single mother who had lost her job following the Russian invasion and had a child to support, and it is likely that many of the other victims had similar profiles [53]. Other parents desperate for money, food and other essentials may either exploit their own children [54] or sanction their exploitation by others. It is likely that the cybersphere will also witness an uptick in such forms of sexual exploitation.

Outside Ukraine, there have been reports of the exploitation of Ukrainian refugees. For the most part, such incidents appear to be of an individual and opportunistic nature, but there have been troubling signs of more organised exploitation. For instance, two 'hackathons' run by Europol highlighted how traffickers were targeting Ukrainian refugees for sexual and labour exploitation online. The first hackathon in May 2022 found 'a significant number of suspicious job offers' targeting Ukrainian women [55], while the second in September found 30 online platforms related to vulnerable Ukrainian refugees, five suspected traffickers of Ukrainians and 25 possible Ukrainian victims [56].

Trafficking risks are also high for Ukrainian refugees returning home to a devastated country where jobs are scarce and living conditions are dire. Returns began after the liberation of Kyiv in mid-April 2022 and have since gathered pace. In September 2022, the International Organization for Migration (IOM) estimated that more than 6 million Ukrainians (IDPs and refugees) had returned to their habitual places of residence, with 85% indicating that they intended to stay [57, p2].

An alarming development in Russian-occupied territories has been the forced movement of Ukrainians into Russia, especially from the Kherson, Zaporizhzhia and Pryazovia (Mariupol) regions. Estimates of numbers have varied substantially, especially in regard to children: in July 2022, the US State Department estimated that between 900,000 and 1.6 million Ukrainians had been forcibly deported to Russia, including 260,000 children [58]. In December 2022, the Office of the Ukrainian Parliament Commissioner for Human Rights said that it had confirmed instances of more than 12,000 Ukrainian children in Russia, of whom approximately 8,600 had been forcibly deported [59]. These forcibly dislocated populations will be extremely vulnerable to exploitation in Russia.

The border channels that opened to facilitate the mass movement of refugees also facilitated increases in other forms of illicit activity and helped redraw the map in terms of illicit smuggling flows in, through and into Ukraine, which were heavily disrupted by the intense fighting in eastern and south-eastern Ukraine and the naval blockade of Odesa.[5] Formerly, the dominant flow was from the east and south to the west (the gateway to Europe). As a result of the looser border controls and the suspension of customs duties to help the flow of refugees and humanitarian and military aid, there has been a boom in smuggling from the west of the country (although the south–west connection is still operational). In particular, illicit flows through Poland have grown because Poland is the main channel for the humanitarian aid that has been pouring into Ukraine. This aid has been granted a simplified customs procedure [61] that criminals have taken advantage of to smuggle illegal goods, such as drugs and weapons, into the country [62]. There has also been evidence of theft of humanitarian aid and military items that have been entering Ukraine from the west. In June 2022, the Ukrainian interior minister said that most cases of theft of such aid (some of which was domestically produced) were registered in Kyiv, Lviv, Kharkiv and Kirovohrad, including the theft of cars intended for the army, as well as fuel, medicines, body armour, and food [63]. One high-profile instance came in October, when it was reported that the deputy head of the Office of the President was driving an SUV that General Motors had donated to Ukraine for humanitarian purposes [64].

Looking ahead, one of the major areas of criminal opportunity will be that of reconstruction, which will take place on a massive scale. As of 1 September 2022, the Kyiv School of Economics estimated the cost of the total amount of damage caused to Ukraine's infrastructure at more than US$127 billion [65]. The costs of reconstruction and recovery will be even higher. In July 2022, the Ukrainian government set out a 10-year reconstruction plan predicated on US$750 billion in investment [66]. These reconstruction funds may enable Ukraine to reshape itself as a stronger country than it was before the war [67], but they are also vulnerable to seizure from corrupt actors and criminal groups. For instance, corrupt officials may take advantage of the lower levels of transparency that are characteristic of wartime to divert funds to chosen partners.

At the lower end of the organised crime spectrum, reconstruction efforts may be hampered by widespread theft of materials, while more sophisticated depredation may see organised crime groups inserting themselves in to reconstruction projects, both on the ground and at the procurement stage. The construction industry in Ukraine was already plagued with allegations of criminality and corruption before the invasion, which ranged from the illegal granting of permits and sales of land to raw materials (for example, illegally mined sand). A key development in this space will be Law 5655, passed in December 2022, which is intended to increase transparency and urban planning control, though some have flagged that it may also give developers greater control and so increase the risk of corruption in certain quarters [68].

Two egregious examples of government funds being misappropriated in 2022/3 highlight the nature and scale of the corruption risks in Ukraine. In November, two media investigations found that UAH1.5 billion (approximately US$40 million) had been paid out in the course of 2022 to a relatively small company known as Budinvest Engineering for the repair of roads in Dnipropetrovsk region [69, 70]. This was far more than had been paid out to any other region – an especially glaring fact considering that the region had suffered relatively little damage as a result of the war. Suspicions were further aroused by the revelation that 49% of Budinvest Engineering was owned by a female fitness instructor who was romantically connected to the head of the Dnipropetrovsk Regional State Administration; the instructor was removed from the company ownership after the investigation became public [71]. Although the investigations flagged suspicions of overpricing and possible inventory fraud of purchased raw materials, the wartime suspension of the publication of state contracts makes it impossible to ascertain the existence or the extent of any illegality.

A second example highlights that the war economy has generated opportunities for corruption. In January 2023, the deputy defence minister resigned over a scandal regarding food procurement for the military [72] after a journalist had revealed that the army had signed a contract in December 2022 for food for units stationed well away from the front line [73]. Comparing the military purchase price with the price of food both before the invasion (adjusted for inflation) and in Kyiv's supermarkets, the journalist found that the military was paying between twice and three times over the going rate for certain staple goods. For example, the military's purchase price of eggs was UAH17 per unit, while eggs were retailing in Kyiv at the same time for UAH7 per unit; potatoes were purchased at a similarly inflated mark-up. In the context of a contract worth UAH13 billion (approximately US$353 million, as of mid-December 2022) these differentials amount to millions. It is also worth noting that this contract was signed without any public scrutiny due to the suspension of the ProZorro procurement system, again highlighting the risks of reducing transparency and accountability during wartime.

Corrupt public servants siphoning off state cash may appear to be merely a sophisticated form of theft, but it also has profound ramifications for governance. Such actions hamper the delivery of civic services, while corruption also builds patronage networks, enriches criminal middlemen, and undercuts democratic principles of transparency and accountability. This phenomenon is already well entrenched in Ukraine, where corrupt officials have turned many regions and localities into 'feudal estates', in the words of Andriy Kaluzhynskyi, the head of the main unit of the National Anti-Corruption Bureau of Ukraine's (NABU) detectives [74]. As billions of dollars flow into the country for reconstruction, there is a real risk that these estates may be strengthened into criminal fortresses.

Conclusion

Past evidence indicates that planning for the post-conflict period cannot wait for peace to come – and that includes analysing and reducing the influence of organised crime. While the battles on the ground and in the political and economic space understandably dominate attention, there is a broad body of research that points to the long-term risks of putting aside considerations of the illicit economy in a time of conflict. Indeed, Ukraine itself is a case study of such risks, as highlighted by the GI-TOC's 2022 assessment of the evolution of organised crime in the self-proclaimed people's republics of Luhansk and Donetsk [75]. As such, it is essential that trends in organised crime remains a priority area of focus for policymakers, researchers, civil society and other key stakeholders.

Acknowledgements

This article was authored by the GI-TOC's Observatory of Illicit Markets and the Ukraine Conflict, established in March 2022 with GI-TOC core resources, as well as contributions from two donor states. The GI-TOC would particularly like to acknowledge and thank our field network coordinator based in Kyiv, and the growing network of journalists, analysts, civil society and local authorities with whom we consulted across the region. In particular, we commend our in-country colleagues for their work under difficult circumstances. The article also benefits from the critical guidance of members of the GI-TOC Network of Experts.

Notes

[1] This article was adapted from New Front Lines: Organized criminal economies in Ukraine in 2022 [1].

[2] It was not possible to verify this claim, and it is unlikely that such a complete sweep of Russian actors was achieved [4, 5].

[3] In the context of Ukraine before the Russian invasion, see the efforts made by Blackwater founder Erik Prince in Ukraine before the conflict [9].

[4] GI-TOC assessed human trafficking as the second most pervasive market in Ukraine (arms trafficking being the first) in the Global Organized Crime Index 2021 [49].

[5] Law enforcement and insider sources we spoke to in both Kyiv and Odesa confirmed that there is nothing coming into the port city: the ships using the grain corridor come in empty and leave with grain. There are no more ships coming in from Latin America and China; the only route is via Turkey under international supervision [60].

References

1. Global Initiative Against Transnational Organized Crime. New Front Lines: Organized criminal economies in Ukraine in 2022.

Research Report; 2023. https://globalinitiative.net/wp-content/uploads/2023/02/New-frontlines-organized-criminal-economies-in-Ukraine-in-2022-GI-TOC-February-2023.pdf.
2. Interview with underworld source. Odesa; 2022 May.
3. Interview with underworld source. Germany; 2022 May.
4. Interview with law enforcement source. Kyiv; 2022 May.
5. Interview with law enforcement source. Kyiv; 2022 December.
6. Interviews with underworld sources. Lviv; 2022 May.
7. Interview with journalist. Kyiv; December 2022.
8. Follorou J. Ukraine's clandestine war to neutralize the pro-Russian mafia. *Le Monde*. 2022 December 9 [cited 2023 January 11]. https://www.lemonde.fr/en/international/article/2022/12/09/ukraine-s-clandestine-war-to-neutralize-the-pro-russian-mafia_6007085_4.html.
9. Shuster S. Exclusive: Documents reveal Erik Prince's $10 billion plan to make weapons and create a private army in Ukraine. *Time*. 2021 July 7 [cited 2023 January 11]. https://time.com/6076035/erik-prince-ukraine-private-army/.
10. Hurska A. Making sense of the 'Semenchenko's PMC' affair. *Eurasia Daily Monitor*. 2021; 18(71). 2021 May 4 [cited 2023 January 2023]. https://jamestown.org/program/making-sense-of-the-semenchenkos-pmc-affair/.
11. Encounter during fieldwork in Bakhmut. 2022 November.
12. У будь-який час і в будь-якому місці. Військових перевірятимуть на алкоголь і наркотики за новими правилами в Україні. NV. 2022 December 15 [cited 2023 January 11]. https://nv-ua.translate.goog/ukr/ukraine/events/perevirka-viyskovih-na-alkogol-i-narkotiki-de-i-kogo-budut-pereviryati-zakonoproekt-8271-50289775.html?_x_tr_sl=uk&_x_tr_tl=en&_x_tr_hl=en&_x_tr_pto=sc.

13. Government approves UAH 100,000 in salaries for military on the frontline. *Ukrinform*. 2022 February 28 [cited 2023 January 11]. https://www.ukrinform.net/rubric-ato/3416086-government-approves-uah-100000-in-salaries-for-military-on-the-frontline.html.

14. Середньомісячна заробітна плата за видами економічної діяльності за період з початку року. Ukrstat [cited 2023 January 11]. https://ukrstat.gov.ua/operativ/operativ2005/gdn/Zarp_ek_p/Zp_ek_p_u/arh_zpp_u.htm.

15. European Monitoring Centre for Drugs and Drug Addiction. Overview of drug markets in the European Neighbourhood Policy-East countries. 2022 November 11 [cited 2023 January 11]. https://www.emcdda.europa.eu/publications/regional-reports/overview-drug-markets-european-neighbourhood-policy-east-countries_en.

16. Vorobyov N. War deepens suffering for Ukraine's drug users. *Al Jazeera*. 2022 March 16 [cited 2023 January 11]. https://www.aljazeera.com/news/2022/3/16/war-deepens-suffering-for-ukraines-drug-users.

17. Офіс Генерального прокурора. Правоохоронці викрили нарколабораторію та склад з «продукцією» на 10 млн грн і арсеналом зброї. Telegram. 2022 August 25 [cited 2023 January 11]. https://t.me/pgo_gov_ua/5376.

18. Ukraine State Bureau of Investigation. The territory of sales – the whole country: the SBI exposed and stopped the large-scale amphetamine production in Bukovyna. 2022 September 29 [cited 2023 January 11]. https://dbr.gov.ua/en/news/teritoriya-zbutu-usya-kraina-na-bukovini-dbr-vikrilo-ta-pripinilo-diyalnist-masshtabnogo-virobnictva-amfetaminu.

19. INTERPOL deputy executive director. Briefing to the G7. Berlin; 2022 September.

20. Ukraine State Bureau of Investigation. The SBI rigorously counteracts attempts of drug distribution in frontline areas. 2022 September 22 [cited 2023 January 11]. https://dbr.gov.ua/en/news/dbr-zhorstko-protidie-sprobam-rozpovsyudzhennya-narkotikiv-v-prifrontovih-rajonah.

21. Europol. Europol statement on the cooperation with Ukraine. 2022 July 22 [cited 2023 January 11]. https://www.europol.europa.eu/media-press/newsroom/news/europol-statement-cooperation-ukraine#:~:text=Regarding%20the%20war%20in%20Ukraine,once%20the%20conflict%20has%20ended.

22. Abramson J. West rushes weapons to Ukraine. Arms Control. 2022 April [cited 2023 January 11]. https://www.armscontrol.org/act/2022-04/news/west-rushes-weapons-ukraine.

23. Jakes L, Ismay J. U.S. program aims to keep sensitive weapons in Ukraine. *New York Times*. 2022 October 27 [cited 2023 January 11]. https://www.nytimes.com/2022/10/27/us/politics/weapons-aid-ukraine-russia.html.

24. Parliament creates commission to monitor movement of Western weapons in Ukraine. *Kyiv Independent*. 2022 July 19 [cited 2023 January 11]. https://kyivindependent.com/news-feed/parliament-creates-commission-to-monitor-movement-of-western-weapons-in-ukraine.

25. European Commission. Informal Home Affairs Council: EU launches the Support Hub for Internal Security and Border Management in Moldova. 2022 July 11 [cited 2023 January 11]. https://ec.europa.eu/commission/presscorner/detail/en/IP_22_4462.

26. Korenyuk M, Swinnen L, Goodman J. Undercover with Russia's fake arms dealers. *BBC*. 2022 September 24 [cited 2023 January 11]. https://www.bbc.co.uk/news/world-62983444.

27. Russia says West's Ukraine weapons are going onto the black market. *Reuters*. 2022 October 20 [cited 2023 January 11].

https://www.reuters.com/world/europe/russia-says-eu-party-conflict-ukraine-2022-10-20/.

28. Lindybeige channel. Back from the front: A British volunteer in Ukraine. *YouTube*. 2022 December [cited 2023 January 11]. https://www.youtube.com/watch?v=TCbD4WBqPg4&t=1666s.

29. Myroniuk A, Khrebet A. Investigation: International Legion soldiers allege light weapons misappropriation, abuse by commanders. *Kyiv Independent*. 2022 November 30 [cited 2023 January 11]. https://kyivindependent.com/investigations/investigation-international-legion-misappropriation.

30. Interview with a media source. Kyiv; 2022 December.

31. Prentice A, Zverev A. Ukraine has become a trove for the black market arms trade. *Business Insider*. 2016 July 25 [cited 2023 January 11]. https://www.businessinsider.com/ukraine-trove-black-market-arms-trade-2016-7?r=US&IR=T.

32. Gibbons-Neff T, Yermak N. A frontline shadow economy: Ukrainian units swap tanks and artillery. *New York Times*. 2022 August 30 [cited 2023 January 11]. https://www.nytimes.com/2022/08/30/world/europe/ukrainian-soldiers-weapons-front-line.html?smid=nytcore-ios-share&referringSource=articleShare.

33. The SBU detained an arms dealer and discovered a stash of weapons in Zaporizhzhia. *Odessa Journal*. 2022 July 30 [cited 2023 January 11]. https://odessa-journal.com/the-sbu-detained-an-arms-dealer-and-discovered-a-stash-of-weapons-in-zaporizhzhia/.

34. Pereiaslav City. Поліція Київщини показала відео затримання підпільного торговця зброєю з Переяслава. 2022 October 28 [cited 2023 January 11]. https://pereiaslav.city/articles/246432/u-pereyaslavi-zatrimali-torgovcya-zbroeyu-ta-vibuhonebezpechnimi-predmetami-video.

35. Ukraine president orders general mobilization. *DW*. 2022 February 25 [cited 2023 January 11]. https://www.dw.com/en/ukraine-president-orders-general-mobilization/a-60908996.

36. National Agency on Corruption Prevention. Departure from Ukraine abroad under martial law: How to eliminate corruption. The NAZK presented the research. 2022 October 26 [cited 2023 January 11]. https://nazk.gov.ua/en/news/74914/.

37. Interview with conscript. Lviv. October 2022.

38. Ковалева А. Незаконно переправляли через границу призывников: в Киеве разоблачена преступная схема. StopCor. 2022 December 8 [cited 2023 January 11]. https://www.stopcor.org/section-suspilstvo/news-nezakonno-perepravlyali-cherez-kordon-prizovnikiv-v-kievi-vikrito-zlochinnu-shemu-08-12-2022.html.

39. Ukrainian Office of the Prosecutor General. Незаконний перетин кордону військовозобов'язаними за 12 тис доларів США – трьом особам повідомлено про підозру. 2022 October 20 [cited 2023 January 11]. https://www.gp.gov.ua/ua/posts/nezakonnii-peretin-kordonu-viiskovozobovyazanimi-za-12-tis-dolariv-ssa-tryom-osobam-povidomleno-pro-pidozru.

40. Волинського лікаря затримали за виготовлення довідок для ухилянтів. Zaxid.net. 2023 January 13 [cited 2023 January 11]. https://zaxid.net/volinskogo_likarya_zatrimali_za_vigotovlennya_dovidok_dlya_uhilyantiv_n1556055.

41. NAZK. Departure from Ukraine abroad under martial law: How to eliminate corruption. The NACP presented the research. 2022 October 26 [cited 2023 January 11]. https://nazk.gov.ua/en/news/74914/.

42. Visit Ukraine. Running away from Ukraine: How men flee from war. 2022 November 3 [cited 2023 January 11]. https://visitukraine.today/blog/1109/running-away-from-ukraine-how-men-flee-from-war.

43. MVS. Майже 3,8 тисячі підроблених документів з початку воєнного стану прикордонники виявили в пунктах пропуску. 2023 January 13 [cited 2023 January 11]. https://mvs.gov.ua/uk/news/maize-38-tisiaci-pidroblenix-dokumentiv-z-pocatku-vojennogo-stanu-prikordonniki-viiavili-v-punktax-propusku.

44. GI-TOC expert personal communication with lawyer. London; 2022 December 16.

45. The Security Service of Ukraine eliminated three more schemes for evaders to flee abroad. *Odessa Journal*. 2022 November 10 [cited 2023 January 11]. https://odessa-journal.com/the-security-service-of-ukraine-eliminated-three-more-schemes-for-evaders-to-flee-abroad/.

46. Ukrainian Office of the Prosecutor General. Організація незаконного перетину кордону через систему «Шлях» – керівнику благодійного фонду та посереднику повідомлено про підозру. 2022 November 1 [cited 2023 January 11]. https://www.gp.gov.ua/ua/posts/organizaciya-nezakonnogo-peretinu-kordonu-cerez-sistemu-slyax-kerivniku-blagodiinogo-fondu-ta-poseredniku-povidomleno-pro-pidozru.

47. GI-TOC. The vulnerable millions: Organized crime risks in Ukraine's mass displacement. 2023 March 29 [cited 2023 January 11]. https://globalinitiative.net/analysis/ukraine-conflict-crime-displacement-risk-trafficking-smuggling/.

48. Statement by Osnat Lubrani, UN Resident & Humanitarian Coordinator in Ukraine. "The war has caused the fastest and largest displacement of people in Europe since World War II". UN. 2022 March 24 [cited 2023 January 11]. https://ukraine.un.org/en/175836-war-has-caused-fastest-and-largest-displacement-people-europe-world-war-ii.

49. GI-TOC. Global Organized Crime Index. 2021 [cited 2023 January 11]. https://ocindex.net/country/ukraine (2021 profile).

50. International Organization for Migration. IOM warns of increased risk of trafficking in persons for people fleeing Ukraine. 2022 March 16 [cited 2023 January 11]. https://www.iom.int/news/iom-warns-increased-risk-trafficking-persons-people-fleeing-ukraine.

51. Siegfried K. Ukraine crisis creates new trafficking risks. UNHCR. 2022 April 13 [cited 2023 January 11]. https://www.unhcr.org/uk/news/stories/2022/4/62569be24/ukraine-crisis-creates-new-trafficking-risks.html.

52. Information received via a Ukrainian activist. Washington, D.C. 2022 November 3.

53. Tondo L. Ukraine prosecutors uncover sex trafficking ring preying on women fleeing country. *The Guardian*. 2022 July 7 [cited 2023 January 11]. https://www.theguardian.com/global-development/2022/jul/07/ukraine-prosecutors-uncover-sex-trafficking-ring-preying-on-women-fleeing-country.

54. Андаліцька І. На Миколаївщині мати знімала своїх маленьких дітей в порно. Unian.ua. 2022 February 4 [cited 2023 January 11]. https://www.unian.ua/incidents/na-mikolajivshchini-mati-znimala-svojih-malenkih-ditey-v-porno-i-prodavala-v-interneti-novini-ukrajina-11693806.html.

55. Europol. Human traffickers luring Ukrainian refugees on the web targeted in EU-wide hackathon. 2022 June 23 [cited 2023 January 11]. https://www.europol.europa.eu/media-press/newsroom/news/human-traffickers-luring-ukrainian-refugees-web-targeted-in-eu-wide-hackathon.

56. Europol. 20 countries spin a web to catch human traffickers during a hackathon. 2022 September 21 [cited 2023 January 11]. https://www.europol.europa.eu/media-press/newsroom/news/20-countries-spin-web-to-catch-human-traffickers-during-hackathon.

57. International Organization for Migration. Ukraine Returns Report. 2022 September [cited 2023 January 11]. https://displacement.iom.int/sites/g/files/tmzbdl1461/files/reports/IOM_UKR%20Returns%20Report_R9%20GPS_FINAL_0.pdf.

58. Blinken A. Russia's 'Filtration' operations, forced disappearances, and mass deportations of Ukrainian citizens. US Department of State. 2022 July 13 [cited 2023 January 11]. https://www.state.gov/russias-filtration-operations-forced-disappearances-and-mass-deportations-of-ukrainian-citizens/.

59. Ukraine Media Centre. It is confirmed that more than 12,000 Ukrainian children are in Russia, about 8,600 of them are forcibly deported — Ombudsman. 2022 December 14 [cited 2023 January 11]. https://mediacenter.org.ua/strong-it-is-confirmed-that-more-than-12-000-ukrainian-children-are-in-russia-about-8-600-of-them-are-forcibly-deported-ombudsman-strong/.

60. Interviews with law enforcement and insider sources. Odesa and Kyiv; December 2022.

61. Ares. Rules for customs clearance of humanitarian aid in Ukraine are simplified. [Cited 2023 January 11]. https://ares.ua/en/how-clear-cargo-humanitarian-aid.

62. Interviews with law enforcement source and journalist. Kyiv; May 2022. Interview with activist. Dnipro; May 2022.

63. Most cases of humanitarian aid fraud registered in Kyiv City, Lviv, Kharkiv, Kirovohrad regions – Monastysky. Interfax Ukraine. 2022 June 22 [cited 2023 January 11]. https://en.interfax.com.ua/news/general/840841.html.

64. Опанасенко М. Заступник Єрмака їздить на позашляховику, який General Motors передав Україні для гуманітарних цілей. Bihus.info. 2022 October 27 [cited 2023 January 11]. https://bihus.info/zastupnyk-yermaka-yizdyt-na-pozashlyahovyku-yakyj-general-motors-peredav-ukrayini-dlya-gumanitarnyh-czilej/.

65. Kyiv School of Economics. The total amount of damage caused to Ukraine's infrastructure is more than $127 billion — KSE Institute's report as of September 2022. 2022 October 21 [cited 2023 January 11]. https://kse.ua/about-the-school/news/the-total

66. National Recovery Council. Ukraine's National Recovery Plan. 2022 July [cited 2023 January 11]. https://uploads-ssl.webflow.com/621f88db25fbf24758792dd8/62c166751fcf41105380a733_NRC%20Ukraine%27s%20Recovery%20Plan%20blueprint_ENG.pdf.

67. Lewarne S, et al. The reconstruction of Ukraine: Historical lessons for postwar reconstruction of Ukraine. Deloitte. 2022 October 10 [cited 2023 January 11]. https://www2.deloitte.com/uk/en/insights/industry/public-sector/ukraine-reconstruction-plan.html.

68. Shashkova M. Urban planning reform Ukrainian-style: What's behind the controversy. *Kyiv Post*. 2022 December 15 [cited 2023 January 11]. https://www.kyivpost.com/post/5767.

69. Седлецька Н, et al. Велика відбудова. Керівник Дніпропетровщини платить бюджетні мільярди своїй супутниці – розслідування. *Radio Svoboda*. 2022 November 2 [cited 2023 January 11]. https://www.radiosvoboda.org/a/skhemy-velyke-budivnytstvo-dnipropetrovshchyna/32111136.html.

70. Ткач М. Фітнес-тренерка на мільярд. Як компанія близької подруги керівника Дніпропетровської ОДА стала найбагатшою під час війни. Pravda. 2022 November 2 [cited 2023 January 11]. https://www.pravda.com.ua/articles/2022/11/2/7374579/.

71. Myroniuk A. Investigative Stories from Ukraine: Russian soldiers involved in Bucha massacre identified. *Kyiv Independent*. 2022 December 28 [cited 2023 January 11]. https://kyivindependent.com/investigative-stories-from-ukraine-russian-soldiers-involved-in-bucha-massacre-identified/.

72. Deputy defense minister summoned his resignation in wake of corruption scandal. *Kyiv Independent*. 2023 January 24 [cited 2023 January 27]. https://kyivindependent.com/news-feed/deputy-defense-minister-summoned-his-resignation-in-wake-of-corruption-scandal.

73. Ніколов Ю. Трапилося найгірше, хоч і передбачуване. ZN.UA. 2023 January 21 [cited 2023 January 27]. https://zn.ua/ukr/economic-security/tilovi-patsjuki-minoboroni-pid-chas-vijni-piljajut-na-kharchakh-dlja-zsu-bilshe-nizh-za-mirnoho-zhittja.html.

74. Ведернікова І. Керівник головного підрозділу детективів НАБУ Андрій Калужинський: «У нас люди, яких підозрюють чи обвинувачують у корупції, — рукопожатні. Їх підвищують по службі, у них беруть інтерв'ю та запрошують на заходи». ZN.UA. 2022 December 23 [cited 2023 January 11]. https://zn.ua/ukr/internal/kerivnik-holovnoho-pidrozdilu-detektiviv-nabu-andrij-kaluzhinskij-u-nas-ljudi-jakikh-pidozrjujut-chi-obvinuvachujut-u-koruptsiji-rukopozhatni-jikh-pidvishchujut-po-sluzhbi-u-nikh-berut-intervju-ta-zaproshujut-na-zakhodi.html.

75. Galeotti M, Arutunyan A. Rebellion as racket: Crime and the Donbas conflict. GI-TOC. 2022 July 11 [cited 2023 January 11]. https://globalinitiative.net/analysis/donbas-conflict-crime/.

PART 4
The West

12. War in Ukraine in a Polarised America

Peter Harris, Iren Marinova and Gabriella Gricius

America's response to the Russian invasion of Ukraine surprised many analysts, both because of its severity, and because of the speed and vigour with which it was implemented. Yet President Biden's policy toward the war in Ukraine has also been noteworthy because of the bipartisan support it has enjoyed at home. Americans have become used to hyper-partisanship as a defining feature of their government and politics, but Biden's policies of support for Ukraine have engendered a rare instance of cross-party unity in Washington, DC. For how long will US support for Ukraine endure? And what are the limits of bipartisanship? In this chapter, we argue that the key to answering these and related questions is to ascertain the national interests that US leaders view as being at stake in the war. After considering three rival explanations of US policy toward Ukraine, however, we conclude that it is difficult to determine whether there is any stable intersubjective understanding of the US interest in Ukrainian security. The future of America's engagement in Ukraine will depend upon how the war is experienced, processed, and politicised by actors on the home front.

To what extent does Ukraine 'matter' to the United States? Before the war, it was fair to assume that a sizable gap existed between US rhetoric about Ukrainian security and Washington's willingness to act in defense of the country. At least, Russia's annexation of Crimea in 2014 and eight years of war in the Donbas had elicited only a modest response from the United States. President Obama, for example, imposed economic sanctions and diplomatic punishments upon Russia from 2014 onwards but refused Ukraine's requests for lethal military aid with which to combat Russian-backed separatists. President Trump, meanwhile, cared so little about Ukrainian security that he infamously threatened to withhold aid unless his counterpart President Zelensky would agree to investigate alleged corruption involving Joe Biden's son, Hunter Biden. This apparent 'quid pro quo' was what led to Trump's first impeachment by the US House of Representatives. Assessing the situation in late 2021 and early 2022, it would hardly have been surprising if Russian leaders had concluded that US support for Ukraine was nothing more than cheap talk. The revealed preference of America's leaders, it seemed, was to avoid the vertical or horizontal escalation of the smoldering war in eastern Ukraine, even if this meant tolerating Russia's violation of global norms regarding sovereignty, territorial integrity, and the non-use of military force.

In the event, of course, the United States responded to Russia's full-scale invasion of Ukraine in February 2022 with vigour and resolve. Helped by the fact that US intelligence services had correctly assessed Moscow's intention to invade, President Biden wasted no time mobilising US allies and a large number of non-aligned countries to condemn the Putin regime at the United Nations and in other international fora. Biden also unleashed economic sanctions of unprecedented breadth and depth on the Russian economy, despite the predictable costs that these measures would entail for US firms and consumers [1, 2]. Most importantly, the Biden Administration involved itself in the physical conduct of the war by sharing intelligence with the Ukrainian military, by providing essential financial and humanitarian assistance to Kyiv, by supplying vital arms and ammunition, and by providing training to Ukrainian forces. The scale of this support has been impressive, including thousands of Stinger (anti-aircraft) and Javelin (anti-tank) missiles, dozens of howitzers and high mobility artillery rocket systems ('HIMARS'), Abrams tanks, and even the Patriot missile defence system [3–5]. Indeed, the quality and quantity of US involvement in the conflict led some astute observers to question whether Washington could accurately be described as anything other than an active belligerent [6]. Yet despite the high level of risk that obviously comes along with participating in a third party's war with Russia – a nuclear-armed power that borders several US treaty allies – President Biden's support for Ukraine enjoyed broad bipartisan support in Congress and the country at large. This is a rare instance of cross-party consensus in an era defined by polarisation, hyper-partisanship, and political dysfunction [7].

What explains the contrast between America's lacklustre support for Ukraine before February 2022 and its robust engagement in the conflict since Russia's full-scale invasion took place? In this chapter, we consider three stylised rationalisations of US policy toward Ukraine and explore the implications of each explanation. While the available evidence does not permit us to make any strong claims about which account of US policy might be superior to the alternatives – not least of all because the war in Ukraine is still ongoing – our analysis at least suggests that the future of US support for Ukraine will be critically dependent upon how the war is experienced, processed, and politicised at home. America's response to the war has been robust over the past year, but there are reasons to suspect that this level of support could be become unsupportable if the domestic context shifts.

Belated Balancing, Overreach, or Bloodletting?

One way to understand why the United States rushed to support Ukraine in February 2022, despite having done relatively little in Ukraine's material defense for the prior eight years, is to frame the response as an overdue balancing behaviour. From this view, the United States should have done much more to contain the Russian threat from 2014 to 2022 given the obvious, real, and present danger that Moscow posed to transatlantic security [8]. The correct response to the annexation of Crimea would have been to check Russian aggression through the provision of lethal aid to Ukraine, the expansion of US deployments to Eastern Europe, and perhaps even the admission of Ukraine into the NATO alliance. The implied counterfactual is that Russia would never have invaded Ukraine in 2022 if the United States had done more by way of credible deterrence. That the Obama and Trump administrations failed to take such measures must have been the result of some set of domestic-level pathologies such as the war-weariness of the US public, the personal failings of individual leaders, or political dysfunction in Washington,

DC [8]. Following the full-scale invasion of Ukraine, however, any domestic impediments to balancing against Russia were pushed aside. Popular revulsion at Putin's war, stirring media coverage of the invasion, and a swell of elite-level support for intervention gave the Biden Administration the political cover necessary to mobilise the United States behind an adroit foreign policy the likes of which should properly have been in place since 2014 or perhaps even 2008.

An opposite view is that US leaders before February 2022 had been wise to prioritise peaceful bilateral relations with Russia over the absolute security of Ukraine. From this perspective, President Biden has not so much skilfully recalibrated US policy toward Ukraine as he has overreacted, overreached, and deviated from a more sober course. The invasion of Ukraine was an appalling violation of international law, but did not come anywhere close to threatening US national security. While the United States does have some limited interests at stake in Ukraine, these do not justify the level of risk that Biden has assumed with its bold measures to defend Kyiv [9]. This view of US policy toward Ukraine is typically favoured by realist (or 'restrainer') scholars and analysts, who worry that the United States risks sparking a full-blown conflagration with Russia over an issue that, at base, has little relation to core US interests. As Ben Friedman has argued, 'The war has a low probability of a serious escalation, but the longer you continue to roll those dice, even if the odds are low, the more likely you are to hit on a future disaster' [10]. Instead of providing Ukraine with a blank cheque to prosecute its war against Russia, this line of reasoning holds that US interests would be best served by diplomacy to bring the war to a swift conclusion – even if this means tolerating some territorial gains for Russia [9].

A third explanation is that Ukraine's fate *per se* does not matter much to the United States, but the unexpected opportunity to weaken Russia is one that the US government has been highly motivated to seize post-February 2022. After 2014, the United States was muted in its response to Ukrainian insecurity because there were not obvious options for using the Crimean annexation or the war in the Donbas as entry points for engineering the enervation of the Putin regime. But once Russia initiated its full-scale invasion of Ukraine – and especially after Kyiv's forces began to inflict heavy losses upon the Russian military – officials in Washington were quick to identify an opportunity to turn the war into a blistering defeat for a longstanding Great Power rival. Defense Secretary Lloyd Austin lent some credence to this view when he described US policy as one of ensuring that Russia would never again be able to wage a similar invasion in the future [11], which several commentators took as an admission that US policy was now to destroy as many Russian forces as possible [12–14]. Viewed through this lens, what the United States is doing to Russia in Ukraine is a cynical, opportunistic, and self-serving policy of bloodletting – an attempt to degrade a rival power – rather than a defense of strict national interests or international norms [15 p155].

Which of these explanations is correct? Should US policy toward the war in Ukraine be viewed as a necessary corrective to an ill-fated policy of under-balancing against Russia? Is the United States alternatively guilty of overreach and overreaction? Or are US leaders engaged in a cold and calculated policy of bloodletting against a Great Power rival? These are important questions. If answers could be furnished, then analysts would be far better equipped to understand the present and future contours of US policy toward Ukraine and Russia. If the US political class has truly determined that Ukraine's survival is integral to US national security, for example, then bipartisanship on the question of military support for Kyiv can be expected to persist; the Russian threat will induce leaders in Washington to put aside their partisan differences in service of a well-understood national interest. On the other hand, if the Biden Administration can credibly be portrayed as overreaching in Ukraine then it follows that, at some point, savvy political entrepreneurs in Washington will recognise the advantage in telegraphing this message to the voting public; as a result, it should be expected that leading politicians (especially those in the party out of power) will stake out positions in opposition to the war, perhaps hastening the demise of US backing for Ukraine. The same is true if the White House has primarily been motivated by a desire to weaken and punish Russia. A cynical and unnecessary policy of bloodletting would be hard to justify to the general public, not least of all because it carries high risks of provoking an increasingly desperate Russian regime to attack NATO, and so would ultimately be vulnerable to objections at the domestic level.

Dissecting Biden's Constrained Intervention

Alas, as noted above, the available evidence makes it difficult – if not entirely impossible – to discern at this juncture whether and to what extent US leaders truly view national interests to be at stake in Ukraine. Part of the problem is that President Biden has responded to the war in Ukraine by pursuing what we call 'constrained interventionism'. This is a hybrid approach that blends elements of militarism, interventionism, and risk-taking with instances of restraint, buck-passing, and circumspection. From a foreign policy perspective, there are obvious benefits to such a strategy: the Biden Administration is clearly aspiring to check Russian aggression and buoy the government in Kyiv while still respecting some firm boundaries when it comes to dealing with Russia. But for the time being, constrained interventionism is proving to be a difficult animal to dissect. Elements of the strategy are consistent with all of the stylised models of US policy described above. This makes it challenging to identify clear evidence of what is truly driving America's engagement in the Ukraine War and to what extent disquiet with these policies has the potential to metastasise into fully fledged opposition to the Biden approach.

To some analysts, the 'interventionist' components of Biden's strategy toward the war in Ukraine are evidence that the United States is engaged in overdue balancing behaviour against the Russian regime. The provision of financial and humanitarian assistance to the government of Ukraine; the supply of military aid, and the gradual expansion of this aid to include high-value weapons systems such as Patriot missile systems and Abrams tanks; intelligence sharing with Ukrainian forces; and determined efforts to isolate Russia as much as possible on the world stage – all of these policies and others like them suggest that President Biden views Russia as an existential threat to US national security and the world order upon which a wide range of US interests depend. Viewed from Europe, Biden's clear leadership on Ukraine has been interpreted as welcome evidence that the United States remains committed to the transatlantic alliance despite the tumult of the Trump years, the chaotic (and unilateral) withdrawal from Afghanistan, and the so-called 'pivot' to Asia.

To other analysts, however, the 'constrained' elements of Biden's approach to the war are reason enough to suspect that the White House understands Ukraine's fate to be something far less than an existential issue for the United States. On the contrary, it seems plausible that President Biden's *overriding* goal in Ukraine is not to see Russian forces ejected from the occupied territories but to minimise the risk of a Russian attack on the United States or a NATO ally. Toward this end, the United States has prevented partners in Europe from supplying Ukraine with fighter jets, for example, while summarily dismissing proposals such as the designation of no-fly zones above Ukraine, the blockade of Russian ports, or the deployment of regular US forces to western Ukraine (although a small number of US special forces have been operating in areas of Ukraine under Kyiv's control). Tellingly, the United States has also refused to endorse Kyiv's bid for membership of NATO – an uncompromising position that would seem to betray a hard reality that the Biden Administration does not, in fact, view Ukraine's security as something worth fighting for.

At the same time, there is also compelling evidence to suggest that the United States is engaged in bloodletting in Ukraine – at least to a degree. Secretary Austin's comment about wanting to 'weaken' Russia, noted above, is the most obvious case in point [11]. But which explanation of US foreign policy toward Ukraine is most accurate? Unfortunately, there is precious little evidence to allow objective analysts to discriminate between the rival explanations laid out above. Overdue balancing, overreaction and overreach, and bloodletting – each of these explanations can plausibly account for the strategy of constrained intervention. To understand which causal logic(s) might actually be at play, new evidence will be needed regarding US interests, intentions, and risk-acceptance – evidence that has yet to be observed, and will only become available with the passage of time.

The Home Front

So far, we have argued that the question of how US elites are defining national interests in relation to Ukraine is of critical importance to understanding the future of US policy toward the war, but also that this question is unanswerable at this juncture. However, it is worth emphasising that America's support for Ukraine will also be contingent upon how the war is 'felt' in domestic politics beyond the Beltway. The insight here is that leaders are not always empowered to pursue national interests as they see fit. On the contrary, the ideas and interests of ordinary people often intervene to upend decision-makers' plans or else encourage leaders to change their minds about the desired ends and means of foreign and defense policy. This makes it even more challenging to say with confidence what is causing the US response to the war in Ukraine, and when and why America's support for Kyiv might falter.

In broad terms, the war in Ukraine promises to affect America's domestic politics in three interrelated ways: short-term economic, long-term fiscal, and party-political. First and foremost, there is the short-term economic cost of the war. By moving to buoy the government of Ukraine and supply advanced weapons, America is ensuring that Ukraine does not lose its fight for national survival. Yet the United States will pay an economic price for as long as the war continues [1, 2]. Given that Ukraine is a major supplier of grain and Russia is a major exporter of energy (oil and natural gas) to world markets, it was inescapable that the disruptions of war would push up prices in the United States and around the world – and at a time when inflation was (and remains) high because of the Covid-19 pandemic [15]. Going forward, it will matter enormously whether the US media and voting public remain broadly supportive of Ukraine despite the negative impact upon US households or whether the United States begins to experience some fatigue with the war, perhaps even growing to resent the government in Kyiv for refusing to make peace with Putin's Russia.

There are also long-term costs to the US taxpayer that are taking shape because of the war in Ukraine. While the money spent on the war (estimated at around $75 bn by February 2023) is manageable when viewed in the context of the overall US defense budget, the conflict has been used by the Biden Administration and members of Congress to justify higher defense spending into the future. Any suspicions (or hopes) that President Biden might be intent on downsizing the US military and shifting national resources from guns to butter should therefore be laid to rest. Counterintuitively, however, it is not always Russia being portrayed as the primary exigency requiring the United States to spend more on defense; even after the invasion of Ukraine was well underway, the Department of Defense was describing China – not Russia – as the 'pacing challenge' to the United States.

Since February 2022, the US government has been emphatic that expanded military commitments in Europe will not prevent upgrades to US capabilities in the Indo-Pacific designed to meet the challenges posed by a rising China. Needless to say, waging broad-based strategies of containment against two Great Power rivals on either side of the Eurasian landmass will not be cheap. For these reasons, the long-term costs of the war (and the US response to it) should be considered highly significant from a fiscal perspective.

Third, the war has shown some early signs of becoming a position issue in US politics – that is, an issue that politicians in both parties may choose to seize upon in order to make broader points about foreign and defense policy. In October 2022, for example, progressive Democrats released a letter calling for President Biden to support talks to end the war in Ukraine. While these legislators later walked back their letter (blaming its accidental and unauthorised release on a staff member), the incident at least hinted at uneasiness among left-wing Democrats regarding the Biden Administration's interventionist approach. Perhaps unsurprisingly, Republicans have been even more vocal with their criticisms of Biden's strategy. Even though only a handful of Republicans have called for US support to be terminated, a growing number have found it expedient to caution against giving Kyiv unrestricted aid (a so-called 'blank cheque'), including the two most likely figures to represent the party in the 2024 presidential election: Donald Trump and Ron DeSantis [16, 17].

It is important not to overstate the significance of Ukraine in US domestic politics. The war did not seem to be a high-salience issue during the 2022 midterm elections, for example. But there are emerging signs that the war in Eastern Europe is exerting sizeable effects upon the economy, government, and politics of the United States. The current upshot is that President Biden seems to feel empowered (or even compelled) to 'stay the course' in Ukraine lest he resurrect popular memory of his chaotic withdrawal from Afghanistan. But this calculus could yet shift in response to changing conditions at the domestic level, especially in the run-up to and aftermath of next year's presidential election.

Conclusion: Revealed Preferences or Concealed Fractures?

In the final analysis, the war in Ukraine can be said to have revealed some things about US foreign policy and domestic politics while making it harder to discern other patterns. Counterintuitively, the war might have revealed precious little about the importance of Eastern Europe to the United States. It is tempting to conclude, of course, that America's deep engagement in the Ukraine War is evidence that this region of Eurasia matters more to the United States than had previously been appreciated (the 'belated balancing' explanation). But we have cautioned against treating US involvement in the war as dispositive evidence that Ukraine's security is a national interest of the United States. There are other plausible explanations of America's conduct over the past year ('overreach' or 'bloodletting') that do not assume any strong US interest in Ukrainian security *per se*. To be sure, the available evidence is clear that a broad-based majority of the US political class is willing to back an intervention to defend Ukraine *so far* – but there is also evidence that some US leaders are looking for ways to politicise the war for narrow partisan gain. It is not at all clear, therefore, that the recent history of US support for Ukraine is rooted in immutable material interests.

One thing the war *has* revealed, perhaps, is that policies of retrenchment and restraint remain unpopular in US politics – or, at least, risky for politicians to embrace [18]. Interventionism, on the other hand, continues to enjoy a wellspring of support at home. Even leaders who oppose US support for Ukraine tend to couch their opposition in language much different from restraint, usually arguing that the United States should be doing much more to balance against China in the Indo-Pacific. This general climate of anti-restraint and anti-retrenchment sentiment is nothing new, of course. President Trump ran up against these same ideational roadblocks when he proposed retrenchment from Afghanistan, Syria, South Korea, and elsewhere. President Biden endured some of the strongest criticisms of his presidency when he ended the twenty-year war in Afghanistan. But even so, it is notable that the US political class has (so far) determined that the United States must be engaged in Ukraine and should use its enormous material and soft power to influence the war's trajectory. Even if the political foundations of US interventionism are showing some visible signs of decay, they seem to be in much finer fettle than some analysts (and even President Putin) had suspected prior to February 2022.

Perhaps most importantly for analysts of US foreign policy, however, the Ukraine War might be concealing some long-term fractures among the US political class. Broadly speaking, the strategy of constrained interventionism is one that most national-level leaders can get behind. So far, the two parties and most individual lawmakers have sought to distinguish themselves from each other in ways that do not risk contradicting the overall consensus that the United States ought to be backing Ukraine. But cracks in this consensus are not hard to discern and may yet widen, especially if the war continues for years and the domestic implications for United States become ever more apparent [19, 20]. Indeed, it would be unusual if political polarisation and hyper-partisanship did not emerge as features of the domestic debate over Ukraine, just as they are features of most other national-level conversations. Today, the most obvious signs of dissent come from Republicans [21], some of whom have sensed an opportunity to benefit from public scepticism about 'black cheque' support for Kyiv. Even Kevin McCarthy, Speaker of the House since January 2023, has repeatedly insisted that US support for Ukraine should be provided within limits – a position supported by the far right of the Republicans in Congress as well as conservative think tanks such as the Heritage Foundation [22, 23]. If the Republican Party takes control of the White House in 2024, with or without majorities in Congress, the conditions will be ripe for a significant change in approach.

The war in Ukraine was a major exogenous shock to US politics and foreign policy, jolting the Biden Administration to overhaul its approach to European security and forcing other domestic actors to develop their own coherent narratives to make sense of Russia's war of choice. To some, the invasion was evidence that the United States should do more to combat Russia, China, and other would-be revisionist powers, perhaps at the expense of engagement in peripheral countries such as Afghanistan [24]. To others, the war has been a reminder that the United States must redouble its efforts to minimise the risk of conflict with its Great Power rivals in a multipolar world, lest the war in Ukraine (or a future war over Taiwan) result in calamitous results. For the past year, Biden's pragmatic policy of constrained intervention has succeeded at bridging these rival sensibilities as well as the wider fractures that plague contemporary US politics; most people in the United States have found something to like about the policy, helping to avoid a situation where the war in Ukraine becomes just another issue over which US politicians fight tooth and nail. However, as the war drags on – and as its implications continue to be felt by people in the United States and their elected representatives – more will become clear about the extent of US interests in Ukraine and the likely future of US commitments to the region. Dramatic shifts in policy are not out of the question.

References

1. Eisen N, Klein A, Picon M, Lewis R, Blumenthal L, Johnston S, et al. The Brookings sanctions tracker. 2022 September [cited 2023 March 29]. https://www.brookings.edu/research/the-brookings-sanctions-tracker.
2. Patel D. How sanctions on Russia and the invasion of Ukraine affect the U.S. economy. 2022 March 29 [cited 2023 March 12]. https://penntoday.upenn.edu/news/how-sanctions-russia-and-invasion-ukraine-affect-us-economy.
3. US Department of State. U.S. security cooperation with Ukraine. 2023 April 19 [cited 2023 May 2]. https://www.state.gov/u-s-security-cooperation-with-ukraine/.
4. US Department of Defense. U.S. sends Ukraine $400 million in military equipment. 2023 March 3 [cited 2023 May 2]. https://

www.defense.gov/News/News-Stories/Article/Article/3318508/us-sends-ukraine-400-million-in-military-equipment/.

5. Pemble A. US-made Patriot guided missile systems arrive in Ukraine. *AP News*. 2023 April 19 [cited 2023 May 2]. https://apnews.com/article/russia-ukraine-war-patriot-missile-system-4c79f9110899ca1880a61f2d1f328179.

6. Kristian B. Are we sure America is not at war in Ukraine? *New York Times*. 2022 June 20 [cited 2023 April 1]. https://www.nytimes.com/2022/06/20/opinion/international-world/ukraine-war-america.html.

7. Trubowitz P, Harris P. End of the American Century? Slow erosion of the domestic sources of usable power. *International Affairs*. 2019; 95(3): 619–639. DOI: https://doi.org/10.1093/ia/iiz055.

8. Stravers A. Partisan conflict over grand strategy in Eastern Europe, 2014–2017. Orbis. 2018; 62(4): 541–556. DOI: https://doi.org/10.1016/j.orbis.2018.08.002.

9. Shifrinson J. American interests in the Ukraine War. *Defense Priorities*. 2022 September 14 [cited 2023 February 26]. https://www.defensepriorities.org/explainers/american-interests-in-the-ukraine-war.

10. Hussain M. The war in Ukraine is just getting started. *The Intercept*. 2023 March 9 [cited 2023 March 28]. https://theintercept.com/2023/03/09/ukraine-war-russia-iran-iraq/.

11. Ryan M., Timsit A. U.S. wants Russian military 'weakened' from Ukraine invasion, Austin says. *Washington Post*. 2022 April 25 [cited 2023 March 28]. https://www.washingtonpost.com/world/2022/04/25/russia-weakened-lloyd-austin-ukraine-visit.

12. Borger J. Pentagon chief's Russia remarks show shift in US's declared aims in Ukraine. *The Guardian*. 2022 April 25 [cited 2023 March 28]. https://www.theguardian.com/world/2022/apr/25/russia-weakedend-lloyd-austin-ukraine.

13. New York Post. Thanks, Lloyd Austin, for finally saying the US wants Putin completely defeated. 2022 April 26 [cited 2023 April 2]. https://nypost.com/2022/04/26/lloyd-austin-finally-admits-us-wants-putin-completely-defeated.

14. Galen Carpenter T. NATO's cynical, risky strategy of arms aid to defeat Russia in Ukraine. *Cato Institute*. 2022 June 11 [cited 2023 March 28]. https://www.cato.org/commentary/natos-cynical-risky-strategy-arms-aid-defeat-russia-ukraine.

15. Hannon P. Russia's war in Ukraine to cost global economy $2.8 trillion, OECD says. *The Wall Street Journal*. 2022 September 26 [cited 2023 March 28]. https://www.wsj.com/articles/russias-war-in-ukraine-to-cost-global-economy-2-8-trillion-oecd-says-11664177401.

16. Mueller J. Trump says he would 'solve' war in Ukraine in 24 hours if reelected. *The Hill*. 2023 March 28 [cited 2023 April 2]. https://thehill.com/policy/international/3921574-trump-says-he-would-solve-war-in-ukraine-in-24-hours-if-reelected.

17. Garrity K. War in Ukraine 'distracts from our country's most pressing challenges,' DeSantis says. *Politico*. 2023 March 13 [cited 2023 April 2]. https://www.politico.com/news/2023/03/13/war-ukraine-ron-desantis-00086917.

18. Walldorf W, Yeo A. Domestic hurdles to a grand strategy of restraint. *The Washington Quarterly*. 2019; 42(4): 43–56. DOI: https://doi.org/10.1080/0163660X.2019.1693107.

19. Dress B. House Republican says Congress doesn't need to pass 'Democrat bills' on Ukraine. *The Hill*. 2022 November 27 [cited 2023 February 18]. https://thehill.com/homenews/sunday-talk-shows/3751582-house-republican-says-congress-doesnt-need-to-pass-democrat-bills-that-help-ukraine.

20. Jentleson B. American consensus on Ukraine has fractured. *Foreign Policy*. 2023 March 29 [cited 2023 April 2]. https://foreignpolicy.com/2023/03/29/ukraine-support-us-republicans-democrats-politics.

21. Abutaleb Y., Hudson J. Inside the growing Republican fissure on Ukraine aid. *Washington Post*. 2022 October 31 [cited 2023 February 18]. https://www.washingtonpost.com/politics/2022/10/31/republican-split-on-ukraine-aid.

22. Amiri F., Freking K. McCarthy: No 'blank check' for Ukraine if GOP wins majority. *AP News*. 2022 October 18 [cited 2023 April 2]. https://apnews.com/article/russia-ukraine-donald-trump-humanitarian-assistance-congress-c47a255738cd13576aa4d238ec076f4a.

23. Heritage Foundation. Heritage president: No, Congress shouldn't write a 'blank check' for Ukraine aid. 2022 October 20 [cited 2023 February 18]. https://www.heritage.org/press/heritage-president-no-congress-shouldnt-write-blank-check-ukraine-aid.

24. Vinjamuri L. Biden's realism, US restraint, and the future of the transatlantic partnership. *LSE Public Policy Review*. 2022; 2(3): 1–6. DOI: https://doi.org/10.31389/lseppr.62.

13. Europe and Russia's Invasion of Ukraine: Where Does the EU Stand?

Nathalie Tocci

Russia's invasion of Ukraine is transforming Europe profoundly. Europe has reacted politically, energetically and in terms of enlargement and defence. Unprecedented sanctions, the first ever activation of the temporary protection mechanism for refugees, energy diversification, efficiency and accelerated transition, as well as the revival of enlargement policy, greater defence spending and the development and use of the European Peace Facility, are all ground-breaking developments. Some, like the steps forward made on energy, will make the EU stronger and more resilient than what it was before the war. On other issues, like enlargement, it remains to be seen whether the EU will truly revive its accession policy. On European defence, the challenge is even greater, given that, notwithstanding the significance of the EU's moves, these are insufficient to reverse the trend of greater dependence on the US, reducing European foreign policy autonomy, first and foremost vis-à-vis China.

Russia's full-scale invasion of Ukraine in 2022 threw the European Union into another existential crisis. It raised the question that lies at the core of European integration once again: how far could the EU hold its member states together? Would the crisis be an opportunity for further integration, or would it create fault lines in the Union?

Crises have dogged the EU for almost two decades. The failed Constitutional Treaty, the sovereign debt crisis, migration, Brexit, nationalist-populism, the pandemic and now the war have shaken the foundations of European integration. In some cases, like the financial or the migration crises, the EU barely scraped through. These 'opportunities' to deepen integration and strengthen itself were not taken. It was in those years the Brexit referendum took place, and the Union was threatened by a Eurosceptic wave. During the Covid-19 pandemic, the EU rediscovered the 'Jean Monnetian' art of transforming crisis into an opportunity for integration.[1] It coupled post-pandemic economic recovery with a repowered European green agenda [2]. But just as Europe and the world were beginning to lift their gaze from the pandemic, Vladimir Putin's Russia invaded Ukraine. Since then, the EU has responded politically, economically and in terms of energy. Not only has it supplied arms and resources to Ukraine, but it has accelerated moves for Ukraine to join the EU. Over a year into the Russo-Ukrainian war, how is the EU faring?

Political Unity: A United Europe and Transatlantic Community... Detached from the World

When a crisis hits and European countries are called to address it, the perennial question is whether centripetal or centrifugal forces will prevail. Will European countries overcome their unique domestic interests and work together for the shared European interest or will their divisions paralyze or push apart the Union?

Russia is a particularly polarising issue for the EU. Northern and eastern European countries have traditionally pushed for a tougher stance, while western and southern states used to press for cooperation. The tension between these two camps explains why Russia's annexation of Crimea and military engagement in eastern Ukraine saw the EU take a two-track approach of sanctions and selective engagement [3]. When the full-scale war began, many feared that divisive forces would eventually gain the upper hand. They may have anticipated a moment of unity at the outset, when the shock of Russia's invasion and awe at Ukrainian resistance galvanised joint European action, but feared that this would dissipate as the months dragged on and as Europe reeled from the economic, energy and humanitarian costs of war [4]. Indeed, by the summer of 2022, the concern was the growing European rift between the 'peace' and 'justice' camps, with countries further away from the frontline pressing for an immediate ceasefire, and those closer to the heat of war being convinced that peace could be achieved at the expense of justice. It is this latter group that argue that Ukraine should be supported until it fully liberates its land and its people [5]. Despite this political divide, the EU has mustered and maintained a united policy response, and a response that is becoming more unified, not less, as the war progresses.

EU member states unanimously agreed on 11 packages of sanctions on Russia [6]. The most significant came in the early months of the war and, as time passed, the time lag between one package and the next increased. But this is because having sanctioned finance, technology, coal and oil, seized Russian public and private assets, banned responsible individuals, capped energy prices, and reduced the import of Russian gas to a trickle, there is little left to sanction. Rather than adding many more sectors, the bulk of the work on sanctions now concentrates on closing loopholes and tightening the implementation screws. Over the months, some disagreements surfaced. Victor Orban's Hungary tried to leverage Budapest's veto right to extract both financial concessions and sanction exemptions from the Union. But Orban's manoeuvrings have broadly failed, with the European Commission using a novel form of economic conditionality linked to the rule of law. In December 2022, the Commission, in fact, held back €22 billion in cohesion funds for Hungary until it fulfils conditions related to judicial independence, academic freedom, LGBTQI rights and the asylum system.

Another area that could have proved Europe's Achilles heel is asylum policy. Alongside the eight million internally displaced persons within Ukraine, there are over eight million Ukrainian refugees in Europe, almost five million of whom have received temporary protection in the EU, with the right to live, work and travel across member states [7]. When the war broke out, European publics were overwhelmed by a wave of solidarity. The brutality of Russia's invasion, the heroism of Ukrainian resistance and the shared sense of destiny converged in explaining Europe's unprecedented humanitarian response to the war. Europe's solidarity with Ukrainian refugees was as inspiring as its closure and indifference to the plight of those from elsewhere is shameful. In the end, the fear that Ukraine refugees would wear out their welcome was unjustified, with millions of Ukrainians continuing to live in the EU, and with refugee status extended. Even through Russia's campaign to destroy Ukraine's energy infrastructure in the fall of 2022 in the hope of triggering a new wave of refugees that would break the Union's will to support Kyiv, solidarity held.

To date, politically the EU is standing firm. Divisions have not grown. In fact, they have diminished. In the early months of the war, west European countries – notably France – spoke of the need for negotiations and triggered the ire of north and east Europeans by insisting on the need for Russia not to be humiliated. But there are few in Berlin, Paris or Rome who now believe in the potential for negotiations, ceasefire, let alone a peace agreement with Russia. This unity is not limited to the EU. Russia's invasion of Ukraine has put the poisonous post-Brexit EU-UK relationship on a different footing; it has ushered unparalleled transatlantic unity notwithstanding acute differences over trade and industrial policy, and it has jelled cohesion within the G7 and other like-countries such as Australia and South Korea.

This growing European and transatlantic convergence stands in stark juxtaposition against the views held by many states in the 'Global South'. Although there are only seven countries that openly stand with Russia in the UN General Assembly, 32 others abstain from votes. Of these, setting aside China, which backs Moscow in all but name regardless of European attempts to nudge Beijing into exerting its influence on Moscow, the rest are more genuinely neutral regarding the war, although for different reasons. While there may be some anti-European sentiment, it is interests rather than ideas that are driving the ambivalence.

In most cases, especially in relatively small or distant countries in Africa, Asia and Latin America, with challenges of their own, the war is either viewed as a 'European war', and/or what matters are its consequences, beginning with food security. What they are more interested in is ensuring that the war ends quickly, even if this costs Ukrainian independence, sovereignty and territorial integrity. This is partly because these norms have been violated before (including by the West and Western-backed countries), and partly because not many countries feel directly threatened by invasion, occupation and annexation by their neighbours. Russia does not necessarily garner much sympathy, but nor is it challenged – perhaps *because* it is viewed as relatively weak and unthreatening [8]. Regardless, the war has revealed that many countries in the Global South are disengaged from the war and are not prepared to pay a price for an abstract rules-based international order, particularly one that is largely Western-made [9].

There is also a smaller group of mid-sized powers that do not want to passively stay clear of the war and its consequences, but rather wish to exploit their neutrality to serve their interests and increase their power. They have opportunistically leveraged their neutrality to extract gains from both sides. Countries like India stand out in this respect, as well as Israel, Turkey, Saudi Arabia and the UAE. They may have condemned Russia at the UN General Assembly, but they have also used their relations with Moscow and Kyiv to present themselves as mediators (especially Turkey), send weapons to Ukraine, and to increase their trade and energy imports from Russia.

Europe's Energy and Economic Resilience

A major reason why Europe has remained united so far is because it has weathered the storm of the energy crisis remarkably well. This averted what could have been a devastating economic recession on the continent. In late spring 2022, the International Monetary Fund had predicted a contraction of 3–5% in countries like Germany, Italy, Hungary, Czech Republic and Slovakia. When the war began, few would have bet on the fact that with Russian gas closed off to Europe, the EU would have survived energetically, and therefore economically and politically. Vladimir Putin expected Europe to bend and eventually break over their need for energy, which is precisely why he turned the taps off at the cost of hurting Russia, too [10]. As Robert Falkner discusses in this volume, Europe was partly aided by exogenous factors like a warm winter and sluggish Chinese growth, but the EU and its member states also put in place a set of key measures that ought to be credited. They diversified their gas supplies by increasing imports from Norway, the US, Qatar, Azerbaijan, Algeria, Angola, Mozambique and the Republic of Congo. They met their targets for the refilling of gas storages and developed a European Energy Platform to aggregate demand for the refilling of storages for next winter. They coordinated the reduction of gas and electricity demand and met the targets they set themselves. And they accelerated the development of renewables, with these now representing the primary source of electricity generation in Europe. Notwithstanding the fuel switch from gas to coal and oil, overall emissions in Europe fell by 2.5% in 2022 [11]. All this has meant that Europe, so far at least, has averted the risk of recession, and, albeit sluggishly, its economy continues to grow.

This does not mean that the energy crisis is over and that the EU has squared the circle of energy security and the energy transition through deeper integration. Plenty of challenges remain. These include short-term ones concerning Europe's energy and economic resilience next winter, especially if China's growth picks up, while a hot summer could lead to higher-than-expected gas consumption and lower renewable energy production in Europe. Meanwhile, new-born instruments like the European Energy Platform remain to be tested, and there are even greater longer-term challenges. While energy prices have dropped in Europe from a peak of €340 MWh to around €40 MWh, they are still double what they used to be before the energy crisis and four times as high as in the US. Coupled with the potential impact of the US Inflation Reduction Act that could lure European companies to the other side of the Atlantic, the risk is Europe's deindustrialisation. China aggravates the problem. Beijing's market dominance in areas like renewables, critical minerals and batteries, alongside Europe's heightened awareness of the vulnerability generated by energy dependences, push Europeans to re-shore, near-shore or friend-shore green technologies and industries. Yet doing so is not easy and certainly comes at a high cost that will strain further public budgets. There is no silver bullet to address these problems, and as the EU scrambles for a solution, it could fall into the trap of protectionism and debt unsustainability. It remains to be seen whether the EU's Net Zero Industry Act will strike the right balance between security, affordability and sustainability [12]. However, EU institutions and member states are well aware of the trilemma as they search for solutions, and just like they have navigated the energy crisis relatively well so far, there's no reason to believe they'll necessarily fail in future.

The Challenges Ahead: Enlargement and Defence

The challenges do not stop here, however. In two other areas, the tasks ahead of the EU are daunting. The first is enlargement. While never formally halted, the EU's enlargement process gradually ground to a halt after the big-bang eastern enlargement of the early 2000s. With the exception of Croatia in 2013, no country has entered the EU for almost two decades. The accession process has formally continued with the Western Balkans and Turkey, but it has been increasingly characterised by a double farce: candidate countries have largely pretended to reform, and the EU has pretended to integrate them. The outcome has not been ideal: Democracy and rule of law have faltered, economic development has languished, peace processes have stalled, and powers like Russia and China have increasingly made their presence felt. But the Union was absorbed by its successive existential crises, and by and large thought that stability in its neighbourhood would hold. The results were not great, but they were believed to be good enough.

That illusion was shattered by Russia's invasion of Ukraine. Suddenly it became obvious that stability, while guaranteed within the EU and NATO, cannot be taken for granted on the other side of the 'frontier' [13]. Unsurprisingly, Ukrainian President Volodymyr Zelensky applied for EU membership three days into Russia's large-scale invasion of his country. Now, Ukraine and Moldova are recognised as candidate countries, while Georgia – given its government's authoritarian turn despite public backlash – is now a potential candidate. In the Western Balkans, Albania and North Macedonia have opened accession negotiations, and Bosnia-Herzegovina has been recognised as a candidate. All this does not amount yet to a decisive revival of the EU's accession policy, and plenty of problems remain to be solved both in enlargement countries and in the EU as far as the reform of its institutions and decision-making processes are concerned [14]. However, it is becoming increasingly obvious – to EU Member States and candidate countries – that potentially there is an extremely high cost to non-enlargement: the status quo is an intolerably high-risk gamble for European security.

This brings to a final set of challenges that pertain more directly to security and defence. Russia's invasion of Ukraine has created a contradiction. Europeans finally take security and defence more seriously. The war has led to more defence spending across Europe, from Germany's defence *Zeitenwende* of €100 billion additional spending on defence, to the more diffuse uptick in defence expenditures across mostly northern and east European states. EU member states' defence spending is expected to grow by €70 billion over the next three years, making NATO's 2% of GDP in defence spending finally within reach [15]. EU institutions, that traditionally considered defence a dirty word, have now mobilised a European Peace Facility to support Ukrainian defence. They have also approved a military training mission for the Ukrainian armed forces. Collectively, the EU and its members have provided €12 billion in military assistance to Ukraine as of March 2023 (and a total of €67 billion if economic assistance is included). The EU has also developed a mechanism for the procurement of ammunition for Ukraine, committing a first €2bn tranche to the endeavour.

In times of peace, this would have been read as hard evidence of European strategic military autonomy in the making. In times of war, paradoxically, the opposite is true. Russia's invasion of Ukraine is leading to a dramatic increase in European defence dependence on the US. This is true in operational terms: without US military support for Ukraine, Kyiv would have likely fallen, putting at an unprecedented risk the entire European continent. It is also true in terms of defence capacities: As Europeans are depleting their stocks, they spend to replace them with what is available: this is often American, not European. This does not mean that European defence industrial projects have stalled altogether. There are several that are promising, including: The European Patrol Corvette, including France, Italy, Greece, Spain and Norway as an observer; European space projects, including the Commission and the European Space Agency; the first steps in a European helicopter project including France, Germany Italy and the UK; and – provided ways are found to partner also with west European countries – Germany's missile defence initiative with east European countries. However, in times of war, the bulk of European defence spending is being targeted not to future projects but to short-term fixes, which means that, in relative terms, European dependence on US defence industry is increasing.

This is bad news for Europe. Transatlantic relations have not been so strong in many years, but this could reverse quite soon.

Were a Republican candidate to win the 2024 US presidential elections, the US's commitment to Ukraine and to European security could be scaled down. This would leave Europeans at massive risk. Moreover, aside from who will win the next US presidential election, Europe's greater dependence on the US will most likely translate into its reduced ability to chart its way in the world. Especially regarding China, while European and US views are broadly convergent – with European views having distinctly hardened since the pandemic – they are not identical. There is, in fact, a substantial difference between the US drive for a decoupling of the Chinese and US economies, and the EU's calls for de-risking. This is because Washington's view is essentially competitive in nature. By decoupling in sensitive technological areas, the US aims to slow down China's rise. Whereas Europeans also talk about China as an economic competitor and systemic rival, it is not really competition they are most worried about. What Europeans fear is China's ability to exploit European vulnerabilities to gain strategic gains and interfere in European systems. Against the backdrop of Russia's weaponisation of energy, by 'de-risking' their relationship with China, the EU wants to avoid making the same mistake twice. In short, US and European views on China overlap but they are not the same. Yet Europe's growing defence dependence on the US may well mean that its ability to chart its own way vis-à-vis China has significantly reduced. In mere months, Europeans cannot reverse this situation; it should have been addressed many years ago. A sense of impotence may be part of the reason why, politically, this question continues to be avoided, although it does not make the problem disappear.

Finally, whereas European security and defence vulnerability is an existential challenge for Europe, it is a problem for the United States as well. When the US was an unrivalled global hegemon, it could afford to have relatively weak and dependent allies. Given that no power seriously challenged US supremacy on the global stage, there was no real price to be paid for European weakness. Europe's defence dependence on the US benefited American defence industry and foreign policy given that European allies were generally drawn into US foreign policy adventures, notably in the wider Middle East. That era is gone. Today the US is challenged by China, and it knows it. It has an interest in having partners and allies that are capable and strong, at the very least in order to look after themselves. The potential costs of a vulnerable Europe in security and defence terms far outweigh the economic and strategic gains of a dependent Europe on the US. This realisation is beginning to dawn in Washington, notably at high political level, but it is yet to trickle down across institutional and policy practice.

Conclusions

Russia's invasion of Ukraine is transforming Europe profoundly; in this respect, this war vindicates Jean Monnet's prediction that Europe will be the sum of the solutions to the crises that it will face. Europe has reacted politically, energetically and in terms of enlargement and defence. Crisis has not paralysed the Union into inaction, nor have the solutions found represented a lowest common denominator. Unprecedented sanctions, the first ever activation of the temporary protection mechanism, energy diversification, efficiency and accelerated transition, the revival of enlargement policy, greater defence spending, the development and use of the European Peace Facility, de facto representing an EU defence funding and procurement mechanism – all of these are ground-breaking developments. Some, like the steps forward made on energy, will certainly make the EU stronger than what it was before the war. On other issues, like enlargement, it remains to be seen whether the EU will truly revive the enlargement process. On European defence, the challenge is even greater, given that notwithstanding the significance of the EU's moves, these are insufficient to reverse the trend of greater dependence on the US. And for a Union that wants and must play a stronger role on the global stage, this is bad news.

Acknowledgements

This research was funded by the Europe Futures Fellowship, Institut für die Wissenschaften vom Menschen, Vienna.

Note

[1] Jean Monnet, one of the founding fathers of European integration, wrote in his memoirs that: "Europe will be forged in crises and will be the sum of the solutions adopted for those crises" [1].

References

1. Monnet J. Memoirs. Third Millennium Publishing; 2015.
2. Tocci N. A Green and Global Europe. Cambridge: Polity; 2022.
3. Tocci N. Framing the EU Global Strategy. London: Palgrave; 2017. DOI: https://doi.org/10.1007/978-3-319-55586-7.

4. Tocci N. Can Russia Divide Europe. *Foreign Affairs*. 2022 August [accessed 2023 March 15]. https://www.foreignaffairs.com/europe/can-russia-divide-europe.

5. Krastev K, Leonard M. Peace versus Justice: the coming European split over Ukraine. European Council on Foreign Relations; 2022 June 15. https://ecfr.eu/publication/peace-versus-justice-the-coming-european-split-over-the-war-in-ukraine/.

6. European Parliament. EU sanctions on Russia: Overview, impact, challenges; 2023. https://www.europarl.europa.eu/RegData/etudes/BRIE/2023/739366/EPRS_BRI(2023)739366_EN.pdf.

7. Operational Data Portal. Refugees from Ukraine recorded across Europe. [accessed 2023 March 15]. https://data.unhcr.org/en/situations/ukraine.

8. Krastev I. For many outside the west, Europe is not important enough to hate. *Financial Times*. 2023 February 22. https://www.ft.com/content/01b69c54-d679-4c86-8dc8-1fff649bf424.

9. Ero C. The world isn't slipping away from the West. *Foreign Policy*. 2023 March 8. https://foreignpolicy.com/2023/03/08/russia-ukraine-war-west-global-south-diplomacy-un-putin-g20/.

10. Tocci N. Putin versus Monnet: European Resilience, Energy and the Ukraine War. IAI Papers; 2022 September. https://www.iai.it/sites/default/files/iaip2225.pdf.

11. International Energy Agency. CO2 Emissions in 2022. Report. Paris; 2023 March. https://www.iea.org/reports/co2-emissions-in-2022.

12. Poiters N, Tagliapietra S, Sapir A, Veugelers R, Zettelmeyer J. The EU net Zero Industry Act and the Risk of Reviving Past Failures; 2023 March. https://www.bruegel.org/first-glance/eu-net-zero-industry-act-and-risk-reviving-past-failures.

13. Tocci N. Russia's War in Ukraine turned Europe's 'Buffer States' into Frontier States. *Foreign Policy Magazine*. 2023 March 14.

https://foreignpolicy.com/2023/03/14/ukraine-russia-war-europe-nato-eu-expansion-buffer-states/.

14. Delcour L, Wolczuk K. Ukraine and the EU at the time of war: a new paradigm. LibMod Policy Paper, Zentrum Liberale Moderne; 2022.

15. Grevi G. Centre for Security, Diplomacy and Strategy. CSDS in Depth; 2023 March. https://prod-b4156475194d8706-vub.paddlecms.net/sites/default/files/2023-03/CSDS%20In%20Depth%205%20Shockwaves%20March%202023.pdf.

14. After Merkel: Germany from Peace to War

Kristina Spohr

In the autumn of 2021, after Angela Merkel retired, her successor, Olaf Scholz, assumed power as head of a new coalition consisting of Social Democrats, Greens, and Free Democrats. Scholz had an ambitious agenda to reform Germany. Yet, within months, Russia launched its brutal military invasion of Ukraine. Overnight Scholz had to adapt to a Europe at war, which raised profound questions about Germany's international role. Was its post-1945 'civilian power status' still viable? What about its deep-seated 'culture of restraint'? On 27 February 2022, three days into the war, Scholz addressed the Bundestag, boldly announcing a German Zeitenwende, an 'epochal turn' in the Federal Republic's conduct of foreign and security affairs. This essay evaluates Scholz's grand rhetorical vision, questioning how much his claims for a major German foreign-policy revolution have yielded in practice. It will reveal that although Chancellor Scholz hoped to be seen as a decisive leader, his actions have so far been those of a beleaguered temporizer, unable to shake the age-old constraints tied to history, geography, and party politics. Crucially, his innate caution (reflected in long bouts of silences), his stubbornness, his unwillingness to lead from

> the front, as well as the structural limitations that Germany has long faced, have acted as breaks. Although the biggest tests are still to come, 2022 was a year of forced reinvention for both Scholz and Germany, and neither looked comfortable in assuming their new role.

In fall 2021 the Merkel era came to end. Angela Merkel – a quiet, understated, and pragmatic Christian Democrat – was the West's longest-serving contemporary leader after sixteen years as federal chancellor. Unlike any of her predecessors since the founding of the Federal Republic in 1949, she left office of her own accord. Her successor, Social Democrat Olaf Scholz, seemed like the continuity candidate – at least until Vladimir Putin's invasion of Ukraine. Three days after Russian tanks rolled into Ukraine, Scholz declared a new era in German foreign policy, the '*Zeitenwende*', or 'epochal turn'. Now a year on, it is time to ask what this proclaimed foreign policy shift tells us about Germany's evolution as an international actor in the post Merkel era. Was the speech mere rhetoric, or did it mark a real 'watershed' moment?

From the Merkel Era to the *Ampel*-Coalition: The Arrival of Olaf Scholz in the Chancellery

Merkel's tenure was a time of relative stability despite major ruptures on the international plane. First there was the financial crash of 2008 and ensuing Eurozone meltdown, followed by Russia's annexation of Crimea and invasion of Ukraine in 2014; then came the refugee crisis of 2015 and finally the COVID-19 global pandemic. When she announced her departure, many felt that they were witnessing the ending of a particular type of governance and leadership style. World news since the early 2000s have been dominated by posturing tough guys – from Vladimir Putin to Recep Tayyip Erdoğan, from Kim Yong-Un to Viktor Orbán. And with Donald Trump, Silvio Berlusconi, and Boris Johnson the lines between TV celebrity, clown, and politician became increasingly blurred. Dr Merkel stood out – and not just because she is a woman [1]. She embodied power without vanity [2].

She had her shortcomings: the vagueness of her political program (domestic and European); the absence of sparkling oratory; and the technocratic prudence, verging on hesitancy. In terms of policy, critical voices also pointed to the inner contradictions of her decision-making, particularly when under public pressure [3, 4]. Despite what one might call the paradox of 'Merkelism' [5], she remained popular, still the country's best-liked politician in 2021 [6].

Merkel's popularity was not enough to ensure that the Christian Democrats remained in charge beyond her retirement. Not only had the CDU/CSU been weakened by a rare and rancorous intra-party power struggle over its leader and choice of chancellor-candidate [7]. It also did not help that the party's traditionalist wing had been intensifying its critical campaign against Merkel's steady course towards the political centre, believing that the CDU's conservative, Rhenish-Catholic middle-class values had effectively been eroded by a pinko, Protestant, *Ossi* woman [4]. Yet while in the election run-up the chief beneficiaries of all the political jockeying appeared to be the Greens, it was Social Democrat Olaf Scholz who was sworn in as Germany's new federal chancellor on 8 December 2021.

His ascent to the highest office came to many as a surprise. The soft-spoken federal finance minister and vice-chancellor of the fourth Merkel coalition government had after all lost the SPD's leadership contest earlier that spring to two left-leaning comrades. Indeed, ahead of an election for which German Social Democrats harboured no hopes whatsoever, he had apparently been picked as chancellor-candidate because he could be sacrificed, giving a new generation of aspirants a better chance next time round. Still, on 27 September German voters did embrace Olaf Scholz at the polls – though at 26 per cent of the vote, the SPD's majority hardly reflected the mandate that previous chancellors had enjoyed. As Germany's number two became number one, he decided for his party to work in a new constellation, together with the Greens and Free Democrats (FDP). Thus, the so-called *Ampel* or 'traffic light' coalition was born [8].

Significantly, the elections had been dominated by an agenda based on domestic stability and social renewal. Foreign policy barely featured. By and large, the voters had wanted to preserve their comfortable lifestyles and Germany's welfare state. The country indulged in the peace dividend that the post-Wall order offered, with Germans looking inward not outward. The coalition deal was thus oriented around the idea that Germany needed to 'Dare more Progress' (*Mehr Fortschritt wagen*) [9] on the domestic front. This was an implicit criticism of Merkel's failure to pursue reform, but also a nod to history, the new maxim rooting itself in Willy Brandt's 1969 declaration to 'Dare more Democracy' [10].

The pressure was intense to make progress at home, with much needed socio-economic reforms as well as a push for digital transformation and for climate action [11]. None of this was going to be easy, given the natural tug-of-war games in coalition politics, especially when involving such ideologically different partners: social democrats, free market liberals, and the environmentalist greens. Indeed, three of the main ministries were headed by the two parties that have least in common. Anna-Lena Baerbock and Robert Habeck (of the Greens) would lead the foreign ministry and the ministry for economic affairs and climate protection respectively, whereas, the FDP got the finance ministry, meaning that Christian Lindner would hold Germany's purse strings. So, from the outset it was obvious to all that it would take time for the new government to find its feet on the global stage. Moreover, when it came to world politics, the experience of Scholz and that of his freshly baked ministers was limited.

As chancellor, Scholz initially professed foreign political 'continuity' [12]. However, with Merkel's departure, a vacuum opened up internationally. In this sphere, her timing could not have been worse. Throughout 2021, a crisis had been brewing around Ukraine – a battleground since the *de facto* annexation of Crimea in 2014 by Russia and the Kremlin's support for pro-Russia separatists in the Donbass region. Then in late November Russian President Vladimir Putin began to unleash mass troop deployments on its neighbour's eastern border. Perhaps it was no coincidence that on 17 December, with Scholz only nine days in office, the Kremlin presented the US [13] and NATO [14] with an unexpected ultimatum, formally demanding binding security guarantees while looking for the rewriting of many of the principles upholding European security since the end of the Cold War [15].

Moscow was no longer satisfied with a policy of keeping 'peace at any cost' [16]. Putin's historical grievances over allegedly broken non-NATO-enlargement promises made in 1990 and beyond, and tales of Russia's 'encirclement', wilful humiliation, and victimisation were used to fraudulently legitimise Moscow's actions [17]. By the start of 2022, it looked as though Putin wanted to literally reverse what, according to him, Gorbachev and Yeltsin had gambled away. His aim: to 'gather' [18] the 'historical Russian lands' [19] through the territorial restoration of the former Russian empire, pushing NATO back and the US out of Europe entirely, ending a commitment that dates back to 1949. These were no mere rhetorical power games, and by February, Moscow's risky moves had brought Europe to the brink of war [20]. Scholz therefore had little time to settle into his role, finding himself embroiled mere months into his chancellorship in one of the greatest European diplomatic contests since the Cold War and indeed real war in the heart of Europe.

From Peace to War: The First 77 Days in Office

From its inception, questions also abounded over the *Ampel-*Cabinet's unity and foreign political direction. Whereas Foreign Minister Annalena Baerbock lobbied for a 'feminist' [21] and 'values-led' foreign policy [22], stressing her party's intention to prioritise issues like human rights, the rule of law, and democratic values over Germany's financial ties with Moscow and Beijing, Scholz was keen to follow the pragmatic and mercantilist foreign policy of his predecessors. Hoping to reboot relations with the Kremlin, he concentrated on lucrative 'private-sector projects' [23] – most crucially, the Russo-German Nord-Stream

II Baltic Sea pipeline – which, he insisted, ought not be entangled in debates about geo-politics and geo-ethics. At this time of crisis, given the intra-coalition tensions combined with the perennial quarrels and speculation over who called the shots in German foreign policy – the Chancellery or the MFA [24, 25] – Scholz felt compelled to forcefully state that when it came to the 'Russia problem', the buck stopped with him [26].

By the new year, the novice chancellor was under mounting pressure to take a tougher line with the Kremlin. Critics considered him 'soft' in *Russlandpolitik*, too conciliatory towards his own party's pro-Russia voices, and too slow in addressing Germany's dependence on the 750 mile, $11 bn Nord Stream 2 gas pipeline [27]. Baerbock in turn enjoyed the limelight of the international stage and continued with her outspokenness. During her Moscow-talks with Russian counterpart Sergey Lavrov in mid-January 2022, she produced a sure-footed performance – clear and robust. But, inevitably, the shadow of World War II loomed large, especially the enduring, almost numbing, sense of guilt that Germans still carry. Laying the wreath at the Tomb of the Unknown Soldier close to the Kremlin, Baerbock deferentially spoke of her 'shame and awe' [28]. Russia had shown once more that German emotions are easily manipulated and Berlin's strategic compass disoriented, keeping the country locked into its post-1945 power-political impotence.

All the same, throughout January and February 2022, Berlin toed the NATO line: To boost the Alliance's eastern flank, Germany sent troops and equipment to the Baltic States and Romania. But Scholz was reluctant to do anything else, particularly on the economic front, dithering about whether Nord

Stream 2 should be included in the sanctions-package and whether Russia's participation in the SWIFT international payments system should be suspended. Even more damagingly, while Russia clearly ratcheted up its threat against Ukraine, Germany flatly refused to ship defensive weapons to Kyiv [29]. That the federal defence ministry proposed what it thought was a bold new initiative, supplying some 5,000 helmets and a field hospital was met by Ukrainian derision. It was a 'joke', all about as useful as sending 'pillows' [30], scoffed Kyiv's Mayor Vitali Klitschko, who was well known in Germany for his time there as heavyweight champion-boxer.

The guilt-ridden contortions were endless. Baerbock and Scholz both held that the Federal Republic, despite ranking fourth in global arms trade [31], could not send lethal weapons into conflict zones for historical reasons [29]. Moreover, beyond the danger of crisis-escalation, a German armaments-U-turn over Ukraine risked undermining Berlin's stance of 'never again war' (*nie wieder Krieg* [32]) – a policy deeply engrained in the convictions of the SPD Left and among the Greens with their roots in the 1970s peace movement. This was notwithstanding the fact that in 1999, Joschka Fischer, the first-ever Green foreign minister (under SPD Chancellor Gerhard Schröder), justified his country's participation in NATO's 'humanitarian intervention' in Kosovo with his own impassioned reference to history – that Germany, precisely because of its Nazi-era crimes, had to stand up against aggression, and if necessary, by *military* means [33 ch3]. Yet equally, due to the precedent of 1941, Germans were convinced that Russian soldiers must not end up being killed by German weapons again. Berlin therefore was reluctant to even permit Estonia to give Ukraine some old Soviet-made howitzers that had been formerly East German-owned [29]. Here, and elsewhere, German principles and their interpretations of history collided with Alliance politics, raising serious questions over Germany's NATO solidarity and its reliability as an ally [34].

Unsurprisingly, therefore, Scholz and US President Joe Biden took great pains to put on a display of 'unity' at the White House on 7 February 2022. While Biden reminded the world that 'Germany is one of America's closest allies, working in lockstep,' Scholz stressed that Berlin and Washington 'will act together' while taking 'all the necessary steps' [35]. The chancellor insisted that 'we work very hard to get a way out of this situation'. But if Russia chose to intervene, it would have to pay a 'high price'. While his words were emphatic, Scholz clung onto Berlin's line of 'necessary strategic ambiguity' when it came to questions of details of Germany's actions. Germany may be the 'strongest economic supporter of Ukraine' with $2 bn and it may also be a significant contributor to NATO's Enhanced Forward Presence; yet, these steps still fell short of a real strategy to seriously raise the costs for Russia by strengthening Ukraine's deterrence capabilities, as a way to promote leverage and diplomacy [36].

Of course, arms transfers are not the only way to deter a revanchist power. But there was simply no sign in the winter of 2022 that Germany was prepared to take the lead in the EUs economic response or to formulate any other long-term policy focused on deterring Russian territorial ambitions and enabling the western aspirations of the ex-Soviet satellites and republics. Worse, some of Germany's leading generals came out as so-called

Putinversteher (Putin empathisers) [37] – suggesting that the Crimean Peninsula, annexed by Russia since 2014, would never be returned to Kyiv's control, that Putin deserved more 'respect' [38], and that Ukraine must not become the West's outpost against Russia. This certainly raised eyebrows in Washington and angered many East European allies – as well as causing much debate in Germany.

Still, Berlin's position continued to remain fuzzy – at least in public. Despite all its rhetoric of 'initiative', 'progress', and 'renewal', the *Ampel* under Scholz seemed stuck, especially in its conduct of Eastern European and Russia policies. It even appeared to some to be harking back to an older past.

To be sure, the SPD has many a time reached out to the history books. And few of the party's contemporary politicians talk about Russia without referring to Willy Brandt's *neue Ostpolitik* of the Cold War – the long-term 'change through rapprochement' (*Wandel durch Annäherung*) strategy towards the Soviet Union and its Warsaw Pact clients, adopted in 1969. Olaf Scholz, too, in his first address to the Bundestag on 15 December 2021 had invoked Brandt's approach of easing tensions through engagement with Moscow, though he lobbied for a new EU version thereof; 'In a united Europe, Ostpolitik can only be a European Ostpolitik', he asserted [39]. While some read darkly into these words a German desire under EU cover to negotiate with the Kremlin over the heads of the Central and Eastern Europeans, others raised doubts over what a Europe-led response would look like [40]. Surely that would involve a military dimension, not just dialogue and trade-sanctions to keep the peace? In this vein, French President Emmanuel Macron kept lobbying for the idea that Europe's security would be best served by the reinforcement (under French leadership) of its 'strategic autonomy' [41] from the US, whereas Scholz (and Merkel before him) emphasised their loyalty to the two pillars – America and NATO – in European security affairs [42].

The reference to *Ostpolitik* was confusing in other ways, too. Scholz certainly hoped to appease his party's strong left wing, perhaps hoping to remind them of his activist student days, when as a radical leftie SPD Juso and fierce NATO critic, he had in 1983 protested against the deployment of US intermediate nuclear forces in West Germany [43]. This, however, stood in juxtaposition to his defence of the transatlantic alliance more recently, including as vice-chancellor. Indeed, in almost all his statements prior to Russia's brutal attack on Ukraine, Scholz had made the era of the FRG's second SPD chancellor, the Atlanticist Helmut Schmidt (1974-1982) a reference point. Scholz, rather than seeing himself as an heir of Brandt, appeared to be moving towards pursuing a more pragmatic *Moskaupolitik* in the tradition of fellow Hamburger, Schmidt, who in an inversion of Brandt's approach, had stood for deterrence and defence first and détente second [44 p54].

Scholz's persistent problem of how to deal with the pacifist and pragmatic wings in his Party, however, goes beyond questions of ideational allegiance to either Brandt or Schmidt. It relates to the deeply engrained historical Russophilia [45, 46] and the more contemporary *Putinverstehertum* (largely the result of the Kremlin's successful long-running, enormous hybrid warfare campaign against Germany) among many Leftists in the SPD, Greens, and *Die Linke*, not just the populist right wingers of the

AfD [47, 48]. In its most unhealthy form this pro-Russian tendency is personified in Gerhard Schröder.

Interestingly, as chancellor, Schröder had, between 1998 and 2005, pursued a New Labourite 'Third Way' in economics, and also taken the supposedly 'grown up' [49] and 'normal' [50] Berlin Republic into the Kosovo War in 1999. Then, however, the latent SPD approach of 'equidistance between Washington and Moscow' kicked in, as the Schröder government made its decision of refusal to join in America's war on terror at the start of the millennium [51]. Real unease was caused when, within months of losing the chancellorship to Angela Merkel in 2005, Schröder became head of the shareholders committee on state-controlled Russian Gazprom's North European Gas Pipeline company, Nord Stream AG. The original Nord Stream scheme had been given the go-ahead by the outgoing chancellor in the interim period before Merkel took office and then continued and expanded into a second pipeline project – Nord Stream 2 – under her tenure. In 2017, Schröder was made chair of the Russian oil group Rosneft, then in February 2022 he accepted Gazprom's nomination to its supervisory board of directors – positions he has since quit under immense public pressure [52, 53].

Still, what is particularly ugly and distasteful, is just how deeply Chancellor Schröder's personal networking came to enmesh the SPD (together with former East German Stasi officers!) with Russian state gas companies, and how he, as ex-chancellor, apart from enriching himself with Russian roubles metamorphosed into a lobbyist for the Kremlin and never unfriended Putin [54]. Worse, in late January 2022 he went as far as accusing Kyiv of 'sabre-rattling' while insisting that Putin's Russia had no intention of invading Ukraine [55].

Gas-pipeline deals between companies of the Federal Republic and Russia were, of course, not new [56]. Indeed, they had started with *Osthandel* in the Brandt-Schmidt era of 1969–1982, gaining traction during the global economic crisis in the 1970s coupled to the two OPEC oil price shocks of 1973 and 1979, when Schmidt had warned against over-dependency on any single country or region and stressed the need for diversification of German energy sources – hard coal, lignite, oil, gas, and nuclear. And yet, there was always a second dimension to *Osthandel* under Bonn's *Ost-* and *Russlandpolitik*, and this would reach all the way into the present. The idea being that Russian 'change' could be affected 'through trade' (*Wandel durch Handel*), i.e., that that East-West tensions could be eased and Russia's political unpredictability tamed through economic interdependence [44 chs1–2].

This desire for cooperation meant that by 2021 united Germany had become the biggest western actor with significant and variegated trade ties to Russia. According to Russian Federal Customs Service, data for the first 10 months of 2021 placed Germany (with $46.1 bn) second among Moscow's top five trading partners – after China ($112.4 bn) and before the Netherlands ($37 bn), the US ($28.8 bn) and Turkey ($25.7 bn) [57]. Meanwhile, for Germany, Russia ranked 15th [58]. Due to geography and history, Germany's relationship with Russia was unique (as much as it was complicated) among its European neighbours. Since the 1990s, successive German chancellors had adopted a conciliatory approach towards the men in the Kremlin, apparently sincerely believing that trade and dialogue would not merely improve Russo-German relations, but foster stability and peace in the post-Cold War world. And so, as the two countries' interdependence had exponentially grown, it had become referred to as a 'special relationship' (*Sonderverhältnis*) [46, 59].

Long-term, these calculations vis-à-vis the Kremlin evidently did not work out [60, 61] – just as Berlin's obsession with *Dialogpolitik* above all else appears to have been erroneous when conducted without a serious defence and deterrence policy and without a 'Plan B' regarding alternative energy supplies. Because Putin in his *Westpolitik* certainly seemed to have kept open the option to weaponise energy policy, and particularly the Russo-German Nord Stream project, as he began to wage Russia's non-linear warfare against the 'West'.

That Germany became so fatally gas-dependent on Russia was, then, not down to structural conditions [62] but to German leaders' conscious political choices. It was not only due to the way German *Russlandpolitik* had evolved, but also rooted in Merkel's domestic political power play: her flawed environmental policy decision in the aftermath of the Fukushima accident in 2011 to rapidly phase out German nuclear power while also cutting reliance on coal to reduce CO_2 emissions – all as she sought to garner green anti-nuclear voters for her next election bid in 2012.[1] Ten years on, the bitter irony could not be lost on anyone. Just as the vexed issues of sanctions against Russia and the certification and opening of Nord Stream 2 were on the negotiation table in early 2022, Germany was more reliant than ever before on much-polluting Russian fossil fuels for heating and power generation. All the while its last three remaining nuclear power plants (reliably providing clean energy) were on track for shutdown [63, 64]. Herein lay Scholz's serious trilemma – having to balance environmental and socio-economic factors, as well as military and energy security.

Questions remain why over time united Germany's initial reinsurance policies [65 p180] vis-à-vis Russia increasingly faded from view while the focus began to shift dangerously to outright collaboration, and why this course found eager supporters across the entire political spectrum [66]. Equally, there are those, including well-known US political scientists, who believe that Germany and the West did actually do too little for Russia, and thereby may have emboldened Putin and perhaps even enabled his war [67–73].

Amid all these arguments it is worthwhile remembering that the stillbirth of Russian democracy, the stunted emergence of law and order, the economic chaos coupled with immense corruption, and the formation of a kleptocracy in the Yeltsin era, cannot simply be blamed on the quality of Germans' and other nations' policies of engagement with Russians. In the event, while unified Germany's post-Wall honeymoon with the Kremlin now looks foolish, to say the least, it is Putin's Russian state that has shown itself once more to be an 'empire by imposition' [74 p69] – a revisionist as much as revanchist power.

Scholz may well have fancied himself in the role as 'double interpreter', like Schmidt in 1980 talking to the man in the White House and the man in the Kremlin when superpower relations had totally broken down [44 ch5]. After all, in February 2022, Scholz (just as Macron) made a last-ditch effort to de-escalate the Russo-Ukrainian crisis and to thaw Russo-Western relations by rushing for personal talks to Moscow [75]. But Scholz did not have the clout of Schmidt, and the international circumstances were different and less advantageous.

Certainly, Putin was not to be deterred. He had long decided to go on the warpath; and for some time, US and UK intelligence had been busy issuing warnings. But somehow, as the world emerged from the COVID-19 pandemic with all the national and global societal and economic upheavals that the lockdowns had brought, to most, including Ukraine itself, War in Europe simply seemed inconceivable.

Thus came the day that shook the world: 24 February 2022, the day that Putin launched his military aggression. Russian tanks rolled, missiles were fired, and soldiers marched. Russia's full-scale invasion of Ukraine had begun. Diplomacy with Russia had died a sudden death. For the first time since 1945, great-power 'war of conquest' had returned to Europe [76] – the course of continent's history changed once more.

From Words to Deeds: Putin's Ukraine War and Scholz's Sticky '*Zeitenwende*'

Germany abruptly awoke from its slumber. The Scholz government was forced to re-evaluate Germany's role in international affairs and what this would mean for Germany's *Sonderverhältnis* with Russia, for its World War II guilt, and for its '*nie wieder Krieg*' policy. The chancellor – who had risen to the top without trace, saying almost nothing of note on international affairs, and certainly had thus far not distinguished himself on the big questions of 'peace and war' – found himself under fierce scrutiny. While some pundits had criticised him for his diffidence and constrained leadership style, others blamed him for refusing leadership altogether.

Now, in the face of war, the German chancellor took a moment to consider his options, before, on 27 February, going on the offensive in the Bundestag. There, in the full glare of the world media, he declared a new era in German foreign policy: '*Zeitenwende*'. He spelled out Germany's intent to leave behind the country's post-Cold War negligence of military defence and its passivity in foreign affairs. Berlin would stand with its allies to deter and confront Putin's Russia. The policies of *Zeitenwende* thus represented a direct rejection of Berlin's (and previously Bonn's) *Moskaupoltik*.

In his revolutionary announcement the chancellor set forth a series of sanctions against Russia. He pledged an overhaul of the Bundeswehr, promising 'from now on' to invest more than two per cent of GDP in defence along NATO's spending target and to provide an emergency fund of €100 bn ($113 bn) to implement this increase and to rearm Germany. He declared Berlin's commitment to new European armaments projects, all the while underscoring his country's continued role in nuclear sharing, underpinned by the purchase of new dual-use US F-35 fighter jets to replace the old American Tornados. Furthermore, breaking with Germany's post-war taboo on arms exports to war zones, he now proclaimed the supply of heavy weaponry to Ukraine, so that Kyiv could defend its sovereignty. Finally, he insisted Germany would strive for independence from Russian coal, oil, and gas [77].

With this *démarche*, Scholz – who that day received a standing ovation by almost all MPs – had at once seized the moment and produced a *fait accompli* in matters that had haunted post-Cold War German politics for almost three decades. Riding the wave of popular support during Europe's worst crisis since World War II, the chancellor united the long-sceptical leftist-pacifist strands within both the Social Democratic Party and the Greens, forcing them to accept an abrupt and complete German security policy reversal. And it seemed that Berlin was also willing to sacrifice its traditional order of policy priorities, namely the pursuit of its trade interests – including with autocratic regimes – over a foreign policy based on values, norms, and principles [78, 79].

The '*Zeitenwende*' speech was lauded as a historic milestone – at home as much as in the major NATO capitals where unified Germany's lack of a serious security policy has been lamented for years. Crucially, it seemed to indicate the emergence of a new, pragmatic Germany finally willing to take some responsibility for European security, and ready to act as a leading political power and provider of 'hard security' commensurate with its economic weight. There was a genuine belief that Germany would now move on from its *Zivilmachtstatus* ('civilian' or 'civilising' power status), founded on the post-war strategic culture of military restraint that was coupled to specific constitutional limitations on the country's ability to use of force [80, 81].

Originally imposed by the victor powers on the then semi-sovereign Federal Republic, this tradition – despite some post-Wall legal amendments by the constitutional court on out-of-area deployments – had continued after 1990 when the country re-united and regained its full sovereignty. It is also noteworthy that in those negotiations of the 'Treaty on the final settlement' [82] of the German question, Germans had agreed to a future

Bundeswehr that would operate at a reduced overall force size of 345,000 men and women and not be composed of the sum of its parts, i.e., of West and East German armed forces (some 545,000 plus 175,000 soldiers). By 2022, the size of *Bundeswehr* had further diminished, to around 182,000 soldiers. This reduction of German troops through the 1990s to the 2020s had not merely been a nod to post-war peace-making, or to alleviate Germany's neighbours' historic fears, but was also a conscious step in the effort 'to build a better', less conflictual post-Wall 'world' [83].

In the context of Russia's War of revanchist imperialism, Germany's 'culture of restraint' appeared anachronistic. Evidently, a moment of deep crisis was necessary to end German inertia. And perhaps only a Social Democrat chancellor could carry the left with him, as Berlin would begin its historic turn away from its traditional pacifist stance to renewed rearmament.

The psychological change that Scholz's speech demanded of the German population was certainly extraordinary. For Scholz's Social Democrats and many Greens it was a bitter pill to swallow, even before the €100 bn special defence fund was enshrined in the country's Basic Law in June 2022, voted through thanks to the backing of the conservatives [84, 85]. The severe tensions within and between the coalition parties that accompanied this politico-legal process may well have been one of the reasons why Scholz soon after his daring speech retreated back into his shell while resorting to defensive and at times cryptic communication, if not plain, awkward silences. Mindful of the past and others' suspicions, he certainly soon qualified his ideas on Germany's future military might in public. In a TIME magazine interview in April, he explained 'We have to be strong enough.

Not so strong that we're a danger to our neighbours', he said, 'but strong enough' [86].

As a rule, Scholz clearly preferred for Germany to work within the EU and NATO 'framework for action' [87], as the chancellor liked to call it. In this vein, that spring he also did not travel alone to Kyiv, waiting instead for a joint summer trip alongside Macron and Italian Premier Mario Draghi [88]. Meanwhile, Ukrainian President Volodymyr Zelensky abruptly uninvited his German counterpart Frank-Walter Steinmeier (SPD), due to the latter's 'close [past] ties to Russia' when he had been foreign minister. To be sure, Steinmeier had acknowledged his 'mistake' of 'sticking' to Nord Stream 2 and of holding on to 'bridges that Russia no longer [itself] believed in, and of which our partners warned us'. But then he appeared to suggest joint blame in failing to build 'a common European home' [89] – when, we should note, the War had been Putin's decision alone and the destruction of the post-1991 European security order Russia's making. In this muddle of awkward and conflicting messaging as well as timid and plodding German military efforts, Scholz's perceived hesitant practical response to the War became widely criticised.

This is not to deny that since that day in late February 2022, Chancellor Olaf Scholz has intermittently taken to the stage imploring fellow Europeans to stand firm and together against Russian aggression while reiterating his own promises on fostering deeper European defence integration and economic coordination [90]. Putin's actions have thus clearly revealed a second chancellor in Scholz – one who with his *Zeitenwende* speech showed that he was capable of being forceful and bold, of demonstrating resolve to pursue a radical political 'turn'

(*Wende*). Indeed, there had always been more to the soft-spoken Hamburger than met the eye. Mocked in the 2021 election run-up by a catty conservative rival for his 'Smurf-like grin', Scholz had straight away retaliated: 'smurfs are small, crafty and always win' [91]. But beyond his wry humour and quick-wittedness, beyond the new authoritative rhetoric and determined tone emanating for Berlin, and beyond his unflappability and his quiet doggedness, it has to be said that few consequential deeds have followed the grand words.

Only after much dithering and many delays, did Berlin start shipping heavy weaponry to Ukraine, and it did everything to avoid trumpeting these moves. The shipments included sophisticated Panzerhaubitze 2000 with the air defence system Iris-T SLM, multiple rocket launchers MARS II, and self-propelled anti-aircraft guns GEPARD. By the end of November 2022 all of this amounted to a value of some €2 bn, making Germany the third largest donor of military aid after the US and Britain [92]. In early January 2023, Germany in a coordinated effort with France and the United States, promised to supply Kyiv with Marder infantry fighting vehicles and Patriot anti-aircraft missile systems. And at the end of the month, after EU and NATO defence leaders had failed to resolve their dispute, when meeting at Ramstein Air Base, over battle-tank deliveries, Scholz came round to announcing he would send a company of Leopard 2A6 to Ukraine and to give the required authorisations to other European countries to do the same with their German-manufactured machines. 'This decision', the chancellor declared, 'follows on from our official line to support Ukraine to the best of our ability. … We are acting in close international coordination' [93].

Scholz appeared to believe that he has acquitted himself well: stubbornly sticking to his secret Scholzian playbook, not bending to others' demands, and never going out on a limb. As he explained afterwards in the Bundestag, he had done everything 'right' [94]. To be sure, on a profoundly controversial question, he ultimately kept the SPD and the coalition together; and he argued that he had managed to persuade the Americans to supply their Abrams 1 tanks for Ukraine's defence efforts alongside Germany's. Even so, it was Washington's decision that ended the international cacophony of demands expressed at Ramstein and unlocked the total paralysis in the chancellery and thereby the German shipments in the first place. As a result, Biden succinctly but joyfully proclaimed that Europe was 'fully, thoroughly, totally united' [95].

Scholz's narrative is obviously pointing to short-term gains. And his partners and allies are mainly relieved that for the sake of projecting alliance cohesion, he finally gave them what they had wanted. Because many believe that this is likely just the first of more western escalatory steps in support of Kyiv, as Putin's war of attrition, is expected to continue. From our vantage point in summer 2023, Scholz's biggest test regarding military help to Ukraine, therefore, is likely yet to come.

As we look ahead as much as back to the *Zeitenwende* speech, the chancellor's own vision fails to take into account the long-term fall-out from his actions: the decline of Germany's influence in Europe and also the continent's profound transformation because of the Ukraine war. Indeed, as RUSI-co-director Jonathan Eyal has argued, the 'continent's strategic centre of gravity has shifted decisively from its western tip, where Germany and France used to decide matters, and towards central and eastern Europe'. For it has been the growing pressure especially from Baltic states, the Poles, and the Finns that has forced Berlin to make choices on weapons deliveries. 'These nations have gained moral authority because they were far more lucid and realistic about the danger of an imperial Russia' and were now also 'exercising a more direct and practical influence over the continent's decision-making' [96].

At home, Olaf Scholz with his *Zeitenwende* speech daringly reintroduced his nation to the language of war – a language that after 1990 was displaced almost entirely by the language of trade. Given Germans deep-seated fears of their country being dragged into a seemingly distant war, amazingly, by late January 2023 some 44 per cent of the population appeared to be in favour of sending battle tanks to Ukraine, with 45 per cent opposed [97]. None of this should be deemed a mean feat, considering that Scholz had hardly prepared himself to be a 'foreign policy' let alone a 'war chancellor'.

Generally, the electorate revealed itself nonetheless disillusioned with the *Ampel* on its first anniversary: 64 per cent of German voters were dissatisfied with the work of the coalition (vs 36 per cent the previous year) and 58 per cent were unhappy with the chancellor's performance (vs 22 per cent in 2021). And a year into the War, only a quarter of voters considered him a strong leader [98]. What's more, Germany's allies and European neighbours – unsure of Berlin's future foreign policies and future strategic choices – are frustrated, too. Even though, as if to reassure itself, the Scholz government in 2022–23 was feverishly writing Germany's first-ever national security strategy.

The cold reality simply is that the process of transformative change in Germany has barely begun. Germans know, that as a nation, they will have to practise thinking and acting in a new threat environment; that in a 'time of war, violence and displacement' which, as President Steinmeier put it, might 'spread around Europe like a wildfire', they must commit themselves once more to proactive deterrence and defence [99]. But it cannot be ignored that in 2022 the NATO two per cent spending target was missed again, the schedule on *Bundeswehr* reforms has been delayed, and the complex and fragile coalition is still arguing over how to best spend the €100 bn special fund [100]. All this led Latvia's Deputy Premier and Defense Minister Artis Pabriks openly to doubt whether Germans would defend their NATO allies. 'We are ready to die', he said. 'Are you?' [101] His trust in Germany was 'close to zero' [102].

On 'security' issues Germany by and large has continued to seek cover under the umbrella of multilateralism while looking to others to make the strategic big forward leaps – because, Scholz believes, in this arena there just cannot be any German going-it-alones (*Alleingänge*). Consequently, the public perception of the Federal Republic as economically domineering and as a free rider in matters of defence remains unchanged and the paradox is unresolved of, on the one hand, too little and, on the other, too much self-assertion and emancipation.

Though clearly sensing an externally imposed compulsion (*Zwang*) for Germany to lead from the front and to take on new responsibilities in accordance with its central position and economic might, Berlin under Scholz has struggled for any real political impact in the European arena and on the global stage.

In the end, for fear of his party, of a fissiparous coalition, and of losing the chancellery, he has thus far largely ended up taking decisions under duress and external pressure.

Conclusions

The first year after Merkel, 2022, was therefore one of forced reinvention for Scholz and Germany. Though he did not want to be seen as a mere follower or temporizer, his actions – as he adapted his foreign policy-responses from peacetime to wartime chancellor – were always those of a beleaguered leader, unable to shake the age-old constraints tied to history, geography, and party politics. Seeing him as more reactive than pro-active, Ukrainians in June 2022 coined the term 'scholzing' («шольцовать») [103] to express their exasperation with the German chancellor's hesitancy in supporting their defence efforts and what they perceived as his empty promises [104].² For all his rhetorical efforts to produce a major German foreign policy revolution – underlined by his December 2022 Foreign Affairs essay, in which he expanded his originally domestic '*Zeitenwende*' notion to that of a 'global' turning point [105] – his natural quiet caution (reflected in long bouts of silences), his stubbornness, and the structural limitations, that Germany has always faced, did act as breaks.

German war guilt, the effects of the '*nie wieder Krieg*' policy coupled with '*Zivilmachtstatus*', and the legacies of the Russo-German '*Sonderverhältnis*' plus the perennial complications of German coalition politics have all continued to check Germany's room for manoeuvre. As have its neighbours' never-ending suspicion of German uses of its clout – economic, political, and potentially military. And yet, for all these constraints that all post-war German chancellors have in some form or other been grappling with, it must be noted that there have been those who did step up and who showed great zeal to shape international affairs from day one. Under Schmidt, for example, an institutionally integrated and semi-sovereign West Germany did not stand in the background during a crisis-ridden decade. Instead, in matters of 'hard security' he managed to pursue openly a policy that both sought to enhance the Alliance's defence and deterrence posture vis-à-vis an obstreperous Soviet Union, all the while continuing efforts to push for nuclear arms reduction. This led to the famous NATO dual-track decision of 1979, which earned the Federal Republic international respect and even a seat at the top table of the western nuclear powers.

Confronted with the War – and with the current strongman in the Kremlin determined to sever the transatlantic bonds that have sustained not only Western Europe but also the Federal Republic since the 1940s – Germany, if it truly wants to lead in Europe, must ensure that its *Zeitenwende* is implemented and endures. Scholz will have to keep a potentially increasingly war-weary public and its neighbours and allies on board. He will have to be visible and vocal, tenacious, and consistent in his approach, as he takes on the new responsibilities that have fallen upon Germany in a changing world. Therefore, if he wants to be successful and sustain a Europe 'whole and free' [106], he must communicate clearly and fearlessly and embark on energetic forward-looking steps. Above all, faced with China's growing peacemaker ambitions in Europe, he must press hard for a process that will allow him – in tandem especially with America and France – to build a new post-war continent at peace with itself.

Notes

[1] It was notable that as early as under chancellor Gerhard Schröder's Red-Green coalition government in 2000 Germany's nuclear phase-out by 2021 had been originally decided before being anchored in the law in 2002. Little changed when Angela Merkel from 2005 began to govern through the CDU-SPD grand coalition. In 2009, however, concerned about German economic competitiveness, climate protection goals, and energy security, her new CDU-FDP government sought the extension of the lifetime of German nuclear power plants by another 12 years (until 2033), before undertaking a sudden policy reversal due to the hypersensibility and atomic angst awakened among the German electorate in the aftermath of the 2011 Japanese nuclear accident.

[2] In similar vein, Ukrainians also expressed their frustrations with France. During spring 2022 they had therefore invented the verb 'macroning' («макронить») – a description of a person who pretends to be very concerned about something but refuses to do anything substantial to help. Specifically, it was shorthand for President Macron's repeated phone calls made in vain [107].

References

1. Koelbl H. Angela Merkel: Portraits 1991–2021. Cologne: Taschen; 2020.
2. Spohr K. Angela Merkel o el poder sin vanidad. *El Pais*. 2021 May 14 [accessed 2023 February 8]. https://elpais.com/opinion/2021-05-14/angela-merkel-o-el-poder-sin-vanidad.html.
3. Alexander R. Die Getriebenen: Merkel und die Flüchtlingspolitik: Report aus dem Innern der Macht. Munich: Siedler; 2017.
4. Plickert P. (ed). Merkel: Eine kritische Bilanz. Munich: FinanzBuch Verlag; 2017.
5. The three pillars of Merkelism: How to understand Angela Merkel. *The Economist*. 2017 September 9.

6. Spohr K. The learning machine: Angela Merkel. *New Statesman*. 2017 July 8 [accessed 2023 February 8]. https://www.newstatesman.com/world/europe/2017/07/learning-machine-angela-merkel.

7. Alexander A. Machtverfall – Merkels Ende und das Drama der deutschen Politik: Ein Report. Munich: Siedler; 2021.

8. Feldenkirchen M, Hickmann C, Medick V, Teevs C. Erst verlacht, jetzt Kanzler: Der Weg des Olaf Scholz zum Triumph. *Der Spiegel* 50/2021. 2021 December 10 [accessed 2023 February 8]. https://www.spiegel.de/politik/deutschland/olaf-scholz-weg-ins-kanzleramt-rekonstruktion-eines-politischen-husarenstuecks-a-5b58f48d-86e1-49fc-b34e-a1134ed2fe76.

9. Mehr Fortschritt wagen – Koalitionsvertrag 2021–2025 zwischen SPD, Bündnis 90/Die Grünen und FDP [accessed 2023 February 8]. https://www.spd.de/fileadmin/Dokumente/Koalitionsvertrag/Koalitionsvertrag_2021-2025.pdf.

10. Bundeskanzer Willly Brandt Stiftung. 'Dare more democracy' – Domestic and social policy 1969–1974 [accessed 2023 February 8]. https://www.willy-brandt-biography.com/politics/domestic-policy/.

11. Tooze A. Chartbook #54 (Updated): Germany's new government – 'Dare more progress'; 2021 November 25 [accessed 2023 February 8]. https://adamtooze.com/2021/11/25/chartbook-54-updated-germanys-new-government-dare-more-progress/. DOI: https://doi.org/10.12968/S0047-9624(22)60457-7.

12. Gehrke L. New German Chancellor Scholz vows continuity with Merkel. *Politico*. 2021 December 8 [accessed 2023 February 8]. https://www.politico.eu/article/pre-written-olaf-scholz-sworn-in-as-german-chancellor/.

13. Договор между Российской Федерацией и Соединенными Штатами Америки о гарантиях безопасности. 2021 December 17 [accessed 2023 February 8]. https://mid.ru/ru/foreign_policy/rso/nato/1790818/?lang=ru.

14. Соглашение о мерах обеспечения безопасности Российской Федерации и государств-членов Организации Североатлантического договора. 2021 December 17 [accessed 2023 February 8]. https://mid.ru/ru/foreign_policy/rso/nato/1790803/?lang=ru.

15. Pifer S. Russia's draft agreements with NATO and the United States: Intended for rejection?. 2021 December 21 [accessed 2023 February 8]. https://www.brookings.edu/blog/order-from-chaos/2021/12/21/russias-draft-agreements-with-nato-and-the-united-states-intended-for-rejection/.

16. RFERL. OSCE meeting ends, no movement made in Russia-Ukraine crisis. 2022 January 13 [accessed 2023 February 8]. https://www.rferl.org/a/ukraine-osce-russia-us-diplomacy/31652032.html.

17. Spohr K. NATO enlargement and Putin's war in Ukraine: policy and history between myth and reality, 1989–2022. In: Ellison J., et al. Roundtable: The war in Ukraine. *Cold War History*. 2023; 23(1): 180–93. DOI: https://doi.org/10.1080/14682745.2023.2162329.

18. Oliphant R. Why Vladimir Putin is obsessed with Ukraine. *The Telegraph*. 2022 February 24 [accessed 2023 February 8]. https://www.telegraph.co.uk/world-news/2022/02/24/why-putin-obsessed-ukraine/.

19. Vladimir Putin 'On the historical unity of Russians and Ukrainians'. 2021 July 12 [accessed 2023 February 8]. http://en.kremlin.ru/events/president/news/66181.

20. The Kremlin – Moscow. Address by the president of the Russian Federation; 2022 February 21 [accessed 2023 February 8]. http://en.kremlin.ru/events/president/news/67828.

21. Soric M. Defining 'feminist' foreign policy. *DW*. 2021 December 23 [accessed 2023 February 8]. https://www.dw.com/en/feminist-foreign-policy-what-does-that-mean/a-60218814.

22. 'Values and interests are not opposites' – Baerbock interview with *Die Zeit*. 2021 December 22 [accessed 2023 February 8]. https://www.auswaertiges-amt.de/en/newsroom/news/-/2503468.

23. Eddy M. Germany wants its Russian pipeline: German allies aren't sure it's a good idea. *The Japan Times*. 2021 December 28 [accessed 2023 February 8]. https://www.japantimes.co.jp/news/2021/12/28/world/politics-diplomacy-world/germany-nord-stream-2-pipeline-allies/.

24. Reitz U. Kanzleramt gegen Auswärtiges Amt: Schon an Tag 1 zieht zwischen Baerbock und Scholz ein unüberwindbarer Konflikt auf. *FOCUS-online*. 2021 December 10 [accessed 2023 February 8]. https://www.focus.de/politik/deutschland/schon-an-tag-1-zieht-zwischen-baerbock-und-scholz-ein-unueberwindbarer-konflikt-auf_id_24500191.html.

25. Blank J, Fischer M. Baerbock und Scholz: Rivalen deutscher Außenpolitik? Dpa; 2023 January 30 [accessed 2023 February 8]. https://www.verlagshaus-jaumann.de/inhalt.bundesregierung-baerbock-und-scholz-rivalen-deutscher-aussenpolitik.94a836f8-e170-47c9-924b-82caf4f74d60.html.

26. Doll N, Wergin C. Das Russland-Problem des Olaf Scholz. *Die Welt*. 2021 December 18 [accessed 2023 February 8]. https://www.welt.de/politik/ausland/plus235727838/SPD-Das-Russland-Problem-des-Olaf-Scholz.html.

27. Rinke A. Germany must reassess policy towards Russia, China – ruling party chief. *Reuters*. 2022 February 3 [accessed 2023 February 8]. https://www.reuters.com/world/europe/germany-must-reassess-policy-towards-russia-china-ruling-party-chief-2022-02-03/.

28. Baerbock at Lavrov: 'Respect, interest and respect'. *Time news*. 2022 January 19 [accessed 2023 February 8]. https://time.news/baerbock-at-lavrov-respect-interest-and-respect/.

29. Chazan G. Germany's Russia problem: Ukraine crisis tests new government. *Financial Times*. 2022 January 31 [accessed 2023 February 8]. https://www.ft.com/content/b02434fc-b00b-4e6b-8fc8-218601eb18ec.

30. Huggler J. 'What will they send next? Pillows?': Kyiv mayor Vitali Klitschko hits back at Berlin over helmets. *The Telegraph*. 2022 January 26 [accessed 2023 February 8]. https://www.telegraph.co.uk/world-news/2022/01/26/will-send-next-pillows-kyiv-mayor-vitali-klitschko-hits-back/.

31. Walraff A. German arms exports as part of a coherent foreign and security strategy. *Verfassungsblog*. 2022 March 20 [accessed 2023 February 8]. https://verfassungsblog.de/german-arms-exports-as-part-of-a-coherent-foreign-and-security-strategy/.

32. Braun S. Die Botschaft: Nie wieder! *Süddeutsche Zeitung*. 2019 August 25 [accessed 2023 February 8]. https://www.sueddeutsche.de/politik/nationalsozialismus-die-botschaft-nie-wieder-1.4575353.

33. Bierling S. Vormacht wider Willen: Deutsche Außenpolitik von der Wiedervereinigung bis zur Gegenwart. Munich: C.H. Beck; 2014. DOI: https://doi.org/10.17104/9783406667671.

34. Gebauer M, et al. An 'unreliable partner'? The price of Berlin's hesitancy on Ukraine. *Der Spiegel* 5/2022. 2022 January 29 [accessed 2023 February 8]. https://www.spiegel.de/international/germany/an-unreliable-partner-the-price-of-berlin-s-hesitancy-on-ukraine-a-a3f5a21e-c37e-4ab0-af8d-c75bf6d2c99b.

35. Viser M, Morris L. Biden and German chancellor try to project unity amid threat of Russian aggression. *Washington Post*. 2022 February 7 [accessed 2023 February 8]. https://www.washingtonpost.com/politics/2022/02/07/scholz-biden-germany-russia-ukraine/.

36. Mekhennet S. Scholz says response to Russia will be 'united and decisive' if Ukraine is invaded. *Washington Post*. 2022 February 6. https://www.washingtonpost.com/national-security/2022/02/06/scholz-interview-germany-ukraine/.

37. Schuller K. 'Fehlgeleitete Sympathie für Russland'. *Frankfurter Allgemeine Zeitung*. 2022 January 31 [accessed 2023 February 8]. https://www.faz.net/aktuell/politik/inland/russland-sympathie-in-der-bundeswehr-und-ex-marine-chef-schoenbach-17761216.html.

38. German navy chief resigns over 'ill-considered' Ukraine-Russia remarks. *Sky news*; 2022 January 23 [accessed 2023 February 8]. https://news.sky.com/story/german-navy-chief-resigns-over-ill-considered-ukraine-russia-remarks-12523257.

39. 'Regierungserklärung von Bundeskanzler Olaf Scholz'. Deutscher Bundestag – Berlin; 2021 December 15 [accessed 2023 February 8]. https://www.bundesregierung.de/breg-de/service/bulletin/regierungserklaerung-von-bundeskanzler-olaf-scholz-1992008.

40. Donahue P, Delfs A. Scholz proposes new EU 'Ostpolitik' to ease tensions with Russia. *Bloomberg*. 2021 December 15 [accessed 2023 February 8]. https://www.bloomberg.com/news/articles/2021-12-15/scholz-proposes-new-eu-ostpolitik-to-ease-tensions-with-russia?leadSource=uverify%20wall.

41. Cohen R. Macron tells Biden that cooperation with U.S. cannot be dependence. *New York Times*. 2021 January 29 [accessed 2023 February 8]. https://www.nytimes.com/2021/01/29/world/europe/macron-biden.html.

42. Dittrich B. 'Schlussrunde': Scholz steht klar zu USA, NATO, EU und Frankreich. *Vorwärts*. 2021 September 24 [accessed 2023 February 8]. https://www.vorwaerts.de/artikel/schlussrunde-scholz-steht-klar-usa-nato-eu-frankreich.

43. Knabe H. 'Historiker enthüllt: So nahe stand der Jungsozialist Olaf Scholz den Machthabern in der DDR'. *FOCUS-online*. 2021 September 24 [accessed 2023 February 8]. https://www.focus.de/politik/deutschland/bundestagswahl/gastbeitrag-von-hubertus-knabe-partner-im-friedenskampf-jungsozialistische-ausfluege-in-die-ddr-im-ersten-leben-des-olaf-scholz_id_24256554.html.

44. Spohr K. The Global Chancellor: Helmut Schmidt and the Reshaping of the International Order. Oxford/ New York: OUP; 2016. DOI: https://doi.org/10.1093/acprof:oso/9780198747796.001.0001.

45. Herzinger R. 'Deutsche Russophilie'. *Die Welt*. 2014 March 8 [accessed 2023 February 8]. https://www.welt.de/print/die_welt/kultur/article125569604/Deutsche-Russophilie.html.

46. Lough J. Germany's Russia problem: The struggle for balance in Europe. Manchester: MUP; 2021. DOI: https://doi.org/10.7765/9781526151513.

47. Stegemann B. Die Rückkehr der Putinversteher. *Cicero*. 2022 November 16 [accessed 2023 February 8]. https://www.cicero.de/innenpolitik/ukraine-krieg-die-ruckkehr-der-putinversteher-ukraine-krieg.

48. Kaan S. Germany confronts Russian hybrid warfare. *Carnegie Europe*. 2017 July 26 [accessed 2023 February 8]. https://carnegieeurope.eu/2017/07/26/germany-confronts-russian-hybrid-warfare-pub-72636.

49. Die erwachsene Nation. *Taz*. 1998 December 24 [accessed 2023 February 8]. https://taz.de/Die-erwachsene-Nation/!1309609/.

50. Bahr E. Die 'Normalisierung' der deutschen Außenpolitik. *Internationale Politik*. 1999; 54: 41–52.

51. Germany Says 'No': The Iraq War and the Future of German Foreign and Security Policy. Wilson Center Discussion; 2008 February 22 [accessed 2023 February 8]. https://www.wilsoncenter.org/event/germany-says-no-the-iraq-war-and-the-future-german-foreign-and-security-policy.

52. Bennhold K. The former chancellor who became Putin's man in Germany. *New York Times*. 2022 April 23 [accessed 2023 February 8]. https://www.nytimes.com/2022/04/23/world/europe/schroder-germany-russia-gas-ukraine-war-energy.html.

53. Bennhold K, Solomon E. Shadowy arm of a German state helped Russia finish Nord Stream 2. *New York Times*. 2022 December 22 [accessed 2023 February 8]. https://www.nytimes.com/2022/12/02/world/europe/germany-russia-nord-stream-pipeline.html.

54. Campbell M. Putin's Nord Stream 2 pipeline: the Stasi connection. *The Times*. 2022 February 12 [accessed 2023 February 8]. https://www.thetimes.co.uk/article/putins-gas-pipeline-the-stasi-connection-fklvlkk5q.

55. Gerhard Schröder wirft Ukraine 'Säbelrasseln' vor. *Frankfurter Allgemeine Zeitung*. 2022 January 28 [accessed 2023 February 8]. https://www.faz.net/aktuell/politik/inland/schroeder-wirft-ukraine-saebelrasseln-wegen-kritik-an-deutschland-vor-17760895.html.

56. Metz A. '50 Jahre Röhren gegen Gas: Deutsch-russisches Jahrhundergeschäft und Deutsch-amerikanischer Wirtschaftskrimi. Ost-Ausschuss – Osteuropaverein der Deutschen Wirtschaft e.V. – Jahrbuch; 2020 [accessed 2023 February 8]. https://www.ost-ausschuss.de/sites/default/files/pm_pdf/Special%2050%20Jahre%20Röhren%20gegen%20Gas.pdf.

57. Russia's 2021 exports. Russia briefing; 2022 January 18 [accessed 2023 February 8]. https://www.russia-briefing.com/news/russia-s-2021-exports-by-sector-and-country.html/.

58. Workman D. Germany's top trading partners. World's top exports; 2021 [accessed 2023 February 8]. https://www.worldstopexports.com/germanys-top-import-partners/.

59. Rahr AG. Germany and Russia: A Special Relationship. *The Washington Quarterly*. 2007; 30(2): 137– 45. Project MUSE: https://muse.jhu.edu/article/210577/pdf. DOI: https://doi.org/10.1162/wash.2007.30.2.137.

60. Weber P, Bätz K. 'Es lebe der Handel' – auch wenn er den Wandel nicht zwangsläufig hervorruft. *Handelsblatt*. 2022 November 1 [accessed 2023 February 8]. https://www.handelsblatt.com/meinung/gastbeitraege/gastkommentar-es-lebe-der-handel-auch-wenn-er-den-wandel-nicht-zwangslaeufig-hervorruft/28780204.html.

61. Friedrich V. Handel erst nach Wandel. *Frankfurter Allgemeine Zeitung*. 2022 May 26 [accessed 2023 February 8]. https://www.faz.net/aktuell/politik/ausland/ukraine-krieg-prinzip-wandel-durch-handel-gescheitert-17999762.html?printPagedArticle=true#pageIndex_2.

62. Högselius P. Red gas: Russia and the origins of European energy dependence. Basingstoke, New York: Palgrave Macmillan; 2013.

63. Frum D. The West's Nuclear Mistake. *The Atlantic*. 2021 December 9 [accessed 2023 February 8]. https://www.theatlantic.com/ideas/archive/2021/12/germany-california-nuclear-power-climate/620888/.

64. Umbach F. Strategische Irrtümer, Fehler und Fehlannahmen der deutschen Energiepolitik seit 2002. *SIRIUS – Zeitschrift für Strategische Analysen*. 2022; 6(4): 373–93. DOI: https://doi.org/10.1515/sirius-2022-4003.

65. Spohr K, Piirimäe K. With or without Russia? The Boris, Bill and Helmut Bromance and the Harsh Realities of Securing Europe in the Post-Wall World, 1990–1994. *Diplomacy & Statecraft*. 2022; 33(10): 158–93. DOI: https://doi.org/10.1080/09592296.2022.2041816.

66. Heinemann-Grüder A. Russland-Politik in der Ära Merkel. *SIRIUS – Zeitschrift für Strategische Analysen*. 2022; 6(4): 359–72. DOI: https://doi.org/10.1515/sirius-2022-4002.

67. Kennan G. A Fateful Error. *New York Times*. 1997 February 5 [accessed 2023 February 8]. https://www.nytimes.com/1997/02/05/opinion/a-fateful-error.html.

68. Politisch-strategischer Fehler von historischem Ausmaß – Offener Brief zur NATO-Osterweiterung von Robert McMamara, Paul H. Nitze, Sam Nunn u.a. an Präsident Bill Clinton vom 26. Juni 1997 (Wortlaut*). Blätter für deutsche und Internationale Politik*. 1997; 8: 1023. https://www.blaetter.de/ausgabe/1997/august/politisch-strategischer-fehler-von-historischem-ausmass.

69. Mearsheimer JJ. Why the Ukraine Crisis is the West's Fault: The Liberal Delusions that Provoked Putin. *Foreign Affairs*. September/October 2014 [accessed 2023 February 8]. https://www.foreignaffairs.com/articles/russia-fsu/2014-08-18/why-ukraine-crisis-west-s-fault.

70. Carpenter TG. Four western provocations that led to U.S.-Russia Crisis Today. Cato Institute. December 2021 [accessed 2023 February 8]. https://www.cato.org/commentary/four-western-provocations-led-us-russia-crisis-today.

71. Was NATO Enlargement a Mistake? Foreign Affairs Asks the Experts. *Foreign Affairs online*. 2022 April 19 [accessed 2023 February 8]. https://www.foreignaffairs.com/ask-the-experts/2022-04-19/was-nato-enlargement-mistake. DOI: https://doi.org/10.31278/1810-6439-2021-19-6-44-60.

72. Sarotte ME. Containment beyond the Cold War: How Washington lost the post-Soviet peace. *Foreign Affairs*. November/December 2021 [accessed 2023 February 8]. https://www.foreignaffairs.com/articles/russia-fsu/2021-10-19/containment-beyond-cold-war.

73. Sommer T. Ein Realpolitiker holt zum Rundumschlag aus. *Zeit Online*. 2022 January 11 [accessed 2023 February 8]. https://www.zeit.de/politik/2022-01/klaus-von-dohnanyi-buch-nationale-interessen.

74. Spohr K. Post Wall Post Square: Rebuilding the World after 1989. London: William Collins; 2019. DOI: https://doi.org/10.12987/9780300252361.

75. Marsh S. Push for peace: Scholz wants more diplomacy after Putin talks. *Reuters*. 2022 February 15 [accessed 2023 February 8]. https://www.reuters.com/world/europe/push-peace-scholz-wants-more-diplomacy-after-putin-talks-2022-02-15/.

76. Fazal TM. The Return of Conquest? Why the Future of Global Order Hinges on Ukraine. *Foreign Affairs*. May/June 2022 [accessed 2023 February 8]. https://www.foreignaffairs.com/articles/ukraine/2022-04-06/ukraine-russia-war-return-conquest.

77. 'Regierungserklärung durch den Bundeskanzler zur aktuellen Lage'. Deutscher Bundestag – Berlin. Stenografischer Bericht. 19. Sitzung; 2022 February 27 [accessed 2023 February 8]. 1350–54. https://dserver.bundestag.de/btp/20/20019.pdf#P.1350.

78. Blumenau B. Breaking with convention? *Zeitenwende* and the traditional pillars of German foreign policy. *International Affairs*. 2022; 98(6): 1895–1913. DOI: https://doi.org/10.1093/ia/iiac166.

79. Bunde T. Lessons (to be) learned? Germany's Zeitenwende and European security after the Russian invasion of Ukraine. *Contemporary Security Policy*. 2022; 43(3): 516–30. DOI: https://doi.org/10.1080/13523260.2022.2092820.

80. Maull HW. Germany and Japan: The New Civilian Powers. *Foreign Affairs*. Winter 1990/91 [accessed 2023 February 8]. https://www.foreignaffairs.com/articles/asia/1990-12-01/germany-and-japan-new-civilian-powers. DOI: https://doi.org/10.2307/20044603.

81. Maull HW. Die prekäre Kontinuität: Deutsche Außenpolitik zwischen Pfadabhängigkeit und Anpassungsdruck. In: Schmidt MG., Zohlnhöfer R, editors. Regieren in der Bundesrepublik Deutschland – Innen- und Außenpolitik seit 1949. Wiesbaden: VS Verlag für Sozialwissenschaften. 1996; 421–55. DOI: https://doi.org/10.1007/978-3-531-90258-6.

82. Treaty on the final settlement with respect to Germany. Moscow; 1990 September 12 [accessed 2023 February 8]. https://treaties.un.org/doc/Publication/UNTS/Volume%201696/volume-1696-I-29226-English.pdf.

83. Zelikow P, Condoleezza R. To build a better world: Choices to end the Cold War and create a global commonwealth. New York: Twelve; 2019.

84. 100 billion euros for a powerful Federal Armed Forces. 2022 June 3 [accessed 2023 February 8]. https://www.bundesregierung.de/breg-en/news/special-fund-federal-armed-forces-2047910.

85. Wieder T. Germany's bitter return to arms. *Le Monde*; 2022 June 28 [accessed 2023 February 8]. https://www.lemonde.fr/en/opinion/article/2022/06/28/in-germany-a-bitter-return-to-arms_5988270_23.html.

86. Abend L, Bajekal N. Chancellor Olaf Scholz wants to transform Germany's place in the world: He'd just rather not talk about it. *TIME*; 2022 April 27 [accessed 2023 February 8]. https://time.com/6170974/olaf-scholz-germany-interview/.

87. 'Resolutely committed to peace and security' – Policy statement by Olaf Scholz, Chancellor of the Federal Republic of Germany and Member of the German Bundestag. Berlin; 2022 February 27 [accessed 2023 February 8]. https://www.bundesregierung.de/breg-en/news/policy-statement-by-olaf-scholz-chancellor-of-the-federal-republic-of-germany-and-member-of-the-german-bundestag-27-february-2022-in-berlin-2008378.

88. Goncharenko R. German Chancellor Olaf Scholz makes historic Kyiv visit. *DW*. 2022 June 17 [accessed 2023 February 8]. https://www.dw.com/en/german-chancellor-olaf-scholz-makes-historic-visit-to-kyiv/a-62163543.

89. Oltermann P. Ukraine snubs German president over past 'close ties to Russia'. *The Guardian*. 2022 April 12 [accessed 2023 February 8]. https://www.theguardian.com/world/2022/apr/12/ukraine-snubs-german-president-over-past-russia-links.

90. Speech by Federal Chancellor Olaf Scholz at the Charles University in Prague. 2022 August 29 [accessed 2023 February 8]. https://www.bundesregierung.de/breg-de/impressum/scholz-speech-prague-charles-university-2080752.

91. Scally D. 'Crafty smurf' Scholz carried to power in second political comeback. *The Irish Times*. 2021 December 4 [accessed 2023 February 8]. https://www.irishtimes.com/news/world/europe/crafty-smurf-scholz-carried-to-power-in-second-political-comeback-1.4746185.

92. Military support for Ukraine. Weekly updates [accessed 2023 February 8]. https://www.bundesregierung.de/breg-en/news/military-support-ukraine-2054992.

93. Oltermann P, Roth A. Germany announces it will supply Leopard 2 tanks to Ukraine. *The Guardian*. 2023 January 25 [accessed 2023 February 8]. https://www.theguardian.com/world/2023/jan/25/germany-leopard-2-tanks-ukraine.

94. Scholz zu 'Leopard'-Lieferung: 'Vertrauen Sie der Regierung'. *Tagesschau*. 2023 January 25 [accessed 2023 February 8]. https://www.tagesschau.de/ausland/europa/ukraine-leopard-panzer-105.html.

95. Bose N, Holland S, Stewart P. In change of course, U.S. agrees to send 31 Abrams tanks to Ukraine. *Reuters*. 2023 January 25 [accessed 2023 February 8]. https://www.reuters.com/world/us/reversal-us-agrees-send-31-abrams-tanks-ukraine-2023-01-25/.

96. Eyal J. Amid the smoke of war, power in Europe is shifting decisively to the east. *The Guardian*. 2023 January 29 [accessed 2023 February 8]. https://www.theguardian.com/commentisfree/2023/jan/29/amid-the-smoke-of-war-power-in-europe-is-shifting-decisively-to-the-east.

97. Olterman P, Connolly K. Scholz's caution over tanks for Ukraine echoed on Berlin streets. *The Guardian*. 2023 January 25 [accessed 2023 February 8]. https://www.theguardian.com/world/2023/jan/25/scholzs-caution-over-tanks-for-ukraine-echoed-on-berlin-streets.

98. Block T. Der Ampel-Absturz: Pannen, Krisen, Umfrage-Debakel. *Bild*. 2022 December 5 [accessed 2023 February 8]. https://www.bild.de/politik/inland/politik-inland/ein-jahr-an-der-regierung-der-ampel-absturz-82143358.bild.html.

99. 'Strengthening everything that connects us' – Federal President Frank-Walter Steinmeier at an event with the Deutsche Nationalstiftung. Schloss Bellevue – Berlin. 2022 October 28 [accessed 2023 February 8]. https://www.bundespraesident.de/SharedDocs/Downloads/DE/Reden/2022/10/221028-Alles-staerken-was-uns-verbindet-Englisch.pdf?__blob=publicationFile.

100. Jones S, Chazan G. Poorly equipped German army awaits financial reinforcement from Berlin. *Financial Times*. 2022 November 24 [accessed 2023 February 8]. https://www.ft.com/content/d094cd2f-7807-4e84-b404-83e15cd88975.

101. Vandiver J. Most Germans say no to military leadership role in Europe, poll finds. *Stars and Stripes*. 2022 October 18 [accessed 2023 February 8]. https://www.stripes.com/theaters/europe/2022-10-18/germany-security-russia-7730229.html.

102. Artis Pavriks at the Lennart Meri Conference. Tallinn; 2022 May 15. https://twitter.com/visegrad24/status/1525793901713440769?s=20&t=UOqA_814CR3AWZcVhR1kzg.

103. Ирина Альшаева. В Чехии считают, что Германия отправляет Украине обещания вместо военной помощи. gazeta.ru; 2022 June 25 [accessed 2023 February 8]. https://www.gazeta.ru/army/news/2022/06/25/18004004.shtml.

104. Ash TG. I went viral in Germany for a meme about scholzing – but the chancellor's hesitancy over Ukraine is no joke. *The Guardian*. 2023 February 3 [accessed 2023 February 8]. https://www.theguardian.com/commentisfree/2023/feb/03/germany-olaf-scholz-twitter-ukraine.

105. Scholz O. Die globale Zeitenwende: Wie ein neuer Kalter Krieg in einer multipolaren Ära vermieden werden kann. *Foreign Affairs online*. 2022 December 5 [accessed 2023 February 8]. https://www.foreignaffairs.com/germany/die-globale-zeitenwende.

106. George HW. Bush's 'Remarks to the Citizens in Mainz'. West Germany; 1989 May 31 [accessed 2023 February 8]. https://www.presidency.ucsb.edu/documents/remarks-the-citizens-mainz-federal-republic-germany.

107. Анекдот дня: что значит «макронить» и «валять шольца»? одесская жизнь. 2022 June 24 [accessed 2023 February 8]. https://odessa-life.od.ua/news/anekdot-dnja-chto-znachit-makronit-i-valjat-sholca.

PART 5
The Rest

15. Comrades? Xi, Putin, and the Challenge to the West

Michael Cox

> The relationship between Russia and the People's Republic of China has been the subject of much discussion amongst scholars, journalists and and policy-makers ever since the two countries began mending their fences in the 1980s and 1990s. Developments over the last twenty years from the rise of Putin and Xi through to Russia's decision to launch a full scale invasion of Ukraine on the 24 February 2022 has made that debate all the more important, with on the one side a number of authors claiming the relationship was merely 'convenient' and would not last, and others insisting – correctly as it turned out – that it was precisely what the two leaders described it as being: 'rock solid'. But what continues to hold these two countries together, what impact has their partnership had on Russia's conduct of the war, and how is it helping reshape the world order?

When Russia launched its 'full-scale invasion' of Ukraine on 24 February 2022, two large questions loomed large in the discussion which followed: (i) why did Putin undertake what he called a 'special military operation' when most experts thought it would be folly to do so; and (ii) how would China respond to an action which it claims caught it unawares and which according to most pundits, has caused China no end of problems since?

The jury may still be out thinking about the first question relating to the deeper causes of the war and why Putin decided to initiate it. On the other hand, it has by now returned a verdict when it comes to China – which is that in spite of a war that has caused the PRC great embarrassment in Europe and led to massive problems for the world economy China depends upon, it is remarkable how loyal Beijing has been to the man who launched the invasion in the first place. Chinese officials may of course insist that China is not a party to the conflict; that it has not aided Russia militarily; that it recognises Ukraine's territorial integrity; and that its only interest is in peace. Yet for many, such claims ring hollow. In fact, not only has China's diplomatic and economic support proved crucial through the war, but Xi himself has turned out be a model friend. From the beginning, he has made it obvious that in a conflict involving the US and NATO in opposition to Russia, it was perfectly clear on whose side China stood [1].

Nor has China been shy of investing the conflict with wider significance. Indeed, what might have begun as a minor military operation Putin said would be over in a matter of weeks has by now become a struggle for the future of the international system as a whole. This has not only raised the stakes in both Europe and Asia. It has also divided the world in ways that would have once been regarded as unthinkable. Furthermore, the outcome of the war according to Beijing will determine whether the world will be dominated by the US and its liberal allies, representing the past, or by new powers like Russia and China, representing what they claim will be a bright new future. As a Chinese official pointed out soon after another meeting between Putin and Xi, the 'relationship' between the two nations had by 2023, moved 'far beyond the bilateral scope' and over time had 'acquired critical importance for the global landscape and the future of humanity' as a whole [2].

Understanding both the war and its much wider implications requires us to then explain how two countries like Russia and China – both with very different cultures and systems of governance – have managed to forge such a close relationship. The answer, as we shall now go on to show, has to be sought out not in the present, where most commentators tend to begin, but rather in an exploration of the past. First, we will look at the last two decades of the 20th century, when the two countries started to mend fences after years of conflict. Over the next twenty years, the two nations then went on to build a new kind of 'great power relationship', which today poses a very real challenge to the West. No doubt Putin's rise and Xi's ascendancy to power in China were critical factors here. But so too was the first Ukraine crisis of 2014, a tipping point moment if ever there was one, which forced Russia to tilt more and more towards the 'East', while persuading Xi – if indeed he needed persuading – that China's future belonged with Putin and Russia. This did not mean there were no longer any differences between the two, however. Even so, as time passed, the two countries and their two leaders discovered that much more united than divided them. Some in the West no doubt hope that economic interest and fear of further escalation in Ukraine will over time, lead to a winding down of the conflict with the West. But with trust between the US and China now at an all-time low, Russia as alienated from the West as it was during the Cold War, and the spillover effects of an unfinished war reaching all corners of the globe, there is every reason to be pessimistic and little cause to be optimistic about the future.

Mending Fences

The second half of the 20th century witnessed at least five major turning points in the history of the Sino-Russian relationship. The first came in 1950, when the two communist powers signed a treaty of friendship meant to last thirty years. The next came in the 1960s, when Mao declared that China's old ally-in-arms was now led by revisionist traitors, who amongst many other ideological sins, had had the temerity to reject Stalin while working hand-in-glove with the imperialists.[1] A few years later, China then met with the same imperialists in the shape of Richard Nixon, followed in 1979 with the establishment of full diplomatic relations and increased military cooperation between the two countries. Then, in the 1980s, the 'seemingly changeless' cold war between China and the USSR gradually began to come to an end [4]. Driven by Deng's desire to drag China's economy into the modern world, as well as the recognition on both sides of the pointlessness of exploiting a 'revolutionary global movement' that no longer existed, the two countries slowly but surely began to move closer together [5].

Significantly, however the most serious change in the relationship only occurred in the last years of the Cold War, when relations took a decisive turn for the better – relations that improved further when Gorbachev decided to visit Beijing in 1989, the first such visit by a Soviet leader in 30 years. Unfortunately for Gorbachev, and more worryingly still for the Chinese, not only did his trip coincide with the ongoing drama unfolding in Tiananmen Square (in part inspired by all his talk of reform), but Gorbachev himself was about to do something which deeply concerned China: decamp from Eastern Europe and East Germany, causing a major crisis in the wider communist camp, of which China still saw itself a part. Putin as we know, later became highly critical of his reforming predecessor. But as Arne Westad has shown, the Chinese were perhaps even more shocked because a leader of a great communist superpower not only let Eastern Europe go, but also went on to accept 'the banning of the party and then the dissolution of the Soviet state' itself, 'almost without a shot being fired in anger'.[2]

That said, China was still faced with the task of working out how to manage their relationship with Russia going forward. The obvious answer, which was already in train anyway, was to improve ties in the hopes these would provide both countries – one rising economically and the other collapsing – with some degree of security in a challenging new environment defined by globalisation, and in which democracy, in one form or another, appeared to be the international norm. Thus followed a series of 'joint statements', a series of agreements on borders and military cooperation, a promise not to target each other with nuclear weapons, various discussions on improving economic relations, and quite a few summits (seven in all), all of which concluded in July 2001, with the two putting their names to what they regarded as a landmark treaty. Old time foes had now become 'good neighbours' and 'friends' [7].

Unipolarity and its Discontents

Though these early moves did not in of themselves mean that anything like a new 'axis of authoritarianism' had come into being, the significance of what had transpired should not be underestimated. Admittedly, none of what had happened added up to a formal alliance. The Treaty of 2001 was nowhere nearly as important as that signed by Stalin and Mao back in 1950. Nonetheless, it did point to a new configuration bringing together two countries who still felt like outsiders in a world shaped and dominated by the United States. Beijing may have also been hoping to secure a partner in what some, though not all strategists in China, were already starting to see as a part of the ongoing struggle against US hegemony. Anti-Americanism was hardly a new phenomenon in China. Indeed, following the crisis occasioned by Tiananmen, the CCP had put a great deal of time and effort into linking pride in the Chinese nation with hostility towards the United States. Hence, building a bridge to another outsider country – which by the turn of the century was beginning to move away from its earlier pro-Western phase –made a great deal of sense [8].

Moreover, even though the two countries claimed that nothing they were doing was directed against any 'third party', implicitly of course, it was. As both made clear in 1997 (with Putin making it clearer still ten years later in a famous speech delivered in Munich), they were determined to move the world away from a unipolar system, which did not suit their interests towards a 'multipolar' order which did. Even so, the two insisted they were not hostile to the US; Nonetheless as Russian leader Boris Yeltsin declared at one of his long meetings with the Chinese premier, Jiang Zemin, in the 1990s, there were some unnamed) powers pushing for a world with one centre. This however, was simply unacceptable to either Russia or China, who from now on, would be working together to create a 'new world order … with several focal points' and not just one [9].

In of itself, this may not have led to conflict with the United States and the West. Nothing was set in stone. However, as it soon became clear, unipolarity created conditions on the ground which allowed the US to act with a degree of impunity without much fear of the consequences. How else, according to policy-makers in both Russia and China, could one explain the many unilateral decisions taken by the United States from the bombing of the Chinese Embassy in Belgrade in May 1999, to NATO's continuing war against Russia's ally Serbia, and finally – most importantly according to Putin, writing on the eve of his war against Ukraine – to Bush's war against Iraq in 2003? These were not accidents of history in their view, but rather expressions of an underlying power imbalance in the wider international system. Some in the West may have insisted that unipolarity engendered stability. Others that unipolarity did not really matter. This however, was not the view in either Beijing or Moscow.

Russia and China may of course, have been hoping that they could still work with the US on key issues. After all, they did share Washington's views on the danger posed by international terrorism and nuclear proliferation. China and Russia also saw a future within pre-existing international institutions like the UN. And from a purely economic point-of-view, Russia and China clearly needed the markets and the investment only the West could provide. Yet the logic of economics would never be enough to overcome the logic of power politics. Slowly but surely, what began as an attempt by all sides to find a way of working together, came to nothing in the end.

History however, never moves at the same speed for all actors, and as it turned out, relations between Russia and the West deteriorated even more quickly than they did between China and the West. Putin's brutal war in Chechnya, his use of the fight against terror to clamp down on democracy, his own vast wealth (accumulated by controlling the apparatus of state), and the imprisonment of key opponents – including one of the richest men in Russia, Khodorkovsky – taken together certainly did nothing to reassure Europe or the United States that this was someone with whom one could easily do business (though many in the West still hoped it would be possible) [10]. Nor was the West much assured either, with Putin's oft-repeated assertions that his main goal now was to make his country 'great again' – especially as it was now firmly under the control of an ex-KGB man with an inner circle whose ruthlessness at home was only matched by a willingness to do anything to prevent change in either Russia or in its so-called 'near abroad' states (most especially Ukraine) as the work of foreign agents [11].

Nor did the relationship show any sign of improvement in the years thereafter. If anything, worse was yet to come, when at the Bucharest Summit in 2008, Bush called upon NATO to open its doors to both Ukraine and Georgia (a move which Putin claimed at the time 'complicated' his 'position').[3] Relations cooled further when Russian forces invaded Georgian territory a few months later in what one writer called 'the first European war of the 21st century [13]. And they became cooler still when three years later, the Arab world was convulsed by a series of upheavals, which not only caused consternation in both Beijing and Moscow – people power was not something they wished to encourage – but also a great deal of anger when the West, in their view, turned what had initially been an R2P operation designed to save lives in Libya, into a policy of regime change. As they pointed out in a joint declaration signed in June 2011, they had been looking for a 'political solution' to the Libya crisis. The West on the other hand, was using military means and taking sides in ways that went far beyond that originally agreed at the UN [14].

But if the crisis in Libya provoked disagreement, then the war in Syria caused something close to a near breakdown in relations, especially when Russia decided to throw its military weight behind the brutal regime of the Syrian president, Bashar al-Assad. Diplomatically, things became even more fraught when both Moscow and Beijing both exercised their veto power at the UN to prevent any sanctions being imposed on Assad's government [15]. Russia's decision may have been perfectly understandable given the long-standing relationship it had with the Baath regime ever since the Cold War. China's reasoning was probably different, but as one observer noted, its decision was probably less driven by any interest it might have had in Syria, and more with demonstrating that it would from now on, be adopting a more assertive, more proactive foreign policy – and significantly doing so alongside Russia [16].

From Xi to the First Ukraine Crisis

Thus the wider crisis in the Middle East was already drawing the two nations closer together, even before Xi became China's 'paramount leader'. But having become leader, Xi lost no time in establishing a close relationship with Putin and Russia. Indeed, within a week of becoming president, Xi was already making his first overseas trip, and the first country he chose to visit was none other than Russia. He even told a small group of invited journalists that the fact he was visiting Russia shortly after assuming the presidency was itself a 'testimony' to the great importance that China placed on its relationship with its 'friendly neighbour' [17]. Moreover, by making Russia what Xi himself called 'a priority', he was also sending a message to the United States, who were by now taking what he felt was a dangerously intrusive interest in the affairs of the Asia-Pacific. The message could not have been clearer: China was no longer prepared to sit back and watch Washington dominate the field of international affairs [18].

Putin was clearly delighted by the visit and Xi's words, and responding in kind, even announced that not only did he look forward to increased economic cooperation (by 2013, trade between the two countries had risen eightfold over a ten-year period), but also to China and Russia working closely to produce what he termed 'a more just world order' [19]. In a joint declaration issued by Putin and Xi after their talks, they also made it clear who they believed was standing in the way of creating such an order. Indeed, without even mentioning the United States, the two governments concluded that together they would 'oppose' any country (or even a 'bloc of countries') that 'unilaterally and without limit', harmed 'strategic stability and international security' [17].

But perhaps the real test of the relationship came just a year later when Russia intervened to change the status quo in Ukraine by force. China may have been less than enthusiastic about this particular move, and even made it clear in its official statements that it continued to support the 'independence, sovereignty and integrity' of Ukraine. Yet in spite of its various declarations, there was little doubt in the end whom China would be backing. As critics at the time pointed out, what Russia was now doing in Ukraine – encouraging secession, using force to settle disputes and intervening in the internal affairs of another state (a state with which China had a significant relationship) – contradicted every single principle upon which Chinese statecraft had hitherto been based.

This however, made very little difference to policy-makers in China, nor to those in the official Chinese press who made clear which side Beijing was on. Indeed, in one fairly typical newspaper article published at the time, readers were informed that there were (unspecified) 'reasons' why the situation in Ukraine 'is what it is today'. Then, having hinted that the situation was more complex than many outside Russia were suggesting, the article went on to attack what it termed the 'West's biased mediation' in the crisis. This, it opined, only 'made things worse'. Putin meanwhile, was almost given a clean bill of health. After all, all he was doing, we were told, was protecting Russian interests and those of Russian-speakers living in Ukraine. The West, it concluded, should thus stop wagging its finger at the Russian leader and 'respect Russia's unique role in mapping out the future of Ukraine' [20].

Best and Bosom Friends

Putin in turn, lost little time reinforcing his position with those now prepared to turn a blind eye to Russian actions. At the sixth BRICS Summit held in Brazil in July, not only did he get the other four states there – including China – to say nothing about Russia's actions in Ukraine, but he also persuaded them to oppose any Western sanctions then being directed against Russia itself [21]. Meanwhile, even though China did not formally recognise Russia's incorporation of Crimea – impossible to do so, given its own views on secession and sovereignty – it nonetheless used the opportunity presented by the crisis to pressure Russia to sell China gas below market rates, while strengthening the economic ties it was already developing with Russia. As one Russian analyst at the time observed, the new 'rapprochement ... accelerated projects' that had been under discussion for decades, resulting in agreements on a natural gas pipeline and cross-border infrastructure, among many other deals. As a result, China now began to import larger and larger quantities of Russian oil and gas, while Russia became one of the five largest recipients of Chinese outbound direct investment in relation to the Chinese government's Belt and Road Initiative [22].

Even so, a number of analysts were still unconvinced that a serious strategic partnership was in the making. We were even informed by at least one writer (there were many more) that the West should not be too concerned about what was happening because 'underlying tensions' between the two countries were bound to keep them apart [23]. Two Russian writers even asked whether this 'strengthening of relations' constituted a 'durable strategy' or was mere 'temporary rapprochement' between two countries with very different interests [24]. Beijing and Moscow soon provided an answer, and as if to prove their intent, signed another strategic agreement right in the midst of the crisis.[4]

By 2015, they were even talking of creating a 'Greater Eurasian Partnership' by bringing their two spheres of economic interests (the Belt and Road Initiative, and the Eurasian Economic Union) much closer together [25]. In 2016, Russia then moved to officially back China in its ongoing struggle with the Hague Court and the West's regional allies over the South China Seas dispute [26]. A couple of months later, following 'a string of high-level meetings' in both Beijing and Moscow, it also announced measures similar to those already in place in China to bring the internet under tighter control [27]. Significantly too, in the light of what happened later, Russia (and 36 other nations) wrote to the UN in 2019 supporting China's policies in the western region of Xinjiang [28].

Nor did the rapidly improving relationship conclude there. In 2015, for example, Russia finally agreed to sell China 24 Sukhoi-35 (Su-35) combat aircraft and four S-400 SAM systems [29]. Sino-Russian military ties also became much closer, especially in the area of joint military exercises, 'the most important' part of Russian-Chinese military cooperation according to Russian Defence Minister Sergei Shoigu [30, 31]. Indeed, by early 2021, one senior Chinese official was even moved to declare that there now appeared to be 'no limit' to Chinese-Russian military cooperation.[5] What followed only appeared to confirm this, when in October, Chinese and Russian warships conducted joint naval drills in the Western Pacific for the first time, followed only a month later with both militaries sending bomber flights into Japanese and South Korean air defence zones. The message could not have been clearer: this was a partnership that needed to be taken extremely seriously [33]. As one well-informed Western analyst pointed out at the time, it was by now clear that relationship was 'the strongest, closest and best' the two countries 'have had since at least the mid-1950s ... possibly ever' [33].

Deep Freeze

Meantime, as relations between Beijing and Moscow moved in one particular direction, those with the West moved in another. Earlier during his presidency, Obama had tried to 'reset' relations with Russia and 'tilt' the US more towards Asia in an effort he claimed to take advantage of the economic opportunities presented there. But as we now know, the reset soon collapsed, while America's so-called rebalancing act was read in Beijing as just a cover for a new and more effective means of containing its rise [34]. Moreover, when Obama was followed by Trump, who had already declared that the US was being economically 'raped' by China, it had become abundantly clear to policy-makers and foreign policy experts in China that they were now engaged in a long-term competition with Washington from which there would be no easy escape [35]. Trump alone was not the cause of this. But reflecting as he clearly did a decisive shift in US attitudes towards China as expressed most clearly in a raft of official reports detailing the threat China now posed to US national security, Beijing drew the logical conclusion that to offset the challenge posed by an increasingly hostile America, it needed all the friends it could get [36].

But what in the end may have driven the final nail in the proverbial coffin of China's relationship with the West was not what Beijing saw as the 'China threat' lobby in Washington, but Europe's increasing concerns about the direction China was now travelling. Hitherto, neither the EU, nor even NATO, had seen China in the same way as Russia. No doubt the lure of its huge market influenced this judgement. But there was also a feeling that even if China was no longer a simple 'stakeholder', it did have an ongoing interest in a stable global economy and indeed in globalisation itself. Soon however, the rhetoric coming out of Brussels started to change. The EU may have continued to see China as a country it could continue, and possibly needed, to do business with. Even so, by 2020 and 2021, it was already starting to view the PRC as a 'systemic rival', pursuing human rights policies as well as economic ones, inimicable to its core interests. When China then decided to adopt sanctions against members of the European Parliament, including the Chair of its Delegation for Relations with China, relations inevitably deteriorated even more rapidly [37].

NATO found itself in a not dissimilar position. As late as 2020, it too was still refusing to see China as a threat or as an enemy. However, by the time of the NATO summit in 2021, it was already arguing that China's policies now presented a serious challenge to the 'rules-based order'. NATO in fact, left little room for misunderstanding, and in a lengthy communique of its own, talked in increasingly tough-minded terms about Beijing rapidly expanding its nuclear arsenal, China's opacity around its own military modernisation and its significant ties working ever closer with Russia in the Euro-Atlantic region [38]. Even more worrying from China's point-of-view was NATO's growing inclination to see security in increasingly globalist terms with a discernible tilt of its own towards what it now called the 'Indo Pacific' region. Admittedly, it was only after the war in Ukraine had begun in early 2022 that NATO began to think seriously about 'practical and political cooperation' with a number of key allies such as Australia, Japan, New Zealand and South Korea. But even before the invasion began, it was clear enough in which direction the alliance was moving [39].

The impact of all this back in Beijing was entirely predictable. Facing as it felt it did a 'collective West' and not just the Americans alone, Beijing concluded that it now had fewer, if any, reasons not to move ever closer to Russia. Meanwhile, as the two began to coalesce around issues such as Taiwan, China began to step up its attacks on the West more generally. Indeed, having been careful hitherto not to attack NATO openly, it started to do so – nowhere more unambiguously than in the communique on 4 February 2022, where it talked, probably for the first time (and very much like Russia) of the organisation being some relic of the Cold War whose continued existence not only threatened the security of its close friend Russia, but provided no long-term basis for European security overall. By the middle of 2022, it was even referring to NATO as a 'systemic challenge' to global security and stability, as well as a 'tool for the United States to maintain its hegemony' in order 'to instigate a "new cold war"' [40].

Conclusion

As we have tried to show in this historical survey of the Sino-Russian relationship leading up to Russia's invasion of Ukraine in 2022, the partnership between the two began to take shape just as the Cold War was winding down, continuing through the 1990s and thereafter going from strength to strength – in part driven by the two nations' overlapping interests, their own ideas about the kind of international system they wished to inhabit, and also by what they perceived to be the liberal, democratic West's underlying refusal to accept their right to be either illiberal or undemocratic. Putin and Xi also played a key role here. The fact that they have met over 40 times, even before Russia invaded Ukraine, may well have been pure coincidence. Powerful leaders of significant states often talk to one another. But the obvious ease Xi and Putin felt in each other's company certainly lent weight to the view that that the wider relationship between the two countries they represented was very special.

But something else was also uniting the two men: a shared view about the direction they thought the world was now moving towards. Both of course, were well aware of how much power the US and its allies could still muster. Even so, underlying their partnership was a belief that the West in general (and the US in particular) were in decline, and that history was at last moving in their direction. Long-term changes in the structure of the world economy followed in short order with the rise of populism, the West's failure (as they saw it) to deal effectively with the Covid pandemic, and finally, NATO's ignominious withdrawal from Afghanistan in late 2021. This only proved to them what Putin and Xi had been saying for years: that the West was failing, and that the future belonged to the East [41].[6]

This in turn, leads us to reflect not just on how durable the Russia-China relationship is likely to be going forward – that question has already been answered by how Putin and Xi have responded to any suggestion that theirs is a 'bad marriage' likely to hit the rocks soon [42] – but also on what the relationship means for the world at large. There is no doubt that if the war had come to a speedy end (with Ukraine overcome as Putin had planned), we might have been in a very different place. However, the fact that it has continued for so long with no end in sight means that there is now much more at stake. Short conflicts can be deadly. But long wars often change everything, and what in effect began as a regional conflict on the edge of Europe, has in the eyes of many come to define the future of the whole international order. Many years ago, all the talk in the West was of how globalisation would turn all states into 'responsible stakeholders'. Even today, many continue to believe that even if Russia is a 'lost cause', China still has an interest in finding a way to work with the West. One can but hope. Yet the signs are not good, and as long as China stands by Russia – and at the time of writing, there is little sign that it will not continue to do so – then what some are already calling a new Cold War is likely to get colder still. Dangerous times lie ahead [43].

Notes

[1] For a useful collection of Mao's thoughts about Stalin spanning the period between 1938 to 1966, see [3].

[2] For a discussion of how China officially reacted to the Soviet collapse, see [6].

[3] Putin could not have been clearer. Opening the door for Ukraine and Georgia to join NATO put Russia in a 'very complicated position' [12].

[4] In May 2014, President Xi Jinping and Russian President Vladimir Putin signed the *China-Russia Joint Statement on a New Stage of Comprehensive Strategic Partnership of Coordination.*

[5] The quote on 'no limit' military cooperation between China and Russia can be found in [32].

⁶ As early as 2012, Putin had been arguing that 'domestic socio-economic problems that have become worse in industrialised countries as a result of the (economic) crisis are weakening the dominant role of the so-called historical West' [41].

References

1. 'Greeting to PRC President Xi Jinping on re-election to post of China's Communist Party Central Committee'. *President of Russia*, Moscow; 2022 October 23 [cited 2023 June 15].

2. Xi and Putin pledge to shape a new world order as the Chinese leader leaves Russia with no peace in sight for Ukraine. *NBC News*. 2023 March 22 [cited 2023 June 15]. https://www.nbcnews.com/news/world/xi-putin-pledge-new-world-order-chinese-leader-leaves-russia-rcna76048.

3. Single Spark: Mao's Evaluations of Stalin: a Collection and Summary. 2006 September 6. https://massline.org/SingleSpark/Stalin/StalinMaoEval.htm.

4. Levine LI. Some thoughts on Sino-Soviet relations in the 1980s. *International Journal*. 1979; 34(4): 649. DOI: https://doi.org/10.2307/40201817.

5. Zubok V. The Soviet Union and China in the 1980s: reconciliation and divorce. *Cold War History*. 2017; 17(2): 121–141. DOI: https://doi.org/10.1080/14682745.2017.1315923.

6. Westad O. A Restless Empire: China and the World Since 1750. London: The Bodley Head; 2012. p 427–428.

7. Peace Agreements Database: Treaty of Good-Neighborliness and Friendly Cooperation Between the People's Republic of China and the Russian Federation. 2001 July 16 [cited 2023 June 15]. https://www.peaceagreements.org/view/1735.

8. Xu G. The Chinese Anti-American Nationalism In The 1990s, Asian Perspective 1998; 22(2): 193–218.

9. China, Russia sign Pact. *CNN World News*. 1997 April 23 [cited 2023 June 15]. http://edition.cnn.com/WORLD/9704/23/russia.china/.

10. Belton C. Putin's People: How The KGB Took Back Russia and Then Took on the West. London: William Collins; 2020.

11. Dickinson P. How Ukraine's Orange Revolution shaped twenty-first century geo-politics. 2020 November 22 [cited 2023 June 15]. https://www.atlanticcouncil.org/blogs/ukrainealert/how-ukraines-orange-revolution-shaped-twenty-first-century-geopolitics/.

12. Putin V. Putin's speech at NATO Summit. 2008 April 2; Bucharest [cited 2023 June 15]. https://www.unian.info/world/111033-text-of-putin-s-speech-at-nato-summit-bucharest-april-2-2008.html.

13. Emerson M. Post-Mortem on Europe's First War of the Twenty-First Century. *CEPS Policy Brief*. 2008; 167. DOI: https://doi.org/10.2139/ssrn.1333553.

14. Terry PC. The Libya Intervention (2011); neither lawful nor successful. *The Comparative and International Law Journal of Southern Africa*. 2015; 48(2): 162–182.

15. Security Council Fails to Adopt Draft Resolution on Syria as Russian Federation, China Veto Text Supporting Arab League's Proposed Peace Plan. 2012 February 4; United Nations Meeting Coverage, Security Council [cited 2023 June 15]. https://press.un.org/en/2012/sc10536.doc.htm.

16. Wong N. China's veto on Syria: what interests are at play?. *Open Democracy*. 2012 July 25 [cited 2023 June 15]. https://www.opendemocracy.net/en/chinas-veto-on-syria-what-interests-are-at-play/.

17. Herszenhorn DM, Buckley C. China's New Leader, Visiting Russia, Promotes Nations' Economic and Military Ties. *The New York Times*. 2013 March 22.

18. Keck Z. China-Russia Relations Endure? With Xi JinPing in Moscow and Beijing's interests overlap on more issues than is often realized. *The Diplomat*. 2013 March 23.

19. Chinese President Xi JinPing in Russia for first foreign tour. *BBC News*. 2013 March 22 [cited 2023 June 15]. https://www.bbc.com/news/world-asia-china-21873944.

20. Tiezzi S. China Backs Russia on Ukraine. *The Diplomat*. 2014 March 4.

21. Putin seeks BRICS moves to protect against U.S. "sanction attacks". *Reuters*. 2014 July 14 [cited 2023 June 15]. https://www.reuters.com/article/us-ukraine-crisis-brics-putin-idUSKBN0FJ2ID20140714.

22. Gabuev A. Friends with Benefits? Russian-Chinese Relations after the Ukraine Crisis, Carnegie Endowment for International Peace; 2016 June 29.

23. Chandran N. Serious rivalry still drives China-Russia relations despite improving ties. *CNBC*. 2018 September 14 [cited 2023 June 15]. https://www.cnbc.com/2018/09/14/china-russia-ties--more-rivalry-than-allaince.html.

24. Alexeeva O, Lassere F. The Evolution of Sino-Russian Relations as seen from Moscow: the Limits of Strategic Rapprochement. *China Perspectives*. 2018; 3: 69–77. DOI: https://doi.org/10.4000/chinaperspectives.8197.

25. Shakhanova G, Garlick J. The Belt and Road Initiative and the Eurasian Economic Union: Exploring the "Greater Eurasian Partnership". *Journal of Current Chinese Affairs*. 2020; 39(1): 33–57. DOI: https://doi.org/10.1177/1868102620911666.

26. Nouwens V, Lain S. What's Behind Sino-Russia Exercises in the South China Seas?. *RUSI*. 2016 September 22 [cited 2023 June 15]. https://rusi.org/explore-our-research/publications/commentary/whats-behind-sino-russian-exercises-south-china-sea.

27. Soldatov A, Borogan I. Putin brings China's Great Firewall to Russia in cybersecurity pact. *The Guardian*. 2016 November 29 [cited 2023 June 15]. https://www.theguardian.com/world/2016/nov/29/putin-china-internet-great-firewall-russia-cybersecurity-pact.

28. Russia Among 37 States Backing China's Policy in Xinjiang. *The Moscow Times*. 2019 July 13 [cited 2023 June 15]. https://www.themoscowtimes.com/2019/07/13/russia-among-37-states-backing-chinas-policy-in-xinjiang-a66401.

29. Wezeman ST. China, Russia and the shifting landscape of arms sales. Stockholm International Peace Research Institute. 2017 July 5 [cited 2023 June 15]: Commentary.

30. Blivas A. Sino-Russian Military Exercises Signal a Growing Alliance, U.S.Naval Institute: Proceedings. 2021; 147(6): 1420.

31. Weitz R. Sino-Russia Security Ties. *National Bureau of Asian Research, Special Report*. 2017; 66.

32. Putin V. Joint Statement of the Russian Federation and the People's Republic of China on the International Relations Entering a New Era and the Global Sustainable Development'; 2022 February 4 [cited 2023 June 15]; Moscow. http://en.kremlin.ru/supplement/5770.

33. Rasheed Z. Why are China and Russia strengthening ties? *Aljazeera*. 2021 November 25.

34. Zhang F. China's Response to the U.S. Rebalance to China. *Security Challenges*. 2016; 12(3): 45–60.

35. Zhao M. Is a New Cold War Inevitable? Chinese Perspectives on US-Strategic Competition. *Chinese Journal of International Politics*. 2019; 371–394. DOI: https://doi.org/10.1093/cjip/poz010.

36. U.S Views of China Turn Sharply Negative Amid Trade Tensions. *Pew Research Center*. 2019 August 13 [cited 2023 June 15]. https://www.pewresearch.org/global/2019/08/13/u-s-views-of-china-turn-sharply-negative-amid-trade-tensions/.

37. Noonan E, Wieringen K. Trends in Chinese reporting on the European Union, Briefing. European Parliament; 2021. https://www.europarl.europa.eu/RegData/etudes/BRIE/2021/690710/EPRS_BRI(2021)690710_EN.pdf.

38. International Institute for Strategic Studies: China's place on the NATO agenda. *Comment.* 2021; 27. DOI: https://doi.org/10.1080/13567888.2021.1957324.

39. Bartlett-Imagawa R. NATO, Asia Pacific partners agree to bolster cooperation. Nikkei *Asia.* 2022 April 8 [cited 2023 June 15]. https://asia.nikkei.com/Politics/Ukraine-war/NATO-Asia-Pacific-partners-agree-to-bolster-cooperation.

40. NATO is Systemic Challenge to Global Security and Stability. *People's Daily.* 2022 July 5.

41. Grove T. Russia's Putin says the West is in decline. *Reuters.* 2012 July 9.

42. Kupcha CS. The Right Way to Split China and Russia: Washington Should Help Moscow leave This Bad Marriage. *Foreign Affairs.* 2021 August 4.

43. Seven Ways Russia's war on Ukraine has changed the world. Chatham House. 2023 February 20 [cited 2023 June 15]. https://www.chathamhouse.org/2023/02/seven-ways-russias-war-ukraine-has-changed-world.

16. The Global South and Russia's Invasion of Ukraine

Chris Alden

Russia's invasion of Ukraine inspired a unity among Western democracies not seen since the first Gulf War. However, Western expectations of global unified condemnation and action against Russia were dashed by the response of the Global South. Far from endorsing the Western position, over 40 member states consistently abstained or voted against resolutions proposed in the United Nations General Assembly that sought to condemn Russian actions. In April 2022, in the wake of overwhelming evidence of human rights violations, 50 members voted against expelling Russia from the Human Rights Council. These included many African, Asian, Middle Eastern and Latin American countries who were adamant that, irrespective of who started it and how it was conducted, the most important response should be to bring the conflict to an immediate end. What is behind the seeming indifference and even hostility in the Global South to the Western position on Russia?

This chapter will review and assess how Russia's invasion of Ukraine has been seen through the lens of the Global South. It will examine how Global South countries viewed the Western response to Russia's invasion; ensuing debates

> over non-alignment generated by Russia's invasion amongst Global South countries; and, how the Russia-Ukraine war has reignited discussion on reform the multilateral system.

Russia's invasion of Ukraine inspired a unity among Western democracies not seen since the first Gulf War. Indeed, it was the expectation that this egregious violation of sovereign territory would galvanise the world to a wholesale condemnation of Russian aggression and, with that, support for a battery of legal, economic and military measures designed to turn back the tide in Ukraine. Led by a revitalised transatlantic alliance, an unprecedented array of sanctions barred businesses from commercial activity with Russia, while Western states did whatever they could to support Ukraine. Ukrainian refugees found shelter all across Europe, while the governments provided significant military resources and training to the Ukrainian troops.

The West's unity was compounded by the nature of the Russian invasion. Finding Ukraine less passive than expected led to a burgeoning catalogue of military failure, with Moscow resorting to indiscriminate bombings of civilian targets while permitting (if not encouraging) human rights abuses by its forces, all of which sparked outrage in the West and shook the confidence of Moscow and its allies. Putin's inevitable threat of nuclear force raised the stakes even higher.

However, Western expectations of global unified condemnation and action against the Russian invasion were dashed by the response of the Global South. No Gulf War-style support was forthcoming from this quarter, counter to presumptions in Washington, Brussels and London. Far from endorsing the Western position, over 40 member states of the United Nations (UN) consistently abstained or voted against resolutions proposed in the UN General Assembly that sought to condemn Russian actions.[1] In April 2022, in the wake of overwhelming evidence of human rights violations, 50 members voted against expelling Russia from the Human Rights Council. These included many African, Asian, Middle Eastern and Latin American countries, who were adamant that irrespective of who started it and how it was conducted, the most important response should be to bring the conflict to an immediate end. Its position was echoed by the BRICS grouping, which increasingly presents itself as a challenger to the G7 industrialised countries for global leadership. And even those countries which did support condemnation of Moscow's invasion were reluctant to impose sanctions against Russia, making the action toothless.

The Global South Defiant

What is behind the seeming indifference and even hostility in the Global South to the Western position on Russia? The arguments put forward by leaders from Africa, Asia, the Middle East and Latin America can be clustered into three categories. The first is exasperation at Western hypocrisy towards violations of sovereignty, the second is the neglect and damage done by the war to the global development agenda and the third centres on the escalation of Russia's 'special operation' to the apparent brink of nuclear war with the West.

Concurrently, something that gets little to no airplay in the West is the fact that the Russian invasion has ignited a broader debate within the Global South as to what it means to be non-aligned in the contemporary context. There is widespread recognition that the form of non-alignment adopted by developing countries during the bipolar Cold War and institutionalised through the Non-Aligned Movement (NAM) does not resonate with the emerging multipolar system. Moreover, despite the protestations of leading emerging powers that they both identify as and are representative of the Global South, middle and small states are under no illusions as to the impact that power asymmetries with China or India have on global initiatives, not to mention on their own national aspirations.

Finally, the crisis in liberal international institutions has set the stage to resume pushing for reform of the UN system by China and the Global South. The dysfunctionality of the UN is embodied in the fact that there are persistent violations of the UN Charter by the Security Council's Permanent members, despite their role being to preserve international peace and stability, and this has undermined faith in the multilateral system. A new round of initiatives is underway through multilateral and plurilateral organisations that aim to reform the institutions of global governance. Should its declared ambitions be realised, it will produce, a more representative, legitimate and effective multilateral system.

This chapter will review and assess how Russia's invasion of Ukraine has been seen through the lens of the Global South. It will first examine how Global South countries viewed the Western response to the Russian invasion in the UN – focusing on the key issues of sovereignty, development and nuclear threats. Second, it will look at the debates generated by Russia's invasion within the Global South over non-alignment – a traditional policy approach to great power competition. Third, it will investigate how the Russia-Ukraine war has reignited the impetus to reform the multilateral system amongst Global South countries and, concurrently, how this feeds into the Russian-Chinese declaration of a 'New Era in International Politics'.

Before embarking, however, on this analysis, it would be important to say a few things about the terminology being used in this chapter. While once an obscure phrase, 'Global South' is a term that has become common currency in academic and advocacy circles, especially among those arguing for economic and political concerns on an international stage, even to the point of being utilised by Western leaders.[2] Loosely employed to cover developing countries and emerging powers who share the historical experience of Western colonialism and imperialism, and a set of shared post-colonial challenges around nation-building and development, Global South geography spans Asia, Africa, Latin America and the Caribbean as well as the oceanic island states [2]. It no longer exhibits the uniformity in material power (or its absence) that was true in the first decades of the Cold War and it continues to be divided along nationalist, ideological, sectarian and other indicators of difference. At the same time, these divisions have not prevented countries from coming to some common policy positions. For instance, most support values such as sovereignty, development rights and international peace, in line with the core principles of the UN Charter. Although, much like Western states, such positions are not always reflected in the actions of Global South states.

Its greatest significance in international politics is as an organising principle for these countries in multilateral settings.

In these settings, coalition politics between regionally based groupings and like-minded members drives policy formulation and the voting process. The most prominent of the Global South coalitions is the G77, established in 1964 (and now with 182 members), which was the instigator of the UN Conference on Trade and Development. It is one of the foundational groupings of the Global South in the UN, and while its fortunes have waxed and waned over time, like the NAM, it continues to serve as a collective voice for developing countries [3]. In this respect, the platform of the UN – especially the UN General Assembly, the Economic and Social Council and the Human Rights Council – is the arena where the Global South primarily puts forward its collective position on issues.

The impact of the Russian invasion of Ukraine was felt in the Global South in three distinct ways: (i) as a great power challenge to their interests; (ii) in generating a debate on non-alignment policy that was traditionally applied to great power competition and (iii) renewing questions as to the viability of an international system which is increasingly paralysed by great power competition.

Global South Reactions to the Russia-Ukraine War
Sovereignty and Intervention

Violations of sovereignty are characteristic of the post-Cold War era, as is patterns of Western indifference, as well as committal of, such violations. The long road from Western intervention in Iraq in 2003 to Russian intervention in Ukraine in 2022 – which passes through breaches of sovereignty in Libya, Syria and Yemen amongst other places – emphasises the disinterest and inertia of Western capitals. Moreover, the tepid response of Western governments' reaction to Russia's invasion and occupation of Crimea and the eastern littoral of Ukraine in 2014 paved the way for other states to also prefer inaction. Western states may have eventually imposed sanctions after Russia conducted a faux-referendum to affirm popular support for its occupation and annexation of the region, but they did so on one hand while propping up Russia's economy on the other. For instance, the EU continued with Nord Stream 2 pipeline construction, pumping Russian natural gas into Germany, a policy emblematic of the EU's unwillingness to sacrifice domestic needs to support core principles of international law [4, 5].

In considering Russia's invasion of Ukraine, South African President Cyril Ramaphosa even suggested that the 'war could have been avoided if NATO had heeded the warnings from amongst its own leaders and officials over the years that its eastward expansion would lead to greater, not less, instability in the region [6].' Brazilian President Lula da Silva echoed this assessment, stating that 'Zelensky is as responsible as Putin for the war [1].' This is a view articulated by many governments in the Global South and finds considerable support on social media in countries as varied as India, Turkey and Malaysia [7, 8, 9].

Finally, as David Miliband points out, Western protestations of the violation of rule of law sound hollow against the catalogue of violations of the same principles by the United States (US) in particular. America has continued to fail to ratify the Statue of Rome, a failure which eased the way for Russia which withdrew from the treaty in 2016 and China, which refused outright to sign up to the treaty China [1]. Western states seem unable to practise what they preach.³

Development as Collateral Damage

While the war goes on, to the Global South it remains a 'European war, far away'. The same sorts of arguments heard time and again when conflict breaks out in Africa, that the Western public would not support intervention in a country so geographically remote from North America and Europe, were played out in the Global South.

However, this does not mean that the Global South does not feel the impact of the conflict. First, there is the sharp rise in energy and food prices, led by the uncertainty around vital Russian grain and fertilizer shipments and second, there is the imposition of economic sanctions on Russia, and their consequent restrictions on commercial exchanges with Russian firms [11]. According to an IMF report published in March 2022, the energy price spike corresponded with a 30% rise in global wheat prices [12]. The negotiation of a deal between Kyiv and Moscow, brokered by Turkey's President Recep Tayyip Erdogan, was a welcome step in easing the immediate concerns about food security, but it is still subject to periodic review and inflationary pressures remain a grave threat to domestic stability in many developing countries. Regarding sanctions on Russian firms, the weaponization of the US dollar has enabled the West to impose costs that hurt developing economies as well as the Russian economy [13]. It is here that the prospect of securing support for sanctions against Russia is inhibited by the Global South's economic needs in the Global South, yet this receives only limited attention amongst Western leaders. As German Chancellor Olaf Scholz said in response to African concerns of the sanctions impact, 'There are many stories that are a distraction from Russia's war in Ukraine – we shouldn't accept that [11].'

The key point here is that the perspective on the Russian invasion held by the Global South places greater focus on its disruptive effect on their economies and the consequent need to restore stability, rather than concern with the territorial and human rights violations. The immediacy of the painful economic spill over of conflict translated into a position that supported a cessation of the war, even if that – as some in the West argued – would play into the hands of Putin.

Threats of Nuclear War

Russia's unexpected failure to sweep aside the Zelensky government in a few short weeks put on display the sub-standard condition of its military. Putin's willingness to brandish the threat of nuclear weapons – not once but many times over the course of the conflict – to coerce and divide the transatlantic alliance over the question of support for Ukraine set off alarm bells across the world [14]. Coupled to this was the dangerous game that was played with the Zaporizhzhia nuclear power facility in eastern Ukraine, where Russian troops had occupied the site early on and put Ukrainian plant managers under their control. The proximity of the facility to ongoing conflict contributed to fears of a nuclear accident on a scale greater than Chernobyl.

This loosening of norms of conduct on nuclear weapons by one of the UN Security Council's Permanent five (P5) has come at a time when the battery of arms control treaties, that guided superpower behaviour for decades, have either run out and are not being renewed [15, 16]. During debates in the UN Security Council, representatives from Ghana and Brazil spoke to the fears in the Global South that nuclear disarmament had 'gone into reverse since 2020 [15]. Moreover, regimes in North Korea and Iran have demonstrated that with sufficient determination and investment, the technical obstacles to becoming a nuclear state can be overcome. All of this raises the possibility that a set of regional nuclear arms races in areas like Asia and the Middle East could be in the making.

Non-Alignment in an Era of Great Power Competition

For the Global South, the Russian invasion of Ukraine and the accompanying Western pressure to support countermeasures like sanctions generated debates over non-alignment. This has been the traditional policy approach to great power competition since the bipolar Cold War era. The conditions of US-led unipolarity, which prevailed from the Cold War's aftermath until 2017, began to evolve towards multipolarity with its impact on the distribution of power across the international system. However, the rise of US-China competition and its manifestation in everything from trade to technology is beginning to bring pressure to bear on the Global South to choose a side. Russia's invasion brings the threat to the liberal international system and the abuses of its principles by the P5 under the spotlight. The default policy of non-alignment looked out of date in this evolving context.

Alongside the evolution of the international system from bipolar to multipolar is a deliberate re-positioning of emerging powers away from non alignment over time. While the bipolar conflict between the US and the Soviet Union inspired Nehru and others to adopt non-alignment from either superpower, the post-Cold War era marked a reconsideration of non-alignment that emphasised a search for 'strategic autonomy' in foreign policy. For example, China while espousing the 'Five Principles of Peace Co-existence' derived from the Bandung Conference as pillars of its foreign policy continues to maintain a distance from traditional Global South organisations like the G77 – the formulation being 'G77 + China' – as a signifier of its special leadership status within the Global South. India, though long associated with the Nehruvian non-alignment policy and formally adhering to the same five principles nonetheless has formally adopted a foreign policy of 'strategic autonomy' [17, 18]. Indonesia, which leaned towards the US under the Suharto regime's long reign, has effectively rediscovered non-alignment with the advent of democracy and even sponsored two major international conferences aimed at reinvigorating the 'Bandung Spirit' [19]. Brazil too has adopted a policy of 'strategic autonomy' as the basis of its foreign policy since the end of the Cold War [20]. Even the European Union, undisputedly a key part of the Western alliance system and obviously not an emerging power, characterises its foreign policy aspirations as one of seeking greater strategic autonomy (presumably from the unnamed US).

This repurposing of non-alignment from its inherently defensive connotations – that is, neither signing up as a partner in the Western alliance system nor deliberately supporting an alternative to the liberal international system spawned by Western governments, seems to be the approach being taken by some countries of the Global South. Seeking to capture this evolving phenomenon, former Chilean ambassador, Jorge Heine and Carlos Ominami have characterised this new approach as 'active non-alignment'.

> Active Non-Alignment (ANA) calls on Latin American governments to not accept *a priori* the positions of any of the Great Powers in conflict. They must act, instead, in defense of their own national interest, without giving in to pressures from hegemonic powers. The term 'active' refers to a foreign policy in constant search of opportunities in a changing world, evaluating each of them on their merits. It recognizes the historical roots of the policy of Non-Alignment but adapts it to the 21st century [21].

Active non-alignment in this respect involves taking a policy position that may cut across the interests of great powers in the service of Global South countries' national interests. It is transactional in content, not embracing the values-framed ideologies characteristic of the Cold War, and aims at the accumulation of greater political space for action, i.e., strategic autonomy. And it is suited to a multipolar system where power is distributed more readily across the system. For IR theorists, active non-alignment constitutes neo-realism's 'balancing' and 'hedging' strategies though more rooted in a collective action approach honed through participation in international organisations.

Geopolitics and Fast Tracking the Global Transformation

The unequal distribution of power across international institutions is a longstanding issue for the Global South. In the wake of great power abuses of the UN Security Council producing systemic instability, countries of the Global South are joining like-minded multilateralists to re-examine how this ongoing crisis can inspire a new wave of reform. At the same time, many of these countries are also looking beyond the liberal international system for a means of addressing what they see as its structural deficiencies and glaring abuses of power which threaten Global South interests.

Permanent members of the UN Security Council continue to be the object of other members states' ire. The violations of sovereignty by Russia have precedents of course amongst the US in Iraq, China in the South China Sea and Britain and France in Libya. The recent passage of a non-binding resolution requiring permanent members of the Security Council to justify their use of the veto by permanent members of the Security Council points again to the resentment and concerns across the UN General Assembly as to the power of the P5 [22, 23].

Even more than the P5's violation of the UN Charter, however, is the more immediate and destabilising impact that US-led sanctions campaign is having on the economies of many countries in the Global South. What this has demonstrated unequivocally is that US power resources have a depth and breadth not fully understood by many in the Global South up till this point. Though Washington's ramping up of financial sanctions against Iran, back in 2014, provided a clear case of the reach of US financial power, even that did not have the level of international impact of the current round of sanctions against Russia.

All of this has reopened the debate on the pervasive use of the US dollar as the default currency in international trade, with Global South countries focusing not only on the cost of conducting trade in dollar but also the denomination of loans in dollars. The use of the dollar results in loan packages whose value is affected by the strength of the US currency and, consequently, contributes to unsustainable debt on their books [24, 25].

Amongst the initiatives operating outside the liberal international institutions against the hegemony of the US dollar is the plurilateral BRICS grouping. Led by China, BRICS countries are accelerating their own initiative to de-dollarise the global economy. The BRICS' New Development Bank (NDB) is already engaged in a range of initiatives from RMB currency swaps to provisions for short term liquidity pressures [26]. The intense interest amongst Global South nations in involving themselves in these initiatives can been seen in the uptick in RMB trade in a number of Asian, African, Middle Eastern and Latin American economies in recent years. And perhaps the most vivid expression of Global South interest is the submission of applications to join BRICS by over forty countries in the past few months.

Conclusion: A New Era in the Making?

During the G7 Summit held in the United Kingdom in June 2021, the Chinese embassy issued a telling statement:

> The days when global decisions were dictated by a small group of countries are long gone. We always believe that countries, big or small, strong or weak, poor or rich, are

equals, and that world affairs should be handled through consultation by all countries [27].

This stinging critique of Western presumptions of global leadership in the service of their interests has been galvanised by the West's response to the Russian invasion of Ukraine. It undergirds the renewed to overhaul the liberal international system either from within or without. It is this vision of a new world order, a 'New Era of Global Development', that coheres most closely with the Bandung principles and promises to deliver global equity in governance and development and is attracting the countries of the Global South.

At the same time, the perpetual critique of the UN system by the majority of states, however valid, does carry with it the seeds of another turn in the system. Should the West see liberal internationalism as no longer worth fighting for then the rebirth of a world where Thucydides' realist logic of the rule by the most powerful will surely eclipse those very interests of many small and middle states in the Global South.

Notes

[1] The vote tally in first UNGA resolution to condemn the invasion was 141 for condemnation to five against, with 47 absences or abstentions.

[2] Emmanuel Macron speaks frequently about the Global South, for example at the Munich Security Conference in 2023 where he said 'I am struck by how we have lost the trust of the global South' [1].

[3] For more on this debate, see Lawson and Zarakol [10].

References

1. Miliband D. The World Beyond Ukraine: the survival of the West and the Demands of the Rest. *Foreign Policy.* 2023 April 18 [cited 2023 June 4]. https://www.foreignaffairs.com/ukraine/world-beyond-ukraine-russia-west.

2. Alden C, Morphet S, Vieira MA. *The South in World Politics.* London: Routledge; 2010. DOI: https://doi.org/10.1057/9780230281196.

3. Satyabraha P. *The Group of 77 in a Changing World.* UN Chronicle. no date. https://www.un.org/en/chronicle/article/group-77-changing-world.

4. Nix S. Responding to the Russian Invasion of Crimea: Policy Recommendations for US and European Leaders. *European View.* 2014; 13(1): 143–152. DOI: https://doi.org/10.1007/s12290-014-0297-3.

5. de Maio G. Nord Stream 2: a failed test for EU unity and trans-Atlantic coordination. *Brookings Institution.* 2019 April 22 [cited 2023 June 4]. https://www.brookings.edu/blog/order-from-chaos/2019/04/22/nord-stream-2-a-failed-test-for-eu-unity-and-trans-atlantic-coordination/.

6. Walsh M. US-South Africa ties explode on Russia Arms claims. *Asia Times.* 2023 May 17 [cited 2023 June 4]. https://asiatimes.com/2023/05/us-south-africa-ties-explode-on-russia-arms-claim/.

7. Garten Ash T, Krastev I, Leonard M. United West, Divided from the Rest: global public opinion one year into Russia's war on Ukraine. *European Council on Foreign Relations.* 2023 February 22 [cited 2023 June 4]. https://ecfr.eu/publication/united-west-divided-from-the-rest-global-public-opinion-one-year-into-russias-war-on-ukraine/.

8. Azmi H. Ukraine war: how the battle on social media has become a propaganda tool for Russia and Ukraine. *South China Morning Post.* 2022 March 19 [cited 2023 June 4]. https://www.scmp.com

/week-asia/article/3171049/ukraine-war-battle-malaysias-social
-media-propaganda-tool-russia-and.

9. Al Jazeera. Why are Indonesians on social media so supportive of Russia. 2022 March 19 [cited 2023 June 4]. https://www.aljazeera.com/news/2022/3/19/why-are-indonesians-on-social-media-so-supportive-of-russia.

10. Lawson G, Zarakol A. Recognizing Injustice: the 'hypocrisy charge' and the future of the LIO. *International Affairs*. 2023; 99(1): 201–218. DOI: https://doi.org/10.1093/ia/iiac258.

11. Mallet V, Bounds A. African Union warns of collateral impact as EU's Russia sanctions hit food supplies. *Financial Times*. 2022 May 13 [cited 2023 June 4]. https://www.ft.com/content/e558de33-6064-4b10-a784-eb344cb17915.

12. Kammer A, Azour J, Selassie A, Goldfajn I, Yong Rhee C. How the War in Ukraine is reverberating Across Regions. IMF Blog; 2022 March 22 [cited 2023 June 4]. https://www.imf.org/en/Blogs/Articles/2022/03/15/blog-how-war-in-ukraine-is-reverberating-across-worlds-regions-031522.

13. Heitzig C, Ordu A, Holtz L. How currency sanctions against Russia could disrupt trade with Africa. Brookings Institute; 2022 May 23 [cited 2023 June 4]. https://www.brookings.edu/research/how-currency-sanctions-on-russia-could-disrupt-trade-with-africa/.

14. Vaddi P, Blanchette N, Hinck G. Expired: The Last Nuclear Arms Treaty. Carnegie Endowment for International Peace; ND. https://carnegieendowment.org/publications/interactive/new-start#.

15. United Nations. Risks of nuclear war are higher than at any time since the Cold War, Disarmament Affairs chief warns. UN Security Council; 2023. Meeting Coverage SC 15/250. https://press.un.org/en/2023/sc15250.doc.htm.

16. Kariuki J. No other country has raised the prospect of nuclear use, no one is threatening Russia: UK statement at the Security Council. Foreign, Commonwealth & Development Office. 2023 March 31

17. Chaturvedi P. India's Strategic Autonomy does not mean Unilateralism. *The Diplomat*. 2022 October 18 [cited 2023 June 4]. https://thediplomat.com/2022/10/indias-strategic-autonomy-does-not-mean-unilateralism/.

18. Weigold A. Nehruivanism in Indian Foreign Policy – embedded in the Modi Doctrine? Future Directions International; 2018. policy report. https://apo.org.au/node/133961.

19. Anwar DF. Indonesia's Vision of Order in East Asia Amid US-China Rivalry: continuity or change? *Asia Policy*. 2018; 13(2): 57–63. DOI: East Asia Amid US-China Rivalry: continu.

20. Vegivani T, Cepaluni G. Brazilian Foreign Policy in Changing Times: the Quest for Autonomy from Sarney to Lula. Boston: Lexington Books; 2009.

21. Heine J. Non Alignment is Back in the Global South, Albeit in a Different Incarnation. Boston University Global Development Policy Centre. 2023. https://www.bu.edu/gdp/2023/02/27/non-alignment-is-back-in-the-global-south-albeit-in-a-different-incarnation/.

22. United Nations. General Assembly holds first ever debate on historic veto resolution, adopts texts on infrastructure, national reviews, Council of Europe cooperation 26. General Assembly Seventy Seventh Session. 2023. Meeting Coverage GA12500. https://press.un.org/en/2023/ga12500.doc.htm.

23. United Nations. Amidst strained multilateral system, states must recommit to United Nations Charter obligations, prioritize human rights, Secretary-General tells Security Council. Security Council; 2023 April 24. Meeting Coverage SC/1526. https://press.un.org/en/2023/sc15263.doc.htm.

[The reference before 17 continues:] [cited 2023 June 4]. https://www.gov.uk/government/speeches/no-other-country-has-raised-the-prospect-of-nuclear-use-no-one-is-threatening-russias-sovereignty-uk-statement-at-the-security-council.

24. Ranasinghe D, Chatterjee S, Chavez-Dreyfuss G. Russia sanctions hike US dollar borrowing costs in global markets. *Reuters*. 2022 February 28 [cited 2023 June 4]. https://www.reuters.com/business/finance/russia-sanctions-lift-borrowing-costs-dollars-funding-markets-2022-02-28/.

25. Debt Justice. Global South debt payments increase almost 50% in two years. 2017 March 13 [cited 2023 June 4]. https://debtjustice.org.uk/press-release/global-south-debt-payments-increase-almost-50-two-years.

26. Sullivan J. A BRICS Currency Could Shake the Dollar's Dominance. *Foreign Policy*. 2023 April 24 [cited 2023 June 4]. https://foreignpolicy.com/2023/04/24/brics-currency-end-dollar-dominance-united-states-russia-china/.

27. BBC. G7 Summit: China says small groups do not rule the world. 2021 June 13 [cited 2023 June 4]. https://www.bbc.co.uk/news/world-asia-china-57458822.

PART 6
The Economics of War

17. Mr Putin and the Chronicle of a Normalisation Foretold

Jagjit S. Chadha

Major central banks have been caught in a low interest rate trap for over a decade. The temporary response to the financial crisis of 2008–9 has become something of a regime. The Federal Reserve, for example, attempted to ease quantitative easing in 2013 but this stalled following the 'taper tantrum' and commenced a normalisation in the Federal Funds rate from 2015 but during COVID major central banks around the world rapidly returned policy rates to around zero. Low policy rates have been the response to tighter credit conditions, excessive global savings, low levels of investment and fiscal consolidation, but they have also played a role in propelling asset price growth and increasing levels of indebtedness. The accommodative stance in monetary policy, as well as the impetus from previous monetary and fiscal interventions, seems to have stoked inflation to a higher level that might otherwise have been the case following the shock of a war on the European continent. However, it may also have finally secured a normalisation in policy rates.

Mr Putin's invasion in Ukraine has imparted a considerable shock to the world economy. At the end of 2020, inflation in the OECD countries stood at 1.2%. By the end of the first quarter of 2023, it had risen to 8.8%. Over the same period, global policy rates rose from −0.5%, 0.2% and 0.1% in the Euro Area, USA and UK respectively to stand at 3.25%, 5.0% and 4.5% by April 2023. Accordingly, in February 2022 the National Institute of Economic and Social Research had forecast world GDP to grow at 4.2% and 3.5% in 2022 and 2023 but by February 2023 this had been heavily revised down to 2.3% and 2.8%, respectively.[1] The sharp increase in energy and food costs since the Russian invasion of Ukraine has not only threatened price stability but has also asked serious questions of the monetary and fiscal frameworks which coped so well with stabilising the global economy over the previous quarter of a century. Many had argued that this period of extraordinary monetary policy, while helpful in avoiding an extended depression after the global financial crisis, had been extended too long and expanded too far. The consequence of this was an unnecessarily large amount of quantitative easing, burgeoning public debt, and an increase in the fraction of unproductive firms, as well as the mispricing of risk in financial markets. If not a secular stagnation, by which I mean a period of slow structural growth that has required historically low interest rates to prevent deflation, the period seems to have had many of the characteristics of a liquidity trap, with firms hoarding cash rather than investing. It would be ironic indeed if an act of international aggression were to be provide the impetus to correct a misalignment in the stance of monetary policy.

Context

The invasion of Ukraine came at a precarious moment for a global economy still trying to recover from the impact of the COVID pandemic. Output had barely reached its pre-COVID peak in most OECD[2] economies when Russia's tanks crossed Ukraine's border. Across the world, the fiscal response to COVID, in terms of additional expenditure and foregone revenue, amounted to some 18% of advanced economies' GDP in 2020 prices, as well as another 10% of GDP in terms of equity loans or guarantees [1]. While many maintained that the COVID shock was primarily one to the supply-side, with real markets in dysfunction and workers withdrawn from the labour force, there were also impacts on the demand-side. These were manifest most obviously with a radical increase in the savings rate, with some of this rise forced and some precautionary. As the pandemic receded, the world entered into a period of readjustment from around 2021. Such a world was not business as usual, or even coming close to it, not least as a result of significant supply chain disruptions, with China maintaining a strict COVID regime with manufacturing and with global shipping still facing disruptions. Monetary policies had been accommodative over the COVID period with the period of abnormally low rates extended further and fresh bouts of central bank balance sheet operations re-ignited. In the UK, for example, the quantum of QE[3] rose from £495bn to £895bn at a peak at over 35% of GDP [2].

It was into this fertile mix of loose monetary and fiscal policy that the impact of war was unleashed in February 2022. The immediate impact was that energy and food prices practically doubled [3]. As a result of the increase in the cost base for consumption and for production, economic policy makers were presented with the problem of stabilising inflation and providing support for those households that would find it difficult to bear the impact on their disposable income. In ordinary times alone, this would have been pretty difficult. But simultaneously engineering an emergence from the expansionary policy stance amplified the nature of the problem. The initial position meant that the impact of the negative supply shock was exacerbated and that countries had levels of public debt, at 100% of GDP or more, far above notions of peace-time normality. In the language of the post-financial crisis, fiscal space was limited and monetary policy had a considerable distance to travel.

The emerging prospect of a prolonged war of attrition in Ukraine has further exposed some of the limitations of the economic settlement that was established following the end of the Cold War in 1991. The acceleration in de-industrialisation in the West since the 1990s has contributed both to a reduction in global inequality, but an increase, or at least an entrenchment, of domestic inequalities that have probably promoted a move towards populist movements. But a war asks directly whether some of the peace dividend that allowed defence expenditure to fall may now need to be claimed back. OECD defence expenditure had fallen from 3.5% of GDP in 1988 to 2.4% of GDP in 2020 [4]. Furthermore, would the discovery that Ukraine accounted for some $27bn of global food exports, accounting for significant fractions of sunflower oil, wheat, corn, rapeseed and barley exports, bring forward the move to onshoring? And if the calls for greater economic resilience in the light of COVID were also to be addressed, there would have to be an extended period over which public and private investment would build up domestic supply networks and inventories. Each of these responses will tend to put upward pressure on domestic absorption around the world, and accordingly on domestic interest rate. And so, I focus the rest of this essay on why we may observe that it was the invasion in Ukraine that finally led to the reversal of global rates back to historical norms.

The Case for Normalisation

Policy rates hovering around zero were a rare phenomenon prior to the global financial crisis. In the immediate aftermath of World War I and World War II, there were periods when policy rates supported the creation of fiscal space and fiscal consolidation [5]. In more normal times, the monetary authorities were typically handed an exchange rate target and, latterly, an inflation target by their governments that was thought both to be reasonably consistent with price stability and yet not likely to induce too many costly deflations. Typically, a target of around 2% for the CPI was settled upon. This was coupled with a natural rate, which ensured that the market was cleared for savings and investment or at least directed path towards market clearing, which was generally of around 2–3%. Together, this meant that policy rates were expected to lie in the region of 4–5%.

In the face of economic shocks, monetary policy decisions set a temporary rate that offsets the shock or accelerates the economy's adjustment to the new economic circumstances. Let us suppose, for example, that a greater degree of economic uncertainty drives down investment demand. Monetary policymakers might seek to offset this uncertainty shock by reducing the policy rate so as to provide a lower hurdle for investors to surmount, and thus promote demand and offset the shock. The policy function in normal times, when monetary policy was actively trying to offset shocks and stabilise the economy efficiently, involved changing the policy rate by more than any change in actual or expected inflation, so that the temporary deviation in the real interest rate brought forward or delayed demand in such a manner as to bring inflation under control at the policy horizon.

In a nice, compact world with small shocks, we have a good idea of what the central bank may do, as its policy rate will follow inflationary pressure in a uniform manner. But with a sufficiently large negative shock to overall activity, the policy rate might have to fall to zero and then find itself in a bind. Indeed, hypothetically the central bank might prefer even lower rates but this may not be possible. Because, as policy rates tend to zero, cash will give a similar rate of return to bank deposits, which are linked to policy rates, which will prevent or limit the extent to which central banks can affect even lower policy rates. In principle, people would rather hold cash than see their bank balance diminish through negative interest rates. This observation implies that the policy function with respect to inflation is not linear and at, or close to, zero may become horizontal, with policy facing little room for manoeuvre in response to a large enough or sustained negative shock. In such a scenario, we have a world in which monetary policy is 'passive'. By this, it is meant that policy rates move by less than any change in inflation and cannot by itself get the economy back to the 'normal' equilibrium.

Such a situation leaves monetary policy authorities with a choice over affecting longer-term rates by making signals about the future stance of policy or influencing premia by exchanging central bank liabilities for assets held by the private sector. There are two separate interpretations of this situation. One is that it allows activism by other means by determining longer term interest rates promoting. The other is that there has been an acceptance of 'passive' monetary policy, which allows fiscal policy to take the strain. And yet after the financial crisis fiscal policy was, at least in terms of the normal perception of the acceptable level of public debt to GDP, already exhausted, so activism by other means was the prescription if it could be found. The weight of controlling nominal demand was placed on central banks who embarked on policies that expanded their balance sheets. While it seems to have prevented a prolonged depression, most advanced economies have subsequently been in the doldrums with stagnation in the growth of real incomes per hour worked. I maintain these two outcomes are unlikely to be independent. But could the change in the forces acting on the global economy in light of COVID and the war, allow monetary policy to escape the bind?

The War and Easy Money

There has been much written on how to escape from a growth or liquidity trap or what popularly came to be known as a secular stagnation. Some have argued that such a trap was highly unlikely and should not have been too much of a concern in the design of monetary policy operating procedures [6], particularly if central banks had credibility because it would always be expected that the inflation target would be achieved and so rates would be expected to return to normal. And since the 1970s the discussion of the liquidity trap had increasingly fallen out of focus as the problem was rather how to bring down inflation and attain price stability, by reducing demand, rather than how to boost demand. But the theoretical possibility remained. In light of Japan's experience since the 1990s, a number of exit strategies have been offered. Harking back to the original problem of money and bonds being perfect substitute at zero interest rates, Buiter and Panigirtzoglou [7] suggested placing a negative (Gesell) tax on base money – currency and reserves – as a way of discouraging holding. Svensson [8] suggested engineering a large exchange rate depreciation in order to bring about a temporary inflation and a loosening of monetary conditions. Many have argued for the deployment of a temporary expansion in fiscal policy, mostly through expenditure rather than tax cuts, in order to stimulate demand, starting of course with Keynes himself. But do note that attempting to stoke aggregate demand will tend to be most effective when public spending on goods and services or on investment does not offer a good substitute for private sector demand and so adds to demand, ideally by nurturing supply [9].

Could we have escaped with better management of expectations? That is to lower real rates by creating inflationary expectations. A famous strategy developed by Eggertsson and Woodford suggested exploitation of the expectations channel with the central bank proving a credible commitment to create a boom [10]. It is difficult though to conceive of a way that an institution, in this case a central bank, committed to or designed for achieving price stability, might reasonably expect to commit to a boom. A variant of this idea was, however, adopted by the Federal Reserve in 2020 with the inflation averaging regime. I shall return to this regime later, but the idea here is that following a deflationary shock inflation may fall below target for some time but if the long run average inflation target is credible households and firms will start to expect higher than average inflation for a short period which will perforce ease monetary conditions by lowering the real interest rates and so stimulate demand. Others have focussed on the inherent instability of models that rely so heavily on forward-looking expectations and argued that a liquidity trap was always beckoning, and that the way out was to build confidence by raising interest rates and signalling a return to normality [11, 12]. A natural consequence of this form of reasoning was the deployment of various forms of forward guidance which attempted to provide statements as to when interest rates would return to normal, either in terms of a commitment to a time in the future or a particular state of nature. But these forms of verbal guidance have not been judged to have been a great success and I have previously suggested that longer term expectations of policy rates responded more to the actual duration of policy rates at zero rather than any specific statements [13]. It seems more that the market learned more from actually observing that rates would not change rather than being told they would not change. Indeed, Woodford and Xie suggest that 'default expectations are best shaped by systematic action in accordance with a relatively simple rule, since they are learned by induction from past experience' [14].

In all this discussion, over the past 15 years, escape velocity from the zero lower bound looked very hard to achieve. The

US tried both to tune down quantitative easing in 2013 but quickly retreated in the face of a 'taper tantrum'. The Federal Reserve tried to engineer a lift off in rates from late 2015. In a similar vein, the Bank of England started to raise rates in late 2017. But both attempts were stymied by COVID. The irony is that just as it seemed that the US only completed its recovery to full employment in 1942 in the two years from 1940 to 1942, when fiscal policies became instrumental during wartime and mobilisation, a return to normal levels of interest rates seems to have been prompted by a war started in 2022 [15], prompting a large inflation shock and a fillip to public indebtedness. Therefore, it might be that it is a more or less standard response to a large inflationary shock and the build-up of inflationary momentum that allows us to leave the low interest regime once and for all.

The Natural Rate of Interest

There has, of course, been a secular decline in the global real rate since the 1990s and that has increased that likelihood of central banks being caught in a low interest rate trap. The standard explanation for this decline is that households in the rapidly industrialising countries have had a lower rate of time preference and so built-up the stock of globally available savings rapidly. The market for global savings therefore cleared at successively lower rates of interest rates as this stock of savings was built up. The rate at which savings and investment schedules clears is the natural rate of interest and has accordingly drifted downwards over time. And it is deviations from the natural rate that determine the traction of monetary policy.

The increase in global supply capacity without a parallel increase in overall spending tended to reduce progressively the rate at which savings and investment cleared. An impetus to this trend was provided by the financial crisis, which by lowering the quantum of financial intermediation, acted to lower further the natural rate and thus led to both an extended period over which policy rates hovered around zero and prompted extensive purchases of government bonds that acted to lower interest rates at term.

In light of the invasion of Ukraine, there are now a number of factors that are acting both to limit the growth in potential supply and also push up expenditures, which may support a re-establishment of normal policy rates. Higher energy prices will tend to constrain potential growth, as will the fragmentation of trade, which may ultimately lead to the formation of new trading blocs. As the newly industrialised economies reach the productivity frontier, we can also expect their growth rates to fall to advanced country levels. At the same time, the war and COVID have revealed a need for more public expenditure. For example, world military expenditure rose by 3.7% in real terms in 2022, to reach a record high of some $2.2 trillion [16]. These pressures, particularly if they are significant and aggressive, will tend to raise the natural rate of interest. And this about turn may not yet have been fully factored in by financial markets [17], which often adjust more slowly to changing secular trends than one might think optimal.

To illustrate, **Figure 17.1** shows how the natural rate is determined at the intersection of global potential output and clearing in the goods market (IS curve) [18]. Positive global growth with

Figure 17.1: Lower natural rate of interest

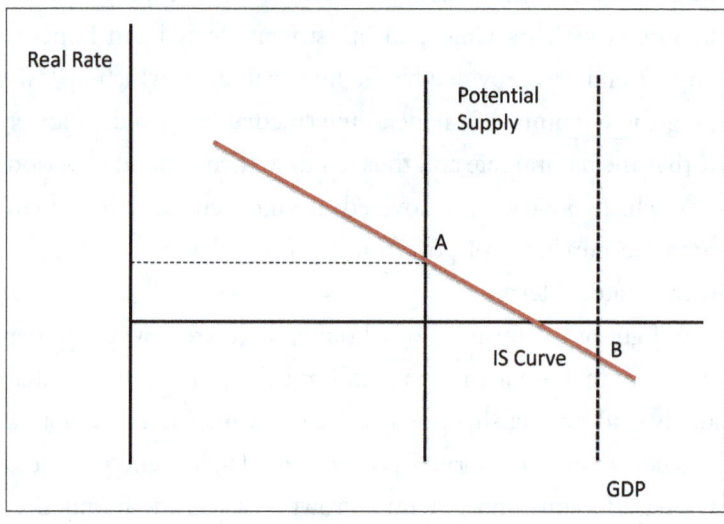

Figure 17.2: Higher natural rate of interest

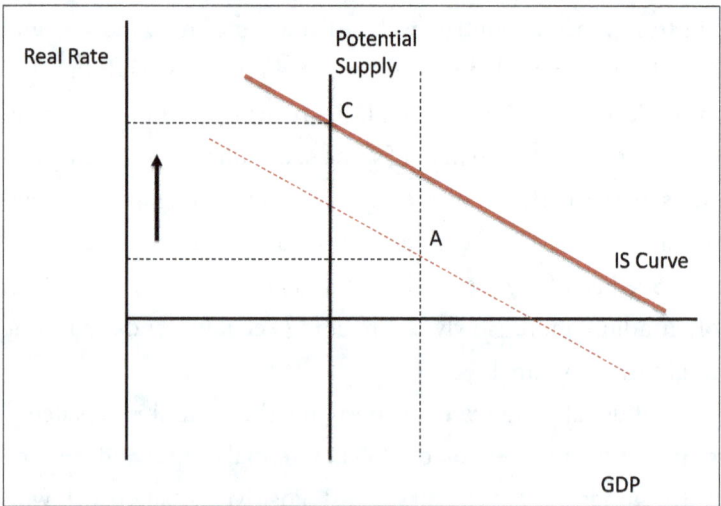

a stable schedule for clearing expenditures on goods will tend to push down the natural rate. In principle, this could lead to fall in the natural rate to a negative level from **A** to **B**. We could choose to characterise the period since the global financial crisis as having obtained that state, particularly if the IS curve has also shifted down (not shown). The war, though, may not only have reversed this step, but provided some impetus for the situation to reverse with the natural rate eventually rising to **C**, as shown in **Figure 17.2**, which will result if the newly industrialised countries start consuming rather than saving. The secular forces that have driven down the natural rate may be about to reverse.

The Monetary Policy Stance

The final part of the jigsaw is the monetary policy stance as we have come out of the COVID cloud. The global monetary support for fiscal policies during COVID was understandable at the time and with hindsight. The absence of a clear exit strategy for reversing emergency support arguably allowed the support to stay in place for too long and caused us to forget that prior to COVID we had sought to normalise rates. The deployment of average inflation targeting and increasing reliance on flexible inflation targeting, along with peripheral monetary issues such as climate change, employment and financial regulation, meant that both the Federal Reserve and the Bank of England may have moved some distance from simple inflation targeting. The European Central Bank has confronted complex control problems as the member countries do not constitute an optimal currency area, which has arguably led to some sluggishness in policy.

In its August 2020 statement on monetary policy the Federal Reserve stated that:

> In order to anchor longer-term inflation expectations at this level, the Committee seeks to achieve inflation that averages 2 percent over time, and therefore, judges that, following periods when inflation has been running persistently below 2 percent, appropriate monetary policy will likely aim to achieve inflation moderately above 2 percent for some time…the Committee seeks over time to mitigate shortfalls of employment…The Committee intends to … undertake roughly every 5 years a thorough public review of its monetary policy strategy, tools, and communication practices [19].

And this statement might be interpreted as involving both an occasional shift in the medium-term inflation target and the adoption of a supplementary target to support employment, which would imply trade-offs in the face of negative supply shocks and possibly a lower aversion to inflation by the central bank. The Bank of England, on the other hand, has had a clear secondary remit to support the economic policy of the government, including objectives for employment and growth [20]. This remit states:

> [T]he objectives of the Bank of England shall be:
> a. to maintain price stability;
> and b. subject to that, to support the economic policy of Her Majesty's Government, including its objectives for growth and employment.

Figure 17.3: The monetary policy trade-off

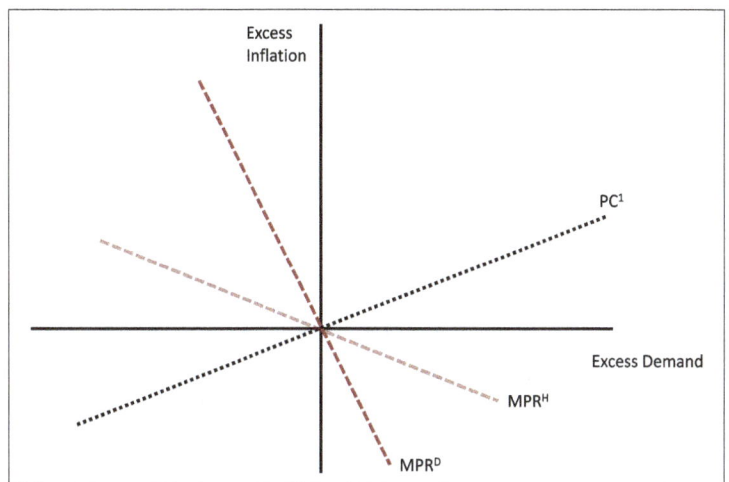

Which allows it to pick the horizon over which inflation is brought back to target following a significant overshoot or undershoot. In this case, the deployment of that path has not been credibly communicated.

How does all this translate into an inflation response when there has been a supply shock? Well, **Figure 17.3** traces a linearised Phillips curve showing how short run supply responds to demand and higher inflation. But also two monetary policy reaction lines: MPR^H when the policy maker has a high level of distaste for inflation, a so-called hawk, and MPR^D when the policy maker is more willing to accept a higher level of inflation temporarily, a so-called dove. We can thus immediately note in **Figure 17.4** that upon a negative supply shock, inflation will rise to **A** or **B**, depending on the inflation credentials of the central bank. In other words what we see in terms of inflation

Figure 17.4: The negative supply shock

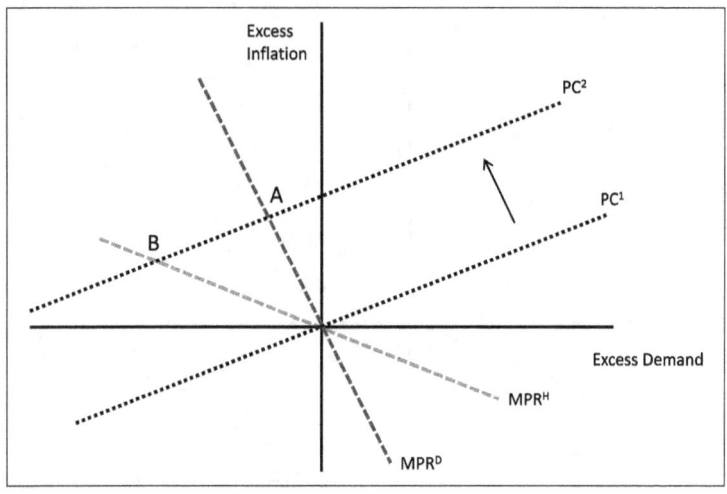

incorporates not only the supply shock but also the assumed policy response. It cannot be stated strongly enough that observed inflation always is a result of shocks and responses, actual or expected. Furthermore, if there are supply chain issues or a break in trade, for example, as a result of Brexit, this Phillips curve may steepen. And in this case, as drawn in **Figure 17.5**, $A^2 > A > B^2 > B$. Finally, as shown in **Figure 17.6**, in the case of the Federal Reserve, which may temporarily increase its implied inflation target or in the case where it is expected that the central may raise its target, in this case I have suggested that even the MPR^H curve may shift up and drive inflation up even further with $A^3 > A^2$. In the UK, the government had stated a wish to halve inflation in 2023, which may have inadvertently introduced a temporary inflation target for 2023 of 5% and played a role in more persistent inflation. My basic point here is that although

Figure 17.5: The negative supply shock and steeper Phillips curve

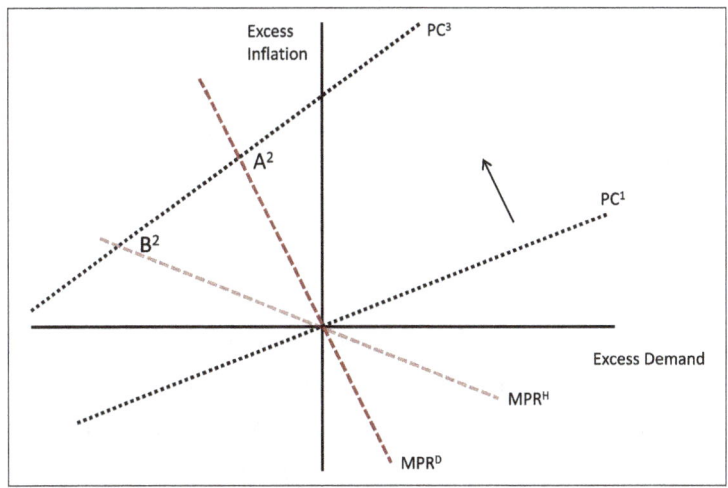

Figure 17.6: The negative supply shock, steeper Phillips curve and shifting target

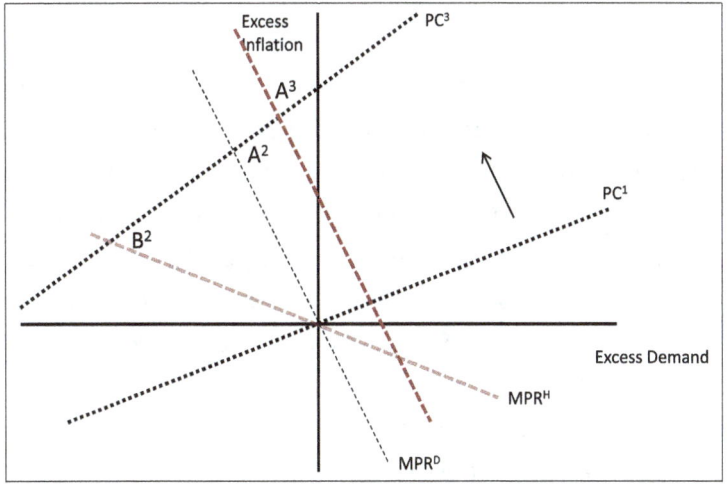

we are right to assign much or the greater part of the inflation shock to the one-off increase in energy and food prices, these interact with the actual or perceived stance of monetary policy to create the actual inflation dynamics we observe. The impact of the war on inflation has thus been amplified by the initial conditions of monetary policy and now produced the long heralded policy normalisation.

Conclusion

One of the consequences of the invasion of Ukraine is that, over a decade after we entered the period of ultra-low or unconventional monetary policies, the combined shock to the fiscal positions and to inflation have finally jolted policy rates back into historically recognisable territory [13]. The good news story would involve a more secure deposit base, under these higher short term interest rates, with incentives to save and financial intermediation operating to locate higher real returns [21], as inflation returns to levels associated with price stability over the next 18 months. The bad news story would be one where the overall deflationary impetus, as we moved from the low interest rate regime back to the normal one, has simply been too large and rates have to correct downwards back towards zero as recessionary forces build up. To the extent that inflation has been more elevated than it might have been, this has increased the possibility of the second and much worse outcome. And to that is at least in part due to some slippage in the actual or at least perceived commitment to price stability [22]. It is important that central banks are not given too many objectives which will require trade-offs against the attainment of price stability when we have a limited number of independent instruments. And that some earlier attention to the exit strategy from extraordinary monetary policies was outlined, particularly following their re-ignition during the COVID cloud. While it is not impossible that we may get dragged back into the liquidity trap, at least for the moment we are out. And that is one monetary benefit from the war.

Acknowledgements

This essay has benefitted from comments and conversations with Tim Besley, Luisa Corrado, Mick Cox, Paul Fisher, Stephen Millard, Paul Mortimer-Lee, Dmytro Natalukha, Adrian Pabst, Nicholas Reed Langen, Silvana Tenreyro and the comments from an anonymous referee. It has been prepared for LSE Public Policy Review: Special issue 'Russia's War in Ukraine and the Future of the Global Order'. Any opinions expressed are mine alone.

Notes

[1] Source: National Institute World Economic Outlook May 2023, Series B. No 10 and the IMF World Economic Outlook, April 2023.

[2] The OECD (Organisation for Economic Co-operation and Development) is a grouping of advanced economies that come together to work on common economic and social problems.

[3] Quantitative Easing (QE) is the attempt to influence long term bond prices by swapping financial market holdings of government issued debt for newly issued central bank reserves. Although first implemented in Japan in the 1990s, it became a widespread and persistent policy tool in Western economies following the collapse of Lehman Brothers bank in 2009.

References

1. International Monetary Fund. Fiscal monitor database of country fiscal measures in response to the COVID-19 pandemic. 2021 October [cited 2023 May 15]. https://www.imf.org/en/Topics/imf-and-covid19/Fiscal-Policies-Database-in-Response-to-COVID-19.

2. Economic Affairs Committee. Quantitative easing: A dangerous addiction? 1st Report of Session 2019–21. *HL Paper 42*. House of Lords; 2021.

3. National Institute of Economic and Social Research. The economic costs of the Russia-Ukraine conflict. *NIESR Policy Paper 32*. 2022.

4. World Bank. Military expenditure (% of GDP). [cited 2023 May 15]. https://data.worldbank.org/indicator/MS.MIL.XPND.GD.ZS?contextual=min&locations=OE.

5. Allen W. Quantitative monetary policy and government debt management in Britain since 1919. *Oxford Review of Economic Policy*. 2012; 28(4): 804–836. DOI: https://doi.org/10.1093/oxrep/grs030.

6. Walsh C. Using monetary policy to stabilize economic activity. Paper presented at the symposium, Financial Stability and Macroeconomic Policy, 2009 August 20–22, Jackson Hole, Wyoming.

7. Buiter WH, Panigirtzoglou N. Overcoming the zero bound on nominal interest rates with negative interest on currency: Gesell's solution. *The Economic Journal*. 2003; 113(490): 723–746. DOI: https://doi.org/10.1111/1468-0297.t01-1-00162.

8. Svensson, L. Escaping from a liquidity trap and deflation: The foolproof way and others. *Journal of Economic Perspectives*. 2003; 17(4): 145–166. DOI: https://doi.org/10.1257/089533003772034934.

9. Christiano L, Eichenbaum M, Rebelo S. When is the government spending multiplier large? *Journal of Political Economy*. 2011; 119(1): 78–121. DOI: https://doi.org/10.1086/659312.

10. Eggertsson G, Woodford M. The zero bound on interest rates and optimal monetary policy. *Brookings Papers on Economic Activity, No. 1*. 2003. DOI: https://doi.org/10.1353/eca.2003.0010.

11. Benhabib J, Schmitt-Grohe S, Uribe M. The Perils of Taylor Rules. *Journal of Economic Theory*. 2001; 96(1–2): 40–69. DOI: https://doi.org/10.1006/jeth.1999.2585.

12. Schmitt-Grohe S, Uribe M. Liquidity traps: An interest-rate-based exit strategy. *The Manchester School*. 2014; 82(1): 1–14. DOI: https://doi.org/10.1111/manc.12065.

13. Chadha J. Interest rate normalisation. *National Institute Economic Review*. 2017; 241: F4–F7. DOI: https://doi.org/10.1177/002795011724100103.

14. Woodford M, Xie Y. Policy options at the zero lower bound when foresight is limited. *AEA Papers and Proceedings*. 2019; 109: 433–37. DOI: https://doi.org/10.1257/pandp.20191084.

15. Vernon J. World War II fiscal policies and the end of the great depression. *The Journal of Economic History*. 1994; 54(4): 850–868. DOI: https://doi.org/10.1017/S0022050700015515.

16. Stockholm International Peace Research Institute. Trends in world military expenditure, 2022. Stockholm: SIPRI; 2023.

17. IMF. Chapter 2: The natural rate of interest: Drivers and implications for policy. In World economic outlook, April 2023: A rocky recovery. USA: International Monetary Fund; 2023.

18. Laubach T, Williams JC. Measuring the natural rate of interest. *The Review of Economics and Statistics*. 2023; 85(4): 1063–1070. DOI: https://doi.org/10.1162/003465303772815934.

19. Federal Reserve Board. *Statement on longer-run goals and monetary policy strategy*. 2020.

20. Bailey A. Monetary policy remit, Autumn statement 2022. London, UK: HM Treasury; 2022.

21. Banerjee R, Hofmann B. Corporate zombies: Anatomy and life cycle. *Working Papers No 882*. Bank for International Settlements; 2022. DOI: https://doi.org/10.1093/epolic/eiac027.

22. Chadha J. The money minders – The parables, trade-offs and lags of central banking. Cambridge University Press: Cambridge; 2022. DOI: https://doi.org/10.1017/9781108975414.

18. Reconstructing and Reforming Ukraine

Erik Berglöf and Vladyslav Rashkovan

> Helping Ukraine to reconstruct and reform its economy is arguably the most important project for Europe this century. It will require extraordinary collaboration from within and outside of the country. We establish a set of principles that should guide these efforts, based on international and Ukraine's own experience. This experience also suggests key building blocks of a reform and reconstruction architecture that can help ensure that these principles are successfully applied. We assess the current institutional arrangements in this light and suggest adjustments that will increase the likelihood of success. The core of the argument is that the unfathomable choices involved in reconstruction and reform, including the use of donor resources, must be made by the Ukrainian people and its elected representatives, and the outcome must be owned by them.

Reconstructing Ukraine will possibly be the most important political project for Europe this century. It will require extraordinary collaboration from within and outside of the country. The complexity of the tasks and amounts of funds involved (World Bank estimates suggest that Ukrainian reconstruction will cost

US$411bn, which corresponds to 2.5 times the country's estimated GDP) go far beyond the capacity of existing international financial institutions and the amount of concessional development assistance available globally [1]. There are many past national reconstructions that provide invaluable guidance, but we must ensure to draw the right lessons from history.

The project is not only important for Europe, but also for the world. It could become an example of how the world can come together to reconstruct a country ravaged by war. Divisions over the responsibility for the damage done to Ukraine and to its people should not be allowed to interfere with the ambition to help the country to reconstruct and reform itself. Of course, there are other places in the world that should also receive such help, but Ukraine offers a unique opportunity to test the modern international system, and to learn for other efforts in the future. We must seek to achieve the broadest possible coalition behind this project.

An instinctive response would be to call for a Marshall Plan 2.0 [2, 3]. This mostly successful scheme, which saw the USA fund much of the reconstruction of Europe after World War II, may be an effective slogan for galvanising support, but this does not mean it is the right model for Ukraine. The Marshall Plan provided macroeconomic support to the physical rebuilding of countries with essentially sound institutions. In contrast, Ukraine requires root-and-branch reform of its entire economy.

Few potential contributors would be convinced to provide unconditional aid to post-war Ukraine, with any international funding likely resting on its commitment to reform. Making and guaranteeing such commitments should be the lead principle for those designing the reconstruction and reform architecture.

While the Marshall Plan may not be the perfect model for Ukraine, neither were the post-war occupation administrations in Germany and Japan. No one is seriously arguing a wholesale adoption of this approach, but many suggestions have elements of imposing institutions from the outside [2]. History is littered with failed attempts to change institutions from the outside [4]. Not even in completely failed states do we now believe in this approach [5]. And Ukraine is not a failed state. While it has some institutional fragilities, many parts – such as the central bank, the public procurement system ProZorro, and the gas monopoly Naftogaz – have been profoundly transformed and are functioning well. Ukrainian civil society is extremely well developed and responsive, as demonstrated in the war.

What must remain a focal point for Ukraine's builders is that reconstruction and reform remain entwined. They must be implemented under an integrated institutional architecture, one which unifies the domestic and foreign efforts to repair and reconstruct the country. The design and implementation of this framework must grow out of a process that is owned by the people to whom it will apply, given that it first requires making decisions about priorities and choices that no outsider could or should decide on. Second, the government must be able to take responsibility for any design flaws in the architecture, or any unintended consequences of the institutions created or modified to achieve reconstruction and reform.

The likelihood of success of the reform and of reconstruction efforts will be greatly enhanced by the EU accession process.

The "EU dream" is a strong political anchor in Ukraine. The cumulative experience of Central and Eastern Europe and, more recently, Southeast Europe provides important guidance on the sequencing and complementarities of the different elements of accession. A hallmark of the accession process has been that while the EU framework creates a clear sense of direction, and sets out reasonably well-defined targets as well as incentives to reach them, the decisions how and when to achieve those targets are left to the countries.

This chapter establishes some basic principles for the combined reconstruction and reform effort and discusses the experiences from some previous reconstruction projects. It then proceeds to identify some elements of a viable reform architecture and a structure for donor coordination. The chapter also briefly looks at how the EU can enhance the effectiveness of its support. Finally, conclusions are drawn for the Ukrainian reform and reconstruction process.

Principles of Reconstruction and Reform

Principles for reconstruction and reform in Ukraine have been discussed in multiple papers, including Gorodnichenko et al [3], German Marshall Fund [6] and Ukrainian Recovery Council [7]. These analyses highlight the importance of partnership, coordination, transparency, rule of law, democratic participation, multi-stakeholder engagement, inclusion, sustainability, alignment of goals, and accountability. Such principles apply to all cases of post-war and post-natural-disaster reconstruction [8] and link up with the Busan Principles of Aid Effectiveness [9].

The overriding principle for any reconstruction and reform is Ukrainian ownership. Only Ukraine can determine its future and define a vision of the post-war country it wants to build. For investment decisions to be undertaken efficiently and for reforms to stick, they must be viewed as legitimate by the citizenry. Aid will be dispensed most effectively when it is seen as consistent with Ukraine's own interests. Ownership should rest on broad domestic support achieved through inclusive and transparent consultations with local authorities, civil society, and business, while Ukrainian civil society offers interesting models for the involvement of citizenry (e.g., Center for Economic Strategy [10]).

A second important principle is that reconstruction and reforms that are designed to enhance both efficiency and growth must go hand in hand. Even while addressing urgent tasks of rebuilding, the government and donors should work to advance Ukraine's structural reform agenda. Reconstruction is an opportunity for Ukraine to leapfrog generations of technologies and should facilitate significant economic and institutional modernisation. The goal should be a post-war Ukraine that is structurally transformed to be more green, more inclusive, and more dynamic.

Institutional reform should be guided by and be consistent with European Union values, given that EU membership is the economic and political endpoint for Ukraine. The EU integration process provides an anchor for Ukraine's efforts to become a modern, democratic, prosperous country by aligning its incentives with those of Europe and ensuring sustained external support. Consequently, it serves as an important guide for the decision-makers and reduces the need for other conditionality. However, the EU path is also beholden to internal EU politics, which must not become an obstacle to reconstruction.

The EU accession process is associated with significant transfers of funds. First, there are pre-accession funds, and then all the resources available to members. These funds are particularly large for poorer members, and they can be used to leverage other funding from bilateral and multilateral financial institutions. Yet the most important financial flows – both portfolio and direct investments – will come from the private sector as risk premiums decrease. Improving the investment climate then becomes essential to attract private and institutional capital.

EU funds mostly come in the form of grants, but most other flows will use various financial instruments, including debt, guarantees, and equity, received from bilateral and multilateral donors and international organisations. It is important that in the end, a significant component of the money transfers are grants – a country devastated by war is unlikely to be able to service and repay additional debt, at least in the short term. Excessive reliance on loans will raise the risk of a debt solvency and will potentially distort investment decisions. The aim must be to design grant structures that are helpful and come with proper governance without undermining the ownership and incentives of Ukrainian decision-makers.

While providing grants has many advantages, the amounts needed to build the new Ukraine will far exceed available concessional resources globally, so solutions will have to be found to combine these grants with other financial instruments. Debt has the distinct advantage in that it is disciplines the contracting parties while equity confers the risk on its owners – and both can potentially be traded. The problems associated with debt can be resolved through later restructurings or debt extensions; debt can also be linked to economic performance or to the delivery of important public goods, such as climate change mitigation or nature conservation and biodiversity.

Moreover, reconstruction cannot rely on the funds of governments and international organisations alone. The participation of private capital, for example, in the form of inward foreign direct investment and public-private partnerships, is essential. Such partnerships will convey not only money but also technologies and managerial expertise. Private flows will be particularly vulnerable to any remaining threats of war actions and are unlikely to come in large sums until a lasting peace has been achieved, but some foreign investors are continuing to commit capital at present, mainly in the parts of Ukraine less affected by the war.

The first stages in reconstruction are planning and institution-building, which can take place even under the threat of missiles and drones. Critical structural reforms also should not wait for the end of the war. Even while the war continues, Ukraine can strengthen market mechanisms, promote competitive market structures, and foster market development. The major players can start now to put in place the prerequisites for a comprehensive reconstruction. Some measures, for example, investing in a more decentralised energy infrastructure based on renewables, can also help to reduce the country's short-term vulnerability to military threats.

International Reconstruction Experiences

There have been previous national reconstruction efforts that were initiated or at least partially engineered by outsiders. At a very superficial level, two distinct approaches can be identified. First, there is the radical US approach, perhaps best symbolised by the efforts after World War II in Germany and Japan, but also in Iraq and Afghanistan. Within this approach, there is an emphasis on building institutions for democracy, rule of law, and human rights from scratch. Second, there is the more gradual European approach, which focuses on long-term change that build on existing institutions, often relying on the outside anchor of membership in the European Union.

The Marshall Plan contained elements of both, using massive transfers of financial resources for the post-war rebuilding of Europe. To administer the Marshall Plan, the US government created a self-standing agency, the Economic Cooperation Administration (ECA), with a hierarchical structure that clearly delineated responsibility and authority. The ECA administrator was the ultimate decision maker, situated at the top of a well-defined chain of command. It had a 600-employee regional office in Paris and missions of American government officials to advise and observe in each country receiving aid.

This structure contrasted with other post-World War II efforts to rebuild Europe – for example, the UN Relief and Rehabilitation Administration (UNRRA) where a lack of personnel and leadership as well as uncertain budgets plagued the program. UNRRA controlled resources unilaterally, and it often ignored local input. Gradually, UNRRA ramped up coordination with other organisations providing relief, and so became more effective.

The Marshall Plan's top-down, army-style organisation, differs from those used for subsequent US reconstruction efforts, and for reconstruction efforts more broadly. Some of these efforts, as detailed below, have been effective and efficient, leading to a swift and genuine recovery from disaster. Others have been bedeviled by poor organisation and consequently, insurmountable challenges.

In Iraq there was no single administrator with the power to resolve interdepartmental disputes, despite the efficacy of the ECA in Europe. Consequently, reconstruction was plagued by poor planning, weak oversight, poor coordination (if not rivalries) across agencies, weak security, poor involvement of locals, low capacity to absorb aid, and understaffing. Similar problems afflicted the recovery of Puerto Rico after Hurricane Maria in 2017. Four years after the hurricane, Puerto Rico still lacked electricity and many homes and buildings still had only temporary roof covers in place. As of the summer 2021, only US$18.6 billion of an allocated US$64 billion had been spent. Among the reasons for this were red tape (specifically, extensive bureaucracy at the Federal Emergency Mitigation Agency (FEMA) responsible for reconstruction), a debt overhang that discouraged new investment, the non-transparent use of funds, and the fact that Puerto Rico's government had little engagement with or influence in the process.

Pakistan's experience of reconstruction after the 2005 earthquake is more positive [11]. The scale of the natural disaster was such that line ministries and local authorities lacked the capacity to effectively organise a comprehensive reconstruction effort. That effort required extensive coordination and a considerable degree of centralisation if it was to deliver the key objectives of mobilising funding and external aid, building back better (especially in terms of seismic safety), achieving a rapid recovery, allocating funding efficiently, enhancing sustainability, and achieving inclusivity. The government therefore established a special authority: the Earthquake Reconstruction and Rehabilitation Agency (ERRA). This new body had several desirable features. First, it was headed by the prime minister, which provided strong political backing and a clear sense of ownership. ERRA had the necessary centralisation to achieve uniform policies and standards, and a sustained flow of funding. At the same time, it involved the international community in a variety of roles (providing technical expertise, oversight, etc.).

Second, the government developed a plan for reconstruction to be undertaken quickly (ERRA itself was launched only three weeks after the earthquake). This was instrumental in securing external funding and laying the groundwork by, for example, providing early and credible damage assessment. ERRA developed a set of sectoral policies and priorities to concentrate resources on key programs. Early planning at the national level was instrumental in achieving a holistic approach and the prioritisation necessary for cluster projects and sustainable recovery.

Third, although a centralised agency oversaw and coordinated aid, implementation was decentralised, employing the subsidiarity principle. Local authorities could approve and implement projects up to a specified price tag. Larger projects involved regional governments, while the largest projects were determined by the central authorities. This tiered approach enhanced ownership by, inter alia, local governments and improved information sharing and coordination. To ensure that funds were not diverted, project results were reported to the relevant steering committees, and funding was provided in tranches. ERRA's organisational structure emphasised horizontal linkages to provide forums for dialogue between stakeholders.

Fourth, to ensure sustained support of donors, ERRA allocated projects (or sectors) to specific donors. This attached donors to specific responsibilities and provided an opportunity for donors to report achievements to their stakeholders. ERRA ran monthly meetings of donors to cultivate relationships and prevent donor fatigue. Overall, ERRA attracted US$2.5 billion in grants and US$4 billion in loans. Although Saudi Arabia, the United States, China, Iran, the United Arab Emirates, and development banks accounted for the bulk of these funds, ERRA established a dedicated window to coordinate funding from smaller donors. This approach provided a single interlocutor for potential donors, lightening the burden of attracting and managing aid.

Fifth, ERRA had a strong legal mandate and sunset provisions. The former was necessary to overcome inertia and bureaucratic bottlenecks, while the latter were needed to ensure that ERRA did not turn into a new bureaucracy, substituting for line ministries and other authorities. ERRA also provided much needed data gathering and data processing to evaluate progress and to strengthen accountability. Importantly, ERRA only financed construction of seismically safe houses, consistent with the 'build back better' principle.

The reconstruction of Sri Lanka after the 2004 tsunami provides similar lessons. Sri Lanka established a dedicated reconstruction agency with a clear structure. Its Taskforce for Rebuilding the Nation (TRN) was composed of high-level officials and businessmen; it was structured to minimise red tape and ramp up quickly. Sri Lanka pursued policies consistent with the 'build back better' principle: new houses were built according to higher standards; new regulations on construction, fishing and tourism in coastal areas were introduced; and education programs were developed on what to do in the event of disasters. However, a lack of a well-planned land-use policy and of construction guidance resulted in a somewhat chaotic process of land allocation and a varying quality of construction, while over-reliance on local governments created disparities between regions. Further, the reconstruction agency was dismantled too early, which prevented institutionalisation of its experience and knowledge transfer.

Finally, Indonesia's recovery from the 2004 earthquake and tsunami was highly effective, thanks to the Agency for Rehabilitation and Reconstruction of Aceh and Nias (BRR), which was established in early 2005. The BRR operated for four years, with a mandate directly from the constitution of Indonesia to restore livelihoods and strengthen communities in Aceh and Nias. It designed and oversaw a coordinated, community-driven reconstruction and development program that was implemented according to the highest professional standards. This temporary but powerful agency was given full authority to manage all aspects of the tsunami recovery in Aceh on behalf of the central government, which allowed for a much smoother coordination process, devoid of any potential inter-ministry politics and bureaucracy. A coordinated approach to planning, fundraising and implementation ensured that the reconstruction program was effective, duplication was minimised, and donor funds were used optimally.

Ukrainian Reconstruction and Reform Architecture

Ukraine needs both reconstruction and root-and-branch reform, building on the achievements of previous efforts, but also recognising the failures and the remaining challenges. Fundamental choices about what and how to rebuild and reform, and in what order, will have to come out of an inclusive domestic political process in which all domestic stakeholders are adequately represented and where decisions are owned by the Ukrainian population. The country needs an integrated architecture for both reconstruction and reform firmly rooted in the democratically elected institutions.

Yet to succeed, a reconstruction effort will require external support of extraordinary magnitude. Contributors will need to be reassured that the resources they provide will be used in an efficient, effective, and transparent way and, in the case of loans, that they will be repaid. This will have to be achieved under time pressure, as the expectations of citizens will be high after the sacrifices incurred. "Donor fatigue" is also likely to set in as the memories of the war fade away among external contributors.

Any reconstruction and reform architecture must balance these two objectives. This is not an unusual ambition for any rebuilding program, but what makes the Ukrainian situation stand out is the scale of the challenge and its geopolitical significance. The process has necessarily begun in the middle of a war and – once outright hostilities have ceased sufficiently to scale up reconstruction – may have to accommodate the risk of future military disruptions and sabotage. The challenge to create a sense of local ownership with an ongoing war, and while more than 15 million citizens are displaced internally or abroad, should not be underestimated.

So far, the Ukrainian population has demonstrated remarkable resilience and ingenuity, and civil society has responded in extraordinary ways. Every effort must be made to reach out to the dispersed community of organisations to canvas and to consult on ideas and concrete proposals. The hope for Ukraine is that the groundswell of community activity and acts of solidarity can, in due course, be channeled into the restructuring of the war-wrecked Ukrainian economy and reforming its economic and political system.

Like any country trying to reform with external support, there is a historic context of previous reform attempts and already entrenched interests. The war experience has provided a jolt to established patterns and has shifted relative positions of stakeholders, but preexisting obstacles to reform are unlikely to have gone away completely, and new special interests will emerge from the war experience and in the reconstruction effort. Sustaining the reform momentum will require maintaining the broad support internally, and also externally. Designing a robust reform architecture will be critical.

After the 2014 Maidan Revolution, Ukraine had an interesting experiment in how to build a domestic reform architecture. A gathering of more than 200 Ukrainians representing different parts of society met for three days in July 2014 at a time when the country did not have a democratically legitimate legislator and found itself thrust into a war with Russia. Among other elements, the group came in behind a proposal for a coordination body generated by reformers inside the government. This was later supported by the country leadership, which established a National Reform Council (NRC). This was staffed by a hundred reform-oriented civil servants in different ministries trained under the EU-financed Ukraine Reforms Architecture (URA) program implemented by the EBRD.

The NRC built up a dialogue platform that included representatives from all relevant stakeholders: economic officers of the President's administration; economic fields ministers (economy, finance, infrastructure, agriculture); the National Bank governor; members of the economic committees and heads of the coalition parties of the Parliament (opposition party leaders didn't participate); representatives of the key business associations; and representatives of the civil society. Considerable donor resources for technical assistance were channeled to support a Secretariat that was supported by at least one or two people of its project implementation unit in each of the line ministries.

The NRC was envisaged to become a platform to present and to discuss the key reforms Ukraine needed with the main stakeholders. As a result of the dialogue, there was a general agreement to support the reform through different implementation stages. They agreed on the concept of the reform, turned it into legislation approved by the Parliament, supported the rollout and created the feedback loop to evaluate its results.

Indeed, the NRC was important in 2014–2016. All the major reforms within the financial and fiscal sectors, energy sector, public procurement, health, and educational reform, etc. were discussed at the NRC meetings every three weeks. Part of the meetings were televised. The responsible minister was tasked with presenting his or her vision, and the measures planned to achieve the goals were set out. From 2017 onwards, the Council was less useful – the country had run out of steam for reform.

In April 2022, just two months after the full-scale invasion, the Ukrainian government created a similar institution – the National Recovery Council (also NRC). Unfortunately, the new institution never became operational as initial management was weak and got dragged into political infighting. These initial mistakes do not mean that the idea of a National Recovery Council was wrong. Times are different today and the magnitude and urgency of action even greater, but the experience of the National Reform Council should become an important element of a new state-of-the-art inclusive reconstruction and reform architecture that also integrates experiences from other parts of the world.

Donor Coordination

The massive external flows necessary to build the new Ukraine will require massive coordination. Several proposals have suggested the creation of a new agency within the EU for this purpose. The magnitude and complexity of administering EU support to the Ukrainian reconstruction and reform effort might require the creation of a new agency inside the EU, but this must not be confused with the arrangements needed to coordinate all of the country's external donors and lenders. Accumulated post-WWII development experience, manifested in the Busan Principles for aid effectiveness, emphatically states that donor coordination will only work when owned by the recipient country. Thinking has recently coalesced around 'country platforms', which would bring together all major stakeholders to ensure that financing and associated conditionality are internally consistent and in line with the government policies [12, 13].

Country platforms were originally conceived by a G20-appointed group as tools for the coordination of international financial institutions, linking them in an overarching system to increase their efficiency and effectiveness [12]. But regardless of the strength of any overarching system, it is in the individual recipient country where the system will be ultimately tested. The parties to a country platform would agree to meet certain common core standards (for a set of potential common standards, see the Eminent Persons Group (EPG) Report [12]) to help coordinate efforts and facilitate collaboration, but also to reduce the scope for corruption and other governance problems.

In a first effort to coordinate outside stakeholders for the reconstruction of Ukraine, the leaders of the key International Financial Institutions (IFIs) – the International Monetary Fund (IMF), the World Bank, the European Bank for Reconstruction and Development (EBRD), and the European Investment Bank (EIB) – and the European Commission established a temporary coordination mechanism during the 2022 IMF-WBG Spring meetings in Washington D.C. The country representatives of these organisations have been organising EU-IFI coordination meetings to discuss Ukrainian short-term financing needs, the first important stage for the reconstruction. While these meetings have been instrumental for sharing information and coordinating operations, they never envisaged more strategic discussions.

On this front, the first major strategic coordination platform for Ukraine was created at the end of 2022 when the G7 established a multi-agency Donor Coordination Platform. This platform aimed to support Ukraine's immediate financing needs, and its future economic recovery and reconstruction. The platform has a Secretariat with two seats: in Brussels, within the European Commission, and in Ukraine – within the Government. Since being established, it has worked with Ukrainian authorities to define, prioritise, and sequence strategic needs. It envisages the coordination of international efforts to support a sustainable, resilient, inclusive, and green economic recovery which enhances strong democratic institutions, rule of law, and anti-corruption measures.

During the G7 Leaders' Summit in Hiroshima, Japan in April 2023, the Development Finance Institutions (DFIs) of the G7 countries and the EBRD agreed to establish the Ukraine Investment Platform. This platform focuses on the private sector and aims to strengthen cooperation and promote information exchange on the question of co-financing. It will also consider the needs of neighboring countries affected by the war. The parties, in close consultation with respective governments, will address the lack of financial capacity, especially in the private sector, and contribute to the recovery of the economy, industry and infrastructure, and to the reconstruction of people's lives.

Another EU coordination mechanism (the European Development Finance Institutions coordination group (EDFI)) has also been established to coordinate a further part of international aid to Ukraine. EDFI brings together European DFIs that foster private sector finance in countries outside the EU. This group has been a good mechanism of coordination, but with limited impact on recovery and reconstruction: many of the institutions have not previously been active in Ukraine, while their financial firepower is limited. Instead, EDFI members are likely to focus on technical assistance to existing clients, disbursing grants, restructuring portfolios, and offering forbearance, rather than providing strategic guidelines for the post-war reconstruction.

During the Ukraine Recovery Conference in London in June 2023, the EBRD, members of EDFI and other G7 Development Finance Institutions (DFIs) signed a Memorandum of Understanding (MoU) that provides a framework for collaboration and co-investments in Ukraine, with a primary focus on the private sector. With the addition of new participants, the total number of signatories now stands at 19. This welcome development should help promote coordination among official financiers.

The question is though whether any of these arrangements fully respect the leading principle for the governance of country platforms, i.e., genuine country ownership. For this to be achieved, the arrangements must be integrated into domestic economic decision-making and subordinated to the overall priorities of the government and to the democratic governance of the country. A good example for the country platform to follow is the Egypt's Nexus of Water Food and Energy (NWFE) platform, in which the Egyptian government displays a pipeline of renewables projects, mainly solar and wind, and its program for phasing out fossil fuel assets. The participating international financial institutions, which include EBRD, EIB and Asian Infrastructure Investment Bank (AIIB), and national development finance institutions, such as Kreditanstalt fur Wiederaufbau (KfW), are then invited to collaborate in the financing of these projects.

Access to grants and other forms of concessional finance will be an essential feature of the Ukrainian reconstruction effort. The NWFE platform has attracted concessional resources from the US, for the retraining and potential early retirement of workers connected to fossil assets; and from Germany, in the form of performance-linked debt related to fulfillment of climate policy commitments [14]. Interestingly, the platform has also helped to bring in equity capital in the form of foreign direct investment in the production of intermediate goods for renewables. Attracting parts of the renewables value chain should also be an important objective for the design of the reconstruction effort in Ukraine.

The country platform concept is now also being used by the G7 in the form of so-called JET-P (Just Economic Transformation Platforms) to implement climate policies in collaboration with individual countries in the emerging and developing world. The first one was a collaboration between the UK and the US in South Africa from 2021. Early lessons from this exercise illustrates several important challenges facing Ukrainian reconstruction, e.g., differing perceptions of what "just" means, what "transformation" trajectory is most desirable, and the lack of follow-through on international promises. The South African example is now being followed with collaborations in Vietnam and Indonesia, and a further platform is being considered in India. There should be rich opportunities to learn lessons for Ukrainian reconstruction and reform from these experiments in donor coordination on climate policy.

Implementation

To manage the herculean task of implementing the reconstruction, the proper institutional arrangements must be prepared. Ukraine needs to put in place the organisational structures, policies and procedures to plan, manage and implement recovery. One model is that suggested by Eichengreen and Rashkovan, who propose creating a specialised, self-standing agency led by the European Commission, but with majority of its staff in Ukraine, and with management representation from each non-European G7 country [15]. According to their view, such an agency should have clear lines of command and independence in operations, oversight by donors, and civil society should be provided by a supervisory board and by the publication of detailed information on reconstruction initiatives and projects. The agency should communicate regularly with donors, local governments, Non-Governmental Organisations (NGOs), businesses and other stakeholders to ensure that the reconstruction takes into account the interests of multiple stakeholders.

While we support Eichengreen and Rashkovan's overarching principles and broad objectives, and agree that IFIs and foreign donors have an important role to play in the implementation of the reconstruction and reform program, they cannot replace domestic institutions. Rather, the reconstruction effort should be used to strengthen existing institutions and to stimulate the creation of the new ones. The Ukrainian government (in a broad sense at all levels) should therefore also build an implementation framework that will formulate and implement policies, and will understand how the recovery will be managed and governed.

Ukraine has already taken the first steps. In December 2022, the Parliament created a Ministry for Restoration – a government body responsible for policies in the field of physical infrastructural recovery, and for setting policies for the restoration process. A new Vice Prime Minister leads this ministry. In January 2023, the Government also created the State Agency for Restoration (Restoration Agency), which will be responsible for the effective and transparent implementation of the country's rapid recovery and post-war reconstruction projects.

The Restoration Agency is a merger of the State Road Agency (Ukravtodor) and the State Agency for Infrastructure Projects (Ukrinfraproyekt). While the latter had delivered several large-scale construction projects that involved both budgetary and external financing, its expertise was mostly lost after the Euro2012 football tournament. The Restoration Agency has inherited a strong capacity in road construction, built by Ukravtodor in partnership with international financial institutions over the past three years. Building on this capacity should help the agency gain credibility among key stakeholders.

An important question for the Restoration Agency to address during the Ukrainian reconstruction is how to reinforce the decentralisation of decision-making initiated in earlier Ukrainian reform efforts after the Revolution of Dignity? Local authorities have been merged and given stronger mandates, but the war will limit options to finance themselves. One way to strengthen their ability to raise resources would be to pool their funding efforts, e.g., the Swedish KommunInvest model or the Bulgarian version implemented together with the EBRD to support municipalities in infrastructure development.

But "to make reconstruction happen", the implementation engine of the Ministry for Restoration and Restoration Agency must learn from the good and bad lessons available from the experience of similar agencies created to tackle post-war or post-natural disasters recoveries: (ECA, BRR, ERRA, CNO, CERA, GREPOC, GSDMA, ONEMI, FAAARO, FEMA, etc.) and to avoid the mistakes in principles and design [16, 17]. One important lesson is the necessity of creating a separate project implementation unit (PiU) that can help foreign experts to support reconstruction. The PiU of the National Reform Council had an important role in the implementation of reforms.

Finally, a designated national development bank could help to raise financing for the efforts of the Restoration Agency, serving as a credible co-financing partner for multilateral and bilateral institutions. The German development finance institution, KfW, originally established to promote Germany's reconstruction after WWII, is an interesting model. Alternatively, the government could establish a dedicated development bank owned by the multilateral and bilateral development banks involved in the reconstruction: EBRD, EIB, KfW, IFC and Ukraine. Such an institution could be focused solely on the reconstruction of Ukraine (just as EBRD was originally set up to support the market transition of the region), and would benefit from the capital, technologies, project expertise and governance of the European institutions, but would not be overburdened with its bureaucracy and geopolitical limitations.

Lessons for Ukraine

Starting from a set of principles for reconstruction and reform, we examined previous international experiences and some of Ukraine's own attempts to establish a reform architecture, including the most recent changes in the ministerial set-up and the establishment of a reconstruction agency. In this final section, we summarise the conclusions for Ukraine's reconstruction and reform efforts and point to potential improvements to better meet the objectives of the government.

The EU accession process and the conditionality involved in financing the restructuring effort will point the way, but the Ukrainian people must do the hard work of rebuilding trust in the political system and cleaning out the oligarchic structures in the economy. Evidence from previous enlargements of the European Union suggests that bureaucratic independence and judicial capacity are at the core of the institutional reforms supported by the accession process. Building these elements must also be central to Ukraine's reconstruction and reform architecture.

The discussion so far suggests that the reconstruction architecture should be designed along the following lines:

- The reconstruction architecture should be based on a country platform, along the principles outlined in the EPG Report – the core principle being the strong ownership by the Ukrainian government. It should generate the vision, strategy and priority list of projects based on its superior local knowledge. Reconstruction will require an all-government approach with the newly formed the Ministry for Communities, Territories and Infrastructure Development of Ukraine (Ministry for Restoration) as the natural hub for internal coordination in Ukraine (a merger of two previous ministries [18]).

- The reconstruction effort needs to be plugged into an inclusive reform architecture that involves all the branches of the Ukrainian government, including the parliament and the president's office, but also civil society and other internal stakeholders. The National Reform Council from 2014 could serve as a model for such an architecture.
- The country platform should have a reconstruction agency associated with it to ensure proper preparation and implementation of decisions taken by the stakeholders responsible for the platform. The recently formed State Agency for Reconstruction and Development of Infrastructure of Ukraine [19] has some of the core features, but the new agency will have to be strengthened along several dimensions and should be formally tied to the country platform.
- The Multi-Agency Donor Coordination Platform [20] launched in January 2023, is a step in the right direction, but it does not yet fully reflect the principles of proper country ownership and inclusiveness. It can still fill a useful role for internal EU coordination, but to qualify as a proper country platform it should be re-weighted in favor of the Ukrainian side and provide more space for non-EU stakeholders.
- The Reconstruction Agency should coordinate closely with domestic stakeholders, most importantly the Ukrainian government at multiple levels, but also businesses and civil society, both before and after projects are implemented. It should organise regular donor conferences; and collect and disseminate pertinent data

on reconstruction projects to ensure accountability and learning, working with internationally recognised accounting firms with offices in Ukraine.
- Ultimately, of course, the entire financial system of Ukraine will have to be involved. Institutional innovation could strengthen the current system which has been thoroughly reformed and has held up well during the war.
- A national development bank can serve as a credible co-financing partner for multilateral and bilateral institutions. There are several interesting models to explore and special attention should be paid to the need to strengthen the finances and implementation capacity of local authorities.
- As the endgame for Ukraine is membership of the EU, the European Commission will have to play an important role in the coordination within the European institutions and among member states. The newly created multi-agency mechanism can help EU's own coordination efforts, but it cannot be the ultimate coordinator of all assistance. It would undermine the incentives of other contributors and, most importantly, of the Ukrainian government itself.
- The international partners may want to establish a multi-donor trust fund (MDTF) to pool donor resources, as the World Bank has done with the Ukraine Relief, Recovery and Reconstruction and Reform Trust Fund [21]. If established, such a fund should have a certain independence and should be run by a managing director selected on a competitive basis with experience of

working closely with the European Commission. It would be natural for such a fund to also have representation for the intended recipient.
- Effective functioning of the MDTF will require not only inclusive representation of key multilateral and bilateral donors but also strong political backing for coordination, technical expertise, and local knowledge via on-the-ground representation in Ukraine (via embassies and local offices of international financial institutions). Technical assistance should be organised as a permanent task force consisting of high-level experts (perhaps seconded from participating institutions).
- Overall, the reconstruction effort will require massive recruitment and continuous training of staff. The positions in the core institutions of a Ukrainian reconstruction and reform architecture should be part of the country's future civil service reforms. The recruited staff will form the future civil service of the country; secondment programs with ministries and agencies in countries participating in the effort could help to enhance state capacity in the country.

With all these elements, the reconstruction and reform of Ukraine could become an important "proof of concept" for similar efforts in other parts of the world. The staff involved could be used to transfer experience and work with representatives of recipient countries to adjust the model to fit local conditions and the regional context. The lessons could be applied not only to post-conflict situations but also to other states with deep fragilities, and to achieve broader development objectives in emerging and developing economies more generally.

References

1. World Bank. Ukraine Rapid Damage and Needs Assessment. Washington, D.C.: World Bank Group. 2023 March 20 [cited 2023 July 20]. http://documents.worldbank.org/curated/en/099184503212328877/P1801740d1177f03c0ab180057556615497.

2. Becker T, Eichengreen B, Gorodnichenko Y. A Blueprint for the Reconstruction of Ukraine: Introduction. London: CEPR Press. 2022 April 7 [cited 2023 July 20]. https://cepr.org/publications/books-and-reports/blueprint-reconstruction-ukraine.

3. Gorodnichenko Y, Sologoub I, di Mauro BW. Rebuilding Ukraine: Principles and Policies, Centre for Economic Policy. London: CEPR Press. 2022 December 7 [cited 2023 July 20]. https://cepr.org/publications/books-and-reports/rebuilding-ukraine-principles-and-policies.

4. Rohner D, Zhuravskaya E. Nation Building: Big Lessons from Successes and Failures. London: CEPR Press. 2023 February 14 [cited 2023 July 20]. https://cepr.org/publications/books-and-reports/nation-building-big-lessons-successes-and-failures.

5. Collier P, Besley T, Khan A. Escaping the Fragility Trap. International Growth Center. 2018 [updated 2020 October; cited 2023 July 20]. https://www.theigc.org/publications/escaping-fragility-trap.

6. Conley HA. A Modern Marshall Plan for Ukraine: Seven Lessons from History to Deliver Hope. German Marshall Fund of the United States. 2022 October 3 [cited 2023 July 20]. https://www.gmfus.org/sites/default/files/2022-10/A%20Modern%20Marshall%20Plan%20for%20Ukraine.pdf.

7. National Recovery Council. Ukraine's National Recovery Plan. Ukraine: National Recovery Council. 2022 July [cited 2023 July 20].

https://uploads-ssl.webflow.com/621f88db25fbf24758792dd8/62c1
66751fcf41105380a733_NRC%20Ukraine%27s%20Recovery%20
Plan%20blueprint_ENG.pdf.

8. O'Driscoll D. Post-Conflict Reconstruction Good Practice. Brighton, UK: Institute of Development Studies. 2018 November 2 [cited 2023 July 20]. https://opendocs.ids.ac.uk/opendocs/handle/20.500.12413/14263.

9. OECD. Busan Partnership for Effective Development Co-operation: Fourth High Level Forum on Aid Effectiveness. Paris: OECD Publishing. 2011 December 1 [cited 2023 July 20]. DOI: https://doi.org/10.1787/54de7baa-en.

10. Vyshlinsky H, Repko M, Gaidai Y, Goriunov D, Kolomiets O, Samoiliuk M. Ukrainian economy in war times: rapid assessment. Center for Economic Strategy. 2022 April 11 [cited 2023 July 20]. https://ces.org.ua/en/ukrainian-economy-in-war-times-rapid-assessment-april-2022/.

11. World Bank. World Bank Annual Report 2014. Washington D.C.: World Bank Group. 2014 October 9 [cited 2023 July 20]. DOI: https://doi.org/10.1596/978-1-4648-0245-4.

12. G20 Eminent Persons Group. Making the Global Financial System Work for All: G20 Eminent Persons Group. 2018 October [cited 2023 July 20]. https://www.globalfinancialgovernance.org/files/g20epg-full%20report.pdf.

13. Carney M. Country Platforms Action Plan. Global Infrastructure Hub. 2021 November 3 [cited 2023 July 20]. https://assets.bbhub.io/company/sites/63/2021/11/Country-Platforms-Action-Plan.pdf.

14. Ministry of International Cooperation. Egypt's Country Platform for NWFE Program. 2022 July [cited 2023 July 20]. https://moic.gov.eg/page/nwfe.

15. Eichengreen B, Rashkovan V (eds). Rebuilding Ukraine: Principles and policies. London: CEPR Press. 2022. https://cepr.org/chapters/how-organise-aid.

16. United Nations Development Programme. Handbook on Recovery Institutions: A Guidebook for Recovery Leaders and Practitioners. UNDP. 2022 January 19 [cited 2023 July 20]. https://www.undp.org/publications/handbook-recovery-institutions-guidebook-recovery-leaders-and-practitioners.

17. United Nations Development Programme. Case Studies on Institutional Arrangements for Recovery. UNDP. 2021 September [cited 2023 July 20]. https://www.preventionweb.net/publication/case-studies-institutional-arrangements-recovery.

18. Ministry for Restoration. Who we are – Ministry for Communities, Territories and Infrastructure Development of Ukraine [cited 2023 June 27]. https://mtu.gov.ua/en/content/hto-mi-e.html.

19. DBDH. A newly created state agency will manage Ukraine's reconstruction. 2023 March 10 [cited 2023 June 27]. https://dbdh.dk/a-new-state-agency-will-manage-ukraines-reconstruction/.

20. European Commission. Recovery and reconstruction of Ukraine [cited 2023 June 27]. https://eu-solidarity-ukraine.ec.europa.eu/eu-assistance-ukraine/recovery-and-reconstruction-ukraine_en.

21. World Bank. Ukraine Relief, Recovery, Reconstruction and Reform Trust Fund (URTF) [cited 2023 June 27]. https://www.worldbank.org/en/programs/urtf.

Annex A: Ukraine's Timeline: From Independence to War

1990s

December 1991: Ukraine votes 92% for independence from the former USSR and elects Leonid Kravchuk as its first President.

January 1992: The Russian Foreign Ministry and Parliament condemn the transfer of Crimea to Ukraine in 1954.

July 1994: Former Prime Minister Leonid Kuchma defeats incumbent President Leonid Kravchuk.

December 1994: The *Budapest Memorandum* confirms the transfer of all Ukrainian nuclear warheads to Russia which in turn promises to recognise the territorial integrity of Ukraine.

June 1995: Presidents of Ukraine and Russia negotiate terms for dividing the Black Sea fleet based in Sevastopol, Crimea.

May 1996, Ukraine sees the last of its nuclear arms transported back to Russia.

June 1996: New Ukrainian Constitution ratified giving President considerable powers.

May 1997: *Treaty on Friendship, Cooperation, and Partnership* signed between Ukraine and Russia recognising the inviolability of existing borders.

August 1999: Vladimir Putin named Prime Minister of Russia.

October 1999: Putin orders a ground offensive against breakaway republic of Chechnya.

2000s

February 2000: Grozny, capital of Chechnya, becomes 'the most destroyed city on earth'

March 2000: Putin wins Russian presidential election.

July 2001: China and Russia sign twenty-year *Treaty of Friendship*.

September 2001: Putin becomes first foreign leader to contact President Bush following 9/11 attack, declaring to 'the American people that we are with you'.

December 2001: Putin insists that the brotherhood between Ukraine and Russia is 'not a legend but a historical fact'.

May 2003: Putin declares that Russia is an 'inalienable part of Europe'.

September 2003: President G W Bush meets with his 'friend' President Putin at Camp David.

December 2003: Putin says US-led war in Iraq 'cannot be recognized as fair or justified'.

October 2004: Ukraine presidential election contest between pro-Russian Prime Minister Victor Yanukovich against Victor Yushchenko, whose supporters stage mass protests that came to be known as the 'Orange Revolution'. Yushchenko becomes President.

December 2004: *Putin states that* 'Russia is not indifferent to what is happening in Ukraine, for every second Ukrainian family, if not more, has family and personal ties with Russia'.

April 2005: Putin declares that 'the collapse of the Soviet Union was a major geopolitical disaster'.

May 2005: Putin argues the 'expansion of NATO does not bring greater security to the world.'

September 2006: Putin criticises 'our European and American partners' who 'decided to support the Orange Revolution'.

February 2007: Putin attacks the idea of a US-led unipolar world 'which means one single centre of power, one single centre of force and one single master.'

October 2007: Putin insists 'that NATO expansion represents a serious provocation that reduces the level of mutual trust.'

April 2008: NATO summit announces Georgia and Ukraine 'will become members of NATO'

August 2008: Russian military begins invasion of Georgia.

January 2009: Russian exports of gas to Ukraine cut off.

Early 2010s

January 2010: Presidential election reveals deep split between pro-Russian Yanukovych and pro-*EU* Yulia Tymoshenko. Yanukovych finally wins the presidency.

April 2011: Putin attacks NATO intervention in Libya.

19 December 2011: The conclusion of the negotiations on the EU-Ukraine Association Agreement.

March 2012: The EU and Ukraine initial an Association Agreement.

June 2012: Russia steps up support for Syrian President Bashar-al Assad.

March 2013: Putin welcomes Xi Jinping to Russia on his first foreign visit as China's President noting that Xi's visit would give 'Russian-Chinese ties a new and powerful impulse'.

Summer 2013: Russia imposes restrictions on Ukrainian exports and warns that signing the Association Agreement with the EU would be 'suicidal' for Ukraine.

16 September 2013: The full Association Agreement ratified by the Ukrainian and European Parliaments.

November 2013: President Yanukovych withdraws from signing an Association Agreement with the EU, instead accepting a Russian trade deal and loan bailout. Russian spokesman Dmitry Peskov says, 'we welcome the desire to improve and develop trade and economic cooperation [with Russia] describing Ukraine as 'a close partner'.

December 2013–February 2014: Mass protests against Yanukovych, dubbed the 'Euromaidan'. These peak in February 2014 when almost 100 protesters are killed by security forces.

February 2014: Russia accuses the European Union of seeking to create a 'sphere of influence' on its borders.

February 2014: Yanukovich flees Kyiv for Russia. Ukraine's parliament votes to remove him from post and schedules early elections.

Seizure of Crimea and after

28 February 2014: Russian troops without insignia begin seizing strategic points throughout Crimea, following several days of organised pro-Russian demonstrations.

March 2014: Putin signs a law sanctioning the Russian takeover of Crimea saying that Ukraine's Maidan revolution 'was an anti-constitutional takeover, an armed seizure of power'.

March 2014: Western leaders issue a joint statement condemning Russia's 'clear violation of the sovereignty and territorial integrity of Ukraine'. Russia is expelled from the Group of Eight (G8).

April 2014: Putin insists that 'if we don't do anything, Ukraine will be drawn into NATO sometime in the future'.

May 2014: Pro-Russia separatists in Ukraine's easternmost areas, Donetsk and Luhansk, announce landslide victories in referendums on 'self-rule'. Ukraine and Western countries condemn the vote.

May 2014: Petro Poroshenko is elected president of Ukraine.

June 2014: 'What actually happened there [in Ukraine]? There was a conflict and that conflict arose because the former Ukrainian president refused to sign an association agreement with the EU. Russia had a certain stance on this issue. We believed it was indeed unreasonable to sign that agreement because it would have a grave impact on the economy, including the Russian economy' (Putin).

July 2014: Malaysia Airlines flight MH17 is shot down over eastern Ukraine with the loss of 298 lives.

July 2016: NATO endorse the Comprehensive Assistance Package (CAP) for Ukraine, enhancing NATO's assistance for Ukraine.

June 2017: Ukraine's Association Agreement with the EU is ratified by all signatories.

December 2017: The US approves the largest commercial sale of lethal arms to Ukraine since 2014.

May 2018: President Putin opens the 12-mile Kerch bridge between the Russian mainland and Crimea.

February 2019: An amendment to Ukraine's constitution, setting NATO membership as a strategic foreign and security policy, enters into force.

April 2019: In a landslide victory taking over 70% of the votes former actor and comedian Volodymyr Zelenskyy defeats Petro Poroshenko in the presidential election, promising to tackle corruption and end the conflict in eastern Ukraine.

June 2019: In an interview with the *Financial Times* Putin says western liberalism has 'outlived its purpose'

October 2020: Zelenskyy and Boris Johnson sign a landmark Strategic Partnership Agreement, paving the way for stronger cooperation between the UK and Ukraine.

February 2021: President Zelenskyy's government imposes sanctions on several Ukrainian politicians with close ties to Russian President Putin, including political heavyweight Viktor Medvedchuk, the Kremlin's most prominent ally in Ukraine.

April 2021: Russia announces the start of mass military drills, raising tensions with Ukraine amid Western concern about the risk of renewed fighting.

July 2021: Putin authors essay *On the Historic Unity of Russians and Ukrainians* arguing they were always 'one people – a single whole'.

December 2021: Russia presents a list of security demands including a legally binding guarantee that Ukraine will never join NATO and that NATO will give up any military activity in eastern Europe and Ukraine.

January 2022: The US and NATO deliver separate written responses to Russia's security demands, ruling out Russia's demand to halt NATO's eastward expansion.

4 February 2022: Xi Jinping and Putin sign a joint statement calling upon NATO to 'abandon its ideologized cold war approach' and announcing a 'no limits friendship' between the two countries.

14 February 2022: Russia's ambassador to the EU says Moscow would be within its rights to launch a 'counterattack' if it felt it needed to protect Russian citizens living in eastern Ukraine.

18 February 2022: President Biden says he is 'convinced' Russia's president has decided to invade.

21 February 2022: President Putin recognises the independence of the two breakaway territories in eastern Ukraine – the Luhansk People's Republic and Donetsk People's Republic.

Russian Invasion and War

24 February 2022: Putin announces Russian forces will carry out 'a special military operation' in Ukraine.

25 February 2022: President Zelenskyy decrees a full military mobilisation and all men aged 18–60 are forbidden from leaving Ukraine.

26 February 2022: Fierce fighting breaks out around Kyiv as Russian forces try to push their way towards the city centre from multiple directions. President Zelenskyy rejects a US offer to evacuate him from Ukraine's capital.

27 February 2022: President Putin orders Russia's military to put the country's nuclear deterrence forces on high alert in response to 'aggressive statements' by NATO countries.

3 March 2022: UN votes to condemn Russia with 141 states voting in favour of the resolution, 5 against and 35 (including China and many countries from Africa) abstaining.

5 March 2022: President Putin describes sanctions imposed by Western nations over his invasion of Ukraine as 'akin to a declaration of war'.

6 March 2022: Chinese foreign minister Wang Yi warns against any moves that would 'add fuel to the flames' in Ukraine.

3 April 2022: Zelenskyy blames former German Chancellor Angela Merkel and ex-French President Nicolas Sarkozy for fourteen years of failed diplomacy vis a vis Russia.

7 April 2022: The UN General Assembly votes to suspend Russia's membership in the UN Human Rights Council. The resolution receives a two-thirds majority, minus abstentions, with 93 nations voting in favour and 24 against. 58 nations abstained.

May 2022: Finland and Sweden confirm they intend to apply for membership of NATO.

June 2022: Leaders of the G7 pledge to stand with Ukraine 'for as long as it takes' by ramping up sanctions on Russia and backing security commitments for Kyiv in a post-war settlement.

July 2022: Syria and North Korea recognise the self-proclaimed Donetsk People's Republic and the self-proclaimed Luhansk People's Republic.

August 2022: The United Nations refugee agency, the UNHCR, reveals more than 10.5 million people have crossed the border from Ukraine since Russia's invasion began on 24 February.

September 2022: Putin signs 'accession treaties' formalising Russia's annexation of four occupied regions in Ukraine He goes on to declare that the West is seeking to 'weaken, divide and finally destroy this country'.

October 2022: Russia's Foreign Minister, Sergei Lavrov, says Russia no longer sees a need to maintain a diplomatic presence in the West.

November 2022: Iran acknowledges that it has supplied Moscow with drones.

December 2022: Putin admits Russia's war in Ukraine could turn into a 'long-term process'.

January 2023: US rules out sending fighter jets to Ukraine.

February 2023: Former Russian PM and President Medvedev says Russia will disappear if it loses in Ukraine.

March 2023: Xi Jinping meets Putin for the 40th time, after Putin had been arraigned before the International Criminal Court.

April 2023: Russian Foreign Minister Sergei Lavrov declines to say if a pre-existing deal allowing Ukraine to export grain through the Black Sea will continue.

May 2023: Putin attacks 'neo-colonialism' of West and claims Russia is working to achieve a more equitable multipolar world order.

June 2023: The Wagner Group stages a rebellion.

20 July 2023: According to the latest Eurobarometersurvey, 64% of Europeans agree with purchasing and supplying military equipment to Ukraine with Sweden (93%), Portugal (90%) and Denmark (89%) having the highest approval rates. On the other hand, Bulgaria (30%), Cyprus (36%) and Slovakia (37%) have the lowest approval rates. In Hungary, 75% of respondents are in favour of an immediate ceasefire. Two in three Americans say that the U.S. should provide weapons to Ukraine (65%).

July 2023: US intelligence claims China is becoming increasingly important to Moscow's war in Ukraine. China insists it 'upholds an objective and just position' on the conflict.

1 August 2023: War enters its 525th day with Russian attacks on grain stores in Odesa and Ukrainian drone attacks on Moscow.

5–7 August 2023: Two day 'peace' talks in Jeddah, Saudi Arabia involving 40 nations including Ukraine, US and China but not including Russia. Russia attacks 'western efforts to mobilize the global south to support Zelensky's formula', saying they were 'doomed to fail'.

10 August 2023: Poland stations up to 10,000 troops at its border with Belarus, sparked by the arrival of Wagner troops in Belarus after the group's aborted rebellion against Moscow. Russia says it downed 13 drones overnight near Moscow and Sevastopol, in Russian-occupied Crimea, accusing Kyiv of being responsible for the attacks.

Annex B: The Geography of War

Figure A.1: Assessed control of terrain in Ukraine and main Russian manoeuvre axes as of 8 August, 2023, 3pm ET

Source: Map courtesy of the Institute for the Study of War and AEI's Critical Threats Project. Available from: https://www.understandingwar.org/sites/default/files/DraftUkraineCOTAugust%208%2C2023.png.

www.ingramcontent.com/pod-product-compliance
Lightning Source LLC
Chambersburg PA
CBHW072129220426
43664CB00013B/2185